From Copper Camp...

Butte is different from all the cities of the world. There is only one Butte—there will never be another. Those who know her, love her, and wouldn't trade her for the most beautiful city on earth.

Butte, Montana, in the late 1800s and early 1900s, where...

The miners worked like slaves, and they played like kings; they asked no quarter, and no quarter did they give; they took their whiskey straight, and they took it often
.

There were Irish, Welsh, Cornish, English, Finns, Serbians, Scotch, Italians, Swedes, Greeks, Afghans, Norwegians, Mexicans, Germans, Turks, Chinese, Austrian, French-Canadian, Polish, Spanish, African-Americans, Native Americans, and more—all mining, building, tending, cooking, hauling, serving, boarding, chopping, raising, and otherwise growing Butte all together, all at once.

They don't ask who you are, but what can you do.

And Butte, where...

A pickpocket fleeced a judge, while the judge was in court, ruling on a case against the pickpocket.

The ice-cream maker saved money by using ice discarded by the mortuaries.

Doors of hundreds of saloons were built without locks, because they never closed.

A bartender indignantly remarked to a newcomer who ordered a glass of milk: "Do you see any room in here for a cow?"

Freight clerks amused themselves by tapping a barrel of pure grain alcohol, only to discover when it was nearly empty that it was a medical shipment containing three human heads.

A riot took place at a miner's picnic over a tug-of-war match. It was reported that during the free-for-all the afternoon sun was obscured by hundreds of flying beer bottles.

The miracle of the dead voting on Election Day was beheld for many years.

Two professional boxers stopped fighting to watch a sudden, wild melee in the audience, where two-thirds of the spectators were engaged in hand-to-hand combat inspired by political differences.

On election day a Democratic "committee man" made frequent rounds of the polling places with jugs of whiskey, and, in that way, "kept the Republican officials…in a more or less comatose state, which greatly simplified the counting of ballots later in the evening."

For the fun of it, a gang of kids climbed aboard a railroad flatcar loaded with steel rails, released the brakes and rode it, yelling and whooping, as it careened down a mountain at sixty miles an hour.

For Halloween, some kids used a heavy rope and a passing ore train to uproot a cabin and drag it down the street, with the owner inside.

Mules in the mines developed a fondness for chewing tobacco.

Kelly the Ghost, a pure white cat that roamed mine shafts hundreds of feet below the surface, scared the wits out of miners who saw its luminous green eyes glowing in the dark tunnels.

A third of the population answered to some sort of nickname, such as Long Distance Mike, Shoestring Annie, Chicken Liz, Filthy McNabb, Crying George, Jere the Wise, Blasphemous Brown, Callahan the Bum, Fat Jack, Lousy Pete, Paddy the Ghoul, Mary the Ghost, Telephone Tshaikowsky, Con the Horse, Mike the Mule, and Paddy the Pig.

Neighborhoods were called Nanny Goat Hill, Seldom Seen, Dogtown, Cabbage Patch, and Chicken Flats.

Saloons were called The Alley Cat, Open-All-Night, Graveyard, Collar and Elbow, and The Cesspool.

Mines were named the Late Acquisition, Neversweat, Orphan Boy, Orphan Girl, Speculator, and Wake-up, Jim!

COPPER CAMP

Stories of the World's Greatest Mining Town
Butte, Montana

Compiled by
Workers of the Writers' Program of the Work Projects Administration
in the State of Montana

First published in 1943

RIVERBEND
PUBLISHING

Published by Riverbend Publishing, Helena, Montana

Printed in the United States of America.

8 9 0 MG

Cover design by DD Dowden.
Text design by Teresa Record.

ISBN 1-931832-04-8

Cataloging-in-Publication data is on file at the Library of Congress.

Riverbend Publishing
P.O. Box 5833
Helena, MT 59604
1-866-787-2363

Preface

IF THE regulations of the Montana Writers' Project did not prevent, the cover of this book would bear the name of William A. Burke as author.

Except for assistance later acknowledged, the book is based entirely on his observations, memories, and research as a native son of the Copper Camp.

Through the years, Bill Burke, crack publicity man and newswriter, has garnered the anecdote and color of Butte. This nostalgic love of every facet of the camp, both tawdry and glorious, has resulted in this work which tells the lusty, rip-roaring story of the "richest hill on earth."

In 1939 *Montana, A State Guide Book* appeared. Although it reveals the lively doings of a frontier state more succinctly than any previous volume, ten pages were all the editors could devote to the coverage of the largest and strangest city, the copper camp of Butte.

To those who were at that time planning a state-sponsored program to replace the Federal Writers' Project, under which the guide had been written, there appeared one obvious undertaking—the compiling of the story of Butte.

It required only the shallowest sampling to reveal that the richest veins of this profligate mining camp had not yet been uncovered. The hidden lode which the historians, the fiction writers, and even a few poets had missed, was the wealth of human interest held within the folds of the "richest hill on earth." Previous writers had prospected only the sensational leads. They had exploited the obvious, gargantuan battles of the Copper Kings and had revelled in the drama of the relatively few men and women who played for incredible stakes in an orgy of intrigue, shooting, power-politics and other blood curdling frontier-town irregularities. Like the early placer miners most of these writers had gleaned only the largest and most easily found nuggets.

In Copper Camp we have sifted through every available old digging and dump for the wealth of ore which the others left behind. In our anecdotal grubbing few leads have been unexplored. Instead of the Copper Kings, emphasis has been placed on the life and antics of the majority of folk; kids and characters, ministers, miners, mothers, girls from the line, bankers and barkeeps. We have attempted to capture this mood through simple, objective anecdote. Our selections can not possibly be construed as either sociological or economic although the implications, we hope, have not escaped documentation. If *Copper Camp* captures only a bit of the raw mood of this mining town, with its hurried veneer of cosmopolitan contacts; its immense wealth and dismal poverty, rubbing elbows; its godliness, charity and normal family life interspersed with violence and sin, all molded by the constant threat of death in underground depths, then we have succeeded in our objective. Of such stuff as strikes, parades, politics, and people—above all, of rawboned, lively, honest-to-God people—is a mining camp composed; and Butte, in the opinion of many experts, is *the* mining camp.

In a broad sense, this can well be the story of all such places, past and present, which dot the vast Western reaches of the United States. Whether Leadville or Lead, Cripple Creek, Tombstone, or Deadwood, the picture has been similar.

Mike Kennedy, former State Supervisor, was one to whom the story of the Copper Camp meant much. His part in the planning of the book was ended when he enlisted in the United States Army.

Acknowledgment is given to Frank Stevens, State Supervisor of the WPA Art Project, who contributed much through his technical knowledge and advice, and to John McHatton, Bob Hall and Walter Mead, artists, for their illustrations.

To George McPhee, credit is due for much of the chapter on early-day sports and the chronology of important events and dates. Gerald Shepherd, Paul A. Rooney, and Emmet T. Burke also aided with research for "John Chinaman," and the sport chapter.

GEORGE D. MARSH,
Editor and State Supervisor

Acknowledgments

Copper Camp could never have been written without the cooperation and assistance of many people. We extend sincere thanks to the following, and any others whom we may have overlooked:

Johnny Sullivan, old time miner. Michael Kelly, attendant at the County Hospital. Mrs. Minnie Cummins, widow of the late James Cummins newspaperman, whose day-book was invaluable. Frank Sullivan, pioneer printer. Joe Foley, former miner, shiftboss, and foreman. Phil (Phileen) Sullivan, ex-saloonkeeper. Joe Choquette, early-day teamster. Charley White, wood cutter and carpenter. Pat Shea, former yardmaster in the Dublin Gulch yards of the Butte, Anaconda & Pacific Railway and Frank O'Brien, old time special agent of the railway. Joe Duffy, laundryman and city alderman. Thomas Hosty, pioneer mine engineer and one time resident of Chicken Flats in Walkerville.

"Belgian Annie," rooming house proprietor of the old days. "Filthy" McNabb, who once carried messages for the red-light district. Michael Rowan, pioneer B. A. & P. engineer. "Judge" Abe Cohen, oldest living resident. M. G. O'Malley, Law Risken and Si Stoddard, newswriters. Jack Duggan, night chief of police. Hancock Mooney, police officer and ex-pugilist. Jack Gerry, detective. Fred Martin, longtime fire chief. Hugh Daly, pioneer undertaker. Mose LaFontise, old time pugilist. Joe Nyman and I. Goodman, pawnbrokers. Sam Kenoffel, cafe operator. Joe Burns and "Watermelon" Burns, one-time messenger boys. "John the Boy" Sullivan, old time hammer-and-steel man.

"Mickey the Bird" Sullivan, Fred Froehlich, and Charlie Holly, barbers who shaved the Copper Kings. Members of the Symons Store "Twenty Year Club," and the Butte Pioneer's Club. Richard Opie and Matt Aho, old time miners. Sam Treloar, longtime leader of the Butte Mines' Band. Walter Roach, assayer. "Dick" Farmer, stage hand of earlier days. Frank Reardon, plumber and member of the school board. Judge McNamara, pioneer blind judge and musician. Ella Swift, Kate Stafford, Gertrude Rosenstein, Mollie Jackson, Sue Baldwin, Buck Weaver and Helen Laird, veteran teachers in the public schools.

Pete McNulty, miner. Mrs. Katherine Hawe, city hall clerk. Pete Grogan, ex-livery stable proprietor, and Al McLeod, old time blacksmith, now sheriff. "Shawn" Sullivan, whose father was foreman under Marcus Daly. Dan "Tango" Culhane and Martin Burke, early day shift bosses. The Rev. Fathers J. M. Venus, F. X. Lechner and Michael McCormack. Henry Young, stage hand. Merle Davis early day theatrical impresario and Kitty Brady, entertainer and actress. Joe Briney, well-known businessman. Mike Milkovich, miner, and Gus Swanson, saloon man. Dan Shea, miner, orator and man-about-town. Howard Opie and Harry Oates, miners and ex-pugilists, and Charles Hauswirth, late mayor and pioneer merchant.

Books which proved helpful in establishing background, which we recommend to those interested in further reading, include:

Butte Above and Below Ground by Harry C. Freeman; *Sketches of Butte* and *Sulphur Fumes* by George Wesley Davis; the autobiographies, I, *Mary MacLane* and *The Story of Mary MacLane*; *Clowning Through Life* by Eddie Foy; *Butte Was Like That* by Joe Duffy; *The Devil Learns To Vote* by C. P. Connoly; *Humorous History of Butte* by Jere Murphy; *Pegasus Pulls A Hack* by Berton Braley; *Wars of the Godly* by Reuben Maury; *War of the Copper Kings* by C. B. Glasscock; and the chapters on Labor and the City of Butte in *Montana, A State Guide Book*, produced by the Federal Writers' Project

Fiction which may prove of interest, although some of it should be taken as such, is represented by the books:

Born of the Crucible, Charles Cohan; *Perch of the Devil*, Gertrude Atherton; *High, Low and Wide Open*, R. Francis James; *Red Harvest*, Dashiell Hammett; and Myron Brinig's *Singerman, The Sisters* and *Wide Open Town.*

We are likewise indebted for reference and source material to the files of the old Butte *Miner*, *Inter Mountain*, *Evening News*, *Montana American* and *The Reveille* and for the use of several copies of Warren Davenport's leaflet, the Butte, Montana *X-Ray*, obtained from the McKee Printing Company. Also helpful were the old minstrel show programs and copies of the magazine *240* of the Butte Elks Lodge, the Rotary Club booklet of 1915, Polk's city directory for 1884-85, and the pamphlet, *Montana's Opportunity*, by Charles A. Hauswirth. We owe much to the unstinting cooperation of the former librarian, Mrs. Margaret McCarthy, and the present librarian, Mrs. Julia McMullen and her staff of the Butte Public Library.

Contents

Preface v
Acknowledgments vii
Introduction to Butte, the Bizarre 1
Assaying the Lode 13
Shacks, Shanties and Mansions 19
Forgotten Man 26
Paradise of Parades 29
Rulers of the Roost 31
Brickbats on Election Day 47
Butte Blows Its Top 56
The Centerville Ghost 72
Cabbages and Kings 76
Printer's Ink 97
Smells of a Camp 103
Indians 105
The Battle of the City Dump 108
John Chinaman 113
Finlandia 128
Crazy over Horses 130
The Bohunk Scare 139
Kids of Butte 145
Disasters 169
Skibereen's One Mile Limit Ranch:
Mountain Oasis 180
Girls of the Line 183
The Old Comique 191
Wakes for the Dead 195
The Callaghans
The Priest and the Bum 198
Naming the Mines 202
Mules in the Mines 208

Men of the Mines 213
Melting Potpourri 222
Sports in the Early Days 229
Copper Camp Cuisine 251
Fabulous Females 260
Play Boys 267
Limbs of the Law 269
Cabbage Patch Corsage 278
Frontier Belascos 285
Chronology of Events in Butte, Montana 296
Index 316

LIST OF ILLUSTRATIONS

Butte, Montana, "The Richest Hill on Earth." 20
Corner of Broadway and Main (ca 1900) Butte 23
Marcus Daly . . . William Andrews Clark 32
W.A. Clark and supporters 35
F. Augustus Heinze 41
Miners Hall Union Hall 69
Fat Jack character 81
Wah Chong Tai Co., ca. 1905 Butte 116
Butte Jockey Club 131
Fourth grade class in Meaderville School, 1892 146
Butte boys try their luck at mining 160
Busy volunteers after explosions, 1895 179
Columbia Gardens, ca. 1925 181
The Comique Theatre 192
Miners station at 1600 level, Original mine 204
Miners at the Mountain Con 205
Mule train working on 1100 level, Rarus Mine 209
Swamper loading ore car from chute 210
Ready to blast at 1900 level 216
Shoestring Annie 262
Nickel Annie 265
W.A. Clark, Mayor Mullins, Fat Jack 270
Jere "the Wise" Murphy with two Butte law officers 273
Uncle Dick Sutton 289

Introduction to Butte, the Bizarre

BUTTE is unpredictable. Yesterday, today and probably tomorrow she is a city of paradox—virtuous yet wanton, vindictive and forgiving, hard headed or charitable, kind, cruel, religious, agnostic, sordid, exalted, gay and tragic.

Magnificent when viewed by night from the Continental Divide, Butte has been likened to a diamond set in jet, but by day she is an uncorseted wench, dissipated from the night before. "Perch of the devil," she has been called by some, and "merciful mother of the mountains," by others.

This is the city where in 1901, a ghost, haunting the environs of adjoining Centerville shared space in the nation's press with Mary MacLane, a precocious young writer who was then communing with devil at a cemetery on Montana Street, southern extremity of the camp, while writing her sensational autobiography, *The Story of Mary MacLane.* About the same period, Callahan the Bum spent the better part of a summer afternoon trying to hang himself from an awning rope on one of the main streets of the business district. When no heed was paid by the passing throng, he finally gave up in disgust, remarking that he would have succeeded but for the fact "the damn roped liked to choke him to death." Two sparrows in a fight to the death in front of a newspaper office caused a crowd of several hundred to gather and urge on the tiny gladiators, the newspaper holding up its presses so as to announce the victor in its afternoon edition.

Butte boasts of suburbs called Nanny Goat Hill, Hungry Hill, Seldom Seen, Dogtown, Chicken Flats and Butchertown. The society pages of the daily papers often feature side by side the likeness of a West Side society matron and that of a promised bride, whose address might be the kitchen of a Finnish boarding house on the "wrong" side of town.

Her saloons have been named The Alley Cat, Bucket of Blood, The Water Hole, Frozen Inn, Big Stope, The Cesspool, Collar and Elbow, Open-All-Night, Graveyard, The Good Old Summer Time, Pick and Shovel, The Beer Can, Saturday Night, and Pay Day.

And not only the saloons had unusual names. Skip Chute, Tipperary Mary, Colleen Bawn, Mag the Rag, Hayride, The Race Horse, Take-Five Annie, Ellen the Elephant, Kitty of Kildare, Finlander Fannie, and Little Egypt were the nicknames of hard-working waitresses at early day miners' boarding houses.

An old-timer, commenting on Butte's numerous saloons, remarked: "Sure, she's a town where they never allowed the dust to settle." Once a miner bequeathed his two thousand dollar insurance policy to a North Main Street taproom specifying that after his funeral expenses were paid, the remainder was to go into a fund to buy morning "eye openers" for his cronies.

The proprietor of a liquid-refreshment parlor filled out his bar bottles from the same whiskey keg, labeling them "Coming Off Shift Special," "Morning After Special," "All Day Special," "Good Night Special,"—and kept aside an ornately decorated bottle, filled from the same keg and bearing a label: "For wakes, weddin's, births and holidays."

Once a year in past days Tolerance Day was held, with Butte's Protestant clergymen, Catholic priests and Jewish rabbis speaking from the same platform. During Lent, theaters report a fifty per cent decrease in business. In earlier days a Jewish rabbi killed his congregation's Sabbath chickens on the sidewalk in front of his South Main Street store before the gaping eyes of the public, and a Jesuit Missionary stated from the pulpit, "There are more saints in Butte than in the city of Rome."

Department stores and newsstands have special departments devoted to the sale of rosaries, prayer books and assorted religious articles. The leading dry-goods store in the city gives its employees the day off with pay on Yom Kippur, and every business establishment in the city is closed down for three hours on Good Friday. But Billy Sunday, the evangelist, once remarked, "The bottles consumed in Butte on a week-end, when empty would build a stairway from the top of its highest peak to the utmost depths of hell."

The two largest funerals on record are those of Father Callaghan, a kindly priest and of Frank Little, the I. W. W. labor leader. Victim of a vigilante rope, Little's body was carried to its last resting place, a distance of some five miles, on the shoulders of husky comrades.

At Midnight Mass on Christmas Eve, the congregation for years has extended from the crowded church out onto the steps and sidewalks, kneeling regardless of the falling snow.

It was also in Butte that a Jewish expressman, Sam Gordon, named his horse "Jesus Christ"—and did a thriving business.

In the early days millions of dollars worth of jewels glittered a welcome to the new year at a New Year's Eve Ball at the swank Silver Bow Club. Twenty years later a Sunday night jitney dance was being featured at the Silver Bow Club by the Miners Union—the labor organization of several thousand members had purchased the club including its art treasures, bars, tapestries and furniture.

Butte is a city where justice is literally blind, with three sightless ex-miners today handing down their decisions in three justice of the peace offices. In the old days, when millions were involved in the litigations of the copper kings, justice was blind for other reasons. Judge Clancy once fined a pompous member of the bar for contempt of court, the lawyer's oratory having aroused the judge from his afternoon nap. Another judge declared that a miner was entitled to get drunk once a week and privileged to beat his wife once a month, adding that any miner who overstepped this limit would be jailed and fined.

Berton Braley, later prominent as an Eastern writer, serving his apprenticeship as a cub reporter on the old Butte *Evening News*, often wrote widely-read columns of the police court happenings in rhyme. At this time the underworld referred to the district judge of the criminal court, Michael Donlin, as "Long Distance Mike," because of the inordinately long sentences he imposed.

In the environs of the old "Cabbage Patch," a fantastic slum area, such characters as Mexicali Rose, Goldie Davis and Fay the Lady Barber proved one long headache to the Butte Police Department.

Rimmer O'Neill and Sean-Soul Sullivan once did the hirin' and firin' at the Anaconda, while Mickey Carrol ruled the north side of the hill; Jerry Mullins sold the "biggest scoops in the city," and the twenty-seven varieties of free lunch were supervised by Pig Nose Gaffney. Uncle Dick Sutton, theatrical impresario, wore a ten-carat diamond in lieu of a necktie ... and gray-haired "Lemons" was the town's leading messenger "boy." In a good old-fashioned free-for-all Stuttering Alex McLean and Watermelon Burns were names to contend with. Mrs. Fitzpatrick ran the "Hog Ranch," and the Centerville marshal was known as "The Limb of the Law."

Such a place was Butte, where "Colonel" Buckets, a camp roustabout, and United States Senator W. A. Clark, the copper millionaire, might often be seen walking through the streets arm in arm. Where Leu was mayor of Chinatown and never failed to become thoroughly drunk on Chinese New Year's and St. Patrick's Day; where Judge Clancy slept and "batched" in the courthouse, chewing constantly a special brand of tobacco which he imported from Hannibal, Missouri. Where Fat Jack, the hack driver, Ike Hayes, a colored heavyweight, Jimmy July, naturalized Chinese, and Paddy the Pig, a boardinghouse keeper, might be seen sitting in the same poker game.

Lulu Sutton, Irene Lorton, Fred Hagen and Charlie Malloy played *Chinatown Charlie* and *Queen of the White Slaves* to a hysterical audience at the old Grand theater; but a local beauty, Myra Quarles by name, driving a cow hitched to a light buckboard, caused no more attention on her daily visits to the camp than would now be caused by a '29 jallopie; and "Pup Milk" Gertney delivered his milk behind a dancing circus horse.

The City Hall clock has never kept the right time. But why should it in a place where the residents tell time by the mine whistles?

Before the day of the radio the voice of the town crier, leather-lunged Harry Clifford, could be heard crying out the news, events, and bargains of the day.

Here the "Divine Sarah" Bernhardt played *Sappho* to five thousand cheering miners in a drafty roller rink on the outskirts of the town, and Harry Lauder interrupted an uptown theater performance to sit down on the stage and listen to a Scotch miner sing *Loch Lomond* from his seat in the audience. When the first marathon dance was held at the old Renshaw Hall forty years ago, some twenty couples who danced continuously for more than twenty-four hours were finally stopped by the police for breaking the cruelty-to-animals ordinance.

What is believed to have been one of the first public barroom weddings in the United States was held in 1886 at a notorious dive known as Clipper Shades, in the heart of the red-light district. The participants were Mollie De Murska, a lady of the district, and Jack Jolly, town marshal. Many years later Dominic Foresco, an Italian from the "Meaderville" section, advertised in one of the daily papers for a wife, explaining that he would be present at the main intersection of the city—corner of Park and Main Streets—for three hours daily wearing a white carnation in his lapel. Because of the crowds which gathered to witness the show, the prospective bridegroom was jailed for obstructing traffic. Upon being released he was met at the jail door by a score of prospective brides, word having leaked out that Dominic was the possessor of some twenty thousand dollars in government bonds.

In earlier days when dapper miners wearing box-backed coats, high-heeled shoes and high-roller hats gathered at the Coliseum dance hall to give the girls of the camp a glimpse of what the best-dressed men were wearing, a leading bagnio displayed a half-million dollars worth of ornate furnishings. And long before Earl Carroll's time, the madame of this establishment had placed on an engraved plate at its entrance the inscription: "Herein Reside The Most Beautiful Girls In The World."

When William Jennings Bryan visited the copper camp on August 12, 1897, after his defeat for the Presidency he received "the greatest welcome ever accorded him in his years of campaigning" and the poem, *When Bryan Came to Butte*, by a Butte newswriter became, for a time, an American classic.

For here, ten thousand people will appear on five minutes notice to witness a parade. Yet circuses and carnivals approaching the Continental Divide always pass the word to "keep everything above board"—for sad experience has taught them that this camp is not a "sucker town."

The copper camp has always been a great sports town. Two world's championship fights, welterweight and lightweight, once were held within a period of twenty-four hours; and a native miner, Jack Munroe, almost achieved the world's heavyweight championship. A colored champion of his time, Joe Wolcott, was refused a drink in an East Broadway saloon, although one of Butte's most popular citizens was the colored pugilist, Ike Hayes. But what would be expected in a camp where Chinese Jimmy July once delivered the principal Fourth of July oration?

On one occasion a local theater ordered a ticket box from a Scotch cabinet maker, the dimensions being given as twenty inches by twenty-four. The slightly deaf craftsman made the box in feet instead of inches and became indignant when the theater refused to accept the monstrosity when it was delivered on a huge truck. He brought the case to court and forced the theater to pay for the lumber.

By the turn of the century, Butte school teachers found it useful to have at least a smattering of six different languages and dialects. Many Irish miners spoke Finnish as fluently as the Finns. A person named "Mike" might be an Irish or Serbian miner, a Greek bootblack, an Afghan tamale peddler, a Turkish coffee-house keeper, a waiter at a Chinese chop suey joint, a "Cousin Jack" newsboy, an Austrian smelterman, a French-Canadian wood chopper, an Egyptian barber, a Polish bartender, a Syrian rug vendor, a Jewish pawnbroker or a Spanish-born resident of Crib 19, Pleasant Alley.

Cornish boarding houses served pie for breakfast. Gypsy caravans considered Butte a highlight stop on their annual migrations. Into the camp, surrounded by their dogs came pleasure-bent sheepherders from the wool country of southwestern Montana. They gathered at the old Swiss Home on South Arizona Street. One wild evening in the company of the neighborhood charmers was the usual extent of their brief holiday, then back to the hills for several months of loneliness.

Where but in Butte would one hear of an Irish miner crawling into a dangerous mine cave-in to rescue his Afghan partner, a Mohammedan;

and, on seeing that the non-Christian was pinned down by a large rock and dying, proceed to baptize him in the Christian faith using copper water from a nearby ditch?

And there were the Irish. After Marcus Daly made Butte the greatest copper camp on earth, they came in by the thousands, bringing with them the Irish flair for politics, a spirit of independence, of broad humor, ambition, superstition and hot temper, which, coupled with an inherent ability for hard work and hard play, complemented perfectly the rugged spirit of the camp.

In half an hour's travel in the old days one might meet up with such notables as Con Kelly, now of New York and chairman of the board of the Anaconda Company and some of the nation's other large corporations; the young newsboy, Frank Walker, present Postmaster General of the United States; W. A. Clark, the copper king; W. W. McDowell, later United States Minister to Ireland; and others who became nationally famous.

The notables rubbed shoulders with the street characters known as Shoestring Annie, Chicken Liz, Nigger Riley, Crazy Mary, Lutey the Box Thief, Liz the Lady, Filthy McNabb, Lousy Pete, Crying George Rooney, The Irish Gentleman, and a score of others.

Yes, this was the "Shamrock City," where McNamara an old country Irishman, was king of the "Cabbage Patch," and with an iron hand ruled several hundred Mexicans and Filipinos. Where once presided "Jere the Wise" Murphy, chief of police, whose name was known to the underworld from New York to San Francisco.

Where, for some obscure reason, the "Far-Downs" as North-of-Ireland Protestants were known, shoveled and blessed themselves with their left hand. Here a lad's ambition in earlier years was to ride astride a black horse in the Miners Union Day parade, with a white cockade stuck in his hat. Here the name Sullivan even today leads all others in the city directory.

Here Mary Maloney, a widow, once accumulated a comfortable fortune gathering up the dropped particles of ore from the tracks of W. A. Clark's electric ore-line, and several similar fortunes have been made from picking over the waste dumps of the company's mines. A shoveler at the Black Rock Mine, winner of $4500 in a baseball pool years ago, celebrated by buying a ticket to Ireland. Instead of returning from the Emerald Isle he remained, and today is a member of President DeValera's cabinet.

Once the Irish miners celebrated on St. George's Day, and their Cornish friends, the Cousin Jacks, whooped it up on St. Patrick's Day. For many years St. Patrick's Day was celebrated twice—on March 17, and again on Easter Monday. But an orange necktie on that sacred day still represents the near-equivalent of a death warrant for the wearer.

When President Theodore Roosevelt visited the city, Mayor Pat Mullins in his speech of greeting referred to Teddy's daring charge at San "Diego" Hill. When the President, later that momentous day, sat down to eat in the luxurious Thornton Hotel dining room, Mullins ordered the waiters to raise the window blinds in order to "let the boys out on the street see the President eat."

Today Butte is this kind of a melting pot: the third generation of an original Tipperary Irish family now boasts a mixture of Spanish, English, French, Serbian and Cherokee Indian stock—although strangely, this brood of eight retains the flaming red hair of their original ancestors.

In this camp the miracle of the dead voting on election day was beheld for many years and some people claim it is so today. Here a black eye is still considered a mark of distinction, and a "Shawn O'Farrell" is not to be confused with a man's name. It's simply whiskey with a beer chaser.

Yes, this is Butte, where Jerry Buckley, a purveyor of moist goods, indignantly remarked to a stranger who ordered a glass of milk: "Do you see any room in here for a cow?"

And where but in Butte could this have happened? While the Reverend Bulgin, self-styled "sin buster," led his two-week attack on wickedness in a huge tented tabernacle, an enterprising saloonkeeper in the vicinity ordered huge banners painted, to be flaunted in the faces of the departing worshippers. They read: REMEMBER—AFTER THE SERVICES, AT DUBLIN DAN'S A BIG COLD SCOOP OF BEER FOR A NICKEL. ADDITIONAL BARTENDERS DURING REVIVAL WEEK.

Motion picture theater cashiers still are members of the Cooks and Waiters Union. Years ago, one of the camp's gay young blades, a scion of banking and mining interests, on reaching maturity, spent forty thousand dollars on a birthday party. Matty Kieley made his weekly visit to Marcus Daly's statue and in a voice that the town could hear, commented on the latest news of the day. A crowd on North Main Street cheered "Shoestring Annie" as she belabored a spectacled tormentor, and then took up a collection to purchase a new pair of spectacles for the victim of her wrath when a blow from Annie's umbrella shattered the ones he was wearing.

At the beginning of the century Butte boasted that its copper mines had yielded almost two billion dollars, and in the same breath admitted that it was the only Western city whose cemetery population exceeded that of the living residents.

Many years after most cities of comparable size were "modernized," most copper camp homes had their little backyard sanctuary, and Lyon's Best flour sacks until quite recently were considered excellent material for an undergarment. While most children picked great bouquets of pansies at W. A. Clark's Columbia Gardens park on Children's Day, one family of boys called the "Ringtails" bought their mother a new axe for a Christmas present.

Reminiscent of New York's Ghetto, old time Jewish clothing dealers on East Park Street pulled all passers-by into their stores in spite of vigorous protests. One of these merchants for years used a stock of smoke-damaged goods which he would dump in his window; then he held a fire sale every time there was a fire within ten blocks of his establishment. Another of these dealers had a "Closing Out—Going Out of Business" sign in front of his establishment for five consecutive years.

This is the Butte where all boarding house chambermaids were once referred to as "Admirals." "Tom and Jerries" are still one of the few mixed drinks regarded as manly. In earlier days, "cocktails" were what flew in the air at the rooster fights held in the Timber Butte Saloon. Down in the mine, bib overalls and union suit underwear were considered effeminate in the days when Jim Brennan, shift boss of the Mountain Con Mine, would pat a miner's back in a fatherly manner to see if his shirt was damp from sweat. If it wasn't it meant the "pink slip" or notice of discharge.

In those days a heavy dose of Epsom Salts was thought to be a most efficient remedy for any number of ailments, but when there was any doubt, one could never go wrong on whiskey. Cow manure was prescribed for copper water sores. It was not at all uncommon for groups of girls from the red-light section to be seen on a summer afternoon cantering through the business district on blooded saddle horses, clad in the latest riding habits. Yet, it was only in the red-light district that the saloons would serve liquor to a woman at the bar. In all other places, rear or side entrance and winerooms only were available for thirsty females.

Peerless or "Michigan Hay" was chewed and smoked by any miner who was worth his salt. A youth, reaching puberty, if able to survive a chew of Peerless without becoming ill, was considered qualified for work in the mines. Greenhorns, on arriving from the Old Country, first looked for "the mine with the seven stacks." The name "Anaconda" was a twister for foreign tongues, but the newly arrived immigrants could count the stacks. Miners frequently sent the porcelain chamber pot from under their beds in East Side rooming houses to be filled with beer. And these miners very early learned the trick of greasing a lunch bucket with lard so as to eliminate foam on the beer. One crew from the Moonlight Mine daily climbed two hundred and fifty feet to surface in the dark up a rickety ladder so as to have a fresh "growler" for the lunch period.

Yes, there has always been a certain amount of drinking in Butte. The old Atlantic Bar, which termed itself the longest bar in the world, was a full block in length with as many as fifteen bartenders serving the customers. It is claimed that twelve thousand glasses of beer were sold there on a Saturday night. By comparison the "Success" Cafe on East Broadway claimed the distinction of being "the smallest restaurant in the world"—four customers crowded the place.

Twenty-five four-horse brewery wagons trod copper camp streets in the summertime during the years when doors of hundreds of saloons were built without locks. On opening night many of the saloons that did have locks made a ritual of throwing the key into the lavatory. Bibulous miners often endeavored to place their hats on the bare head of Saint-Gaudens' bronze statue of Marcus Daly opposite the post office. It was not uncommon for the miners to toss any change smaller than a dime to the newsboys and a stack of twenty dollar gold pieces was the accepted admittance fee into a faro or poker game. The floor of a leading saloon was embedded with hundreds of silver dollars. Custom for years decreed that any small change dropped in the barroom sawdust rightfully belonged to the swamper.

Many old-timers will swear to the story that in the nineties a transient fell in a faint from hunger. Scores of generous citizens had bought him drinks—but not a person offered to buy him a meal.

When national prohibition became law, Butte was temporarily stunned. A half-century way of life was to be altered. But soon prohibition came to be regarded as a crank law, enforced in Pocatello, Idaho but not in Butte. During this "dry era," Federal prisoners at the county jail staged an elaborate wedding, the principals being a convicted counterfeiter and a comely girl-about-town. The list of guests read like a *Who's Who* of copper camp.

From the beginning, throughout the "dry era," many residents annually received engraved invitations: "YOU ARE CORDIALLY INVITED TO ATTEND THE ANNUAL BOOTLEGGERS' PICNIC, SUNDAY, AUGUST 25TH, 1929, AT ROSS' RANCH. TAKE RESERVOIR ROAD. EXECUTIVE COMMITTEE. KINDLY PRESENT THIS INVITATION." The copper camp continued its old way of life and many new fortunes were created during this period.

Today many of the natives long for the "good old prohibition days, when whiskey had a bite in it," and when there were considered to be three pints to a quart, local measurement. A traveler remarked on his first visit in the early days of depression: "Butte—a great town—they sole their own shoes and make their own whiskey."

In 1912, a newswriter in reporting a free-for-all at a miners' picnic at a nearby resort, Gregson Springs, stated: "The afternoon sun was obscured by the flying beer bottles." The nucleus of a family fortune estimated at over a million dollars, was obtained from salvaging the camp's empty bottles. Yet in this same camp a popular saloon once advertised it would refuse to sell a miner a drink if his children were in need of shoes. And in the late nineties a convivial band of barflies and rounders gathered at a local bar on Christmas Eve, to organize the Josher's Club, an organization which continued for a quarter of a century to provide every needy family in the city with a Christmas dinner and toys for the children.

Because of the smelter smoke nuisance, not a blade of grass, nor a tree, nor shrub would grow until the smelters were moved. But years ago a lemon tree was found growing a thousand feet underground, sprouting from a seed dropped from a miner's lunch.

It's hard for Butte to outgrow many things from the past and it probably never will. There's something both sensible and cockeyed about it all.

It is a cockeyed place, where a tailor patches a United States Senator's forty-dollar suit while his assistant stitches on a new hundred-dollar overcoat ordered by a Finn miner. Where "Nickel Annie" who once made her piteous plea from the church steps, never asking for more than five cents, was believed to have accumulated a neat fortune . . . and a crippled beggar on Park Street has for years employed a chauffeur to take him back and forth to work.

It's the place where the twenty thousand miners who paraded on Miners Union Day, and risked their life daily, considered the display of a gold-nugget watch chain the very height of sartorial perfection. Where a local newspaper had more linotype machines on the job than any newspaper in the city of New York.

While the Salvation Army held lonely meetings on the streets, their "lassies" passing tamborines in the countless saloons and sporting houses were enthusiastically received, treated respectfully and generously tipped.

Early day "skinners" on the six- and eight-horse ore teams were never without a quart of whiskey in the wagon box.

The kids, in wintertime, once started their bobsleds at the top of the hill in Centerville and coasted nearly two miles to the cemeteries at the edge of the camp.

A former mayor and restaurant man, W. H. Davey, won a sizeable fortune, estimated in the tens of thousands, by betting year in and year out that rain would fall twenty-six days during June.

Over a hundred mine and smelter whistles once blew for a full hour on New Year's Eve.

Amid such hilarity there was always tragedy. In 1906 Butte had five suicides from dynamite alone.

Mohammed Akara, a rug peddler, had his name changed in court to Mohammed Murphy—"for business reasons."

Perhaps "Nigger Liz," a pioneer prostitute, old, half-blind and toothless, indicated something of the nature of the camp when she bemoaned: "I'se got a million dollars worth of chawm, but Ah can't get a nickel foh hit."

Maybe there's a clue in the fact that despite the vast fortunes which have been made here, it finally remained for WPA to pave hundreds of miles of streets, lay a vast network of sanitary sewers, develop parks and playgrounds and provide an Art Center for the community, while symphony orchestras, libraries and art galleries endowed by the copper kings are enjoyed in the cities to which the millionaires moved.

Butte has been and always will be, it seems, a paradox of rags and riches. Miners' wives wear fur coats and Fifth-Avenue-model dresses and hats. Jewelry stores do a thriving business. In years of depression or shutdowns, the Christmas shopping is done at the five and ten cent stores, but when "copper is high" there is a rushing business for imported perfumes.

It is the city that Gertrude Atherton claimed had only forty minutes in every hour.

No one can be found who will accept the dog catcher job, although the job pays six dollars a day.

Fully half the town labors while the other half sleeps. . . . The Cousin Jack pasty is as popular as beans in Boston.

Once, during a clerks' strike, a picket carrying a banner in front of the largest department store, blithely entered and purchased himself a pair of gloves to warm his numbed fingers.

Thousands of people annually visit the five cemeteries on Memorial Day, and it is rare to find a neglected grave. . . . Snow on the Fourth of July is not unheard of.... A talent for singing has often proved a valuable adjunct in the seeking of public office.

Butte has never had a Miss America chosen from her ranks, but of her girls, the late Chauncey Olcott, famous Irish tenor, once remarked: "I met more pretty girls in Butte on my walk from the hotel to the theater than I saw in a year's engagement in New York and the last six months on the road."

Butte even today is a frontier camp where a farmer is often referred to as a "sheepherder" and anyone hailing from farther east than Meaderville was once called a "Missourian" and is now styled as "Arkie" or an "Okie." . . . Where holidays are celebrated a week in advance and nursed for a week afterward. . . . Where pigeons roost in the Library and City Hall and are fed with religious care by the residents.... Where the leading chain store reported "no sale" on a carload shipment of mauve- and pale-green-tinted toilet paper. . . Where summer nights are so cool that blankets are needed. . . . Where ten thousand miners hoist twenty thousand tons of copper and zinc ores to the surface every twenty-four hours to produce one-third of the nation's copper.

Her people are proud of one of the lowest temperatures ever recorded in the nation, minus 61°. When a series of earthquakes shook the city several years ago they were not noticed by any of the miners working underground.

A barren, deserted knoll on the southwest part of the town is known as "Lovers' Roost." It was an unwritten and unbroken law never to divulge the name of male or female encountered there. Over two-thirds of the town answers to a nickname, and the camp's daily baseball pool has averaged six thousand dollars.

Butte volunteers in the Spanish-American War wrote a round robin to the President stating that they would desert in a body if the Government did not stop feeding them embalmed beef.

Here Bylo, the original ice cream and hokey-pokey vendor of the gay nineties, proudly admitted he saved money by obtaining his ice from the undertaking parlors of the city—"putting it to good use instead of letting it melt in the hot sun on the sidewalks."

Yes, that was Butte—and that is Butte today.

Assaying the Lode

SINCE that day long ago when the first grizzled prospector thrust his pick into the metal-rich surface of what is now known as "the richest hill on earth," Butte, Montana has been different. She is different from all the cities of the world. There is only one Butte—there will never be another. Those who know her, love her, and wouldn't trade her for the most beautiful city on earth. She's dirty, she's rough, and she's wide open, but she's the World's Copper Metropolis. And that explains it in any man's language.

And yet her story is in large part the story of the other best-known mining camps of the West—Leadville, Central City, Cripple Creek, Virginia City, Deadwood, Lead, Tonopah, Tombstone, Rhyolite and the rest. But with one difference. Many of the others are now "ghost towns," while Butte, because of her importance to the nation's war effort, was never more important than today.

Once there was a time when gold was *the* precious metal, but that was before we realized that all the gold at Fort Knox cannot make one shell casing for the defense of Democracy. Today, in the greatest war effort of all time, the precious metals are steel, aluminum, tin, zinc, chromium, manganese, and copper. Of these, Butte has vast deposits of zinc and manganese but—above all—copper, of which the country is a million tons short this year and may face even greater deficiencies.

The story of copper mining here is the story of adversity, which faith and good luck turned into fortune. For after its beginning as a short-lived gold camp, seventy-seven years ago, a rich silver strike later spurred the camp to boom proportions—only to fade as the silver veins, after several years digging, began to turn more and more to the gray, heavy rock and the peacock-colored ore which miners threw aside as worthless waste. Depression settled on the camp and it appeared headed for the cobwebbed status of so many of the Golcondas before and after it.

It remained for a staunch emigrant lad who "landed in America [at 15] with nothing in his pockets save his . . . Irish smile," who learned about mining the hard way in California and Nevada mining camps and gained the backing of Salt Lake bankers—despite the complete derision of the mining experts—to save the day for Butte. Marcus Daly brought it up to the generally undisputed claim of the world's greatest mining camp.

But what is the background of the "richest hill on earth"—this copper camp of 40,000 people sprawled on the gaunt, gray slopes of the Continental Divide, a mile above sea level in southwestern Montana, from which has been extracted the fantastic total of three billion dollars in mineral wealth in only three-quarters of a century?

* * * * *

The first authentic record of white men visiting the spot where the city now stands was in 1856, when Judge C. E. Irvine and party from Walla Walla in Washington Territory stopped on a tour of exploration. They found an ancient prospect hole, four or five feet deep, upon what is now the Original lode. Scattered about the edge of the hole were decayed and weatherbeaten prongs of elk horns sharpened for use as picks. Whether this was the work of Indians in search of metal or of a still earlier white prospector is unknown.

The discovery of gold on Butte Hill was made in July 1864 by G. O. Humphrey and William Allison just as placer gold mining in the fabulous territorial camps of Bannack, Virginia City and later at Confederate and Last Chance Gulches—all within a hundred miles—were approaching their peak. Humphrey and Allison worked the dry gulches, particularly Town Gulch, by hauling the gold-bearing dirt down to Silver Bow Creek and there washing it. News of their luck brought hundreds of miners, many from the Alder Gulch diggings, to the camp, and all of them more or less unsuccessfully panned the nearby gulches. The miners christened the settlement of Butte City, taking the name from the sentinel-like peak (Big Butte) which stands northwest of the town. It was an exciting, boisterous, typical camp, not sensational but steady.

Several miles to the west and south a few cabins and rough shacks made up a settlement known as Silver Bow, where the yellow metal had been discovered a month before Humphrey and Allison located farther up on the meandering course of Silver Bow Creek. An occasional placer digging was found along this stretch of rocky, sagebrush terrain. By autumn the thin cold air from the mountains which hemmed in this area, and the deep snows and cold blizzards which followed, prompted the building of several more cabins at Silver Bow and a false-front store structure at Butte City. By spring the entire creek channel from Silver Bow to Butte City, and a new camp, Rocker, midway between the two, echoed with the scrape of miners' tools, the swish of gravel in gold pans and flumes, and the creaking of crude hand-made rockers.

Four or more men usually toiled in every two-hundred-foot claim. They lived in tents and crude shanties. Labor began with the first crimson slant of dawn across the jagged outlines of the Continental Divide. It continued until a cold ball of fire settled on the shoulders of the great hulking mass of the Rocky Mountains to the west. They worked six days of the week always—but generally showed up in one of the three camps on the seventh. This was the business day of the week. Gambling and drinking flourished. The merchant made his weekly clean-up and the dance halls panned out more gold dust than the richest placers.

An unknown writer of this time described the physical appearance of the structures—mostly saloons—which lined the abbreviated streets of the camps:

"We should judge the prevailing style of architecture to be the Pan-Doric—a heathenish one of many evils. The material used is log and lumber. Last year houses were hauled from Silver Bow to Butte City; this year the movement is reversed," concluding sarcastically: "This was to save timber, we suppose, as there is not more than a million or two acres of good timber in this vicinity."

"In 1865 and 1866 the moral character [of Butte City] was probably the most deplorable of its placer days," wrote Harry C. Freeman. "It is said that . . . no man was safe without a brace of revolvers in his belt and a bowie-knife tucked in his bootleg. No small percentage of the numbers who had flocked to the district were of that daring, lawless type whose greatest pleasure was found in pastimes similar to shooting up the town, which type has given to the entire West a name of wild and wooly and which name to this day [1900] has not been wholly effaced. . . ." Actually Freeman was only proving that Butte at the beginning was not entirely an orthodox camp. Time has proved that convincingly.

As the placers gradually worked out, just as they did elsewhere, miners began leaving the diggings. By 1874, the population of the camps had dwindled to a handful. Silver Bow was a ghost. Rocker was crumbling into decay. Butte City, with less than sixty inhabitants, was dying.

But there was one man who held a deep faith—Butte City was not played out. William L. Farlin in the early placer days had seen some rock taken from a shallow prospect hole. Later when he traveled to Owyhee, Idaho he had the specimens assayed and found them rich in gold, silver *and copper.* He kept his discovery to himself, and being a poor man, continued to work in the waning placer diggings to make a living. Farlin never forgot that mineral-bearing quartz lay under the placer workings.

A few others were aware of the potential quartz properties of the area, but they did little about it. In the first year of the camp, Charley Murphy and others had gone beyond placer gravel, uncovering leads they named the Missoula and Deer Lodge lodes. Three years later Joe

Ramsdell, afterward credited as the "father of quartz mining in Butte" struck a good character of ore in the Parrot lode. A company composed of himself, W. J. Parks, Dennis Leary, T. C. Porter and others was formed. A small arastra smelter was built by Charles E. Savage to handle the silver ores from this mine, but it was quickly abandoned and all traces of the smelter soon disappeared. Some ore from this mine was shipped to Swansea, Wales, but nothing came of it. In 1868, the Davis mill was built and a furnace erected for the smelting of ores from the Parrot lode which had been developed to a depth of 155 feet through the persistence of W. J. Parks. Inability to properly flux the ore again caused abandonment of the idea.

After several years Farlin found his opportunity when Congress passed a law compelling owners of claims to perform a certain amount of labor or forfeit their claims on January 1, 1875. Few had done this. At 11:30 in the freezing mountain air of New Year's Eve, Farlin was on the ground. He relocated the claim and commenced development work at once. With every stroke of the pick, his Travonia Mine revealed its hidden treasures.

From the mediocre placer diggings of ten years standing and the dying camp of the year before, Butte—as it was now called—in three months became the leading mining town of the Territory. With the permanency of the camp seemingly assured, many miners soon were encouraged to bring their families with them. The town as a silver camp quickly took on an air of stability.

"Now following an exposure of the true facts concerning the value of the ores of the camp, the news spread like wildfire far and near, and newcomers flocked in great numbers. Old locations were renewed and new ones made in rapid succession. The discovery of the Alice, La Plata, Burlington, Late Acquisition, Great Republic, and other less famous mines followed quickly, and the movement toward Butte resolved itself into a stampede. The town had become metamorphosed. From the hopeless, abandoned camp of a year before, it was now the Mecca of all who could possibly reach it, and its growth was magic-like," wrote Freeman, twenty-five years later.

Smelters for the proper handling of the silver ore of the camp were constructed almost immediately—and this time they worked. The Dexter and Centennial plants were the first of note, but three years later when the first post office was established, there were others.

Just before Christmas, 1881, an old-fashioned locomotive puffed and chugged up the newly-completed Utah and Northern narrow-gauge railroad to officially connect Butte with Ogden, Utah—and the outside world—by rail. It was an occasion for real and ribald celebration, and few of the camp's four thousand people failed to take advantage of it.

Hard-bitten and experienced miners, late of the mother lode mines of California, the hard-rock workings of Arizona, Nevada and Colorado, and a few of the advanced guard from the free-copper pits of Michigan, mingled with strong-backed "greenhorns" from the old sod of Ireland and the collieries of Wales. Many miners were soft-handed "pilgrims" from the cities of the East.

They struck their drills, swung picks and mucked heavy ore in numerous mines in the Travonia district to the southwest, north to a point a mile beyond "the Hill" where the famed Alice and Lexington mines were pouring forth a prodigious stream of silver in the midst of the mushroom town of Walkerville. Above the base of the hill proper, for a stretch of almost two miles where the city was already beginning to cluster, were many mines of good promise: the Original, Parrot, Clark's Colusa, Ramsdell's Parrot, Mountain Consolidated, and Leonard. New smelters were being erected and others already belched black smoke at convenient places over this large area, to handle ore from the many mines.

Silver was the metal exclusively sought. Copper was encountered in no great quantity, except in W. A. Clark's Colusa.

One adventurous Irish miner, Michael Hickey, ex-soldier of the Union army, had read an editorial by Horace Greeley in the *New York Tribune* stating that, Grant's army was "encircling Lee's forces like a giant anaconda."

"That word struck me as a mighty good one," said Hickey. "I always remembered it, and when I wanted a name for my mine I remembered Greeley's editorial and called it the 'Anaconda.'"

Hickey's famous property in which was discovered, in 1882, a great copper lead, gave its name to the largest copper mining, smelting, and fabricating organization in the world—the Anaconda Copper Mining Company, now sole owner of the mines of Butte.

In Nevada, at the time Hickey climbed the Butte hill with his location notice, was a "hotwater man," as the miners of that state were known, working in the silver veins of the Comstock lode. He was the bright, ambitious young Irish immigrant, Marcus Daly. Brought to Butte as manager of the Alice silver mine, Daly was on the lookout for new ventures. He became a partner of Michael Hickey, and pushed development work. Soon he and other backers bought Hickey's share in the Anaconda.

At the three-hundred-foot level, good luck in the guise of tragedy struck Daly. Instead of silver, he found ore predominantly copper. The disappointment of Daly's backers is easy to understand. Few of the hard-rock mining men of the West were then familiar with the red metal. As a matter of fact, only gold and silver generally were considered worth the gamble. The camp had no facilities for treating copper ore. No one knew if the ore body was large enough to warrant an investment in equipment for smelting copper. There appeared many other drawbacks.

Daly, himself, was optimistic. The mining engineers were skeptical, but the unschooled Irishman proved all of them wrong. Neighboring properties were bought up. Thousands of men probed their way to orebearing veins—this time for copper as well as silver and the always present gold. The surface of the hill became unlovely from the scars of the waste dumps, the piles of black slag, and gray-green tailings, and the scene was set for the tremendous years to follow.

The year 1882 stands as a great mark in the records of events. The effect of the discovery of the huge copper body in the Anaconda Mine was revolutionary, and it was this discovery that established the scope and permanency which resulted in the greatest mining camp on earth.

Advent of the railroad had removed all obstacles that previously blocked every effort to handle recovery of any mineral except silver and gold. The new strike trebled the importance of previous discoveries in the district. It gradually dawned upon the miners, the operators, and many capitalists, that "the Hill" was a veritable mountain of copper ores. Almost without exception it was found that in the mines of that portion of the hill lying south of Walkerville, the ores closest to the surface were rich in silver, but as depth was gained and the water level passed, copper ores predominated.

Additional and larger mills and smelters were constructed on all sides. The development of the mines was expanded in scope. Men skilled in mines and mining all over the world were attracted by favorable reports—the copper kings who controlled out-of-state properties, imported geologists—men trained in the art of detecting new and richer ore bodies. The stage was set for the greatest mining boom the world has ever known.

By 1884 more than three hundred mines were working and paying handsome dividends. In addition, more than four thousand location notices were posted on the hills surrounding the copper camp. Smoke from nine quartz mills and four smelters, working three shifts, seven days a week, clouded the growing city. Five thousand miners, woodchoppers, and teamsters were making the wheels turn for the huge mine-machine. The payrolls of the various companies on "the Hill" aggregated around $600,000 a month. The yield of silver and copper for that year was estimated at $14,000,000 and in a decade this was almost quadrupled. By the turn of the century almost a quarter of the world's copper supply and seventy-two million fine ounces of gold and silver were being produced annually.

Small wonder that Butte grew overnight and that she developed some rare characteristics. In the cradle days of the camp, only the hardiest of men ventured this far into the wilds. They were rough, tough, and as hard as the metal they mined, but many of them were the "salt of the earth." They worked like slaves, and they played like kings; they asked no quarter, and no quarter did they give; they took their whiskey straight, and they took it often. Humor played a leading part in the lives of those underground boys. The humor was coarse, often bawdy. It was rough men's fun, and rough men enjoyed it. To be sure there were worries but real men didn't show them. Grief was a thing to be expressed briefly—at wakes. Tragedy and sorrow were under the surface. On top it was, "Hey Jack, what the hell, we're here today and gone tomorrow!"

Money came the hard way, but it took wings with the greatest of ease. In the tinseled confines of the sporting houses and gambling joints money was merely something that had the power to purchase fun. As long as the money lasted, John Miner was cock of the walk. When it was gone—well, what the hell! There was always more money waiting on "the Hill."

Few were "family men" in those days. Home was where the single man hung his hat. Fights were numerous. The city jail was never without occupants. The black wagon of the police roamed the streets night after night looking for customers and business was always good. But through it all Butte smiled, and built her reputation—a reputation that is known wherever men gather and talk.

Shacks, Shanties and Mansions

IN a brightly-hued, illustrated folder, *Butte—Center of the Montana Wonderland*, the Chamber of Commerce relates: "Butte is not one, but really two cities, one above and one below ground, both worth crossing the nation to see." On other pages one reads that "Beautiful by night and unique by day, Butte is literally a city set upon a hill which cannot be hid."

It explains pointedly that "Butte is the richest hill on earth"; that "one third of all the copper mined in the United States comes from Butte." The fact that a million and a half dollar pay-roll is paid out to fifteen

MONTANA HISTORICAL SOCIETY, HELENA

Butte, Montana, "The Richest Hill on Earth."

thousand wage earners is cited, as is the fact that "Butte has 42 churches, 19 public schools, 11 parochial schools and the Montana State School of Mines."

Detailed statistical mention indicates that Butte's population of sixty thousand (including suburbs) uses 10,300 telephones, ten thousand gas and sixteen thousand electrical connections; that there is always abundant sunshine with days never uncomfortably warm and nights always cool, and that the elevation of the city at the courthouse is 5,755 feet.

All of which is true—from a public relations standpoint—but what a little folder does not tell is the unbeautiful fact which fairly smacks any first-time visitor right between the eyes during the first few minutes within the city's boundaries. Butte *is ugly as sin.*

At night, miles of neon and thousands of lights serve to hide its bleakness. Their glare tends to brighten up the town's shabby appearance. After dark one sees the camp at its best. But in the pitiless light of day Butte can never be mistaken for anything but what it actually is—a lusty, sprawling mining town, just a handful of several-story buildings but little ahead of being as much a frontier camp as it was sixty years ago.

Two miners of the Marcus Daly era aptly described it when on their way to work early one morning they paused on the top of Anaconda Road and gazed down over the awakening camp.

"Butte's a great old town," reflected one of them. "There's none better. But, do you know, I've never yet looked down on her in the sun's light that she doesn't remind me of a painted, old trollop waking up after a wild night."

"Aye," agreed the other, "a painted, old trollop—but with a heart as big as a mountain."

One of the first impressions gained by the visitor is that the camp appears old—centuries old. The barren, gray mine dumps with faded cottages in clusters at their feet; the huge steel and wooden gallows frames of the mines; the smoke-belching stacks; the crooked, crazy dirt roads and crumbling sidewalks leading up the hill to the mines., the rickety, unpainted, bulging and leaning brick and frame buildings —all look as if they had been there for generations. Yet Butte is relatively young. To quote an old-timer: "If you had lived as hard and excitin' a life as old Butte has, you'd be a bit prematurely aged yourself." That is Butte—prematurely aged, but tough and defiant.

The six or seven blocks comprising the business district, if not exactly an architect's dream, is a bee hive of activity. Night or day, there are crowds on the streets. If times are good and the mines are working to capacity, the stores will be packed and jammed. The silver dollar is king in Butte, and paper money in small denominations is hard to find. Saloons dot the shopping district. They will be found next door to anything but a church or school, and usually they are crowded, with two and three bartenders behind every bar. The "lounges" as many of them are now called, though ultramodern in equipment with stainless steel and chrome fronts, still present the old camaraderie of their sawdust-floored predecessors. Good fellowship predominates. Over three hundred saloon licenses are issued each year.

Tell almost any resident there isn't beauty in the town, and he most probably will answer: "Sure there's beauty—have you ever piped more beautiful girls than walk our streets?" If you should explain that you were speaking of beauty of other types, he most likely would interrupt: "Oh, you mean flowers and trees and things. Certainly, plenty of them. Have you been out on the West Side or the Flat? Have you been out to Columbia Gardens?"

It is as though the camp, aware of her ugliness and half ashamed of it, points with pride to the few residential sections of the city which have beautiful homes, some semblance of landscaped lawns, and well-laid-out streets. These, with their garden clubs, imported trees, shrubs and flower borders are not often the homes of miners, but of business and professional men, or of the executive staff of the mining corporation.

Nevertheless Butte is a city of home owners and builders. Three-quarters of the homes are owned by their occupants. Those frame and brick cottages huddled up against the mine dumps and scattered up and down the hills and gulches were built and paid for by the early day miners. Cornish, Irish, Italian, Swede, and a dozen other nationalities built their houses near the Hill in order to live closer to their work. Every house is a saga of saving, skimping and self-denial to keep up the payments through boom times and shutdowns. On the Flat, south of the camp, where there are hundreds of miners' homes, many of the workers and their families during the biggest boom years lived in tents and temporary shacks while the houses were under construction.

Even today while many miners' homes, especially in the uptown and eastern parts of the city, are outwardly uninviting, one has but to accept an owner's invitation to enter to receive a surprise. They are spotlessly neat. The rooms will likely be furnished more than comfortably. One will see up-to-date plumbing fixtures, built-in features, modern lighting equipment, a late model radio, an electric ice box, electric washing machines, gas ranges and heaters, vacuum cleaners and other appliances, all bought and paid for on the installment plan. You will find the homes stocked with books and paintings of a better quality than would ever be expected. One finds magazines, too, of the better class, but sometimes they may be mixed with cheaper pulps. Butte people for unexplainable reasons are inveterate readers, and, as one old-timer put it: "They'll read the labels on the grocery cans, if they can't find anything else."

The greater part of these homes house large families. Here you will see in the making the spirit that keeps Butte unique—the love of home and the loyalty of each member of the family toward the others and a spirit of family cooperation in keeping the home fires burning. This is but a part of the copper camp's beauty that the visitor does not see on the surface—and there are a score of others.

Butte is democratic. There isn't a man, woman or child in the community who doesn't believe that he or she is as good as his neighbor. The miner or mucker doesn't look up to the banker or merchant and the banker or merchant doesn't look down on the miner. There is little class distinction. The roughly clad miner whom one sees hurrying down the street with his lunch pail under his arm leaning up against a Park Street bar could be a Harvard graduate with a degree or two in his trunk—and again he might be a hobo who rode in on a freight last month.

Since that wintry New Year's Eve in the early sixties where Chastine Humphrey and Bill Allison staged Butte's first party with themselves the only guests, snobbery has had no place in the town. As early as 1901, a

Blue Book, a tiny social register with about two thousand names, was published. In addition to an advertisement for "Herpecide," a popular dandruff remover, and two full-page ads for whiskey and brandy, the little book contains a preface by its compiler:

> "All of Butte's society ladies have dreaded the task of preparing a list of persons who might be desirable as guests for a reception or other important social function. It is with this in mind that the author after the closest investigation, has prepared the following checked and rechecked list."

Butte has no use for such a certified list of the "elect," and the publication was discontinued after the first year. They don't ask who you are in Butte, but what can you do. That and the ability to mind one's own business and be a good fellow are the main requisites of citizenship.

MONTANA HISTORICAL SOCIETY, HELENA

Corner of Broadway and Main (looking down Main) in turn of the century (ca 1900) Butte.

While the camp can by no stretch of the imagination be called metropolitan, the people themselves are cosmopolitan. There are over fifty nationalities among its population and they all know their way around. They have a big-city polish, and there is very little of the rustic in their makeup. On the contrary, they look down upon the rural inhabitants of the state.

Butte people possess a fierce civic pride, the like of which can be found in few places. They love the camp with such an intense devotion that it blinds them to the physical bleakness and ugliness of the town. When away they are clannish. In Seattle, San Francisco, Los Angeles, Washington, New York, or wherever there are numbers of former Butte residents, one will find them getting together socially. Their principal topic of conversation will invariably be of happenings in the old camp, current and past.

When death comes, it is the desire of many of them to be buried in Butte. Morticians point out that an average of a hundred bodies of former residents are shipped back every year. There is an incident on record of a resident who died while visiting his boyhood home in Ireland. He requested on his deathbed that his remains be shipped back—and the request was carried out. As Matty Kieley, that sage of the camp, once said: "Sure, the people of Butte are like the Chinks, they never rest easy until their bones are planted in their homeland.

The town grows on one. The average person visiting for the first time is horrified at the shabbiness and bleakness of the place, and he that he cannot get out of the camp fast enough. He gets a job and decides to remain only long enough to obtain a small stake. He becomes acquainted, makes friends, accepts the overt hospitality of the place, and, like an enveloping cloak, the good fellowship and cordial spirit sweep over him. Within a short time he is as loyal a citizen as will be found in the camp. Several prominent writers have proclaimed this fact repeatedly.

Joe Pasquale, an Italian resident for fifty years, tells it: "Disa Butte, she'sa like a being seasick. Firsta two-three day she's a given you pain in belly. You geta used to da boat, pretty soon you feela fine. Butte is lika da boat. You get used to it, she'sa besta damn town in United States.

And the copper camp, despite its love of play, has equally as deep a religious feeling. As the Chamber of Commerce booklet points out, there are forty-two churches of almost every major denomination in the town. Attend any of these, and you will be fortunate if you obtain a seat. Some enthusiastic Saturday night celebrators go direct to early morning services from the scene of all-night festivities. Sunday is God's day in Butte and the citizens do not let it interfere with the balance of the week or vice versa. To again quote the late Matty Kieley, who had been around a long time: "God keeps His eye on Butte People, and He wouldn't have them split up in the next world. So that they'll all be together, He sees that they get under the wire at the last minute and make their peace with Him before they pass away."

The camp is charitable and generous. Drives and campaigns for any worthy cause are always oversubscribed. It has always been a mecca for beggars. Several legless, blind, or maimed are always present begging on the pavements of the shopping district. The shaky alcoholic in search of his "mornin's mornin'" is rarely turned down.

The average resident assumes unmistakably the attitude, "There, but for the grace of God, go I." And most of her people realize from experience that there are few ailments more miserable than a hangover.

Butte has an honest and a sharp sense of humor. It can both laugh at itself and take a joke. It has often rewarded its pranksters and laugh makers with public office. Time can always be found to listen to a good story. Indeed, many of the yarns spun underground while the miners are "taking five" have been repeated the nation over.

Butte is patriotic. While frowning on the flag-waving type of chauvinism, whenever war comes the town's record for voluntary enlistments per capita has always led the state and compares favorably with any city in the nation.

The camp is proud of its schools. The average miner has a burning desire to see his children receive a good education, if for no other reason than to keep them out of the mines. No sacrifice is too great in attaining this end, and if the average high school student cannot get at least a year or two in college, it is not that his parents didn't want to send him.

When the mine wheels are turning and copper is selling high, Butte goes in for luxuries. A casual visitor is always surprised at the high percentage of bright, large, new-model automobiles driven by the miners. When the shutdown comes, as it always does, the finance companies get them back as they have before; but while times are good the camp rides to work and to play in style. Five out of ten women wear fur coats. They might be dyed rabbit, but they are fur, and if prosperity perches on the Hill for two or three years in a row the coats will be predominantly mink. Nothing is too good for the miners' wives and daughters. Long lines in front of the theaters, and standing room only in the "Keno" gambling parlors and cocktail lounges prove that.

During the depression, it was the dime second-run houses that received the play, but when times are good the sky's the limit.

The state-owned liquor stores do a capacity business to meet the needs of the camp's famous rawboned hospitality. Butte eats and drinks only the best. Some might sacrifice a little of the former for the latter, but not many.

As for the ugliness of the town, there has been a decided improvement in the past few years. With the exception of the "for rent-furnished" shacks, flats, and tenements owned by certain real estate interests who seldom do any more than absolutely essential repair work on their properties, the miners' homes are beginning to perk up. The city government with the aid of Federal agencies has graded and oiled the streets, sewers have been installed, and the decay has been at least stemmed.

All this has helped. Someday, perhaps, the mining company will find a way to process the mine dumps, at least removing some from the center of the town, but it is doubtful if Butte will ever be pointed to as a beauty spot.

Butte's beauty is within—the big-hearted spirit and unequalled neighborliness of the town and its people.

Forgotten Man

BUTTE was laughing in 1869. Its whole population of some three hundred fifty was laughing long and loudly at the efforts of one William J. Parks to prove that his claim on the Parrot lode contained a vein of copper ore of fabulous richness.

Parks was one of the original quartet comprising Dennis Leary, Joseph Ramsdell, Thomas C. Porter and himself, who in 1866 had built a crude smelter on the site of the Parrot lode, which had been by Leary and others in 1864. The smelter venture had proved a dismal failure for the four miners, and after spending around seven thousand dollars on it, they had dropped the project. General Charles S. Warren explained it in 1876: "They did not understand how to flux the ore."

The idea of building the smelter was Parks'. Its failure had marked him as something of a crackpot. Vision and genius have often been rewarded with scoffs, however, and if not a genius, Parks was surely a man of vision. Through his association with his former partners he owned a full claim on the Parrot lode. Parks believed that in this claim he had a high-grade copper mine in the making. Surface indications were that the only mineral content was a copper ore of too low a quality to ship the long distance to Swansea, Wales, for smelting and retain a profit.

But Parks had a pretty good hunch that if a shaft were to be sunk to a greater depth, the value of the lead would increase, and perhaps ore rich enough to make shipping worth while might be uncovered. He told his belief to his associates and did his utmost to convince them of the feasibility of the venture. The truth is that his former partners had the same hunch but did not care to risk their slim bankrolls on the project. Their attitude was "Let George do it." "George" in this case was Bill Parks and they reasoned, "Let Parks do the work and sink his hole, and if he uncovers anything of value, we will then sink our own claims." Of course they didn't tell Parks this. They made many excuses and at the same time encouraged him to sink his own shaft.

Parks, alone and unaided, started his hole on the present site of hundred block on Anaconda Road. His only tools were a pick and shovel and a "moil," a sort of primitive drill. It was then that the laughing began. Butte was a placer camp, and any fool who had lost his sense so far as to start a quartz mine on that side of the hill where everyone knew there was no trace of gold, deserved to be laughed at.

Parks, however, had a thick skin, and ridicule and laughter were not new to him. Slowly the shaft took form. For the first fifteen feet or so, the dirt was laboriously shoveled by hand out of the hole. As the shaft deepened, he erected a crude windlass and attached a rope and bucket fashioned from a half whiskey keg. Working alone, this meant Parks must climb down the shaft, fill the bucket, and then climb out again and hoist it to the surface. For ten to twelve hours a day he followed this tiresome procedure. He had obtained a set of hand drills. With the aid of a small blacksmith's forge he kept the drills sharp, and day after day put in the rounds of powder and blasted.

He had erected a makeshift shack on the place. In this he slept and prepared his simple meals. At times his supplies of grub and blasting powder ran out and he found it necessary to work at some of the placer mines to replenish them. But he grimly stuck with it. Day after day, month after month, year after year, the dauntless Parks kept at it and the shaft gradually reached lower depths. From time to time, he erected timbers to prevent the shaft from caving. These, he patiently hewed from green timber with a hand axe.

And Butte continued to laugh. The joke was getting ancient now. Pity was mingled with the mirth. "Parks' Gloryhole," they called his mine. It was a point of hilarious interest that the camp jokesters pointed out with glee to new arrivals. Parks' former associates were frequent visitors to the mine and cabin. The visitors never offered the tired miner any help, but were most liberal with veiled sarcasm and advice. They also kept a close watch on the samples that Parks faithfully scraped from the bottom of the shaft each day. As Parks later told his friend, General Charles Warren, according to the latter's statements, "I do not mind so much their visits and advice, but every time they come up to the cabin they eat up my grub and drink my whiskey."

Down, down, down went Park's shaft. At last a depth of a hundred feet was reached, then a hundred and ten and a hundred and twenty. As the latter depth was reached, climbing up and down the shaft for ten to twelve hours a day became a herculean task, but Parks persisted. Samples from the shaft were showing higher and higher returns. This tended to whip up his flagging spirits and urged him on to greater efforts.

At last the shaft was down one hundred and forty feet. The air at the bottom was poor now—any work was a great effort. The long climb up and down the shaft was telling on Parks. Slower and slower the work proceeded. There was a short period when Parks was taken ill. He doctored himself and dragged his weary limbs back to the mine and his well-worn windlass.

Then came the memorable day in 1876 when he reached one and fifty feet and saw at last that which he had so long sought. Pure copper-glance ore that, as he put it. "They could ship to hell and back for smelting and still make a profit." And the lead was wide and gave promises of getting wider at greater depth.

Parks dug no longer. He had a mine and the townspeople stilled their laughter. They shook his calloused hand and bought him drinks. Parks' "gloryhole" became the Parrot, Number One, and eventually turned out over a million dollar's worth of high grade copper, before it was abandoned to be worked through other mines.

Parks' former partners and owners of other claims on the lode cashed in. After Marcus Daly had proved in his Anaconda, that Butte was virtually a hill of copper ore, they hired hundreds of miners, put them to work, and soon many shafts and gallows-frames made their appearance. They had let Bill Parks do the heavy work, and now they cashed-in on his vision and perspiration. Parks worked his mine for a short time and then sold out for ten thousand dollars, a fraction of its real value. By now local operators had discovered how to flux the ore, smelters were erected and Bill Parks' associates held on to their properties and became men of note in the community. Many of their biographies are listed in the histories of the state.

There are no biographies of William J. Parks. A few words in passing is all. He soon spent the money received for his Parrot, Number One, and unobtrusively passed from the scene. He married, died and was buried in the nearby village of Twin Bridges. But to the courage and perserverance of Bill Parks is due no small part of the building of Butte. He at least hastened by a number of years its claim as the greatest mining camp on earth. Butte's first big laugh at Parks' expense indeed paid handsome dividends.

Paradise of Parades

EVER since the arrival of the first settler the copper camp has been willing and anxious to stage a celebration on a moment's notice. Any occasion will suffice. National holidays, local holidays, religious holidays—any day indicated in red on the calendar is good enough for Butte.

Fourth of July, Labor Day, Thanksgiving, Christmas and all the duly accredited holidays are, of course, celebrated to the hilt. But the special holidays of a score or more different nationalities are not forgotten. The camp, regardless of race or creed, will whoop it up just as enthusiastically for the Irish on St. Patrick's Day, the Cornish on St. George's Day, the Serbs on their Christmas and Easter, the JugoSlavs on Mesopust as they will for Washington's Birthday or Miners' Union Day.

Peculiar, too, is the fact that Butte can never wait until the arrival of the holiday itself. It is always on the eve of the occasion that the doings commence. This is not always true of the sane minority which contents itself with the actual holiday, but most of the camp will begin to cut loose on the evening before the holiday and carry the celebration over into the day marked on the calendar.

Should any dearth of national or foreign holidays present itself, the ingenious minds of the residents will find plenty of excuses for a celebration. Witness the big festival planned in the winter of 1927.

Butte's winters are usually severe and of long duration. After Christmas, the mercury usually drops down below zero and remains there for a good many days—sometimes weeks. The winters of 1926 and 1927, however, were different. Not once had the mercury fallen to zero. January 18, 1927, would mark two years since that mark had been reached.

Confronted by this vagary of the weatherman, what could be more appropriate than a gigantic celebration to mark the event of Butte's entrance on the list of banana belt cities? A date was accordingly set for a colossal demonstration. The Chamber of Commerce, along with all civic clubs, drew up plans for a gala occasion. Among many other events, a straw hat parade was arranged. Newspapers and merchants entered the preparations with vim. Everything was in readiness for a celebration that would go down in the annals.

The morning of January 18 dawned—yes, you guessed it—in the midst of a howling blizzard. Overnight the quicksilver had dropped and dropped, until at 10 A.M., the time set for the parade and opening of the program, a mark of 38° below zero had been reached.

Undaunted, Butte went ahead with the celebration. The parade was held with overcoats and mufflers greatly in evidence, but with a straw hat on the head of every parader. There were scores of frostbitten ears, but the taverns along the line of march dispensed a plentiful supply of "hot ones" and the camp added another party to its long list of celebrations.

According to the late Judge A. B. Cohen, who had spent sixty-four of his seventy years in the camp, credit for the first party goes to G. O. Humphrey and Bill Allison, Butte's first residents. They had erected the first house built here, a log and slab shack at the head of Baboon Gulch, where the Butte Brewery now stands. The gulch ran south through the present business district.

The year 1863 was drawing to a close. It was Humphrey's and Allison's first winter in the placer camp. The story, as heard by Cohen from Allison and Humphrey, indicates that the winter was exceptionally cold, even for Butte. The thermometer on several occasions, dropped to 30° below and colder. The country was wide open, and the little shack at the head of the gulch bore the force of many a blizzard.

Everything within the cabin, however, was cozy and comfortable. An abundance of firewood was at hand, a supply of buffalo and antelope meat had been frozen, and the two miners lived well through the early part of the winter. The had little to do except to keep well-fed and comfortable.

As Cohen relates it, Allison had, among his belongings, a cherished quart of fine brandy that he had been packing around for some time. It was reserved for an emergency—snake bite or such. Christmas passed that year without the bottle being broached, although they later confessed the temptation had been trying.

Now it was New Year's Eve. It was at first Humphrey's idea. What better time for him and his partner to do a bit of celebrating? But still and all, since it was Allison's brandy, the moment called for rare diplomacy.

What manner of persuasion was used by the thirsty Humphrey is not certain, but before midnight had arrived on that New Year's Eve, the bottle was uncorked and a few preliminary drinks had been consumed. As Allison's silver key-winder marked the passing of another year, the bottle passed from hand to hand and a toast to the new year was drunk. A toast to the future of the new camp called for another drink. Now, properly primed, the arrival of another milestone called for something more than drinks. New Year's called for noise. Two rifles were taken from their pegs on the wall.

The wild life of the vicinity—antelope, deer, cottontails and jacks—scurried for shelter as blasts from the rifles echoed and proclaimed to the untamed world that Butte was celebrating its first New Year.

The story does not tell how Humphrey and Allison spent the next day. But most likely the two miners did exactly as following generations in the camp have done for over a half-century since that party. They probably nursed a raging headache and made preparations for the next party!

Rulers of the Roost

THE years from 1889 to 1906 are usually referred to as the period of the "Wars of the Copper Kings." Beginning with the Clark-Daly fight and ending with the Heinze-Amalgamated struggle, these factions used the streets of Butte as their bribery-paved battleground. The prodigious battles involved the entire state and although the principals of the strife have long been dead, the enmities and bitternesses engendered, even yet, occasionally affect the conduct of public affairs throughout Montana.

While bringing good times and "easy money" to the miners, the conflict muddied the public character of many prominent men and left a black mark on hundreds of others involved in the machinations of the Kings. For a period it certainly discouraged the highest type of citizenry and gave an ugly impression of Montana to the nation.

Summed up, the cause of the long and bitter war of the industrial masters was nothing more nor less than petty jealousy between W. A. Clark and Marcus Daly, inflamed later by the promotional genius and larcenous intent of F. Augustus Heinze.

Marcus Daly came to Butte as agent of the Walker Brothers of Salt Lake City seeking promising investments for that banking firm. After leaving Nevada as a miner he had worked his way up to a position of superintendent in one of the firm's Utah mines. Daly bought the Alice Mine, a Butte silver property, for the Walker Brothers.

W. A. Clark's start was equally modest. The foundation of his fortune was laid with money he had earned as wages. Once possessing enough capital to invest in a small stock of merchandise, he opened a frontier store in Bannack,

MONTANA HISTORICAL SOCIETY, HELENA

William Andrews Clark.

Marcus Daly.

W.H. HOOVER, PHOTOGRAPHER; MONTANA HISTORICAL SOCIETY, HELENA

Montana Territory's first capital. Later he became a small banker in the little, nearby mining camp of Deer Lodge. Finally he entered both the banking and mining business in "Butte City." Out of his first gains, Clark obtained a college education which later stood him in good stead in his days of strife. At the time of Daly's arrival in Butte, Clark was already a leading business man well on his way to making a fortune. It was to W. A. Clark that Marcus Daly carried his introduction from the Walker Brothers of Salt Lake City.

About 1880 Daly became interested in the Anaconda Mine, then being worked for silver by Michael A. Hickey, who with his brother Charles X. Larabie, had located it on public ground.

A story that is given much credence is that Daly had accumulated a fair stake from the management of the Alice, and was intending to retire to California when he met Hickey on the street. Hickey is said to have urged Daly to have a look at the Anaconda with the idea of buying it. Daly pretended to be reluctant but postponed his departure and made an examination of the property. He purchased the mine for thirty thousand dollars.

Daly set about mining the silver in his newly acquired property, in the meantime taking in as a partner, George Hearst, of the famous Comstock lode, and father of William Randolph Hearst. Through Hearst, James B. Haggin and Lloyd Tevis were also taken into the deal.

On the three-hundred-foot level, rich veins of copper were found and Daly was at once convinced that the Anaconda would prove one of the greatest deposits of the red metal in the world. Fearing the fact would soon become generally known, he immediately stopped the pumps and closed the mine. Rumors were now current that Hickey had handed Daly a lemon, and that the mine was worthless. Daly's agents, on the strength of the rumor, acquired much of the adjoining ground at a very low figure. He and his associates thus became the owners of practically all that part of the hill which they believed valuable.

The Irish miner was now ready to strike. He opened up Butte hill and overnight the town mushroomed. Fortunes were made and spent in a day. Armies of miners moved into the camp, day and night shifts were employed and smelters were erected to belch forth clouds of greenish, stifling smoke.

Daly was always known to be generous, and the miners were his friends. Loyal to his old acquaintances of Nevada days, he passed out leases with a prodigious hand. Many of the camp's wealthy citizens of today are descendants of those who received these favors.

Meanwhile, as far back as 1872, Clark had turned his attention to quartz mining in the district. At the time of Daly's acquisition of the Anaconda he held controlling interest in the Original, Colusa, Mountain

Chief and Gambetta mines. By 1885 Clark was part owner in no less than forty-six paying silver or copper properties in or around Butte.

Following Daly's first visit, he and Clark had become close personal friends. This pleasant relationship lasted for several years when it was further cemented by the marriage of Daly and Clark's brother, J. Ross Clark, to two sisters. Both men were loyal Democrats and, with Colonel Charles A. Broadwater and Samuel T. Hauser of Helena, comprised what was known as the "Big Four" of Montana politics.

Clark, as he grew unbelievably wealthy, was stung by the political bee, whereas Daly, because of his lack of formal education felt he had no qualifications for statesmanship, hence no personal ambitions in that direction. Politics bothered Daly only as they might affect his private interests.

The first break between the two friends is believed to have started when the dapper Clark made a slighting remark about Daly, ridiculing his uncouthness and referring to his discovery of the Anaconda as "dumb luck." These remarks were promptly carried to the Irishman, probably with several flourishes added.

Open enmity resulted after the defeat of Clark as a candidate for Congress, his first venture in the seeking of public office. The banker claimed that his defeat was caused by the treachery of Daly.

According to Clark, the rival Irish mining magnate while professing to be in accord with his candidacy and the party ticket, so directed affairs on election day that thousands of men in his mines and smelters either were prevented from voting or were influenced to vote for the Republican candidate, Thomas H. Carter, who won by five thousand votes. Daly and his friends offered no explanation.

The Clark and Daly war was then on in earnest. The breach between the two men never healed.

A year later, in 1889, Montana was admitted to the Union and Clark repaid the injury by throwing his entire resources into defeating Daly's pet project of making Anaconda the capital of the state. Before this, Clark had been beaten in his quest for a seat in the United States Senate. Daly fought him openly in the State Legislature causing Clark to miss having a majority by only three votes. For two years Montana was without its constitutional representation in the United States Senate.

In the Helena versus Anaconda fight for the state capital location, the battle was in the open. There was no pulling of punches. Money flowed like water in the initial skirmishes, while bribery and vote buying was rampant. The popular cry among the miners was "How much are votes today?" More champagne and fifty-cent cigars were handed out to

MONTANA HISTORICAL SOCIETY, HELENA

W.A. Clark and supporters celebrate in Helena after winning the fight for the state capital location.

the voters than were probably sold in all of the Rocky Mountain States at the time.

Shortly before the campaign, Clark acquired the moribund Butte *Miner* which he immediately built up by adding a high-priced, brilliant editorial staff. He converted the paper into a sharp weapon for constant, bitter attacks against Daly.

The wealthy Irishman retaliated by erecting an entire newspaper plant in Anaconda. He imported Dr. John H. Durston, a noted editor, from the Syracuse *Standard* who named the new paper the Anaconda *Standard.* Capable newspapermen were hired and the finest mechanical equipment available was installed. At one time more linotype machines were operating on the Standard than on any Manhattan paper. Many men who became prominent in the newspaper field were identified with the paper. Daly is said to have spent $500,000 on the *Standard* to make it an effective competitor against Clark's *Miner.* It had a circulation of twenty thousand in Butte alone.

Clark drew first blood. The slogan of the Daly forces was "Take off your coat, and cast your vote for Marcus Daly and the Capital," but in spite of Daly and his loyal henchmen, Helena was selected with a vote of 27,028 over Anaconda with 25,118 ballots. Daly is said to have spent $2,500,000 in the fight and Clark $400,000.

Helena, as could be expected, was strong for Clark. On election day, one inebriate of that city cast caution to the winds, and on the main street vociferously expressed his choice with a loud "Hurrah for Anaconda." He was promptly thrown in the Helena jail. Hearing of the occurrence in Butte, Daly promptly ordered a special train. Accompanied by a coterie of legal talent, newspaper men and political hangers-on, he went to Helena, and at once had the man released on a writ of habeas corpus. A few days later, the surprised individual was presented with a mining lease which netted him $60,000, for Daly was ever loyal to his supporters, political or otherwise.

With the site of the capital decided in Clark's favor, Daly was beaten for the moment. Clark, flushed with success, announced his decision to again run for the United States Senate. Daly as firmly announced that he would fight such aspirations with every weapon at his command

Round three of the battle was on, and Butte, or few cities regardless of size, ever witnessed a more sordid or spectacular campaign. If money and champagne had flowed during the state capital fight, it now rained in bucketsful. The legislature and state senate were political plums as earnestly sought as was the governorship. It was the legislators who named the United States senator at that time.

During the campaign, the money of the voters was not acceptable in most saloons of Butte, for both Clark and Daly had standing orders in scores of establishments that all drinks were on them—and the refreshments were not limited to beer. The best in the house was none too good for the miners, if they had a scratch coming on election day. There was no middle ground; a citizen was either on Daly's side and drank his liquor, or he was for Clark and partook of his hospitality.

Many of the miners actually acquired a taste for expensive cigars during the period. Clark's employees carried home turkeys to their families, with small cards attached reminding them of the generosity of the man who would be senator. Clark's son, Charlie, made the oft-quoted remark, "We'll either send the old man to the Senate or to the poorhouse!"

Nor was Marcus Daly idle. His money was scattered liberally wherever his lieutenants thought it would do the most good. A story is told of a conservative, money-conscious Daly henchman, who after the campaign was over, aroused the Irishman's ire by returning several thousand dollars unspent. "If you had spent that money in the right place, we would have won the fight," Daly upbraided him.

November 8, 1898, was election day. The vote in Butte and Silver Bow county was close, but late that evening as the returns trickled in, the Daly-Democratic Legislative ticket was leading with a slight majority over the Clark-Republican slate, and the Dublin Gulch precinct, a conceded Daly stronghold, was yet to be heard from. At about four-thirty the following morning, judges of this precinct were finishing the count by the dim light of miner's candles, when suddenly the door flew open and two masked men entered. Guns in hand, they ordered the astonished judges and clerks to "reach for the ceiling."

But the armed thugs had underestimated the loyalty engendered by the Copper King's gold. Dennis O'Leary, an armed checker, grappled with one of the bandits, and John J. Daly, an election clerk, sprang to his assistance. The bandits fired. The election clerk was killed and O'Leary badly wounded. Another of the judges threw himself across the ballot boxes as the election clerk fell. Thwarted in their purpose, the two bandits disappeared in the darkness. They were never identified or captured.

In the ballot boxes were 302 votes for the Daly ticket, only 17 for the Clark forces. The loss of these ballots would have swung the Silver Bow Legislative ticket to the Clark-Republican side. With all of the state returns in, the result indicated an overwhelming Daly victory.

They failed, however, to reckon with the money bags of W. A. Clark. Daly, feeling secure, went East to spend the winter in New York, leaving, he thought, everything under control. But the wiley Clark had other plans. Since the voters had failed to send his supporters to the state legislature, he then and there resolved to buy his way into the United States Senate. As a result, there began in the state capital, a series of astounding briberies and vote buying, which when exposed, astonished and shocked the nation.

Men and women who formerly had exhibited sound traits of character and honesty, began to talk of bribes of amazing size as casually as they had once talked of birthday gifts or monthly salaries.

Members of the legislature were "bought up" singly and in groups. Votes were purchased as housewives buy eggs or oranges—by the dozens. Those who attempted to withstand temptation found rolls of currency in inconceivable places. Bills of large denominations mysteriously appeared under the politicians' pillows and mattresses, or were thrown over the door transoms of hotel rooms. On arising in the morning they occasionally found yellowbacks tucked in their shoes. Clothes and laundry came back from the cleaners with sheaves of century notes hidden in the pockets. Many found themselves receiving exorbitant prices for out-of-the-way and valueless real estate, and rundown or worked-out mines, mills or places of business.

In justice, it must be said that not all legislators succumbed. There were many who held their heads high and fought back. Some even brought charges, but the balloting, nevertheless, started. It continued for eighteen days before a majority could be reached. One by one, personal or public weaknesses were found in the armor of the holdouts. Persuasion, pressure and blackmail followed.

When the final roll call was announced the vote was fifty-four for Clark, a clear majority. It is reported that forty-seven votes were bought during those eighteen days at a total cost of $431,000 An additional $200,000 which had been offered, according to later testimony, to thirteen other state senators, had been refused.

Although the Daly camp was in mourning, they saw to it that news of the corruption and scandal reached Washington. The United States ordered an investigation. A mass of evidence as to rottenness in public affairs in Montana, and particularly in her copper metropolis was gladly furnished to the committee by Daly cohorts. It has been said that a list of the bribe takers as presented to the investigating committee, would read like a page from "Who's who in Montana." The Senate listened with amazement, but Clark, to escape further humiliation, resigned his seat as the Senate at that time was preponderately Republican. In the finals, this round of the grudge battle must be handed to Marcus Daly. Clark didn't go to the Senate.

When the next campaign appeared in 1899, the indomitable Clark again tossed his hat into the senatorial ring. By this time, his rival had consolidated mining interests with the Standard Oil Company under the name of the Amalgamated Mining Corporation. F. Augustus Heinze had already made his spectacular entrance into the Butte field, and was dealing out annoyance to the newly formed corporation. This time it was Heinze whom Clark wanted as a partner, and sagacious Heinze was agreeable.

Heinze was desperately trying to elect "safe" district judges to make his raids on the Amalgamated secure in the courts, and Clark again wanted to pick a legislature that would assure his election to the U. S. Senate. Daly was ill in New York, and in no condition to offer the vigorous and expensive resistance he had shown in former wars. Clark picked a political partner who knew the ropes. With the multimillionaire's pump furnishing an unending stream of money, and with Heinze at the pump handle, victory was practically certain. The first move of the archconspirators was to obtain the backing of labor, simply by establishing the eight-hour day in all of their mines and smelters. The Amalgamated, although their employees outnumbered the Clark-Heinze forces ten to one, shortsightedly refused to change to the eight-hour shift.

On the following Miners Union Day, Clark and Heinze rode side by side in an open hack leading the parade of miners. Heinze's tiny newspaper, the *Reveille*, with the aid of a most able journalistic crew, fought the Amalgamated's powerful Anaconda *Standard* to a finish. Standard Oil was made the issue, and Clark-paid glee clubs sang the campaign song, *We Must Down The Kerosene, Boys* to the tune of *The Battle Cry of Freedom* on every street corner.

Entertainers imported from the big cities made it a continuous twenty-four-hour-a-day show. Once more the latch string was out on the local saloons and two-bit cigars were ground up to be smoked in many miners' clay pipes. William Andrews Clark paid for all of it, but Heinze, the stage manager, was giving the people a show they'd never forget. As an orator, his magic eloquence swayed the miners to a frenzy.

Marcus Daly, desperately ill in a New York hotel, sent a telegram to his Butte friends to stand by him. Copies of the wire were posted in prominent places throughout the town, but Heinze proclaimed the wire a fake and offered to wager five thousand dollars as to the truth of his statement. A rooming house where lived over three hundred Amalgamated voters, developed a mysterious case of smallpox within its walls, and was quarantined until after the election. Only twenty-five of the roomers succeeded in escaping to cast their ballot. Heinze and Clark carried that precinct by a scant two hundred votes.

The Amalgamated forces were snowed under. Heinze elected his judges and Clark elected his legislature which this time quickly elected him to the long-sought office. Butte celebrated at Clark's expense. His liquor bill for the election night festivities has been listed at thirty thousand dollars. But he was Senator Clark at last.

W. A. Clark served the full six years of his term. He was regarded as a capable senator, never known to betray his constituents during tenure of office.

Soon after the election of 1900, Marcus Daly died at the age of fifty-eight. He did not live to see Clark take his seat in the Senate.

Both Clark and Daly are integral parts of the history of Montana. As many an old-timer laments, "Times were good when Clark and Daly were alive." It is true. They circulated their money, and their competition was beneficial to the "little fellow." Every man, woman and child in the camp, from a materialistic standpoint, gained through the wars of the copper kings.

Neither Clark nor Daly was without good points. Both were charitable, generous, religious, and fair to their employees; neither failed to reward loyalty in their friends and workers. They used fabulous amounts of money to gain their ends, but as Clark often stated, "I never bought a man who wasn't for sale." Their spirit of competition served to keep the Butte mines and smelters working to capacity. Shut-downs were few and of short duration, and while Marcus Daly was alive, there was never a strike in the Butte mines. The stories of his charities to widows and orphans are many.

The election of 1899 was not the first Butte had seen of F. Augustus Heinze and it was not the last. Heinze had arrived in 1891, a young man of twenty, fresh from college. He found his first employment in a subordinate position in the engineering staff of the Boston and Montana Consolidated Copper and Silver Mining Company, then the most formidable rival of the Amalgamated Corporation in the camp. Heinze soon discovered that possibilities were open to an enterprising young man. He quickly used his position to acquire a thorough knowledge of underground conditions on the hill.

Heinze was of German-Irish extraction, although it was rumored that his father was Jewish. His mother was of the famous Irish family of De Lacy which traced its ancestry back to the twelfth century. He was raised in Brooklyn, partly educated in Germany, then finished his education with a course in mining at Columbia University. After graduation he spent some time in Colorado making a study of mining and smelting. From there he came to Butte.

Heinze possessed brains in abundance. He had a robust physique, being five feet eleven inches tall and weighing two hundred pounds. He was an excellent athlete and accomplished boxer. Possessed of a magnetic personality and tireless energy, along with a striking egotism, he was a commanding figure—always the "good mixer" and hail-fellow-well-met. It has often been said that "he could drink any group of men under the table, then put the bartender to bed," yet Heinze was never

F. Augustus Heinze.

seen under the influence of liquor. He was a prudent spendthrift, not greatly bothered by conscience or moral restrictions. In his associations with the gentler sex, he was as much at home with the West Side society ladies as with the ladies from the other side of the tracks. Heinze played the field and was sought after by members of all classes.

He made both friends and money rapidly and used them in the accomplishment of his purposes. The knowledge he acquired while working for the Boston and Montana Company made him a valuable ally of Daly in several unimportant earlier conflicts. He soon broke with the latter, however, and moved over to the Clark camp, as related before.

Ever the promoter, in the lull following the Clark-Daly set-to, Heinze traveled to the eastern money marts, where his persuasive manner and inside information won him financial backing from Wall Street. This capital was immediately put into building a smelter for the alleged purpose of reducing the ore of the independent Butte mining operators who had no smelting facilities of their own. A company was formed under the name of the Montana Ore Purchasing Company. His first mine, the Glengarry, leased from Jim Murray, earned him $500,000. Next he leased, then bought outright, the Rarus Mine. This, he explained, was to assure keeping his smelter running to full capacity. It was the Rarus Mine around which a large part of the litigation with the Amalgamated afterwards revolved. Oldtimers assert that all Heinze needed to operate profitably was a hole in the ground near a producing mine.

Heinze soon had several of his "holes in the ground" in scattered localities but always each of his holes was near proven Anaconda or Clark properties. And, too, he had Judge Clancy to make his transgressions legal—at least, during the precious time afforded until the Supreme Court, months later, usually reversed the decision.

Clancy was a bewhiskered, curb-stone lawyer, who came to Butte from a backwoods district in Missouri. Until Heinze's time, he had been noted chiefly as a hanger-on in the cheaper saloons. He had dabbled a bit in minor politics and had wormed his way into some little influence with the bigwigs of the Populist party in Butte. It was to Marcus Daly that he owed his elevation to the judgeship, an act Daly was later to regret more than his defeat in the state capital fight. Daly at the nominating convention, had promised the Populists to fuse his Democrat votes with theirs in the selection of a judge. Clancy's name had been presented along with several others. The latter, being a shrewd Southern trader with a glib tongue, speedily met individual members of the convention and asked them to vote for him on the first ballot, "not that he expected to be nominated, but for the advertising value." This, many of the members agreed to do, never believing a choice could be made on the first ballot.

To the surprise of all but Clancy, when the results of the first ballot were known, he had a majority of two votes. According to the rules he had the nomination, which with the fusion of the two parties, was tantamount to election. The convention offered to rescind the vote, but Daly, ever fair, would not hear of it and Clancy's nomination stood.

The combination of Democrats and Populists triumphed at the polls, and for eight years Judge Clancy kept local courtrooms in an uproar, as time after time, his decisions favored F. Augustus Heinze. Not once in that eight years, do court records show Clancy giving an adverse decision against Heinze or any of his associates. There are scores of newspaper stories concerning the idiosyncrasies of "the Judge."

Judge Clancy had occupied the district court bench about eighteen months when Marcus Daly's plans for the organization of the Amalgamated Copper Company were perfected through the Standard Oil group. Their first act was to enter legal proceedings against Heinze, of whom they had decided to make an example. At this time there were only two district judges in the camp, Clancy and John Lindsay, the latter a man of unquestioned integrity. Under the rules, all cases as they were filed were assigned to either of the two departments according to number, the odd to Clancy's court and the even to Judge Lindsay's. It was soon apparent to all that Heinze's cases somehow got into Judge Clancy's department, even when two cases were filed at the same time. Heinze never played to lose.

Following the death of Marcus Daly, Heinze filled his ranks with ambitious politicians, both in and out of Butte. Turned down by the Clark forces after his aid in electing the latter to the Senate, he then declared war on the combined Amalgamated and Clark organizations, together with any others foolhardy enough to join with his enemies. Cleverly he aroused the ever-willing-to-be-aroused voters against the "dangers of foreign combines and monopolies," who as Heinze explained, "would sooner or later throttle the very life from their bodies."

Heinze was a politician of ability. He made flattering promises to the miners, and shrewdly kept every promise, as when he reduced the hours of labor from ten to eight. After the election, the Amalgamated followed suit, but it was Heinze that the miners credited for the act. From time to time thereafter he raised and re-raised the camp's scale of wages. To the miners, Heinze was no less than a god. He made them feel that his fight was their fight. And so he had but to command and the miners would obey his slightest wish. His "full dinner pail" policy kept them happy and contented, and when election day rolled around, they placed their X's in front of the candidates listed in the Heinze column of the ballot.

For years this buccaneer of the mining camps fought the Amalgamated with that corporation's own money. High grade ore from Amalgamated mines, nonchalantly purloined from under their very noses, was hoisted through Heinze's mine shafts and smelted in his Meaderville smelter. Judge Clancy, on the bench at the court house, approved the legality of the act.

Ever a master of strategy, time and again Heinze proceeded to beat the Amalgamated experts at their own game. Money rolled into his coffers, then was paid out again through the hands of his many campaign managers. The elections were but formalities. Without great effort he secured control of the city and county governments, as well as of the judges of the district court. He also exerted a strong influence in the legislative and administrative offices of the state, for Heinze was the law, and the miners were once again drinking champagne and smoking two-bit cigars.

The magnetic interloper was a born showman. His pre-election vote-getting drives, as shown in his campaign for Clark, have never equalled in the camp.

To his personal newspaper, the *Reveille*, Heinze later added the *Evening News*. More top-flight writers, cartoonists and artists were imported at fabulous salaries. Journalism of the most saffron hue, interspersed with lurid art work, dominated their pages. The papers were sold to the newsboys at a much lower rate than the *Miner*, *Intermountain* or Anaconda *Standard*, and the newsboys accordingly pushed their sale. These were the newsboys who often earned more money selling papers on the streets than did the miners working underground.

The miners carried full dinner pails both *to* and *from* work. Going to work they were filled with lunch, and coming home with foaming lager beer. Workers could afford such luxuries with F. Augustus Heinze at the throttle. Because Clark long had made it a custom to at his employees with a turkey on Christmas, Heinze gave his a bird both for Christmas and Thanksgiving. Grocery stores friendly to the magnate sent candy for the kids with each payday order. Housewives were presented with a bottle of wine each month. The old man was remembered with a demijohn of bourbon on payday. Small wonder that Heinze ran away with the majority of the elections.

Down in the mines, the youthful genius carried the war into enemy territory. The Amalgamated fought him with every conceivable weapon, valiantly striving to keep him from moving off with their entire mines.

Through his Rarus Mine, Heinze complacently moved into the Michael Davitt, an adjoining Amalgamated property, which he claimed "apexed" on the Rarus. Here was discovered an immense body of ore that the Amalgamated engineers themselves did not know existed. Before being stopped, Heinze succeeded in taking out an estimated hundred thousand tons of forty per cent copper ore. Then, dynamite was set off, caving the property for several hundred feet and completely obliterating all evidence.

There was magic in Heinze's pick, and it is a known fact that in his raiding expeditions, he often uncovered veins of rare richness that probably never would have been discovered but for his uncanny sense of mineral locations. This was repeated at his Minnie Healey and other properties. Heinze took the ore, and Judge Clancy took the matter "under advisement," delaying matters sufficiently to allow Heinze to gut the place of its riches, thus giving him the money to fight in the courts. With this, he prepared for another raid.

There are countless tales told of the stirring underground battles, fought in the darkness between opposing factions. Guns were carried underground and used, sticks of dynamite were tossed back and forth, drifts, stopes and cross cuts were caved. One very rich strip of ground, a mile and a half long, lying between the Minnie Healey and the adjoining Amalgamated property, was known as the "firing line." A noted mining engineer stated: "There was more powder burned by the contending forces on the 'firing line' than was burned during the then current Russo-Japanese war."

Two miners in the Amalgamated's Pennsylvania Mine, Sam Oleson and Fred Divel, were blown to bits. Someone dropped a dozen sticks of dynamite down a raise as the two men were attempting to erect a barricade at the foot of the raise to keep the Rarus powder smoke out of the workings of the Pennsylvania. Murder charges were never filed although the widow of one of the victims won a verdict for twenty-five thousand dollars damages from Heinze. Live steam, unslaked lime, ammonia and boiling water are said to have been used by the combating forces in the underground warfare. It is remarkable that these two miners are the only listed casualties. The truth, according to many of the old-timers who were participants in the warfare, is that a majority of the miners on either side engaged in actual combat only while the shift bosses or foremen were present, or in the immediate vicinity. As soon as the bosses were out of sight the two factions usually could be found fraternizing over a friendly game of "seven up" on top of some convenient muck pile. Many stories are repeated of miners who worked the day shift in a Heinze mine, and at the same time were on the payroll for the night shift at an Amalgamated property. They got their nightly sleep at the last one, thus pulling down two checks each month.

In 1906 Heinze sensed that his nuisance value had reached its peak. The mighty Amalgamated forces were ready to call it quits.

On a cold, dismal morning, February 13, Heinze was handed a certified check for $10,500,000 to give up his properties and leave Butte forever. The young mining engineer who, ten years before, had been working in the drifts and stopes at five dollars a day, had a greater fortune than either Clark or Daly ever dreamed of possessing at the same age.

With visions of becoming a second Rockefeller, Heinze went East to the stock markets while the miners of Butte were left to fight their battles without their champion.

On Wall street, Heinze found that the game was played with different rules. Despite his agreement, with twenty million dollars he organized the United Copper Company as opposition to the Amalgamated; bought control of the Mercantile National Bank from George Gould for six millions; and entered into an alliance with Charles W. Morse, the ice king, for a contemplated chain of banking institutions.

But Heinze's old enemies had been waiting. In an interview published in the *Wall Street Journal* in January, 1904, H. H. Rogers, guiding genius of the Amalgamated, was reported to have said: "The flag has never been lowered at 26 Broadway, and I will break Heinze if it takes ten millions or more to do it."

They did "get him." Heinze's enemies in some manner reached his partner Morse, gained control of his banking stock and threw it on the market. This caused a crash which left Heinze stranded. A national banking panic resulted with the Aetna Bank of Butte going down in the crash and taking the savings of the miners with it. President Theodore Roosevelt came to the rescue with a $25,000,000 loan out of the Federal Treasury, but Heinze was cleaned out.

He died in New York of cirrhosis of the liver with complications on November, 1914, a disillusioned man with a few hundred thousand dollars, mostly in insurance policies made out to his young son, constituting all that was left of his once great fortune.

On Heinze's departure, Clark and the Amalgamated Company signed a truce. Clark, accepting the word of one of his trusted mining engineers, that three of his principal mines were practically out, disposed of them to the Amalgamated for a fraction of their true value, only to later learn that he had been betrayed by his employee. The Amalgamated, within a year, took twice the purchase from one of the three mines alone. The judas advisor, his pockets lined, it is said, slipped off to South America.

Clark continued to manage his few remaining Butte business and mining properties until his death, March 3, 1925. Shortly after, in settling the estate, his heirs sold the remaining Clark interests in Butte to the Anaconda Copper Mining Company. Since that day, the "A.C.M." Company, alone has ruled the roost in the city of Butte. Today there exists neither spirited competition nor fabulous battle among the copper kings for there is only one, all-dominant king.

Brickbats on Election Day

"—and the Populists, as you all know, have larceny in their hearts, as well as being bigoted, entirely ignorant and incapable of even associating with, never mind governing, their fellow men. And that goes double for the Republicans."

The speaker was a faithful, third-ward, Marcus-Daly, Irish Democrat. The time was 1893. The Democrats, a thousand strong, had gathered at the Renshaw roller rink to hear the pros and cons of the coming mayoral election.

The perspiring orator mopped his brow, paused, and gazed challengingly down on his audience.

"Am I right, byes?" he thundered.

A roar of approval came from the entranced voters.

"You're damn right I'm right!" The speaker's words rang proudly through the hall.

He poured himself a glass of water from the tumbler at his elbow, drank deeply, wiped his lips and continued:

"But the democratic candidate—Dugan—D-U-G-A-N—E. O. Even the mere sayin' and spellin' of his name strikes a note of pride in me heart. A man of honesty, integrity and truth, destined as Butte's next mayor to lead the miners and the honest residents of this town out of the depths of darkness and despair into the realms of light, freedom, happiness, and contentment."

Once again the speaker paused, cleared his throat and repeated dramatically,

"Am I right, byes?"

A chorus of assent from a thousand throats.

"You're damn right I'm right."

Three days later E. O. Dugan was elected mayor by 296 votes and the speech became a copper camp classic. Yet the election was but one of hundreds that have embroiled Butte year after year and have made it one of the most politically conscious cities in the United States.

Politics comes next only to copper, and more than once the election of "honest stalwart men" has taken priority even over the red metal. According to the old time miner's calendar there are the three regular legal holidays and also the four *Butte* holidays—St. Patrick's day, St. George's day, Miners Union day and Election day, and sometimes, when there is a municipal change of offices due, there are two Election days.

Joe Klaffke, an early day tailor, used to tell of a typical old-school politician, who, upon being measured for a suit of clothes, instructed:

"Joe, this suit of clothes is for me best, to wear to weddin's, wakes and funerals; on Christmas and New Years; Miners Union day and St. Patrick's day; the Fourth of July and Election day—and by golly, come to think of it, you'd better use a bit stronger cloth, there's two election days this year. That's one day that's hell on clothes."

As far back as the files of Butte newspapers record, front pages and nearly every other page teem with political news—city, county, state and national. From reading many of the stories, it would appear that there was little regard for libel laws. Hundreds of the articles put to shame the most scurrilous of those appearing in the rank sheets of later muckraking eras.

There was always a convenient issue. Butte's fourth mayor, William C. Owsley, after a heated campaign in 1882, rode to victory on the slogan of "Cheap Chinese Labor Must Go," although it is doubtful if there were more six hundred Chinese in Butte at the time, counting every man, woman, child and slave girl.

But in 1895 a real issue presented itself. For the first and only time in the history of the camp, religious hatred was an election factor. This was the hard fought A. P. A. anti-Catholic campaign, attendant with rioting, fist fights and gun play.

The A.P.A. ticket won hands down, electing William Thompson by a healthy majority. For two stormy years Thompson held office. The Democrats nominated P. S. Harrington to carry the banner of the anti-A. P. A. forces.

At three o'clock on election afternoon Marcus Daly turned his thousands of miners loose, and they marched from the hill down to the town in their working clothes. Their combined vote turned the tide of battle and the forces of P. S. Harrington won by more than a thousand votes.

As the line of miners passed by the courthouse a Mrs. Gilligan, an aged boarding-house keeper, fell to her knees on the courthouse steps, and, with tears streaming down her withered cheeks, her arms stretched out in supplication, cried: "God bless ye Marcus Daly and yer fine bunch of Christian miners." A fervent amen was voiced by the crowd. This was the last time that religion was a major issue in the politics of Copper Camp.

To be sure, Butte boiled over politically during the oft-repeated Clark and Daly skirmishes of the nineties. It was during those turbulent engagements that the camp politicians gained the finesse that made them second to none in the practice of political strategy, as is shown by the number who have graduated into state and national politics.

Pre-election campaigns are invariably knockdown, dragout affairs with no holds barred. Every man is his own orator and he must be ready to back up his principles with fists, although in the old days it behooved a man to be cautious in choosing the places where he practiced orating.

A story is told of a North Main Street saloonman whose sawdust sprinkled establishment bore the reputation of being an excellent place in which to mind one's own business.

It was during a particularly exciting pre-election campaign that a payday-oiled patron chose the place to do a little orating in the interests of his particular party, whose platform, unfortunately, was one with which the saloonkeeper had little sympathy.

In the midst of his harangue, the amateur Demosthenes was knocked flat by a bung starter in the hands of the saloonman. Returning to his place behind the bar, the latter addressed the fallen orator along with a half-dozen customers lined up before him.

"Free speech is a great institution," he said, "but I don't just happen to like the brand our friend on the floor was giving away." Election day seldom ended the bitterness engendered in the campaign. Recriminations and accusations were passed back and forth for weeks and sometimes months after the balloting. A good example is indicated in the stories carried by the Butte *Miner* and Anaconda Standard, rival copper kings' political papers, the morning after election, November 9, 1898. The *Miner's* story:

> "By coercion, intimidation and bribery the returns show that the Dalycratic ticket has managed to force itself upon Silver Bow County. A more disgraceful election was never witnessed in Montana. The freedom of the ballot and honesty in elections has be-

> come a farce in the light of the methods used by the Dalycratic heelers.
>
> "That the Dalycrats bought all the purchasable element no one in the city doubts. Election day, every irresponsible loafer and bum in the city was shouting for Marcus Daly and jingling in their pockets the price of their votes. The better element, the representative element of Butte, does not appear to be in the majority in Silver Bow County. The returns show that good government by and for the people was beaten."
>
> Reported the *Standard*:
>
> In spite of a wholesale buying of votes, repeating and fraudulent balloted as indulged in by an unscrupulous opposition, the forces of honesty and decency in Silver Bow County were rewarded yesterday when the entire Democratic ticket won by a handsome majority. That the lying and thieving tactics of the Clark forces availed them little is proven by the results of yesterday's balloting.

"The hell of it is," remarked an old time voter, remembering back, "the two papers were both damn near telling the truth, if they only knew it."

Butte's Irish were "one hundred per cent" Democrats. The Cornish were strictly Republicans. Other nationalities were more or less divided. While friendly in other activities, the Cornish and Irish were vigorous political enemies. Whether the Irish outnumbered the "Cousin Jacks," were more adept at winning converts to their cause, or carried some secret vote-getting power cannot be explained; but the fact remains that the Democrats were winners far more frequently than their rivals.

Tabey Daley, an eccentric Cornish miner, has his own explanation. "Thee robbing Hirish," he would say, "they not honly 'ave two votes heach on Helection day, but thee buggers vote seven years hafter they 'ave been dead hand buried."

Butte's present-day pre-election campaigns are not exactly safe or sane, but they can't be compared with those of the horse-and-buggy days. In the words of a veteran of fifty years campaigning:

"The elections in thim days was ghastly. It paid a man to be a citizen. Ye could follow the rallies and speakers from neighborhood to neighborhood, night after night, and a man could keep blind dhrunk for three months before election if he had a mind to."

According to reliable observers, and from what can be gathered from the newspaper files of those dates, his statement seems accurate. Every theater music, dance and lodge hall, as well as every available schoolhouse was utilized for rallies by the different political parties weeks in advance of election. The speakers and politicians with their red fire, fanfares, bands and oratory journeyed from theater to theater and from neighborhood to neighborhood to neighborhood in hacks, buggies and tallyhos. Neighborhoods turned out in force to listen to the spellbinders. It is doubtful if any of the parties succeeded in making any great number of converts, for, according to an old-timer: "So fearful were they that someone might start a free-for-all or disturbance, they wouldn't let anyone in the halls except those belonging to their own party."

Billboards were covered with flaming posters and twenty-four-sheet caricatures and cartoons. Opponents were usually pictured as fat, greedy "corporation" oppressors or as coiled reptiles ready to spring. The telegraph and telephone poles were plastered with posters bearing honeyed-promises along with the likenesses of the candidates. Election cards were printed by the hundreds of thousands and handed out in every conceivable place. Shift bosses in the mines passed them out to the miners with an"—or else" glint in their eyes. Streets and gutters were covered with the pasteboards. The candidates were represented at all card parties, entertainments and other social events. Even the churches were not overlooked, as many of the candidates had representative at the church entrances to pass out tickets as the congregations came from the services.

One story is told of an ambitious candidate who hired two small boys to pass out his cards to the congregation as they came from mass at a Catholic church. The morning was chilly, so the kids had an idea. They entered the church during the services and placed themselves in the front row of pews on either side of the main aisle leading to the altar. As the worshippers, with heads bowed, came down from the communion rail, the kids forced election cards into their clasped hands.

A vote was always a vote in Butte, no matter how it might be gained.

Wakes were considered an excellent place to garner votes, so the death notices in the newspapers were eagerly scanned by the politicians. Often there were more politicians present at a wake than bona fide mourners.

Even the prize fights were not missed in the campaigns, politicians usually being introduced from the ringside along with the pugs. At one prize fight in the Renshaw Hall arena in 1901, featuring two out-of-town middleweights—neither of whom had a vote in Butte and probably not the slightest interest in the coming election—in the middle of the second round an excited and leather-lunged ringsider bellowed:

"Kill the Republican son-of-a-bitch!"

In an instant the cry was taken up by a hundred other spectators, obviously with Democratic party leanings.

The Republicans among the crowd were not to be ridiculed without retort. From scores of seats came an answering cry:

"Kill the Democrat son-of-a bitch!"

In less time than it takes to tell, the arena was a shambles. The fighters in the ring were for the moment forgotten, as back and forth passed the epithets: "Kill the Republican son-of-a-bitch!" "Kill the Democrat son-of-a-bitch!"

Two-thirds of the spectators were engaged in hand-to-hand combat. The two gladiators in the ring stopped to enjoy the melee; then, deciding that self-preservation was the better part of valor, they lit out from the ring for the dressing room, hurriedly donned street clothes, and made tracks for the South Butte depot. A patrol wagon loaded with police soon arrived at the arena, but it was nearly an hour before they succeeded in restoring order and dispersing the crowd.

Election eve brought the hard-fought campaigns to a crescendo. The street in front of the Butte Hotel on East Broadway was usually the scene of the final appeal. From the balcony facing the street, the most gifted orators of the parties addressed the milling thousands below. The election-eve crowds often extended far blocks in either direction. Streetcar service was at a standstill, with often six or seven cars in line, unable to make their way through the dense traffic. On one memorable occasion a motorman was rash enough to attempt to force his car through the mob. Several hundred husky miners lifted the car bodily from the tracks and turned it around in the other direction. Heinze, when addressing the crowd from the balcony of the hotel, in answer to the incessant clanging of the streetcar bells, cleverly would instruct his audience to "Let the corporation go by!"

An unfailing attendant at the election eve rallies was "Deaf Dan" Harrington, who brought some amusement to the crowd and discomfiture to the speakers by his habit of cupping his hand over his ear, and in a loud voice asking, "Eh, what's that?" or "Would you mind saying that over again, I'm a bit hard of hearin'!"

According to the newspapers, election day always arrived to the accompaniment of "clear skies and bracing weather." But clear or stormy, the paramount issue of the day was "Get out the vote." All saloons were closed for the day—that is, the front doors were tightly shut but a side door might open to a knowing rap. Judges and checkers by the dozen were on hand at every polling place early election morning and collusion between the different political parties is hinted at in stories of the appointment of judges. One story which has gone the rounds concerns the appointment of two blind miners as Republican judges in a notoriously Democratic ward in Dublin Gulch. Reports are frequent of the appointment of judges who could neither read nor write. The pay was ten dollars for the day.

Early election day, every hack, horse and buggy or other conveyance had been rented from the livery stables. These were for the use of the "committeemen" whose job was to see that every registered voter turned out to make his scratch. These included the blind, lame, aged, and decrepit, or those who merely wanted to promote a free ride uptown. There were no absent voter's ballot in those days, and at more than one election, patients were taken from the miners' wards of the hospitals on stretchers and transported to their polling places.

The Com-mit-tee Men (they accented the first and last syllables) had other duties, such as seeing that the judges and checkers were kept supplied with sharp pencils and liquid refreshments. An old time "handy man" on election day, now a booster in a hickey game in a local gambling hall, tells of this incident which happened while he was a committeeman:

> "This particular election," he recalls, "I was working out of the Central Democratic Committee offices uptown. I had a horse and buggy, and my job was to go from voting booth to voting booth to see that none of the judges or checkers went dry. I had two jugs of whiskey in the bottom of the rig, one was a brand of good whiskey which I poured out in small glasses for the Democrat judges and checkers. The other jug contained a brand of vile liquid-dynamite which we called 'Republican whiskey.' I filled up a big, tin cup of this for the Republican judges and checkers. Each judge and checker came out, one at a time, to the buggy at the curb in front of the polling place. This way, none of them knew what the other was drinking.
>
> I made the round trip about every hour and a half, and, in that way, the Republican officials were kept in what you might call a more or less comatose state, which greatly simplified the counting of ballots later in the evening.
>
> "It was down in a Republican ward in South Butte, and the Republicans had a big, six-foot Missourian for judge. I drove

down there on my first trip and took care of our boys out of the bottle of good stuff. Then I gave this big mountaineer the wink, and he came out to the buggy. I poured the tin cup full from the Republican jug. He tossed it off and from the face he made, I thought he would choke to death.

"'Land O' God,' he sputtered, 'It's molten lava!'—but I'll be danged if he didn't pass the cup back for another jolt, which I willingly gave him. I made eight or ten trips to that polling place in the course of the day, and each time he made a face like one dying but he emptied the cup. I never saw a man with such a capacity as that Missourian. Do you know, that night he was the only sober man in the polling place, and the Republicans won in that ward by a landslide. I think the Democrats got only four votes, and we had six of our own men working there and they all voted in that precinct."

The ballots cast, the vote counted (the latter, mysteriously, often took two or three days in some precincts), the results meant either jubilation or recrimination and revenge. Miners who were known, or suspected of having voted the "wrong" ticket often found themselves working in the toughest places in the mines, or out of a job entirely. The miners, themselves, had an expression for it: "Which hand do you shovel with?" and it sometimes was a good idea for a man not to be left-handed.

In police court one day after an election about the turn of the century, the judge was in an ugly mood, his party having tasted defeat the day before.

Three prisoners stood before him, each charged with drunkenness and disorderly conduct. He questioned the first one.

"Well, Your Honor, being that yesterday was election day, and me being a good Democrat, I thought I'd do a little celebrating."

"Case dismissed," said the judge. "See that you go back to your work in the mines tonight. Next prisoner."

"Well, Your Honor," explained the second, "I was but celebrating Republican victory:'

"Ten days," snapped the judge. "Next case."

"It was this way, Judge," the remaining prisoner explained. "I went down to vote yesterday morning, and when I got down to the polls, damned if I hadn't forgot to register and they wouldn't let me vote. It made me so mad, I went out and got spiflicated."

"Ninety days," stormed the judge, "such negligence is unforgivable!"

The story is an old one but it illustrates the seriousness of election day in Butte.

Which indirectly explains the influence which the mining companies wielded on the politics of the copper camp. No innuendo is necessary; the mines and the mining companies *are* the politics of Butte, and have been since the first days of the camp.

During the earlier years such power politics were much more interesting, for it was one mining company against another. The forces of W. A. Clark used prodigious amounts of money and every other conceivable means against the political powers of Marcus Daly. A miner was expected to be, and usually was, loyal to the outfit that furnished his bread and butter. Later it was the combined Amalgamated and Clark corporation machines against the powerful independent, F. A. Heinze and "the peoples" interests; but here again it behooved a man to accept the politics of those who were signing the pay check, or at least to keep his mouth shut. If in disagreement, it was a simple matter to go to work for the rival interests.

When Heinze finally capitulated to the Amalgamated forces, and Clark had become but a minor issue, the mighty Anaconda Copper Mining Company became the power on the Hill, and there is no denying that "The Company" controlled the two major parties, Republican and Democrat, and pretty much ran the politics of the town for many years.

The miners, of course, did not like it, but they had little alternative in the matter until 1911, when Butte voters rebelled against the growing abuses of The Company and the two old parties, electing a full Socialist ticket headed by the Rev. Lewis J. Duncan, a Unitarian minister. Duncan proved an honest, efficient mayor and was re-elected again in 1913 despite the strongest kind of opposition from The Company. The miners union riots of 1914 gave The Company an opening, however, and Duncan was removed from office. The camp's politics again came under the domination of the interests. It was about this time that the possession of The Company's rustling card became a requisite for employment, and many an old-timer can tell of being blackballed from The Company's mines because of his political beliefs. The people objected, but the candidates of both parties were handpicked by the Anaconda interests.

During this period there were countless accusations against the Company's assertedly high-handed methods of conducting elections and other political manipulation. Grand juries listened to tales of perjury, intimidation and bribery, but somehow the proof was always insufficient, and no indictments were ever voted. Jobs were scarce, and there was always the threat of a shutdown. It was not again until 1919 that the voters decided for all time to take politics away from The Company. The *Daily Bulletin*, a labor paper, was a deciding influence.

Since that time, with the exception of state and legislative offices, the Company on the surface, at least, has taken a defeat in all local elections which it has entered. Today it is considered political suicide for any county candidate to publicly acknowledge or accept the backing of the mining company or its two daily newspapers, the morning Montana *Standard* and evening *Post*—only two in Butte. As Matty Kieley said, shortly before his death: "She's a free town now, and no man need wear a copper collar but for the eight hours he's down in the holes." The words "copper collar" are a common figure of speech in any conversation touching Montana politics.

Yet Butte remains a decidedly politically-minded town. No two residents can hold an ordinary conversation for any length of time without the subject turning to politics. And it is not restricted to the regular city, county and state elections, for there is usually as much interest in school or bond issue elections as in major contests elsewhere. One of the camp's most bitterly fought issues, several years ago, concerned the proposed combining of city and county governments.

If politics were gold, the copper camp of Butte would be several times as wealthy as it already is.

Butte Blows Its Top

MOST of Butte's old-timers will suggest that the Copper Camp's countless riots, free-for-alls, general uprisings, and other boisterous occasions of this nature should properly be placed in the sport section of this volume.

To quote one spirited resident who has seen many a head cracked the past half century:

> "That was the main fault of Butte. She had a divil of a temper, and any little thing might set her off on a rampage. Everythin' could be quiet and peaceful for months—like a tea kittle bilin' peacefully away, then all of a sudden-like she'd steam over an' there was the divil to pay."

There's no denying it—Butte frequently "biled over."

The camp's first major melee, important enough to make page one of the Nation's newspapers, was the so-called A.P.A. Riot in 1894. As to the cause of the trouble, an Irish engineer, a youngster at the time, who was in the center of the engagement and escaped with a few minor nicks and abrasions, tells it this way:

> "Supposin' you was a bull, and that it was orange or yellow that made you fightin' mad instead of red. And supposin' you loved the color of green better than anything else in the world, and there was others who hated green as bad as you hated the orange or yellow.
>
> And supposin' you woke up in your nice green pasture one Fourth of July mornin', and there across from you on both sides was a big orange flag, and you knew that the flag was being flaunted in your face just to get your dander up.
>
> "What would you do?—You'd fight of course. It'd be the same as a declaration of war—and that's what caused the A.P.A. fight in Butte."

And war it was, with a cracking of skulls that would have put to shame a Donnybrook Fair. Half of the camp's policemen were wearing black eyes, the hospitals were full, jail space was crowded, and there was at least one body on the slabs at Larry Duggan's mortuary before it was all over.

The A.P.A., or American Protective Association, it is said, was an organization antagonistic to the Catholic Church. Its color was a bright orange. Butte, predominantly Irish-Catholic to begin with, and noted for the absence of intolerance, had in no way accepted the precepts of the organization, although the latter had recruited many members in the city. A.P.A. meetings had been secret and there had been no noticeable action until the Fourth of July, 1894, when two West Broadway saloons included in their Independence Day decorations a saffron-hued shield with the letters A.P.A. emblazoned thereon. The buntings had been up the greater part of the day, and most of the afternoon had passed without incident. But as hilarity increased so did the mutterings and there were advance rumblings of trouble.

At 3:30 that afternoon the camp was startled by the roar of a heavy explosion. Someone had placed a half-box of dynamite, taken from a nearby mine, in front of one of the saloon's big bay windows. The front of the building had been blasted to fragments, but the A.P.A. sign and colors remained aloft.

The war was on.

A.P.A. sympathizers dashed out of the saloon into the street. There they were met by a determined, fuming mob of fighting Irish.

In a moment, half a hundred fist fights were in progress. Over the length of West Broadway to Montana Street combatants struggled in the heart of town. Sticks, stones, paving bricks and scantlings were brought into play. Then from the saloon across the way came another outpouring of A.P.A. compatriots. Shrieks, moans and curses crescendoed above the din of flying fists and whacking clubs. Heads were being cracked on all sides. The street was littered with fallen fighters and here and there venturesome spectators saw the occasional flash of a knife.

The camp's entire police force, brandishing upraised night sticks, soon came on the run. They advanced bravely into the midst of the onslaught, then like Coxey's famed army, marched back again on the double, nursing sore heads and blackened eyes. After additional reinforcements came from the sheriff's office, the cops once more advanced into battle, this time engaging in a hand-to-hand struggle with the rioters. Blood flowed freely, but as yet there was no gun play. It was a good old-fashioned knockdown and dragout free-for-all with no holds barred—and biting and kicking in the clinches was strictly encouraged. Again and again the battling bruisers between the two saloons were attacked, but each time the policemen were repulsed by the angered defenders, A.P.A. and Irish patriot, alike.

For two hours Butte's battle royal continued. Ambulances, "dead wagons," hacks and private vehicles removed wounded men to the hospitals.

The cops' strategy, developed through frequent consultations of the general staff, was improving. By employing flying wedges and fighting as a mobile body they succeeded in dragging—one by one—dozens of the rioters to the city jail. In short order that place was filled to overflowing, and the county jail was rapidly filling. Friends of both factions continued to arrive from every part of the camp, even from the hilltop towns of Centerville and Walkerville a mile away. The new recruits were bringing with them pickhandles, clubs and other weapons of the shillelagh type.

"It's the finest fight Butte ever seen," they told each other. "It's getting better every minute—you'd better hurry or it will be over before you get a whack at some damned A.P.A."

West Broadway was a shambles. Half the paving stones of the street had been torn up and used for ammunition. Nearly every window was broken. Mayor Duggan was helpless. Sheriff Reynolds after an hour of the bloody battle had telegraphed the Governor to authorize the use of the militia, a company of which was then stationed in Butte. Finally, D. J.

Hennessy, a leader in the community, along with the mayor, called at the two saloons and pleaded with the proprietors to tear down the A.P.A. banners in the hope of quieting the crowd. After much persuasion one of the saloons agreed to do this. The other vigorously refused.

It was then that the elements, like the boys who were eagerly running to the fray—as though fearful of being cheated out of participation in the battle—turned on Nature's heavy guns. Thunder roared, lightning flashed, and the rain came down in bucketsful. But not for a moment did it deter the mobs which now had their second wind, and thirsted more than ever for the blood of the enemy. At the height of the rainstorm, Judge McHatton and Mayor Duggan mounted a packing case, pleading with the crowd to desist. They may as well have asked the rain to stop. A shower of paving stones greeted their request, and the two were forced to flee for safety.

By now the militia was being assembled. Their members, some of whom had already been participating in the melee, and others at their homes in different parts of the city, were called to assemble immediately, lest half the population be killed and the camp demolished.

As head of the Butte militia post, one Frank Munford was in the center of the embattled miners endeavoring to round up stray members of this guard, when somebody swung on him. The soldier fell to the pavement with a thud, but was up at the count of two. Then another well-directed blow, also to the jaw, brought him to his knees once more. He came up fighting mad, this time with a gun in his hand. The situation was tense. As if by signal, other guns appeared in the crowd. Two shots were fired. A bullet barely missed Munford's head. Then, only, according to his later testimony, did Munford fire. Police Officer Daly, in the thick of the fighting, fell with a bullet in his heart. Other shots rang out, an innocent bystander receiving a fatal wound in the stomach.

At this a score of guns were out with bullets flying in every direction. One man was shot in the leg, another through the head.

The shootings somewhat sobered the fight-mad crowd, and the rioters gave ground. At this moment the fire department arrived. Why they had not come earlier has never been explained. Up to the offending saloon they clanged; unrolling their hose and hooking it up to a nearby fireplug, they turned the full force of the water on the orange-hued A.P.A. insignia floating placidly in the summer breeze. Down came the bunting in a swirl of cascading water. Then the firemen turned their heavy-pressured stream into the saloon itself, driving its occupants out through the rear door. Every glass, mirror and breakable fixture was smashed. The place was a wreck when the white flag of surrender appeared.

The firemen then directed the stream of water across the street, the interior of the other saloon receiving the same treatment as its neighbor. As an afterthought, apparently, the fire laddies pointed their hose in the general direction of the crowd which was once again attempting to renew hostilities. The force of the water tended to dampen its ardor, and the rioters retreated.

By now the militia had been mobilized. As they arrived with fixed bayonets, the crowd gave way before the cold steel. In a short time order was once more restored, with the street blocked off by ropes and heavily patrolled.

It was a field day for Butte's doctors. A newswriter reporting the affair stated:

> "They must have taken ten thousand stitches in the hundreds of cracked heads that appeared at their various offices that evening for treatment.... It was too bad that sewing machines were not a part of the physician's equipment—they could have done much more efficient work. Close to a third of all the miners in Butte exhibited neat samples of medical hem-stitching the following day."

But typical of the spirit of the camp, there were few grudges and in a short time the whole affair was practically forgotten. No serious effort at prosecution was instigated. The two factions, it seems, had relieved their systems of all hates and prejudices in that one gory afternoon of combat.

It was many years before the temperature of Butte again reached fighting heat on a mass scale.

The next time the camp marched forth to riot was on August 20, 1912. This time the scene of battle was Gregson Springs, a resort fifteen miles west of town. The Butte Miners Union, six thousand strong was holding its annual picnic. The Mill and Smeltermens Union of Anaconda—twenty-six miles distant—where the ores of Butte are hauled for smelting, had scheduled a picnic at the resort on the same day. A tug-of-war between the two unions had been arranged as a sporting highlight for the joint affair. The miners of Butte lost to Anaconda team.

This, with the courage inspired by some several thousand quarts of beer, offered an ideal setting for the warfare to come.

And inevitably, as it must in such an atmosphere, it came. Miners disputed the tug-of-war decision. Hundreds of husky smeltermen argued. Somebody swung a fist. Someone else threw a bottle. Women and children ran for the protection of the nearby hills. It was a grand fight while there were enough empty beer bottles to go around.

The smeltermen, outnumbered, but fighting as valiantly as ever did their Croatian, Austrian and Polish ancestors, were finally forced by sheer numerical superiority to retreat in defeat to the sheltering glades of the nearby hills.

Their ammunition exhausted, throats parched and dry, victorious miners adjourned to gather their wounded, then to reduce body temperatures with copious droughts of cooling beer from the numerous refreshment stands. A special baggage car was provided by the B.A.&P. Railway to carry men requiring medical attention to the hospitals in Butte and Anaconda. First aid was given to the less seriously injured.

A reporter from the Butte *Miner*, writing of the affair the following day, may have exaggerated a little when he said, "The afternoon sun was hidden from sight by the clouds of flying bottles."

But there was only one fatality and it, paradoxically, was caused by an outsider, a cowpuncher—the only one probably within miles of Gregson Springs—scouring the nearby hills for stray cattle, took an accurate pot shot at a fleeing smelterman. The cowboy's defense was that "he saw the fellow running, and thinking he must be wanted for something, up and let him have it."

Broken heads and broken hearts healed quickly. For several years the camp maintained a more or less pacific mood. Of course there were minor clashes, such as when the Norris and Rowe circus was chased from town, with tents torn to ribbons and half the roustabouts nursing cracked heads. They had, unfortunately, attempted to sell more seats than their accommodations allowed for. It was a sad lesson on misplaced judgment of the temper of a mining camp.

Of other such occasions there were a few.

A stage show at Sutton's Old Broadway, *Happy Hooligan,* by title, did not measure up to the miners' exacting demands for quality entertainment, and after a thorough pelting with vegetables, ancient eggs, uprooted seats and perhaps a brickbat or two, the disgruntled Thespians were eager to silently fold their tents and scram.

On another occasion, a burlesque show foolishly posted advertising matter which caricatured the hard-working Irish miners. The burlesque troupe arrived at the depot, but that was as close as they ever came to the mining camp. Several thousand miners had gathered to welcome them. The hint was sufficient and the show kept right on going.

Then came the supreme holocaust. A pile of bricks on North Main Street is all that remains of the Miners Union Hall, grim reminder of this dramatic set-to during a hectic June week. John Sullivan, who came to the camp in 1884, and carried a card in the old Miners' Union from the time of its organization, tells his version of the story:

> "I don't know if there's a miner in Butte qualified to tell about the Miners Union trouble. There's a hundred different stories told, and there's a little bit of truth in all of 'em. Things moved too fast them ten days for anyone to keep track of everything. Butte was boomin' high, wide and handsome. It would have taken a dozen police reporters workin' night and day to even begin to see or tell half of it.
>
> I joined the Union in 1888. That's the year they built the hall. I was a member in good standin' through the years and paid my dues every month. Things went along peaceful enough at the meetings, with little trouble until the latter part of 1913. That's the year the miners in Michigan went out on strike. Bein' affiliated with the Michigan boys, the Butte Miners wanted to see 'em win that strike and we dug down for assessments every month to help 'em out.
>
> "Along in 1914 there was the beginnings of rumblings and grumblings, the assessments for the strikers becomin' a little larger all the time until that spring every Butte miner was being assessed a day's pay every month. There was rumors and more rumors. I'm not saying there was anything to them y' understand. I kept payin' the assessments, and, like hundreds of others, let somebody else attend the meetin's and do the talking. That's one of the big reasons we kept away from the meetin's. There was too much talking, and if a man didn't say the right words, someone would accuse him of talkin' out of turn and he might find himself tossed out on the street. We were a tough bunch of muckers them days.
>
> "Things went on like that until June when there was open rebellion. It started at the Speculator and Black Rock Mines. At that time, accordin' to a contract the Union had with the mining companies, a miner had to have his dues and assessments paid up every month before he could go down to work. The Union had appointed committees to visit different mines to see that the rule

was enforced.

"There was a smart young fellow with a glib tongue working at the Spec, named Muckey McDonald. He was well-liked by the miners and finally talked those working at the Spec and Black Rock into breaking away from the Union. Orders were to tell the committee when they come up there, to go to hell. Well the two minin' companies, keeping their part of the contract with the Union, refused to let the miners go down to work under those conditions. It was sort of a lock-out, with members of the committees on hand to see that miners either had paid-up cards or they didn't work.

"On the night of June 12, the committee, six of 'em, was at the Spec, and expecting trouble. All were well-heeled with guns, they say. About a thousand miners gathered outside the Speculator mine-yard and they was in a pretty ugly frame of mind. The committee leaving the mine pulled their guns and forced a way through the crowd at the mine gate. They had called up Sheriff Tim Driscoll. Not wantin' to see any trouble, Driscoll had his car at the gate and with a number of deputies escorted the committee into the car and drove away to town.

"The miners disbanded and came downtown where there was a big meeting at the Auditorium. I was at the meetin'. Muckey McDonald was in charge, and they had a noisy session. Everybody talkin' an' whoopin' it up but not accomplishing much. By then there was quite a few foreign-speaking miners in the camp, and I remember a lad named O'Brien getting up on the stage and talking to the Finns in their language and then next talking to the Serbs in their lingo. He claimed to be able to talk seven different languages. The meetin' finally disbanded, and anyone with a half a eye in his head could see that there was trouble in the wind.

"The next day was June 13, the big Miners' Union Day celebration. Preparations had been made for the parade, and everybody in the line of march had a feelin' that any minute there was going to be hell to pay.

The parade started at the hall on North Main Street, went down Main to Park and then west. Nothin' happened until they came to the corner of Park and Dakota, by Symon's store. The Union officials and the marshals of the day were leading the parade on fine, big strapping horses. Sann Treloar's band was right behind 'em.

"The streets was crowded with people, the band playin' and the officials ridin' their prancing horses, as proud as anything, when all of a sudden a mob surged in off Park Street and started pulling officials off their horses. Old hell—high, wide and handsome—had broke loose.

"The horses, half-scared to death, stampeded into the crowd, then galloped in all directions. That was all that saved the officials. All of 'em got away but one whom the crowd succeeded in pulling off his horse. They gave him an awful thumpin' before he escaped by runnin' into a saloon and out the back way into the alley.

"Someone in the crowd climbed on his horse and yelled, 'How does it look to see an honest man heading a miners' parade?'

By that time Chief Jere Murphy and the police had reached the scene and took the horse away from him. Somebody hit Jere with a bottle. He had plenty of nerve, but the crowd was too big. It was only a scratch and he wiped the blood away. The parade was well broke up and there was a half dozen mobs millin' around the main part of town. The cry went up:

"To the Miners Union Hall—Tear it to hell and get the records! Wreck the house of the grafters!'

"The mobs joined and marched to the hall. They had gone entirely mad by then and there was no controlling 'em. Up into the hall went the men and out the windows came typewriters, cash registers, bundles of records, papers, furniture and anything they could tear loose. Thousands stood in the street and egged 'em on. In a hour the place was a wreck with everything movable torn out and thrown into the street. Some of 'em wanted to set the whole business on fire.

"A big Montenegrin tore the keys out of the piano and threw them in the street. 'No more Big Yellow Tulip,' he said. [referring to the currently popular tune *When You Wore A Tulip, A Sweet Yellow Tulip, and I Wore A Big Red Rose.*]

"Lewis Duncan, the mayor, was in Chicago on business. Frank Curran was the actin' mayor. He rushed to the scene, and from a second-story window begged the crowd to leave. Somebody in the hall pushed him out of the window and he fell to the street on top of a pile of carpet. His arm was broke and his ankle dislocated. They took him to the hospital. Then Chief Murphy gave orders to close all saloons right away.

"There was two big safes in the hall. One was open and had little in it so the angry miners threw it out in the alley. The other was a big one, claimed to be burglarproof. This one had money and books of records in it. All afternoon one after another, with sledge hammers and chisels, men tried to open it. It was sure enough burglarproof. The cops stayed away. It was useless for them to try and control such a mob. It would only lead to bloodshed.

"Along towards evening, the police drove up with a big dray, intending to get the safe and take it down to the City Hall for safekeeping, but the mob sensed what they were up to, and took the dray away from them and loaded the big heavy safe on it. When the safe was loaded, a dozen or so of 'em climbed on the dray and away they went with it, a crowd of five thousand following them yellin' like Indians. Down Main to Park they drove. Then over Park to Montana, and down that street to Front, the crowd following in its trail. Back of the old Butte Reduction Works near the Centennial brewery, on a pile of slag, they unloaded the safe, and proceeded to blow it up.

"Out stepped a lad from the crowd with a big bottle of some white looking stuff. 'That is nitro,' he says. 'I'm an old time safecracker; I'll show you how to open her.

"The mob took him at his word, and he poured the bottle into the cracks of the safe, put in a piece of fuse, and lit it with a match. The crowd backed away to safety. A bright blue flame came out of the cracks of the safe. The stuff was alcohol, and the mob chased the would-be safecracker to hell away. Someone came up with a armload of dynamite. There's a big difference between mining and safecracking, and it took three or four blasts before they finally had it open.

"Inside was a bundle of cash. They counted it. One thousand, thirteen dollars. They put it in a sack and gave it to a member for sakekeeping. There was also a lot of account books and the contract with the company. They put these in a sack too and everybody headed back for town.

It was getting late and things were quietin' down a little. Pretty near everyone was tired; the saloons were closed; they'd had a busy day, so the most of 'em went home to bed. A few gathered up in front of the wrecked hall. It was a sad sight. Only the four walls were standing and everything had been torn from the inside, even the partitions and doors leading into the anterooms.

"A big miner who had been one of the leaders in the wrecking that morning, now cooled off and sober, looked sadly at what was left and made a speech to the few that was still standing around.

"Look what we've done,' said he. 'It's just like gettin' mad at your wife and smashing up the furniture. When you cool down and make up you have to buy it all over again!'

"The next day was Sunday, and things were a lot quieter. The president of the Union had got out of town and no one knew where he was. There were crowds on the streets all day. In the afternoon, a mob went over to the City Hall and demanded that five of the men arrested the day before be turned loose. They called the fire department to break 'em up, but they cut their hose into ribbons. Finally, to avoid any more trouble, Jere Murphy ordered 'em to turn the prisoners loose. The crowd welcomed the men and slapped 'em on the backs like they were heroes.

"The mines was all working as usual. Those at the Spec and the Black Rock had gone back to work, and things started getting calm once more. On the twentieth, Charlie Moyer, president of the Western Federation of Miners, came to town to try and patch things up. They had his picture on the front pages of the papers with a big send-off. He called for the old officers of the Union to resign and those that was still for the Union to hold an election and put in a new bunch.

"In the meantime, on June 21, about four thousand miners met down at the old Holland skating rink near the edge of town and organized a new Union. They elected Muckey McDonald president. Moyer came out in the papers declarin' that the Western

Federation wouldn't break up and called a meeting of that Union at what was left of its own hall for the evening of June 23. That was a bad mistake.

"Well, the night of the meeting came, and I guess it's one that Butte will never forget. Moyer and about a hundred or so of the old Union men were in the hall. Moyer was making a speech. A few thousand had gathered out in front of the hall. There was no great disturbance, only a few catcalls and some kids throwin' empty tobacco cans at the windows—nothing that would set off the wide-open brawl that followed.

"A fellow named Bruneau went into the hall and started up the stairs with his union card held in his fist. He got to the first landing when Bang!—Bang!—somebody up in the hall cut loose. Bruneau went down with a bullet in his shoulder. He was only wounded, but out cold.

"That started the fireworks. In a minute, that stretch of street had earned its nickname of 'Dardanelles.' Guns were in every window of the Union Hall—and they weren't cap guns. Smack into that crowd of miners gathered in front the bullets whizzed. It caused the fastest move a gang of miners ever made. They cleared the street in nothin' flat, but some innocent bystander, standing between Larry Duggan's and Con People's saloon on the corner, had taken a look at his last riot. He was deader than a mackerel with a bullet through his head. Several more had been nicked by the flying lead. One lad from out of town had seen the crowd and thought there was going to be a parade. A bullet creased him across about where his navel was, and I don't think he stopped runnin' till he got back on his ranch.

"The sight of the dead man lyin' in the street with blood running onto the sidewalk drove the mob crazy. Coming back with hundreds more to the front of the hall, they cried for the blood of Moyer and everyone who was in the hall.

"Guns come from everywhere. They blasted into the windows. A gang all armed to the teeth went around the back to cut off escape in that direction. But it was too late. After the first shots, when the crowd scattered, Moyer and everyone in the hall had made their escape.

"But the crowd wasn't sure. They thought there were some of them still in the hall and the cry went up—

"'Blow them to hell out of the hall! Get dynamite!'

"One bunch went up to the West Stewart Mine, half a block away, and made the engineer lower four men down in the mine to get the dynamite. With guns they forced a shift boss to lead them to the powder magazine. They loaded up a cage and took the powder on top and down to the hall. A tall, slim lad elected himself as blaster and piled twenty or thirty sticks close to the bottom of the building. He put in a long fuse and pouched her off. There must have been a couple of hundred guns in the crowd and these were shot in the air as a signal for everyone to clear the street.

"The crowd scattered up and down Main Street far enough away to be safe.

"Boom!

"The old buildin' shook, but she was well built, and they only blew a small hole in the side of it. Again and again they piled powder against the buildin' and set it off, guns firin' their warning each time, and the crowd scatterin'. People downtown were hidden in their houses listenin' to the blasts, and thinkin' the whole town was bein' blown up. Hundreds climbed on the Columbia Gardens cars, figurin' they'd be safe out near the mountains. A thousand stories were going the rounds and half the mothers and kids in Butte were stiff with fright—probably all of 'em.

"It mustn't have been very good blastin', because they were having a hell of a time bringing the buildin' down. Along about the tenth shot they shouted: 'Move away back this time—We've got sixty sticks under her and she's coming down for sure.

"Boom!-Boom! Every window in town rattled, but only a part of one wall fell.

"All evenin' long they kept at it. The police and sheriff's force were helpless. It would only have meant a hundred killings if they interfered.

"Boom! Boom!

MONTANA HISTORICAL SOCIETY, HELENA

Miners Union Hall after a night of dynamite blasts in June 1914.

"Slowly the old hall was crumblin'. She was giving up the ghost. Along towards morning at about the twenty-fifth blast, they decided to call it a day. All that was left was a big pile of bricks and one wall that firemen later pulled down for safety. Thousands of people gathered around the next day to look over her ruins. But the town was coolin' off and going back to work. A pile of broken bricks and mortar along with a thousand headaches was about all that was left the morning after to remind Butte of the old Union Hall and the Western Federation.

"That's about all there was to it. Things got back to normal. The new Union got off to a good start, but it wasn't long before Muckey McDonald himself in trouble with the law for inciting riot—they called it—and got a year in the pen.

"They brought charges against Mayor Duncan and Sheriff Tim Driscoll for not stopping the riot. The two of 'em lost their jobs. Then when the whole business blew over, they brought in the state militia. All the saloons were kept closed for a long spell, and the only place you could get a drink was in an alley. It was a sad period—almost like prohibition."

Butte had a breathing spell for a few years after that. It was not until the hanging of Frank Little in August, 1917, that the camp again gained the front pages of the nation's press.

The lynching of Frank Little has always been a controversial matter. The headlines of the Butte *Miner* on Thursday, August 2, 1917, recapitulate one version of the event:

"Armed Vigilantes Lynch I. W. W. Leader.... Frank Little, First Lieutenant of W. D. Haywood Surprised and Overpowered in His Room and Hanged to trestle on Outskirts of City.... Victim given no time to dress but is bundled into waiting auto by half dozen masked men and hurried to the scene of murder. . . . Desperate struggle apparently ensued and Little shoved off railroad bridge after hemp rope had been placed around his neck, death being instantaneous. . . . Suspended body is found with ominous death warning of the early day vigilantes, written in red on card pinned to underwear.... Initial of others marked on gruesome placard presumably carrying the 3-7-77 to them."

This was the symbol used by the vigilantes of early day Alder Gulch to warn the road agents of impending death. It referred to the dimensions of a grave—three feet wide, seven feet long, and seventy-seven inches deep.

In another column of the same issue was this story: "Act branded as devilish. Federal and County officials unanimous in declaring the lynching of Little despicable piece of business. . . . Reward of $1000 offered by City Council for lynchers."

The Butte *Daily Bulletin*, a labor paper, on July 31, 1920 commented on another side of the lynching:

> "It is probable that the brutal murder of Little has done more than any one thing to discredit for all time to come the copper trust and its hirelings. Alive, Little was merely one of a multitude. Murdered by the agents of a profit-mad corporation, his name and the manner in which he met his death is known wherever workers gather, in whatever tongue they voice their thoughts. He is remembered not because he lived but because he died on the blood-soaked altar of capitalism, a sacrifice to the god of profit.
>
> "August 1st is the anniversary of the murder of Frank Little. He rests peacefully, but his murderers never will."

The *Miner* of August 6, 1917, told of Little's funeral:

> "Funeral paraders in silent protest . . . 2,514 in procession in demonstration against lynching . . . Remains of Frank H. Little, I.W.W. Board Member, are borne down principal streets of Butte on the shoulders of red-sashed pallbearers marching through solid lanes of many thousand spectators. . . Brief services at cemetery."

Butte's next and bloodiest upheaval occurred in April, 1920. "Bloody Wednesday" and "The Massacre of Anaconda Road," it was aptly by the Butte *Daily Bulletin.*

The Metal Mine Workers Union, No. 800 had called a strike of miners. Pickets were engaged on Anaconda Road, principal street leading up to the hill. They were stationed in front of the gates of Neversweat mineyard, attempting to keep strikebreakers from entering the yard. At about 5 P.M. on that day, a shot is said to have been fired in the direction of the mineyard from a boarding house on the south side of Anaconda Road.

Suddenly, a squad of mine guards, armed with rifles and machine guns, came from the mineyard and fired into the ranks of the pickets. Fifteen persons, including a policeman, were wounded. It was over in a minute and the mine guards retreated to the yard. The pickets quickly dispersed.

The *Daily Bulletin* had an extra on the street a short time after the shooting with the following headline set in 96 point type:

SHOOT THE SONS OF BITCHES!

This, they alleged, was the expression used in giving instructions to the guards. Thousands of the papers were sold on the streets before presses were suppressed.

As far as can be learned, all but one of the wounded recovered. The strike itself was short lived, as the Metal's Trade Unions refused to strike in sympathy with the miners. Within a week most of miners were back at work.

Once more the copper camp knocks on decaying mine timbers. Things have been quiet for a long, long time now. The strikes of 1934 brought a few skirmishes, but they were negligible. Perhaps Butte has at last grown up, and there will be no more "biling over." But the citizens knock on wood when they say it.

The Centerville Ghost

MINING camps have always had the reputation of being places of spirits—liquid, ghost, gay—or name your own variety. But, in the spring of 1901, the copper camp was confronted with an entirely different type of spirit, one that was purportedly supernatural and which was reported to have transferred its habitat in unearthly realms to the streets and byways of the suburb of Centerville, a short half mile north of the business district. The entire population of Centerville, together with most of the population of Butte, was frightened half to death before the spectre ceased its midnight prowling.

It was on a Sunday night, March 6, 1901 that the ghost made its first public appearance. As the hour reached midnight, two youthful residents of the little town, homeward bound on Main Street, were astounded to see, what they later described as "a shrouded apparition, partially concealed by a luminous sort of haze, with two balls of fire for eyes and emitting a pungent, sulphur-like odor." The spectre was traveling from the direction of the West Greyrock Mine, and continued its progress until within six feet of the terrified youths, when it suddenly stopped, threw its head back, and in the manner of a wolf, poured forth "a long piercing, soul-tearing scream" and, as suddenly as it came, disappeared as if into the ground in a cloud of phosphorescent vapor."

Upon recovering the use of their legs, the thoroughly frightened young men lost little time in making tracks for their respective homes. There, with labored breath, they told of their fearsome experience. The next morning the ghost was the sole topic of conversation in Centerville.

Over back fences, from house to house—which, because of the steepness of Butte hill, were practically on top of each other anyhow—the story traveled. Each teller enlarged on the details until by nightfall there were over a dozen different stories being told with a score of persons saying that they had personally come in contact with the weird apparition.

The news quickly reached the city, but the skeptical newspapers would have none of it. Not until several nights had passed, and the unearthly visitor had been reported to have made its appearance in widely separated localities of the little town on succeeding evenings, did the newspapers see fit to send reporters to investigate the rumored visitations.

The newshawks learned plenty. Scores of Centerville residents told of personally meeting up with the awesome spook. On the same evening of the reporter's visit, the ghost had been followed by a dozen young men to an abandoned shack on East Summit Street, below the Mountain Con Mine, where it again disappeared. Two of the bravest youths remained on guard at the shack to await its reappearance. Their companions, returning hours later found both boys lying in the shack in an unconscious condition. Upon being revived, they told the strange story of being attacked by the monster, who, they claimed, grasped them with its grimy talons and proceeded to give them a thorough trouncing. They stubbornly clung to this story despite the fact that their bodies bore no visible marks to substantiate the tale.

The newsmen had heard enough. The following morning's papers carried bold-face headlines telling of the marauding apparition and continued with a lurid story describing the ghost's nightly depredations. Their story, sent out over the Associated Press wires, was carried by most of the papers of the nation. Residents of Centerville remained behind locked doors, and the good wives of the little community saw to it that the lights burned throughout the night.

Still the prowling wraith continued its nocturnal ramblings. A Centerville Miss, whose veracity was unquestioned, told a story of being held prisoner in a small alleyway by the luminous figure, who, she stated, had tied her up with pieces of rope and smoked innumerable cigarettes while he stood watch over her. Finally, she told, the apparition apparently tiring of her worldly company, released her and once again disappeared, taking the ropes that held her bound along with him.

On the night of Friday 13 (an excellent night for a spook hunt), the Butte newspapers assigned two armed reporters to the scene. The reporters drafted the services of two Centerville Irishmen, Mike Collane and Jack Murphy, who were armed with double-barreled shotguns. The four decided to trail the phantom to its lair, and once and for all to put a finish to its ramblings.

A page-one story with headlines told the residents of the copper camp the next morning of the eerie adventures of the quartet. It seems that in their plans to track down the apparition the two reporters were to proceed up a seldom-used pathway at the foot of an old mine dump a few hundred feet from the railway tracks. Collane and Murphy were to take the B.A.&P. railway tracks running east. As the latter pair, with cocked shotguns, cautiously approached a string of empty ore cars on the tracks the spectre suddenly appeared before them. This time the ghost had the appearance of a dark figure, very tall and clothed in what appeared to be a long ulster.

As the story read, Murphy, the braver of the two, commanded, "Halt! Are you a man or a ghost?" Receiving no reply, he let go with both barrels, the ghost slowly dissolving before his terrified eyes. His partner, Collane, petrified with fright, had not fired his gun. The two newspaper men hearing the shot, hurried to the scene and learned of the encounter from the trembling lips of the Irishmen. So frightened were they, the story related, that both had to receive medical attention, Murphy remaining in bed for several days recovering from his terrible experience.

That the reporters gave entire credence to the story is shown by the final paragraph of their account:

> "If the appartition or ghost, or whatever the object which was encountered on the railroad tracks last night, is not supernatural, it is certainly one of the most puzzling things which has ever come up for discussion in Butte. There is no question that the appearance of the object was a creation in the mind of the men who went in search of it, and if it had been a man it could not have survived the shots which were taken at it from a distance of less than ten feet by a good marksman."

For several days the ghost was page-one news and the talk of the camp. Centerville was paralyzed with fright. Business on the little main street was at a standstill after sundown. Residents dared not to venture forth after dark, and the men on nightshift coming home from mines in that vicinity gave the spook's domain a wide berth.

On the night of Sunday, March 15, a posse of close to two hundred men was formed to end forever the prowling of the spectre. Armed with clubs, pitchforks, knives and guns of all descriptions, the small army was deployed into squads of from six to a dozen men. Every nook and cranny in Centerville was visited.

Oddly enough, the phantom did not make its appearance on that evening, or, for that matter, any further evenings. Self-preservation, evidently the first law of ghosts as well as humans, presumably kept it at home. There certainly would have been a showdown of man versus spook, if it had dared to face any of the determined armed force abroad that evening.

However, two Walkerville residents claimed to have encountered the apparition that same night in the neighborhood of the old Lexington Mill, a mile distant from Centerville. Their story appeared in the following morning's Butte Miner:

> "The two men stated that they talked to the ghost and that it replied to some of their questions. The spectre was asked why it appeared to disturb people at such unseemly hours and it replied that it was full of trouble and had lots of trouble ahead of it. It had such a heavy burden to carry that it could not rest and it sought the freedom and quiet of the night to help restore its calm. It stated further that after Thursday night, it would appear no more, but would retire to the realm to which it belonged, never again to trouble the earthly."

The ghost's final message reassured the residents of Centerville and Butte and they once more dared forth at night without fear of meeting the spirit.

It was a matter of thirty years before the secret of the Centerville ghost was exposed. Meanwhile, many residents of the hill city believed implicitly that the spook was indeed a supernatural being, and that at some time might return. During this time it was used as a threat to make naughty children behave.

In 1930 at a political gathering in Hibernian Hall in Centerville, an expose of the affair was made. Joe Duffy, Butte laundryman, for years noted for his pranks, held the answer.

As Duffy told it that evening, it seems that he and two friends (who, incidentally, were newspapermen, one on the morning and the other on the evening paper) framed the deal.

Duffy started the rumor around Centerville and played it up for several days. As the story traveled, each teller embellished the tale with fanciful additions of his own. At this point, the two reporters stepped in with stories in their individual papers. The rest, according to Joe Duffy was merely "the power of suggestion." There never had been an actual ghost or anyone masquerading as such.

As to the two Irishmen, who in company with the newswriters had encountered the spectre on the railroad tracks, Duffy claimed they were but a couple of Centerville saloon hangers-on just getting over a terrific "bender" and had been experiencing hallucinations of one kind or another for over a week. The guns provided for them had been thoughtfully loaded with blanks.

Cabbages and Kings

IT IS said that democracy makes for the development of the individual. It would be difficult to find a more democratic city than Butte anywhere. Here in the old days, at least, one could find more rugged, unabashed, unorthodox individualists to the square block than can be found to the square mile in most places.

This is not the copper camp's own opinion. Personages from presidents and queens down to the hobo arriving on the blinds of a passenger train or a hard-rock miner from another part of the globe, at sometime or other all have voiced words to the same effect.

Berton Braley in *Pegasus Pulls a Hack* expressed a bit of it when he wrote:

> "Butte, there was a town. It is easy to gird the 'wide open spaces where men are men' but when Ireland, Scotland, Cornwall, Finland, Italy and Serbia, to say nothing of New England, Texas, California and the Middle West, seemed to have bred their strongest males for the job of mining copper in Butte, the men-ness of men in this rugged town of the wide open spaces is just one of the many facts of life that the intelligentsia don't know. Take any of these. Take, in fact, nearly anybody you met in Butte and you met, not a type but a person. An ugly town, a raw town, a hard-fighting, hard-living, hard-drinking town, but also a gay, careless and tonic town composed of personalities and individuals."

Clark, Heinze, and Daly were here, but for every bigwig there was a score of such personalities as Callahan the Bum, Crazy Mary, Colonel

Buckets, and the countless others previously or hereafter mentioned. All were as well known to the camp as the mining magnates, and were just as important in the eyes of the populace. Here are the stories of a few:

"Cryin' George" Rooney is still alive and has the reputation of being the most arrested person in Silver Bow County. At present he is one of Sheriff Al McLeod's boarders at the Silver Bow County jail.

"Cryin' George" possesses lachrymal glands capable of releasing a floodgate of tears at will. A slight man, gray and stooped, he has been for years a familiar figure around the barrooms where his crying act is always good for a two-bit touch from most strangers. Through a flood of tears his usual story is that he hasn't eaten for several days. George never mentions the cargo of liquid refreshment that he usually has aboard.

"Rooney your name? Any relation to Little Annie Rooney?" he once was asked.

"Yes—a relation of any Rooney in the town," was his answer.

One time a member of the flourishing Rooney clan was getting married. The reception at the bride's home was elaborate. There were handshakes, congratulations, gifts, and plenty of refreshments. The bride and groom were about to depart on their honeymoon, when late in the afternoon came a knock at their door.

"It's your Uncle George," a husky deputy sheriff announced as they opened the door. "At least he claims to be your uncle." Sure enough, there was "Cryin' George." He had been in the county jail but had persuaded the sheriff that being a close relative of the groom, he should attend the festivities. Perhaps some of the guests had a hand, but there was George outfitted in fresh apparel smelling strongly of disinfectant. Then came the flood of tears and George's story that he wished to drink the happiness of the bride and groom.

They invited the interloper in and highballs were passed to him. "Cryin' George" blubbered, wept his thanks, and, when the deputy suggested it was time to return to the jailhouse, he was asked if there was anything he wanted.

"Yes—" he said, "you can pour me out a big shot of whiskey!"

He drank a stiff drink to the bride and groom and shuffled back to the jail.

"Yep, a relation of any Rooney in Butte!" he wept.

Lemons was Butte's gray-headed messenger "boy," who, though only thirty-six years of age at his death, had the appearance of at least sixty. For twenty-five years he had carried trays with his slow, shuffling gait referred to as the "Lemons' stride." A tiny red cap perched askew on his silver hair, Lemons might be seen night or day, as he shuffled his even-paced way, never faster or never slower, about the streets.

Lemons was prematurely gray. His hair, it was said, had turned white when he was sixteen. It was this, set off by a weathered countenance that gave the appearance of old age—this and the countless secrets that he carried in his head. Rich and poor, great and small trusted the messenger boy with their confidences, and Lemons was never known to talk or betray a trust, even though he could have told sensational stories.

Presidents, statesmen, royalty, capitalists, noted pugilists, and celebrities of all kinds were served by Lemons. All were the same to him, except that some gave larger tips than others. He often stated that the ordinary miner was much more liberal than the great and near great.

Colonel Charles A. Lindbergh was paying a short visit to the copper camp after making his epochal flight. Lemons met the flier at six o'clock one morning when he took a tray up to his room at the Finlen Hotel. The aviator invited him to drink one of the half-pint bottles of milk that was on the tray.

"Partner, you're the only man in the world I'd drink this stuff with!" said the tray balancer to the flier, as he disposed of the bottle of milk. Lindbergh tipped Lemons one dollar which the veteran messenger boy kept as a souvenir.

Lemons graduated into the messenger service from selling papers on the streets. During his quarter-century of delivering messages he estimated that he carried at least one hundred thousand trays and an equal number of messages.

He died in harness, suffering a heart attack while sleeping on one of the benches at the Home Messenger Service, awaiting the next call. Lemons claimed he came by his name because of his fondness for the citrus fruit when he was a boy. His name was Elmer Johnson, but Butte knew and remembers him simply as "Lemons."

The camp's miner works hard and plays equally energetically—perhaps at times his play may be too strenuous—but there is one who rarely plays. For thirty years his spare moments away from the mines have been spent in visiting the sick in the hospitals and the prisoners in the jails.

Eddie Mitchell is his name, and there is none who has convalesced in the three hospitals who does not remember this simple little Cornishman with his smiling face and his cheery greeting: "How is everyone in this room tonight? ... That's fine, just splendid. Is there anything I can do for anyone? Any letters to be mailed; any messages to be sent out; need any cigarettes, tobacco, reading material?"

Eddie Mitchell might pass as a minister. Many of the patients at first think he is—but Eddie never preaches. His work is solely an act of kindness and he shuns publicity. No matter what the weather, each evening after he has finished a shift at the Belmont Mine Eddie sets out on his errand.

He has often prayed with the dying, and more than one friendless miner has passed away in the little man's arms. Once each week he goes to the county poor farm. Every Sunday sees him at the county and city jail where he distributes cigarettes and reading material, doing his best to cheer the prisoners and carrying messages to the outside, if desired. His influence has often obtained leniency for prisoners whom Mitchell thought were getting a rough break.

"Sheep's Head" Barry received a small share of passing fame around the year 1907. Sheep's Head was a miner. The kids had hung the moniker on him when he was a youth, although there was no greater reason for the name than there were for half the nicknames passed out in the camp.

Sheep's Head was a handsome lad, and he was wise. So wise, that when he felt the hot boxes of the mines getting the best of him, he quit and obtained a job as a freight trucker at much lower pay but under much more healthful conditions than those prevailing in the mines.

Sheep's Head had one failing, and it was overpowering. He liked his liquor.

For several months while working at the freight house, he had conquered his thirst and remained strictly on the wagon. Sometime prior to Barry's employment at the freight house a thirty-gallon cask had been shipped to a local physician. The latter had made a trip to Europe and the cask had been uncalled for. While Barry was trucking freight, it was gathering dust in a dark corner of the freight house.

One day while nosing around the building, Sheep's Head discovered the cask. He at once had his suspicions, and, obtaining a small auger, he drilled a hole in the top of the cask. Inserting a small rubber tube, Sheep's Head put the end to his lips, inhaled deeply, and a blissful smile came to his face. The cask was filled with pure grain alcohol.

Barry did not keep his secret to himself. Generously, he let his fellow workers in on it, and, for the remainder of the winter, the O. S. L. freight truckers kept themselves well stimulated.

Came spring, and the doctor to whom the cask was addressed arrived home. One of his first acts was to make a trip to the freight depot to claim his shipment. After the payment of freight and storage charges, one of the freight truckers was instructed to wheel out the doctor's cask. It was considerably lighter than at the beginning of the winter, and the doctor, dubious, ordered a hand axe and crashed in the head of the barrel.

Reposing in the bottom of the receptacle in about six inches of alcohol were three human heads. The doctor was a brain specialist. The specimens had been shipped to him from an eastern mental institute for laboratory purposes. Of course, they were ruined. Right then and there Sheep's Head and his fellows took the pledge for life, but it did not save their jobs. The medico sued the railroad company and the entire crew was fired on the spot.

If you drew a picture of Uncle Sam, but substituted ordinary black trousers for the red, white, and blue ones worn by him; and if, instead of the colored swallowtail, you drew a long buffalo-skin overcoat, and changed the stars and stripes in the hat to a plain black topper, the finished sketch would be a perfect likeness of the camp's first and last hack driver, and, incidentally, the most nationally famous character of Butte's early days, "Fat Jack" Jones.

Long and lean with cadaverous features set off by a pointed and well-trimmed goatee, Fat Jack was known to thousands near and far. He was a Civil War veteran, born John Codman Jones in Bangor, Maine. For well over a half-century he made Butte his home and claimed to have driven in his hack more Presidents, royalty, and prominent men and women of all fields than any hack driver in the United States.

His quaint appearance made him a favorite subject for cartoonists. The late Homer Davenport drew many pictures of Fat Jack which appeared in newspapers all over the country. When Davenport, in New York, met anyone who claimed to have come from Montana, he would draw a sketch of Fat Jack, and, if the person could name the character, he was Davenport's friend and guest. If not, the artist knew at once that the person was an imposter.

Fat Jack received his name in the nearby town of Deer Lodge, where in the early days he tried his hand at barbering. At the time he knew very little about the trade, but chose it simply because there was no other barber in the town. One of his first customers was the late Judge Dixon, a widely known early day Montanan. Dixon later claimed that he wasn't certain whether he had received a shave or a surgical operation.

WORLD MUSEUM OF MINING, BUTTE

Fat Jack character (Butte resident Joe Duffy impersonates famous hack driver Fat Jack Jones).

After Fat Jack had once mastered the intricacies of the trade, he set out as a circuit-riding barber, visiting the mining camps of Silver Bow, Rocker and Burlington where once every week or so he cut the locks of the miners and invariably lost the proceeds at faro before moving on to the next town. Fat Jack was an inveterate gambler and never reformed during his lifetime. Like most gamblers, he was usually broke and often had his hack and horses in hock for gambling debts.

It was as a barber that he first visited Butte, in 1871. He did not remain long as there was strong competition, but traveled around the country, barbering as he went, finally ending up in Deadwood, South Dakota where he remained until 1878. Here he won and lost several good stakes, ending up by losing his shop, tools and all. It was then that he returned to Butte, where he went to work for Owsley and Cowan's transfer concern. While on this job Fat Jack checked the first shipment of freight to come in over the Utah and Northern Railroad.

In 1881 Fat Jack leased a hack and team of horses from Jim Murray, a banker and mining man, and John Curtis, a real estate operator. The hack was the first in the camp, brought in from Salt Lake City where it had been the family vehicle of one Judge Hempstead. It was a closed carriage, called in those days a "Rockaway." Fat Jack was now in the hacking business, and, although Butte had a population of but four thousand, he did well. Had he discontinued gambling, which usually kept him in a more or less straitened financial condition, Jack would have been well off.

It was around this time that the cab driver staked his false teeth in a faro game. He lost, and the dealer refused to give him the molars until he had the funds to redeem them. For a week, Fat Jack lived on soup and a very soft diet. His first act on redeeming the teeth was to order three, thick, T-bone steaks which he polished off in one sitting.

It was in February, 1882. Times were tough in the camp and the hacking business nothing to brag of. Most people were walking. Fat Jack was driving his hack up Main Street when the stage came down the hill. A Jerry Cumbro, a friend of the cab driver in his Deer Lodge days, was sitting on top of it.

"Come on," he hailed Fat Jack. "Let's go to the Coeur d'Alenes!"

"I'll go with you," yelled Jack, who climbed down from the cab box, tied his team to a hitching post in front of the old Arcade Saloon and left it there for Murray and Curtis, the owners, to find. Fat Jack hopped on the stage and was off for Idaho.

In later years Fat Jack often told of that trip and his experiences in the Coeur d'Alenes. There were few sleeping accommodations in the town of Eagle City and Fat Jack claimed that he and a miner from Butte obtained a large empty, steel oil-container, built a big fire in it, and charged the sleepy miners fifty cents each to lie within the radius of its warmth. A breakfast of two fried eggs, a plate of beans, and a cup of coffee cost $7.50 Fat Jack said.

Jack remained in Eagle City for six months. He was down to his last ten dollars, so he bet the entire amount against a horse in a poker game, won the horse, and started a freighting outfit which he built up to thirteen horses and a remunerative business. But Fat Jack couldn't keep away from faro. He finally left the Coeur d'Alenes afoot with two sandwiches and a pair of blankets, beating his way to Philipsburg, Montana. Then he walked thirty miles into Anaconda where he borrowed twenty dollars from a friend, bought himself a new shirt and a pair of trousers, and returned to Butte where he persuaded Jim Murray to lease him another hack and team. He remained until shortly before his death, some forty-five years later.

During his last years Fat Jack switched from faro to the horse races. "You are just as sure of losing your money," he would say, "and the bookmakers don't egg you on. You lose it quicker on a horse race and you don't have the painful suspense of a possible win."

The proudest day of Fat Jack's life was in August 1897, when he drove his hack through the streets of Butte with William Jennings Bryan as a passenger. He purchased a special outfit for the Great Commoner's benefit, an outfit which he carefully put away for later occasions when called upon to drive noted personalities. It consisted of a new, tall, silk plug hat and a long dun-colored coachman's coat of broadcloth with big black buttons. Fawn-colored gloves, a red-silk kerchief about his neck, and an eight-dollar whip completed the ensemble.

Fat Jack delighted in telling of the time he drove President Theodore Roosevelt from Butte to Columbia Gardens where Teddy was scheduled for a speech. Fat Jack whipped the horses all the three miles to the Gardens and took many of the curves on two wheels. Although the former President turned slightly pale, he did not complain and when he arrived at the Gardens and climbed out of the hack he turned to Fat Jack, showed the famous Roosevelt teeth and remarked: "Bully!"

Besides Roosevelt and Bryan, other notables hauled by Fat Jack in his hack included William Howard Taft, James Corbett, John L. Sullivan, Bob Fitzsimmons, Jim Jeffries, Sarah Bernhardt, the Kings of Belgium and Denmark and scores of actors, actresses, novelists, artists, and others in the public eye.

When F. Augustus Heinze returned to Butte in 1909, the mining town for weeks had been making preparations to give him a hero's welcome. Of course, Fat Jack and his hack had been secured to carry him from the depot to the town. The cab driver entered into the preparations by having his hack repainted until it glistened like polished ebony. He rented a team of spanking black horses from the Marcus Daly stock farm at Hamilton, Montana. Fat Jack claimed the value of the two thoroughbreds was $30,000.

On the night of Heinze's arrival, twenty thousand Butte people crowded around the depot. Fat Jack and his hack, both resplendent in their new accouterments, were awaiting the train. Heinze arrived and was ushered through the cheering crowd to Fat Jack's hack. It was one of the proudest moments of the old cab driver's life. At last the parade to town was started, Fat Jack and his prancing steeds leading the way. But his pride was short lived. About a third of the way up Wyoming Street, the frantic, joyous miners decided that they would take the place of the horses themselves. Without ceremony they stopped the hack, and over Fat Jack's protestations, unhitched the horses from the hack, and dozens of hands grasped the tongue and pulled the vehicle the remainder of the way to the Butte Hotel where Heinze was scheduled for a speech.

The miners told Fat Jack to remain on his perch on the seat, but the angry and disappointed jehu would have none of it. He climbed down, took his frightened horses by the bridle and sadly led them away. Later he told reporters, "If that bunch of hay-wire miners thought I would sacrifice my dignity to stay on that seat while they pulled my hack through the town, they had another guess coming. I've drove Presidents and kings and queens in that hack, and if it was good enough for them, it was good enough for Heinze." Fat Jack never fully recovered from what he called an insult to himself, his horses and his dignity.

F. M. Hickman, another hackman of Fat Jack's period, tells of "the biggest fare ever given to a hackman." It was handed to Fat Jack by Jim Murray, the noted banker and mining magnate—and Fat Jack rejected it.

Murray and Jack were old acquaintances. Murray had loaned the hackman two thousand dollars on his simple note. One evening Fat Jack picked up Murray at the depot and hauled him to the Thornton Hotel. As Murray left the hack he remarked, "Jack, I am going to pay you the highest fare ever paid a hackman for a ride from the depot or anywhere else." He then handed Jack the two-thousand-dollar note. "That's very liberal of you, Jim," Jack answered, "but if it's all the same to you, I'd rather have the fifty cents. I pay my debts."

As the years rolled along, taxicabs made their appearance in Butte. One by one, the other hack drivers changed to the motor-driven vehicles. All but Fat Jack. For years he tenaciously stuck to his cab and horses. Finally his good friend, Howard Pierce, presented him with a splendidly equipped car of foreign make. Fat Jack drove it for some years, but never thoroughly satisfied, he yearned for the old horse-drawn hack. It was shortly after this that he retired to the Soldiers' Home in Sawtelle, California. Fat Jack died December 16, 1920 at the home of W. A. Clark, Jr., in Los Angeles.

There are few in the camp who do not know a long, thin individual, who, from his seat on the hurricane back of a laundry delivery truck, has viewed and absorbed the local scene for close to a half-century. Joe Duffy, wag, practical joker, and storyteller, has handed the populace as many smiles as any man in the camp.

Duffy is the author of *Butte Was Like That*, a volume of tales of old Butte. The story of his "Centerville Ghost" prank is told in another chapter of this book.

In 1909 Duffy and a man named Carney were co-managers of the famous old Renshaw dance hall. Along with a number of other stunts planned to bring in cash customers, the two hit upon the idea of staging a "Marathon Waltz." The proposed contest was advertised in the newspapers along with the rules which stated that the couple staying on the floor the longest and who were still waltzing when everyone else had quit would be judged the winner. The prizes were a diamond ring for the lady and a watch for the man.

The two dance hall impresarios did not realize what they had started. On the night of the contest seventy-three couples were entered. Sielaff's orchestra banged out a popular waltz and the grueling grind was under way. Five hours passed and there were still thirty couples on the polished floor. The orchestra was already tiring and a relief band was secured.

The floor had been roped off like a prize fight arena, and as the word got around town of the endurance struggle under way in the hall, hundreds of night owls flocked to the scene. The enterprising management taxed them each fifty cents for a "look-see."

At seven o'clock when the lights in the hall turned yellow in the sickly gray light of a cold December morning, there were still half a dozen glassy-eyed dancers moving like automatons to the clash of an orchestra which, though three times relieved, was disheveled and worn. Not for a second had the dancers stopped. They chewed gum and kept wearily moving around and around the hall. Earlier many of the women contestants had fainted in the arms of their partners, while rumors were about town that one woman had dropped dead. This canard served only to fatten the box office receipts for Messrs. Duffy and Carney.

The Butte *Miner* reports:

> "There was something ghastly in the movements of the dancers striving to keep up with the music with the least possible exhaustion. At 10 o'clock A.M. three couples plodded along after their fourteen hours and fifteen minutes of continuous dancing without rest or nourishment. There is little doubt that in a large measure the minds of all on the floor were seriously affected by the exhaustion and continued circular motion. Tommy Donnelly danced thirteen hours with a newly made bride (not his). Her disgruntled husband finally broke up the twosome and took her home to get his breakfast and pack his lunch pail so that he could go to his work in the mine."

The insane dance was still in progress at eleven o'clock. The management at that time walked alongside each couple and suggested that the dance be called off and the spoils divided. There was a strong protest from the dancers, for none wanted to quit.

At the piano an exhausted piano player stooped over the ivories with a bit of cigarette hanging from his lips. The male dancers were coatless, and their lady partners badly in need of makeup. At 1 P.M. the music stopped abruptly. Sheriff John K. O'Rourke in answer to an avalanche of complaints from residents and also from the humane society had arrived.

"Stop the music!" said "Jawn K.," and the long, weary grind was over.

The dance floor was in confusion. The dancers did not want to quit. Men cursed, and women became hysterical. An announcement was made that the prizes would be divided. There was a furor among the audience. How were they going to divide a diamond ring and a watch among three couples?

Butte now held the world's non-stop dancing record, fourteen hours and fifty minutes, which up to then had been seven and a half hours in America and fourteen hours in the town of Johannesburg, South Africa.

The three remaining couples on the floor at the conclusion of the dance were Tom Furey and Julia Driscole, Ed McCormick and Miss McCormick, George Renean and Mary Coyle. They staggered to a Turkish bath for a rub-down and then to their homes for sleep.

Sheriff O'Rourke announced: "I am not in favor of such contests and hope it will be the last contest of the kind conducted in Butte. Foolish as it is, I am just a little proud that Butte dancers have broken the world's endurance record."

Duffy and Carney later gave a sumptuous banquet for the winners where the spoils were amicably divided.

Adding variety to an already varied town was Diamond Tooth Baker and Dublin Dan. Not that the two gentlemen had anything in common. The former was the self-styled king of the red-light pimps and the latter, proprietor of a drinking establishment that made a specialty of catering to the hobo trade.

Diamond Tooth Baker was a big, good looking "McGoofer" who had a fortune in precious gems set into the gold fillings of his teeth. It was his boast that there never was a time when he did not have at least a dozen girls in the district contributing to his support. He was reported to have a hundred different suits of clothes which he changed eight or ten times each day. He employed a valet and had a suite of rooms in an apartment house of the district, furnished with luxurious furniture, paintings, and objets d'art.

At one time he was hailed before Police Judge Boyle on the charge of pandering. Boyle had little sympathy and assessed him the maximum fine, one hundred dollars.

Diamond Tooth pulled out a bale of currency and smirkingly remarked, "That's easy, judge, any one of my girls can make that much in an evening."

Judge Boyle was burning inwardly—"And ninety days in the county jail at hard labor," he added. "Maybe one of your girls can do that in an evening!"

Dublin Dan, a big, devil-may-care Irishman, was the proprietor of "Dublin Dan's Hobo Retreat at the corner of Porphyry and Main Streets. It was regarded as unique in the Northwest. No slumming trip was complete without a visit to the resort. Sawdust, several inches deep, covered the floor. There were only two varieties of drinks passed out over the long, scarred bar: beer, served in quart-sized schooners, and whiskey at a dime a shot.

Lumberjacks, box-car tourists, transient workers, and the roughest class of the miners made the place a rendezvous. In the center of the saloon was a huge, pot-bellied stove on which always simmered a giant pot of stew, served gratis to hungry customers who dipped in empty cans or whatever receptacles were available. To the rear and running back and forth across the room was a series of clothes-lines drying out various garments of a hobo's wardrobe. In a room in the rear were tubs, washboards and other utensils necessary to "boiling out," as the hoboes called it. At night after closing hours the floor of the place was utilized as a flophouse, scores of bums laying out their blankets on the floor. The very novelty of the place insured a steady patronage.

It was in the summer, early in the new century, when the Rev. Bulgin, a sin-buster, held a series of revival meetings. A huge tent was erected on an empty lot on the corner of Wyoming and Porphyry Streets, and immediately in the rear of Dublin Dan's resort. From the point of attendance, the revivals were a distinct success, and thousands of residents attended each evening. On leaving the services, they were confronted by a band of ragged sandwich men in front of the tabernacle entrance carrying canvas banners: "FOR A GOOD COLD SCOOP OF LAGER AFTER THE SERVICES OR A SHOT TO WARM YOUR INNARDS GO TO DUBLIN DAN'S JUST AROUND THE CORNER."

Jacob Ehrlich was a frock-coated, bewhiskered, and derby-hatted rabbi, known to hundreds as "Cockelevitch." Rabbi Ehrlich was the kosher butcher of the old camp, to whom members of his faith brought their Sabbath chickens. These Cockelevitch unconcernedly butchered on the main street sidewalk in front of his store, usually before the eyes of a group of gaping youngsters. As a side line, the rabbi did a thriving business in the unleavened bread called matzoth and in pickled herring. The variegated aroma, which wafted from the establishment, is well remembered by old time residents, to whom the rabbi's activities were but another phase of a cosmopolitan camp.

Slightly over a quarter of a century ago, one cold December night, Old Kris Kringle must have been surprised. The principal instigator of the surprise was Billy Gemmel, a rounder, gambler, racehorse man, and, from that evening on, a sort of head official of a most unusual group, the "Joshers Club," which came into being that Christmas Eve in a North Main Street saloon.

Everyone in the camp knew of the Joshers, or had heard something about them. As an agency for spreading cheer at the Yuletide season, no other secular organization ever approached it.

"Peace on earth, good will to men!" sang the herald angels when the Child at Bethlehem came to lead humanity. It was the same spirit which guided the activities of Billy Gemmel and the Butte Joshers. The club had no elected officers, no constitution or bylaws, no home, But it had a motive—to feed the hungry, clothe the poor, succor the sick, and bring happiness to children at Christmas time.

In Al Green's saloon in 1900 there were a number of good fellows lined up at the bar—typical Western men who worked hard, played hard, and drank hard. They appreciated their comforts, and that night as they enjoyed their Tom and Jerries the sight of a ragged urchin, who crowded up against the radiator to absorb some of the warmth, started them thinking.

"Let's do something!" a frail, but wiry little man suggested. The man was Billy Gemmel and "a damn tough little man in a scrap." The crowd at the bar listened as Gemmel continued:

"There are a lot of hungry people in Butte who need something good to eat tomorrow. Let's get busy, us fellows who have our three square meals a day, and give these people a good Christmas dinner."

The suggestion was like applying the torch to a split fuse. It took. That night several hundred dollars had been contributed, wholesale and retail grocery and butcher shops lined up, and all holiday produce remaining on hand was hastily assembled by scores of volunteer workers. Baskets and boxes were secured, and before the sun rose on that Christmas morning two hundred and fifty homes were provided with a week's provisions.

For better than twenty-five years there were thousands in Butte in actual want and need during the wintertime who were aided by the generous and unselfish work of Billy Gemmel and his Joshers. In later years, contributions were accepted from all who desired to give. Each year a big, local and professional-talent show was held at the Broadway Theater, certain of the reserved seats often bringing as high as a hundred dollars. When times were tough as many as twenty-five hundred baskets were distributed. Delivery of the baskets was a secret and no one but the recipients themselves ever knew who received them.

When not engaged in charitable enterprises the Joshers were inveterate practical jokers, and many are the stories concerning the pranks. At Thanksgiving time, one year, one of their members from the South, received three fat 'possums from his home town. He had planned a Thanksgiving feast for a few of his friends and had secured the services of a colored chef who was to prepare the dinner at the Finlen Hotel.

In some manner, Gemmel and one or two others of the club found out about the fattened 'possums which were in a crate in the Finlen kitchen. By judicious inquiry they also learned that the chef employed by the Southern Josher had been a bit indiscreet with the wife of another gentleman of color, a pugilist of repute.

This information they used as a club to persuade the philandering chef to give them the three 'possums and accept in their stead, three sleek, plump tomcats. They told the frightened cook, he could either prepare the cats instead of the 'possums, or face the prize fighter who would be in no peaceful state of mind if they told him what they knew.

The chef followed their directions. The cats were skinned, stuffed and baked in approved Southern style, and, at the Thanksgiving banquet, the genial host from below the Mason-Dixon line was eloquent on the superiority of Southern cooking as he served generous helpings of the done-to-a-turn " 'possum" to his guests.

Gemmel and a select group of Joshers who had not been invited to the banquet at the Finlen drove out to Barney's roadhouse on the Flat, where the real 'possums had been prepared by one of Barney's cooks. The trick they had played added savor to the meal.

It was a month or so later down at the colored club when the guilty chef with a few too many slugs of gin, let the 'possum out of the bag. Gemmel and his archconspirators went into hiding as on many other occasions when the Joshers rode hilariously high.

"Colonel James W. Rutledge of the Rutledges of Virginia, Suh! A gentleman of the old South whose word is his law. You can lay a million dollars to a dewdrop on the little filly I'm telling you of, and go to bed with money in the bank!"

The speaker was "Buckets"—Colonel Buckets—if you please; for a half-century one of the camp's outstanding residents, racehorse tout, tipster, bookmaker, gambler and walking encyclopedia on horses and events pertaining to the turf.

In appearance Buckets was the typical racehorse fancier and man-about-the-betting-ring. Of average height and weight, freshly barbered complexion, neatly clipped iron-gray mustache, silk shirts of violent stripes, flashy suits running to checks and plaids, the very latest in fashionable headgear, eye-blinding cravats of every hue in the spectrum —this was Colonel Buckets when the horses were running his way. When he picked them, his pockets were lined with folding money, and his lone one-carat diamond stickpin was out of hock and flashing from the silk shirt front. When all his selections had either broken their legs or had been left at the post; or when the Colonel had spent a hard week about the bars of the city celebrating the victory of a nag who romped home at juicy prices, there was a different appearing Buckets—a bit bedraggled—but not for long, because Buckets had marvelous recuperative powers. He might wilt, but he was certain to bloom again, this flower of the South.

Colonel Buckets was born in Virginia. As a youth he learned to "ride the nags to hounds" as he expressed it, to become an accomplished horseman. Because his parents had their hands full with twelve children, he decided to "leave home and make a name for himself."

Going to New York, he secured employment in the famous Vanderbilt stables where he gained first-hand knowledge of fine horseflesh. Gifted with an uncanny memory, Buckets never forgot their history or fine points.

Buckets was breveted colonel by the late Tom Chope, mine foreman and one of the tipster's closest friends. The title was later made official by the late Governor Joseph Dixon of Montana. For a half a century, except for brief intervals while visiting other race tracks, he lived in Butte continuously.

Colonel Buckets thrived in the "good old days" when the "bangtails" were running out at the old race track on the Flat, and the horse races of the country were given as much space in the sport sections of the dailies as is now accorded baseball. Buckets never did like baseball, not that it was to blame for what happened to the "gee-gees," but because as he put it: "There was no baseball news when Proctor Knott won the Derby."

The Colonel knew more about horses than a desert Arab. He could recite the genealogical chart of every worth-while winner that ever scampered down the home stretch of an American track.

When King and Lowry's, the M and M, the Butte Hotel, and most of the camp's gambling resorts ran racetrack poolrooms, Buckets was in his element. He would slip into the poolrooms with some friends who would read him the list of entries and odds.

Buckets had a remarkable photographic memory. One reading of the board was always sufficient. The number of each entry and the track on which the horse was to race was engraved on his mind until the next race. He would stand out in front of the betting board discussing odds, horses, pedigrees, and jockeys as accurately as those who could read and, there were few who knew he could not read or write as well as they.

Buckets passed out his tips with lavish hand. It was his living. Those who benefited by his words of wisdom showed their appreciation in a proper manner—and Buckets flourished.

Then came the eclipse of such sunny days. Racing and the operation of betting rooms were banned in Montana, and Buckets began slipping back until, he stated, "They finally put me in politics and ran me for State office" He was Democratic candidate in the 1924 primaries for the office of Lieutenant Governor under the family name of Rutledge.

James Rutledge didn't get the nomination his friends sought for him, although he polled a complimentary ballot of nearly three thousand votes and ran third in a field of seven candidates—or in race track parlance, he "finished in the show money." Feeling his defeat keenly, Buckets gradually took on the appearance of a disappointed man.

It is said that "they never come back," but Buckets did. In 1928 horse racing was again legalized in Montana. The new Marcus Daly park was opened for a thirty-day run. Buckets, whose talents had been hidden for two decades, again came into his own. With the return to Butte of the sport of kings, Buckets dressed in striking togs, dashing through the streets as though he were walking on air, shouting to the throngs that he "had information of great moment" to impart—the famous "Buckets' Tips"—but always for a consideration.

Noted for his wisecracks, the colonel invariably talked in the language of the turf. "Left at the post" and "Put it right on the nose" were among his favorite expressions. So confident was he in a selection of a winner that at one time he offered to bet "the royal jewels against a broken shoestring."

Buckets was always a commanding personality. Possessed of a ready wit, he was never lost for a word and was the cause of much merriment for old time friends who sought to best him in an argument When horse racing was again discontinued in Butte, he always managed to follow the ponies to other tracks. He was ever ready with the latest tips on "sure winners" and always willing to place a bet on a percentage basis.

A confirmed bachelor, Buckets was like a frisky colt and shied away from the feminine rustle of silks and satins. However, he was always a gentleman when among the fair sex and it angered him to hear disrespectful language being used within the hearing of a lady. But his dealings with the weaker sex were strictly confined to pointing out for them the "sure-shot winners."

It was in 1915 that Buckets went to work in the mines. The lid was on in Butte for racing and everything connected with it. That went for gambling too. Buckets' good friend, Senator W. A. Clark, who often came to his rescue with a meal ticket and a month's room-rent, was in Europe and the biscuits were indeed hanging high for the usually resourceful Colonel. His friend Tom Chope suggested that he consider a job shoveling in the High Ore Mine. Buckets was at first indignant, but after due consideration decided it was his only out.

Reluctantly, he procured a miner's outfit of digging clothes, candlestick and lunch bucket. Word got about of Buckets' decision, and the newspapers ran the story with a photograph of Buckets on the front pages.

The Associated Press picked up the story, put it on the wire, and the tale of Buckets going to work was news for the nation.

The ubiquitous racehorse tout was to report at the mine on night shift. On the evening of his departure for the High Ore, hundreds of his cronies with a hastily gathered-together brass band, followed him up the hill to the mine gate. Buckets labored at the High Ore for a matter of two weeks when some new angle presented itself, and he gave the underground work a glad farewell. But, ever after, he claimed to be a miner.

Among other accomplishments, Buckets also was an entertainer of ability. He often appeared under the sponsorship of his friend Billy Sullivan, manager of the Rialto Theater, on the stage of that playhouse at New Year's Eve shows. In dramatic voice he recited that heart-rending saga of the race track, "The Old Sport Sat In the Grandstand Seat."

To be certain of a Thanksgiving dinner each year, it was Buckets' custom to place twenty-five cents "on a gobbler's nose" at an East Park Street butcher shop early in July, and twenty-five or fifty cents every so often throughout the summer and fall. Thus he was always assured of a gala, convivial holiday feast, cooked and served in true Southern style to many friends at Buckets' abode.

On Buckets' death in 1932, friends planned to give him the honor of a horse-drawn funeral. The state was combed in an attempt to procure an old style hearse, but there was none available. Nevertheless the turn-out for his funeral was prodigious, with the Butte Pioneers Club of several hundred attending in a body. One friend made all arrangements and assumed the entire burial cost. At his graveside in the Pioneer Club plot, a race track crony of the dead man remarked: "There is a divine law that every hoss-racing man has got to die broke."

Buckets was buried on the day of the Kentucky Derby. His selection for the race was Ladysman. Broker's Play won the race. Ladysman was a poor fourth.

Butte has never confined her interest to only human characters. There are many instances when dogs and horses became as well known as the countless two-legged characters.

There was "Old Jim," the firehorse who had the run of the city's streets for a quarter of a century and whose likeness on an enormous oil painting hangs in a prominent place in the fire station. Old Jim was no ordinary horse. He had been to as many fires as he had hairs on his tail.

Coal black, of massive build, he was the only firehorse to survive the disastrous explosion of January 15, 1895, when practically the entire

Butte fire department of seventeen members was wiped out. Jim was terribly injured from the explosion, and it was thought for awhile that he would die, but he was always a powerful animal and he pulled through. To the time of his death, the animal carried the scars of the big explosion.

Jim had a special stall at the fire station, and there were no bars or locks on it. He was free to come or go at will. He knew all the cafes and candy stores of the business districts, and it was an odd sight to see Old Jim poking his head in their doorways, begging for sugar or apples. Old Jim was a great favorite with the fair sex, too. It was often his habit to follow a young lady up the street, nudging her pocketbook in the hopes of a lump of sugar or a bit of hard candy. North Main Street was the old charger's stamping ground, particularly its block of saloons known as the "Dardanelles." Old Jim could tell a drunk, and caused many a laugh as he followed some inebriate up the street, gleefully pushing him along with his head or taking the drunk's hat off with his mouth and dropping it to the sidewalk.

On each Decoration Day, Old Jim, pulling the fire chief's buggy, headed the parade. At the cemetery, as the fire laddies decorated the graves of the firemen killed in the explosion, the horse stood silently by the side of the graves, seemingly proud of his duty. As age and infirmity crept up, the firemen had him removed to pastures in a warmer climate where he finally died. Butte mourned his passing. A memorial was passed and read as the Mayor and City Councilmen stood with bowed heads while the flag on the fire station was lowered to half staff.

In the early nineteen hundreds, one dog claimed much attention. As Sol Levy's dog, his bailiwick was the city jail where Levy was jailer. "Jimmy" was a thoroughbred fox terrier with a stack of papers proving his ancestry. Like his namesake, the firehorse, he made the rounds of the confectionary stores and was also a frequent visitor at the better-class cafes, where scraps and tidbits were saved for him. Jimmy's rotundity bore evidence of this fact. His bed was in a box under jailer Sol Levy's desk, and it was said that the pugnacious little terrier could whip any other dog in the camp within fifty pounds of his size.

Jimmy had originally belonged to the heavyweight champion, Jim Corbett. The latter had purchased him when a pup for $150 from a sailor off an English ship in San Francisco harbor. Corbett named the pup after himself.

When "Gentleman Jim's" show was touring the Northwest Butte was on his itinerary, and the dog had accompanied him. Sergeant Dawson, then of the local police department, had known and admired Jim Corbett for a long time. The sergeant went to the show, and after the performance talked with the pugilist.

When the two men were about to separate the sergeant asked Corbett for a memento, and the champion promptly presented the sergeant with his namesake. Jimmy was at once installed as a pet at police quarters, and he made it and the streets of Butte his home for many years.

Another famous animal of which pages might be written was the famed "Centerville Bull," a coal-black animal with amorous instincts who roamed the streets of the hillside town, causing consternation as he smashed down fences and led the Centerville cows away from their paths of rectitude. His favorite diet was the backyard washings of the housewives.

For several years, The Bull roamed the streets and alleys of the town at will, until finally, a Mrs. Sullivan, tiring of the depredations, decided to take matters into her own hands, and shot at him with her husband's shotgun. She scored a bull's-eye, hitting the bull in a spot that measurably reduced his virility and likewise his amorous prowlings. As the story goes, because of the injury, The Centerville Bull became disconsolate, and one night ended it all by jumping down a mine shaft. At any rate that is where his remains were found the next morning.

Sharkey and Kelly the Ghost were two huge tomcats known to all the camp. Sharkey was a three-legged battle-scarred veteran of a thousand fights whose domain was the Pennsylvania mine-yard. He had been named after the prize fighter, Tom Sharkey. His particular hate was dogs—particularly any dog that chanced to stray within the Pennsylvania Mine fence. The cat, which weighed close to fifty pounds, had lost a leg in a battle with a Great Dane. It was the habit of the miners to coax stray dogs into Sharkey's domain and then stand by to watch the fur fly. It was always the dogs who made a hurried and squealing exit from the mine-yard after the battle. Sharkey met his end when a Missourian miner sneaked three coon dogs into the yard—although the tomcat fought the hunting dogs valiantly for over a half hour. The Missourian, himself, received a severe pommeling for "teaming up" on Sharkey in such an unsportsman-like manner.

Kelly the Ghost was a big white cat whose habitat was on the eight-hundred-foot level of the St. Lawrence Mine. At that time, on account of the feed kept for horses, the mines were alive with mice and Kelly had been taken underground to do his part in ridding the mine of rodents.

He received his name because of his habit off roaming around the level in the dark, frightening the greenhorns. One look at Kelly's green eyes in a darkened drift caused more than one novice miner to rush out to the station and ring for the cage to the surface.

Kelly developed into quite a traveler, finding his way to and from the St. Lawrence to the Anaconda and Neversweat Mines, which are connected on certain levels. One time Kelly appeared on the six-hundred-foot level of the "Saint." How he made his way up there no one knew, but many of the old-timers would swear that he climbed a ladder for the two hundred feet.

Dynamite was Butte's own dog. As far as known he never had any other owner and the City paid his dog tax each year. Dynamite was a large yellow and white collie with a good share of shepherd in his veins. He made his first appearance one morning at the busiest street intersection. Where he came from no one knew, but for many years thereafter, this street corner was his only home. The traffic policeman on the busy corner gave him his name.

Like Jim, the firehorse, and Sol Levy's Jimmy, he obtained his meals at the restaurants. But where the former two welcomed any stray handout, Dynamite frowned on any contribution less than T-bone steaks and chicken or turkey scraps.

He had a great affection for children, accompanying them out to Columbia Gardens on the weekly Children's Day. Dynamite rode the streetcars to and from the resort, and was the only dog in Butte allowed aboard the cars.

He had also a peculiar love for policemen, firemen, or anyone in uniform. At that time, the traffic policemen in winter stood out in the center of the street intersection on a steam-heated grille. It was on this grille, at the feet of the traffic cop, that Dynamite might be found stretched out on the cold winter nights—that is if there wasn't a fire—for Dynamite never missed a fire during his regime. At the first blast of the siren, the big dog was off like a streak, and he had an inherent instinct for locating the blaze, often beating the firemen to the scene. He could be seen cavorting about and barking with delight until the fire had been extinguished; then he would jump aboard the hook and ladder wagon and ride back to his stand on the corner.

Baseball was another of the dog's weaknesses. At that time the Mines Baseball League was in existence, and Dynamite never missed a game. The games were played at Clark Park, south of the city, and took place each evening at 6:15. At six sharp, without fail, Dynamite would climb aboard a streetcar bound for the ball park. Arriving there, the dog's habit was to proudly stride through the main gate and then bound out onto the playing field, where he always received as resounding a cheer as any player. His homage duly received, the dog would then go to one or the other of the team's playing benches, as ardent a booster for his chosen nine as any fan in the stands. A hit, home run, or a score, brought forth mad barking, cavorting and much tail wagging, and Dynamite was usually on the winning team's side. The game over, the dog always rode home in state in one of the player's cars.

For several years Dynamite remained at his post. Rarely a month passed by without some story of him in the newspapers. He loved to be photographed and posed proudly for countless snapshots.

The winter of '27 was cold. Dynamite was growing old, and the infirmities of age seemed to be crawling up on him. Now and then he was late for a fire. As is the custom in the camp, each December, the Union Pacific runs a midwinter excursion from Butte to Los Angeles. Many residents take advantage of the low rates and journey to the California city. Usually, a celebration is held at their departure. That year, with Sam Treloar's Mines Band in attendance, the delegation had chartered a special streetcar to take them to the railroad station. As the car pulled out from the corner of Park and Main Streets, old Dynamite suddenly jumped from his warm grille in the middle of the street and bounded aboard the crowded streetcar.

When the delegation boarded the train at the depot, Dynamite climbed on too, and made the trip to Los Angeles. He never came back, preferring in his old age the balmy winters of California to the chilling blasts at the corner of Main and Park Streets in Butte.

Printer's Ink

THE pressroom of the *Evening Intermountain* in the early days was the basement of a building on North Main Street. Next door was the basement of a large saloon where the beer kegs were placed and kept cool. For some reason, perhaps through an error in construction, it was necessary to run the beer lines of the saloon across the ceiling of one corner of the composing room. The pipes had been there for some time when one day an inquisitive printer discovered that the pipes contained beer. A hand drill was obtained, a hole was bored and corked tight with a small steel plug known as a "dutchman." From then on, it was one continual party for the *Intermountain* printers.

The bartenders in the saloon above thought that something was amiss, but on investigation failed to see the tapped pipe, as the printers had it well camouflaged. They didn't dare press the search too closely for fear that if the printers hadn't discovered the beer lines, any suspicious action might disclose the secret to the ink slingers.

Just after the Butte-Anaconda printer's annual mulligan, a moist affair that lasted several days, many of the boys suffered from parched throats. As a result they began "hitting the dutchman" pretty heavily, and soon several of them were laid out in varying degrees of drunkenness. One printer either forgot to replace the plug or didn't screw it in tight enough with the result that the beer leaked out onto the floor of the print shop. Soon the kegs in the saloon ran dry, and investigation showed where the beer had been going.

Before the discovery of the tapped beer line, however, the printers had magnanimously acted as host at a beer bust for the owner of the saloon, recently elected as county commissioner. The county commissioner, not to be outdone, reciprocated with a party of his own. Later, to his chagrin, he discovered that he had been treated with his own beer.

In those days the camp's newswriters were sharply-drawn individualists, most of whom fell into the category of characters-about-town. Many possessed real talent. Byron E. Cooney was representative of both groups.

One of Cooney's news stories concerned the hot tamale vendors who could be heard nightly crying their wares, as, steaming cans in hand, they wended their way through the streets. Because many were hotblooded Afghans, given to feuding among themselves, cutting scrapes were frequent. Their family name, Kahn, appeared frequently in the police court news.

Remembered as a gem of that golden era of journalism was Byron Cooney's story in the Butte *Evening News* headed: "HOUSE OF KAHN IN WRONG AGAIN." It read:

> "And it came to pass in the valley of Butte, which is hard by the river of Silver Bow, Shad Kahn, a Mussulman, was vending the flesh of birds wrapped up with meal and corn husks at midnight. For Kahn had come far from Afghanistan and the Christian people were strange to him and sometimes they were unkind to him, giving him nothing but abuse and unkind speeches. Came one Stephen Kane, who hailed from the land known as Hibernia, and, liking not the garb of the vendor of food, approached the Mussulman and sayeth:
>
> "'Wherefore sell you the flesh of goats? saying "Rabbi, this is chicken!"'

"And Shad Kahn answered saying:

"'Peace be with ye. By the beard of my father this is chicken, for I am Mussulman and I say only truth, being not like unto the Irish, who lieth like Hades.'

"'Bohunk that thou art,' said Stephen Kane, the Irish one, 'accursed be thou and all thy race. May hostile hordes overcome you and may your wells go dry and your flock sicken and your tribes decrease; may your corn be blighted and may the heathen and barbarian carry off your wives and daughters and your cities be burned and your king be taken captive. . . .'

Thus far had Stephen Kane spake in great anger when Shad Kahn smote him on the mouth. And Stephen Kane kicked Kahn's tamale can forty ways for Sunday.

"Here endeth the first half of the story.

"A harness bull with a hand like a grappling iron pinched the tamale peddler and his tormentor and threw them both in the coop and Judge McGowan heard the story this morning in court.

"'These Kahns are a tough bunch,' said the arresting officer. 'They're in wrong all the time. They couldn't keep the peace if it was in a safe. They're worse than the Bohunks.'

"'It was this way,' said Kane. 'I'm going down the street minding own business and I says to the Bohunk: "Phat have ye in them tamales, chicken or horse meat?" says I, meanin' no harm.

"'Then he calls me a jub- jub- balabo- Karara, or somethin' like that, which no decent man would take. So I makes a pass at him and miss, and he unwinds one to me map and then in comes the bull and saves him from the undertaker, but don't worry, judge, if you'll but let me at him, I'll knock him flatter than the decayed meat he pizens people with in his putrid tamales.'

"Judge McGowan laughed, and Kahn being the aggressor, he fined him $10 and suspended the fine. He let Stephen Kane off with a warning.

"Here endeth the tale."

Although he spent but five or six years in Butte, the camp claims another newspaperman, Berton Braley, poet and author, as her own. And Braley too, born and raised in Iowa, proudly calls Butte his home. In his autobiography, *Pegasus Pulls A Hack*, he takes three chapters in lauding the town. Braley concludes by saying Butte is the only spot in the world that he would care to claim as his own—and he traveled extensively.

Braley arrived as a cub reporter fresh from college in 1903, working first on the old *Intermountain.* He early showed flashes of talent. For some time the cub ran a daily rhyme in the paper—many of them having merit. But a city editor who didn't think much of Braley's rhymes told him he was wasting the paper's time, and to confine himself to straight news gathering. This editor, Jere Murphy, later claimed to have started Braley on his career. At any rate the young reporter quit the *Intermountain* for a job on the Butte *Evening News*, controlled by F. Augustus Heinze. Here Dick Kilroy, the editor, gave him the leeway which enabled him to jump to national prominence. While covering the police court for the *Evening News*, Braley often broke into unorthodox news reporting as indicated in this piece from a 1905 issue:

SCENE
The Police Court of Butte

CHARACTERS
Herman Yutee, Bill Kelly, Tom Coughlin (the Man Eater)

THE CLERK—

"Yutee, stand up!
and you, Kelly, stand too!
And Coughlin, those words
are directed at you.
You are charged with a souse,
which laid you out flat.
Now what is your plea and your answer to that?"

SONG OF THE TANK TRIO—

"We were drunk, we were tanked,
we admit it with pain.
We were plastered and filled to the
brim.
And the sight of our eyes it was
dim.

But it's water for us in the
    future, you bet.
No more of the whiskey or beer.
We've sworn off before, but we
    chanced to forget–
And that is the reason we're here.

"Our good resolutions
    they melted away
In the heat of a terrible thirst.
Our strong constitutions
    grew haggard and gray,
And the bubble of abstinence burst.
We were floating on billows of
    whiskified bliss,
We thought we had purchased
    the town.

"We wondered what heaven is
    equal to this?
When the cop pulled us suddenly
    down.
And now all our thought are
    becoated with fuzz
And our heads are the size
    of a horse,
If a man only knew what a
    damn fool he wuz,
When he gets what is known
    as a souse!

"We know we were pickled—
    We know we were tanked
We were ossified, every man.
    So we will be tickled
And you will be thanked
    If you'll fine us as light as you can."

HIS HONOR—
"Red wine is a mocker,
    and booze is a fright.

But as in the locker
You've spent all the night
Five dollars each will settle the bill."

CHORUS OF DRUNKS—
"We'll never get drunk no more.
We'll never get drunk no more.
We've signed the pledge and forsaken the booze
And we'll never get drunk no more."

Braley's dog Solomon, an animal of doubtful lineage, was as well known about the camp as the newsman himself. The two were inseparable, and when the reporter was covering trials at the court house, Solomon could usually be found dozing outside the doors. Photos of Solomon appear several times in the old issues of the *News.* Braley left Butte in 1909, a local attorney, H. L. Maury, advancing him the money to make the trip to New York. He never returned, stating in his memoirs that although he loved Butte, he preferred to remember it as the wild roistering camp he had lived in from 1903 to 1909.

Many of the newsboys, too, were characters of note. The Walker brothers, Tom, a Federal judge, and Frank, present Postmaster-General of the United States, sold papers here at one time.

Little Stevie was an urchin who slept under the sidewalks on East Galena Street. His plaintive plea, "Give Stevie two bits and he will make a fit for you!" is remembered by many old-timers. Stevie was an epileptic apparently possessed of the ability of bringing on the convulsions at will.

Little Alex Discount's bid to fame came from the odd fact that he had the largest head in the city. He wore an eight and a quarter size hat which some local doctors claimed was due to a double skull. Alex was a prodigy, who at eleven enrolled in a college scientific extension course. Stories and pictures of this newsie appear frequently in the early newspaper files.

Among countless others was Barney Kenoffel, once mayor of the large and prosperous Butte Newsboys Club, and now a Pacific coast business man. Barney had the reputation of being the best hustler among all the newsboys, accumulating a thousand dollar bank account before he was sixteen years of age. Although Jewish, Barney never failed to plant a special brand of clover seed a few weeks before St. Patrick's Day. As the gala holiday arrived, Barney would transplant the clover into individual flower pots. These he sold as growing shamrocks to homesick Irishmen at prices up to a dollar apiece.

Smells of a Camp

ABOUT the turn of the century one local paper screamed in headlines: "IT STUNK TO HIGH HEAVEN."

It was not a pretty expression but the aroma that arose and assailed the nostrils of all residents within a three-mile radius of an odorous half-acre on the Flats was not pretty either. This monstrous caldron of the variegated scents and odors was owned, operated, and controlled by the municipality itself. To be romantic, it was "The Smell of the City." To be vulgarly blunt, it was the city dump . . . and it did stink.

A nose can stand so much, but in spite of public clamor, city officers held their bulbous noses between their thumbs and forefingers. His Honor, the Mayor, upheld his administration in a short denial that to this day remains a classic.

"'Tis not the city dump that smells," said he, "it's that damn Chinese graveyard a half-mile away, and the pork, chicken, and rice those poor heathens lave on top of the graves to spile in the sun!"

As the mortality rate of the camp's Chinese did not exceed an average of one a month the citizens laughed long and loud, and held their noses a bit tighter.

The acres of nasal effronteries attracted indescribable swarms of flies. Packed together tightly in great black clouds they vied with the Cree Indian squaws in reclaiming choice tidbits from the dump. Demand for fly screens brought rushing business to the hardware merchants, and it was whispered that one of the aldermen had his savings invested in this lucrative business. But that—like so much Butte history—is off the record.

Another odor can be laid at the feet of the meat packers. In 1902 and 1903 Butte was the center of the industry for most of Montana and a large portion of North and South Dakota. Thousands of head of cattle and sheep were shipped to the mining city for slaughter in those years. This thriving business kept five large slaughterhouses busy—and rightfully they did not call them packing plants or abattoirs in those days. Several hundred men added their pay rolls to those of the camp's miners. All of the plants were located within a mile of the business district.

Meat packing not having reached the perfection it has today, when everything but the squeal is canned, there was an enormous amount of refuse material. Taking full advantage of the utter unconcern of the city authorities, the packers ordered it all hauled and unceremoniously dumped in a common pit on the city's municipal dump. When one pit was completely filled, another was dug and made ready for the slaughterhouse refuse. As the years passed the number of pits increased, as likewise did the terrific all-overwhelming stench. As thousands of livestock were slaughtered and shipped, Butte held its nose with one hand, and pleadingly sought with the other, some manner of relief from its duly elected officials.

When the slaughterhouses cleaned up or as they termed it, "ran the tank," a general housecleaning of all accumulated dry waste, scraps and tallow, it was rendered for soap in huge iron tanks. This further insult to the camp's olfactory sense, went up the slaughterhouse stacks as smoke, steam and mist. The aura poured forth in black clouds. After rising a hundred feet or so, it would descend and waft in gently billowing, odorous clouds toward the homes of the miners.

Yes, all this could be blamed on the butchers and the livestock industry, but it must be remembered that these were a mile distant from the city. This was not a constant menace. When the breezes changed, which was often, all unpleasant odors quickly dissipated into the fresh sparkling air of the mountains.

There was yet another odor which was distributed into every neighborhood.

Chic Sale, if he had been present, perhaps could have painted a vivid picture of these "night riders" or "moonlighters" or "honey men" as they were variously known. Anyone whose youth was spent in Butte in those days remember the clump-clump-clump-of the solid iron wagons and the racket and din made by the accompanying buckets, brushes, ropes and various paraphernalia. Black horses, black drivers, black night, with running lights both fore and aft. Just why the running lights were used has never been satisfactorily explained. Certainly their coming was heralded by the breeze for over a quarter of an hour before their arrival. And it was certain that no one would be foolhardy enough to dispute their right-of-way. They were a necessary evil of those days and the aroma added novelty to that coming from the dumps.

In time an outraged public gathered at the election polls. A reform administration was elected and its first civic act centered around the abolishment of all odors and their causes. The dump was filled in. Thousands of cubic yards of soil were used. Trees and shrubs were planted and a rather attractive park arose on its site.

Today the younger generation marvels at the luxuriant growth in the park, and wonders at its cause.

The old-timer doesn't marvel, he knows.

Indians

AS IN other mining camps on the fringe of civilization, Indians were much in evidence in Butte's earlier days. Between 1890 and 1910 a large encampment of vagabonds from Canada rubbed shoulders with the miners.

Why they picked on the copper camp has ever been a mystery. But at the foot of the old city dump, close by the slopes of Timber Butte, south of the city, several hundred Cree braves joined later by the belligerent Chippewas—along with twice that number of squaws, papooses and dogs—made their camp. Winter and summer, they lived in the teepees, and added color to the already colorful town.

The Indians were ever a troublesome problem to the authorities; a Democratic chairman of the city council once remarked:

"If it isn't the Populists, it's that damn, heathen, Hole-in-Blanket, and his crew of dog-eaters out by the dump! I don't know which smells the worse or has the most bugs—thim or the slaughterhouse dumps that the people on the West Side are always bellyachin' about!"

In summer the Indians eked out a doubtful existence from the dump piles. When the wintry blasts stormed in from the 11,000-foot peaks of the Highlands, south of the city, the Indians "went on the county" and the mercy of the politicians. To augment the tax-roll contribution, once each year, under the supervision of the city and county authorities, the red men acted as hosts to the citizens of Butte at a gala celebration.

A two-day program of horse races, with a war dance as a grand finale, was offered by the redskins for the entertainment of miners and their families. With the compliments of the taxpayers, ingredients for an old-fashioned Indian barbeque were donated. Viands such as toasted mustang, tastily prepared city-dump rat, gopher and ground squirrel, and the particular *piece de resistance*, a much favored delicacy of the Crees, "Reeky-Reeky-Pookey-Pookey," were served in style. The last dish was prepared by the industrious squaws and maidens in advance of the fiesta.

The principal and important ingredient was a fattened dog, whose bones had been broken while still alive. The bone-breaking was done with a husky club in the hands of a squaw a week preceding the festivities. Allowed to remain in the sun for this interval, the thoroughly ripened delicacy was then served from the original hide on the day of the festival. The Indians, before the gaping eyes of the crowd, ate "Reeky-Reeky-Pookey-Pookey" with enjoyment.

The celebration was usually held in July at the old Marcus Daly race track. The tribe of Crees with its retinue of squaws, papooses, horses and dogs journeyed *en masse* to the race track dragging the teepees and camping paraphernalia behind.

Great were the preparations for the event. Bedecked in savage finery, including blankets, feathers, beads, and with faces streaked with war paint, the Indians presented a vivid aboriginal spectacle.

The squaws, unmindful of personal appearance the greater part of the time, literally "went to town" on the big days. Perfume was a major weakness. Cheapness and a powerful odor were the main requisites. They bought it by the pint, and drenched their persons from head to foot.

As bathing was unknown, the reaction resulting from the meeting of unwashed bodies and cheap perfume, tended to bring forth an odor that could not possibly be duplicated. "Attar of Indian," it was humorously called by an early writer. The squaws revelled in it.

The braves of the tribe looked askance at the squaws' efforts to beautify themselves. To their masculine notion, the use of perfume for personal adornment was utter waste. To them, "smell water" with its alcoholic content was an excellent and satisfactorily potent beverage, and once the thirsty scalp hunters got the scent, the squaws had to guard the perfume with their lives.

Thousands of residents attended the big events. At a dollar a ticket, a tidy sum was turned over to the redskins to help tide them over the cold winter.

Scores of the Indians competed in the horse races. Stripped to their breech clouts and smeared with war paint, the braves wildly rode their small, wiry mounts over the track. No bridles or saddles were used. Bareback, hunched over their mounts, they guided the animals with their knees. The din was terrific, each rider, "wahooing" at the top of voice, the squaws, papooses and Indian spectators emitting blood-curdling yells as they urged on their favorites. Miners in the stands added to the din. Betting was heavy and hundreds of dollars changed hands.

The Indians also wagered to their limit on the outcome. As the Crees did not compute their wealth in dollars and cents, horses and ponies were the stakes; and many head of these animals passed from one Indian to another on the results. It was not an uncommon practice for a brave down to his last pony, and still desiring to wager, to place squaws and girl papooses up as collateral—even up—one young squaw against one pony; one old squaw against one old horse.

The war dances were a spectacle long to be remembered Here the Indians let off the accumulated steam of the year. The entire tribe reverted to type and went native with a vengeance. The Anaconda *Standard* of July, 1894, describes the event of that year:

> "The Crees put on their war whoop dances at the race track yesterday. Chief Hole-In-Blanket, boss musician and Chief of the Indians, led an intricate quick step on the war drum. Chief Little Bear, Buffalo's Coat and Ta-Noose, together with their paint bedaubed and feather bedecked followers, danced, hopped and howled to the delight of several thousand white-faced spectators.
>
> "The orchestra was composed of about six warrior musicians who sat on their haunches around a big drum which they beat in concert, meanwhile chanting a doleful anthem that sounded like a pathetic 'Irish Come Allye.'
>
> "The attire and decorations of the dancers were elaborate. One who was presumably the *premiere danseuse* was attired only in one short breech clout. In lieu of fancy leggings one leg was painted yellow and one green. The facial pencilings matched the leg colors. Another had his face and arms marked bias with red, white and blue stripes, a tribute to his own 'original American' blood or to the flag of the Union.
>
> "They executed the dog dance, the tea dance, the ghost dance, the swill barrel polka and all of the other weird movements with which they celebrated early-day war victories. The Indians danced singly as well as in concert. It was an odd show."

The Battle of the City Dump

"A tribal war has broken out between the Cree and Chippewa Indians both of whom camp on the Flat. Each claims it has an exclusive franchise to plunder the Butte dump for such things as are edible or wearable or sellable. The dump, it seems, will support one tribe but won't support two tribes. The Cree Chief, Ta-Noose, claims two years' priority. Hole-In-Blanket, Chippewa leader, retorts that the Crees are not United States Indians and really belong in Canada. City officials have appointed a mediator to aid the Indians in settling their difficulties. In the meantime, war has been averted by the signing of a temporary truce."

—Butte *Miner*, July 20, 1898.

War was brewing that July morning in
the year of ninety-eight.
Though history's silent on the matter,
And its pages don't relate,
Yet on the lips of each Butte miner,
From the shiv-wheel to the sump,
Was this wordy, bloodless battle held
on Butte's old city dump.

The Crees, brave Indian nation, were the
cause of all the talk.
They, full brothers to the eagle, the
beaver and the hawk.
Yes, the blood of warrior forebears through
their veins did pump.
But now, peaceful in their teepees,
they resided at the dump.

Living quietly with their leader, proud
old Chief Ta-Noose,
Who'd trade his scalp for whiskey or a
chew of white man's snoose.
But for all, a noble redman who kept
the tribal laws,

From the dump he picked a living for
his tribesman and his squaws.

For many moons and springs and winters,
he'd accepted as his right,
To garner refuse from the dump piles
at morning, noon or night.
Those odorous acres on the prairie were
his happy hunting ground,
And his braves and squaws held charter to
salvage what they found.

At times their life was frugal, it
depended on the town.
Sleek and fat when Butte was booming—
starving when the mines were down.
But a living is a living—makes no
difference where you dwell.
So the Crees, from off the dump pile,
all in all, did fairly well.

Rags and bones and bottles, perhaps a
dress or derby hat,
Frozen spuds or ailing onions—now and
then a stray tomcat.
Each morsel gathered careful, washed
and soaked in salty brine,
For the Crees were not exacting when
they sat down to dine.

Not for long, this blissful setting,
'tis sad we must relate.
E'en as today, were despots in those
days of ninety-eight
Who'd cast their eyes with envy on
those who'd live at ease.

Who looked upon with avarice, the
easy pickings of the Crees.
Such was Big chief Hole-In-Blanket,
of the thieving Chippewas,
Who'd been chased across the country
for breaking half the laws.
Hunted, hounded, haunted—his hungry
tribe was on the loose,
And he turned his fleeting footsteps
to the lands of Chief Ta-Noose.

Merely, in the years of plenty, could
a town the size of Butte
Keep one tribe of redskins fattened on
the dump's assorted loot.
So when Hole-In-Blanket's tribesmen
swooped down from afar,
The Cree drums around their campfires
beat out the call to war.

To the wigwam of the paleface at its
councils in City Hall
Came the message of the drumming, and
they heeded to its call.
From its members quick, was chosen, their
most gifted diplomat,
And on wings of speed, they rushed him
to the campfires on the Flat.

Calling both chiefs for a pow-wow, he
declared a hurried truce,
Then bade them tell their troubles, and
he listened to Ta-Noose,
Straight and tall, this brave old fighter,
and his breath smelled strong of gin.
Gaudy war paint streaked his features,
and his words came proud as sin.

"Many Moons, O, Great White Father, my
people live on dump;
Muscles in—this Hole-In-Blanket. Thinks
Ta-Noose must be a chump.
He try to make 'um monkey—make 'um sap
of old Ta-Noose.
You tell 'um move 'um stuff—take 'um
kids and squaws—vamoose.

"Me catch 'um lease on paper—signed by
big shot, Butte white man.
Me savvy rights to dumpground. Hole-
In-Blanket better scram.
Great Spirit comes in vision—Tell Ta-Noose's
braves He help,
Say Chippewa plenty horse thief, maybe
soon they lose 'um skelp.

"Ta-Noose has spoken, O, White Father—
Hole-In-Blanket go too far.
Chippewa jailbird take 'um powder, or
Ta-Noose must go to war.
Brave as eagles are my fighters. Their's
the courage of the bear.
When sun comes in the morning, Cree then
start cutting hair!"

Now, oft' in heated battles in the wars
at City Hall
This envoy'd proved his mettle and ne'er
for help need call.
But palavering with the Indians, at last
had him up a stump,
So he questioned Hole-In-Blanket, "How come
he trespassed on the dump?"

Then spoke that wily warrior. In his eyes
was haughty hate.

He, who was wanted by the sheriffs
    of nearly every state.
"My tribe—brave, fightin' Injun—Plenty
    scalps have Chippewa,
No 'fraid of any red man. At Cree
    we laugh—ha!—ha!

"Plenty plunder on that dump pile—
    Hole-In-Blanket think he stay,
Sell 'um bottles for much wampum—buy 'um
    horses plenty hay.
Catch 'um tobacco for my fighters. They
    no have to shoot 'um butts.
Ta-Noose, if he no like 'um,
    Hole-In-Blanket tell 'um 'Nuts!'

"Cree, no have citizen papers—they just
    cayuse Canuck,
Plenty trouble for those babies, if
    Hole-In-Blanket run amuck.
Me come from old time family—ancestors
    meet Mayflower,
Squaws and papoose plenty hungry, no
    catch 'um bread for many hour.

"Honest man is Hole-In-Blanket—no want
    trouble with police.
If okay with old 'Ta-Noosie', Chippewa
    Injun sign 'um lease.
Pay 'um up in Old Crow whiskey, plenty horses
    and some squaws.
Then Chippewa own part of dump pile, all
    okay by pale face laws."

At the mention of the whiskey, old Ta-Noose
    perked up his ears.
"Old Crow" he'd often dreamed of, but not
    tasted all these years.

He could use a few more horses, and his squaws
were growing old.
After palaver with his tribesmen—at last he
muttered "Sold."

"Okay, Hole-In-Blanket—we'll smoke 'um
pipe of peace.
Call your bravest to the campfire, also
this guy from police.
For nine horses, case of Old Crow, five
squaws and box of snoose,
I sell 'um northside dump pile, and
sign 'um name 'Ta-Noose.'"

And long into the dawning, around a dozen
tribal fires,
The Crees vied with the Chippewas as to
who were the biggest liars.
And when every Old Crow quart was empty, and
vanished was the snoose,
Butte's Indian chiefs lay down together—
Hole-In-Blanket and Ta-Noose.

John Chinaman

IN BUTTE, as was the case of Nevada's Virginia City, Gold Hill and Silver City, and most of the other boisterous early-day camps, John Chinaman followed close on the heels of the first miners. There was a deep-born spirit of adventure in the early-day Chinese, who had, seemingly, an inherent urge to find out what was on the other side of mountain.

As early as the mid-sixties there were scores of the industrious yellow men who had followed closely behind the vanguard of the Montana placer miners on Silver Bow Creek. Here, as elsewhere, they were content with the leavings of the white miners. They panned the overlooked sandbars, dumps and other neglected places, and, as was usually the, case, in the end made more of a success out of their gleanings than did the original locators.

A bowl of rice, a cup of tea, an occasional pipe of opium, and the Chinese were content. They hoarded all except the few pennies expended on these necessities and by the time the white miners were beginning to build more permanent camps and cities, the thrifty Orientals usually were in a financial position to establish themselves as operators of the restaurants and "washey-washey" houses of the new towns.

The Chinaman was tolerated the white miners as a necessary nuisance, and often was the butt of more or less sadistic amusement. On the Fourth of July, 1868, the first victim of a hangman's rope in Silver Bow County was a Chinese gold-panner hanged at the camp of Rocker, four miles from present-day Butte. An 1898 issue of the Anaconda *Standard* posthumously described the affair:

> "It was not a judicial execution. It was simply the cool, premeditated act of a disheartened, yet patriotic and Fourth-of-July conscious miner who hanged the Chinaman to a cottonwood tree just for the devilment and in the hopes that it might bring luck."

It was about this date, when Silver Bow Creek had been worked clean by the placer miners and the white population had moved the four miles to Butte leaving the settlement to the Chinese (over a hundred in number) that the latter changed the name of the little community from Rocker to "Foochow." However, they failed to notify the post-office authorities of the change, and all mail addressed "Foochow" found its way to the dead letter office. The Chinese never could understand this.

Unlike many of the famous camps to the south, Butte did not have numerous Chinese until about 1880. There were few placer diggings yet operating by then but the smelter industry was beginning to flourish. Immense quantities of wood were needed to keep the furnaces running and to provide timbers for the mines. The hills adjacent to the camp were covered with heavy growths of pine and fir and in these forests, brawny, bewhiskered French-Canadians from the timber country of Montreal and Quebec had established a thriving business supplying wood for the smelters. The French Canucks had a camp a few miles northeast of Butte they called Woodville.

Wood chopping was a vocation that the Frenchmen somehow considered their monopoly, and they were wrathful when they discovered that hundreds of Chinese under the supervision of white contractors or "padrones" were muscling in on their lucrative business. The Chinese, when not engaged in the woods, were making Butte their headquarters. They had already established residences and a joss house along the length of lower Main Street, and later had settled in a square block of ill-constructed hovels and shacks within a few hundred yards of the camp's principal intersection.

"Sacre dieu," the French-Canadians said as they took to arms. And the only arms with which they were thoroughly skilled were their steel calked boots and the tools of their trade—razor-sharp, double-bitted axes with which most of them could plane a board or shave themselves—if the necessity arose. Now they put an extra edge on the axes, sharpened the calks on their boots and stalked the trespassing Orientals. In the encounter, several Chinese were sent to the lands of their fathers, minus their heads and queues.

The battle raged for weeks and there was much bloodshed. Posses from the sheriff's office, sent out to intervene, brought back dozens of indignant Frenchmen and battered Celestials. In the end, the Canucks and their axes won and the defeated Chinese were driven back to work in the washey-washey houses or to establish restaurants, begin vegetable peddling, gambling, house-cleaning and other kindred businesses.

Chinatown was growing. By 1882 there were some several hundred Chinese in the camp, and the miners began to fear that they had a yellow peril on their hands.

There were hints of vigilante action, and murmurs of boycotts. Butte, with the rest of the nation, particularly the Pacific Coast area, at this period was becoming Chinese conscious. There were cries for action in Washington. As a mayoralty campaign was in the offing, William Owsley, candidate on the Democratic ticket made "Down with the Chinese cheap labor," his platform slogan and rode to victory on it, although there is no record of the election resulting in any reduction in the Chinese population.

The yellow men paid little heed to the excitement they were causing. They tended to their own peculiar occupations, which few white men would engage in anyway. There is no record of a Chinaman ever working in a Butte mine. The old-timers will tell you that in this they exhibited rare judgment, as many of those old wood cutting Chinese lived ninety to one hundred years.

Chinatown continued to prosper. The shacks disappeared. Substantial two- and three-story structures, done in the Oriental manner, were erected by Chinese who had accumulated far greater stakes than their white persecutors ever made. Chinatown became a show place, with its weird-fronted stores, noodle parlors, gambling joints, drug and herb shops, Oriental knickknack stores and other business establishments. An ornate,

MONTANA HISTORICAL SOCIETY, HELENA

Wah Chong Tai Co., ca. 1905 Butte.

pagoda-roofed two-story joss house was erected with the upper story devoted to religious purposes and the main floor used for tong meetings.

They were colorful and mysterious, those denizens of old Chinatown. They wore their hair in braided queues and dressed in loose, baggy trousers, tight blouses of silk or cotton, buttoned from the throat down and floppy, heelless slippers. Many of them wore broad-brimmed, "high binder" hats or tight, silk skull caps.

Although there were many native women living in Chinatown, they were seldom seen. A brisk trade in slave girls was carried on. It was kept well under cover, but occasionally a case would come before the authorities.

The *Daily Miner* on Friday, November 4, 1889, under the headline: BATHED IN HER GORE—BLOODY TRAGEDY IN CHINATOWN, told the following story of a bartered bride:

> "At 20 minutes to 3 o'clock yesterday afternoon a bleeding Chinese woman rushed into Police court, supported on either side by a fellow Mongolian, and after a five minute torrent of gibberish, gave the court to understand that she was a slave girl and had been chopped in the back with a hatchet by one Gong Sing, her former owner.

> "Gong Sing had sold her for $1,200 to another almond-eyed Celestial, and instead of delivering the goods demanded more money. When this was refused, Gong Sing seized the hatchet, and as the fair slave girl, You Kim, sat in front of him, chopped her deliberately in the back about one inch to the right of the spine, at about the point where President Garfield was shot."

A week later the *Miner* reported the wedding of the slave girl, You Kim, to one Jim Hong. Maybe Gong Sing reduced the price for goods damaged in transit. Anyway a police judge, one John O'Meara, tied the knot after bemoaning the fate of the scores of other slave girls he said he knew were living prisoners in that section of the camp.

There was a well-patronized bagnio in the camp's Chinatown supported exclusively by Orientals. Here many slaves were traded.

That Butte Chinese had anticipated racketeering and gangster methods long before the time of Al Capone is indicated in the *Daily Miner* on Christmas, 1889:

> "A Chinese, Ah Sing reported in municipal court he had been forced pay $300 for the privilege of opening a laundry in Walkerville."

And the sequel, in the *Miner* for December 31, 1889, told of the blackmailing of local Chinese by the "Six Companies" of San Francisco. The newspaper account reported:

> "The following notice, posted on several buildings in Chinatown, was translated in the municipal court:
>
> "The sign of the firm is Lun Han Tong. Three men at Walkerville keep a wash house against the tong law, and the man that goes out and kills those three will be paid a reward of $1,500, and you have to kill them before you get the money.
>
> "Kim Lun, the Chinese lawyer, was put on the stand and testified under oath that the translation given was correct. Whether it is or not no one can tell. The mysterious document which is still posted in China Alley and in many Chinese cafes and laundries may be even more diabolical than it looks."

The truth, as explained years later by old time Chinamen, was that a ring of "cumshaw" blackmailers had imported "hatchet men" to collect tribute from their countrymen. The scarlet and gilt posters emblazoned in native writing on the walls of the buildings of China served as a newspaper. The bulletins were changed daily and the worried Celestials either paid up or went into hiding in the underground and chambers with which Chinatown was honeycombed.

Opium dens and gambling dives flourished despite the cops and detectives assigned to the district. The principal patrons of the opium dives were the Chinese themselves, but many underworld characters—prostitutes, pimps and gamblers—had become addicted to the opium habit and found solace in the dream pipes. Arrests were frequently made, but the offenders usually got off with a small fine.

Yung Lee, a Cantonese Chinaman, was a constant offender. His dive in the main part of the alley was more ornate than the others. Yung catered to a high class clientele. He had mattresses and pillows on his bunks, incense and silk trappings. The charge was anywhere from ten to twenty dollars for a pipe but he guaranteed privacy to his smokers. Yung Lee never denied his operations. He excused himself to Police Judge O'Meara, according to the *Daily Miner* of July 9, 1896:

> "Yung Lee sell dleams-velly nice dleams—if China boy or 'Melican boy or girl want have nice, pletty dleam—Yung Lee, he fix 'em up. They pay Yung Lee money, he bling 'em one- two-hour dleam—pletty dleams—no distlurbance—no botha anybody—just lay down—sleep—dleam. Much blettah than spend money for Ilish whiskey and want to kill evlybody. Much blettah dleam—no hurt anybody!"

The same year, the *Miner* tells how the police court was entertained a full afternoon while a comely girl from the red-light district, who had been picked up in a raid on the premises of one opium vendor, Oola Jack, explained in detail how the pipe smoking paraphernalia was used:

> "The pretty young lady explained that men and women would go into Oola Jack's den, give him two bits or four bits, or more, and lie down for a smoke in one of the four loathsome bunks provided for that purpose. She illustrated with the opium kits, pipes, peanut-oil lamps, etc., which were still in court, the method of preparing the gum opium for consumption.... Her testimony was quite interesting and provoked some applause as she facetiously alluded to the opium den as the 'joint' and the wire roost as the 'anhawk' [used for heating a bead of opium over the peanut-oil lamp; usually spelled 'yen hok']. She offered to cook up a

dream for the judge and court attendants, but was politely refused."

Several gambling dives flourished in the buildings on either side of the principal alley of Chinatown. Fan-tan, bird cage and chuck-a-luck were the principal games. Most of the players were Orientals, although there were always several whites present. A Chinese lottery game received a heavy play, and was a favorite with the camp's colored residents.

The lottery tickets had eighty numbers printed in Chinese characters and each player marked out with a writing brush certain of the characters, usually from ten to fifteen, depending on the price paid for the ticket. If enough of the characters marked out turned up in the drawing, the player won varying amounts. Anything from a "seven spot" up paid big returns. The drawings were held every fifteen minutes. They were purported to have taken place in San Francisco, Boston, London, New York and Hong Kong with the results cabled or wired to Butte, although it has been stated on good authority that the Chinese, being most dexterous in the handling of numbers, figured out in advance a list of the least-played numbers and then held the drawings in another building in China Alley. One thing was certain; there were very few winners.

A Chinese bank was organized, and many Orientals made it a depository for their savings. It was an interesting sight to see pig-tailed bank clerks computing accounts on the "abacus," a frame arrangement which held a hundred or so small wooden beads of different colors on wires, with either addition or subtraction achieved by shifting the beads. They were experts in the operation of these "Chinese adding machines" and could add, subtract and multiply with them much faster than their white neighbors could with pencil and paper.

The native New Year was the big day in old Chinatown. On this festive holiday the alley was a riot of color and a hubbub of frenzied Orientals. They came by the hundreds out of their catacombs and hovels to celebrate. Rice wine flowed freely, and up and down the alley could be heard the dissonant squeaking of the Chinese fiddles. Thousands of long strings of popping firecrackers, suspended from telephone poles, added to the din which lasted from dawn until late into the night.

The *Daily Miner* of February 9, 1893, commented on the celebration:

> "Chinese New Year is in full blast and the Celestial heathen appear to be enjoying the noise, firecrackers, rice wine, feasting and fearful disturbance with which the festive occasion is celebrated. Hundreds of Chinks are celebrating and making China Alley

hideous with their maniacal shrieks. The ugly brute which represents their deity at the Joss house has been duly propitiated by the presentation of two fine dressed hogs, half a dozen turkeys and twice as many chickens; all fancifully decorated with colored ribbons and bits of gaudy, gilt paper. The painted and bedizened image of Joss is not possessed of alimentary organs, and the *Miner* reporter strongly suspects that the almond-eyed janitor, who acts as high priest to that exalted tobacconist's sign, will lay in his winter's supply of pork and poultry before the termination of the New Year's festivities. Judging from the crowd of miners present in China Alley each evening at the celebration, one might be led to believe that the Chinese Joss might have Hibernian or Cornish relatives."

Not all of Butte's Chinese lived in China Alley. The washey-washey laundry houses were scattered about the town. One could be found in nearly every neighborhood. Although the kids made life a nightmare, the laundrymen seemed to prosper, and each laundry employed at least a dozen clothes washers.

Even on the fringe of the forbidden Irish territory of Dublin Gulch, one Fun Gee ran a laundry. A paragraph in the *Miner* of January 3, 1901, might account for the reason that he and his assistants were rarely molested in that usually hardboiled neighborhood:

"Fun Gee, the pioneer Dublin Gulch laundryman, has left for the Orient on a visit. Wealthy and generous he will be missed in Butte. It was as king of the Chinese, 'washee-washee' houses that he acquired his wealth.

"A white widow of Dublin Gulch with about ten small children was in competition with Fun at one time—or was she: The lady wasn't strong physically and frequently became ill. Whenever this happened her competitor, Fun Gee, sent his men over to her house to do her washing, wringing and ironing and distributed dimes and quarters among her children. Fun Gee, it is asserted, has never turned down a needy white man and never turned away a country man on an empty stomach. Yes, Fun is a Mongolian and a heathen, and they are not popular in the United States just now, but the honest man will be compelled to admit that if we had more citizens like Fun Gee this country would be a better place to live in."

Not all the washee-washee houses received the respect accorded Fun Gee's establishment. The *Evening News* of March 18, 1909, played up a story of a one-man riot at the laundry of Hong Huie on East Mercury Street, on the border of the old Cabbage Patch:

> "Mike Mahoney, beau brummell of the Cabbage Patch, is in trouble again.
>
> "Yesterday was St. Patrick's Day and Mike wanted to look his finest in the parade, but his shirt had not come back from the laundry. So Mr. Mahoney girded his loins and fared forth to the wet wash laundry of Hong Huie & Company on East Mercury Street, stopping only to pick up a few quick ones at a couple of Arizona Street dispensaries.
>
> "By the time he arrived at the laundry he was packing a fine, fighting edge, and he, in no uncertain terms, demanded his shirt. Unfortunately, however, he had forgotten the important matter of bringing along the Chinese laundry ticket that served to identify his particular shirt.
>
> "No tickee—no shirtee!" patiently explained Hong Huie, meanwhile keeping a wary eye on Mahoney.
>
> "'Nivir mind your heathenish gibberish about no tickee. Gimme me shirt, it's a phite wan with green stripes, and make it fast, or I'll take your domn laundry ap'rt, tub by tub and find out phat makes *it* tickee!'
>
> "Tremblingly, Hong Huie signalled into the next room for reinforcements, and Mike Mahoney went to work.
>
> "When the police, who had been called by terrified neighbors, arrived, Hong Huie and Company's establishment was a wreck. Packages of laundry were tore open and strewn to the four winds, much of it out on the sidewalk. Three of Huie's faithful assistants reposed in a huge tub suds, tossed there by the irate Mahoney. The latter was personally working over the honorable Huie with a three pound flat iron when interrupted by the police.
>
> "A few hours later, as the St. Patrick's Day parade passed over East Broadway, Mahoney listened to the stirring strains of the Irish bands through the bars of the city bastile. His trial comes up before Judge McGowan this afternoon."

Late in the nineties, discrimination against the Chinese was in full swing. The steam laundries were rapidly driving them out of the washee-washee business, the picket and boycott of the Trades and Labor Council drove them out of the restaurant business, and the Koreans drove them out of gardening and vegetable peddling. Nothing was left for John Chinaman but his "long-noodle—all pork," chop suey and chow mein eating houses, his fan-tan gambling joints and lottery swindles, his opium smoking dives, and his three French lingerie and silk hosiery establishments in the red-light district. These were the only fields the white man did not disturb.

It was in the noodle parlors that Butte became more closely acquainted with the Celestials. The residents of the copper camp had and still have an insatiable appetite for Chinese food.

Shortly after 1900 there were seven noodle parlors in the camp, some gilded and palatial, others dingy, smelly, uninviting holes; but all of them did a standout business day and night. After dance, show, or celebration, it was the custom of the Butte bloods to end the evening by a visit to the noodle parlors. There was a certain camaraderie so typical of all life in the camp—West Side millionaire might rub elbows with Cabbage Patch bum, and Galena Street harlot might be found sitting in a booth across from a prominent society matron, with miners generously interspersed throughout the room.

A steady string of messenger boys carried covered trays from the noodle parlors to the rooms of the gamblers, pimps and madames. Gossip had it that the three latter professions subsisted entirely on Chinese food. Hum Yow, a patriarch of the noodle and chop suey business frequently stated: "Noodle with plenty soy sauce velly good for hangovah:'

Often the noodle parlors were the scene of enormous Chinese banquets arranged and attended by business and social leaders of the community. Sometimes days were required to prepare the enormous repasts. The *Miner* of February 14, 1896, on its society page reports:

> "A number of American friends (James Murray, mining magnate and uncle of the present United States Senator from Montana, a judge, professor, prominent lawyer, three prosperous merchants and Senator Tom Carter) were entertained the evening of February 13 at an elaborate dinner held at the Shanghai Cafe in Chinatown and given by Dr. Huie Pock and Tom Lee in honor of Dr. Huie Pock's newly acquired bride, recently arrived from China....

"A fifteen course Chinese banquet was enjoyed. The chinaware used was the finest imported hand-painted kind, and the cutlery was of coin silver. After the food was disposed of the guests smoked cigars imported from Siam and discussed the future welfare of Butte and China."

The Chinese had their own cemetery in the rear of the white burying grounds on the Flat, which once contained nearly a thousand graves. Since then their bones have been exhumed by the tongs and shipped back to China. In the early years, every dead Chinese was accorded a native burial. Sam White, pioneer undertaker, invariably was called to attend to the obsequies.

Such a burial never failed to cause considerable interest in the camp. The *Miner* of August 30 1891, carried the following story:

"Yesterday the citizens of Butte witnessed another Chinese funeral, and as usual it created no end of interest. Chin Kin Bow, a laundryman known about town as John 'Buck Tooth' and a prominent member of the Celestial race in Butte was buried with all the ceremony and rites of his native land.

"The body was taken from the residence of the deceased, a laundry on South Wyoming street and the neat, gilt-papered coffin was placed inside the hearse and the procession started for the Chinese cemetery on the flats. Scores of friends and relatives clad in Chinese costume, their queues dangling down their backs, walked solemnly behind the hearse, wearing bright ribbons on their wrists. On the top of the hearse two relatives of the dead man sat, one tossing out handfuls of bright-colored paper—to fool the devils. The idea being that the latter would mistake the paper for money, start picking it up, and give the spirit of Chin time to escape, the other tossing handfuls of round papers with holes in the center, the notion being that those devils who were not picking up the money would have to hop through the hole in each paper and thus not make any great progress in following the procession.

"Behind the walking friends and relatives came three hackloads of closer relations to the deceased man, and bringing up the rear of the procession was a spring wagon filled with the bedding, clothes and other personal effects of the dead man.

"At the cemetery more scraps of paper were tossed into the grave and a taper was burned over the grave to attract the devil's attention. Punks burned at the foot of the grave because fire attracts the devil and his crew of fiends!

"When Satan and his gang of demons had theoretically assembled, a fine banquet was set for them at the side of the grave, consisting of roast pork and chicken, boiled rice, apple dumplings, and other delicacies along with several bottles of rice wine and other imported Chinese liquors, all as an offering and bribe to Satan for permitting Chin's spirit to escape to the 'happy land.'

The dead man's personal effects and bedding were then gathered up and made into a large bonfire, after which the body was lowered into the grave amidst much wailing and chanting of the mourners while the devil and his gang were busy eating the repast spread out for them.

"A Chinese priest murmured a prayer and threw in the first shovel of dirt, while the mourners shook hands over the grave. Chinese candy and sweetmeats were then passed around the grave. A bit of China sugar and a dime, wrapped in paper, were given to every person present. The Chinese then solemnly took their departure, leaving Chin to his ancestors. A number of white residents of the camp who had followed the procession to the cemetery were interested observers. Several of them seemed to find much humor in the proceedings, and it is reported that a few of them remained after the mourners departed to help the 'devils' dispose of the liquor and foodstuffs."

Chinatown produced several colorful characters. The careers of Leu, Mayor of Chinatown and Jimmy July, the camp's only naturalized Chinaman, are covered in another chapter of this book. There were several others—among them, Yan Sing, the kleptomaniac, who would steal anything that wasn't bolted down.

One of Yan Sing's most notable bids for fame came with the stealing of a prize winning and pedigreed duck from J. Goldman, Jewish rabbi, who lived near Chinatown.

Sing carted not only the prize fowl but the Rabbi's hot, smoking stove to an empty house on the outskirts of Chinatown. When Officer Gillette appeared at the house on a hot tip from an informer, the stove was smoking and crackling merrily, while Yan with a happy look upon his moon face was turning the now-plucked and sizzling duck on an improvised spit over the flames, smacking his lips in anticipation.

Seeing the officer, he shrieked, grabbed the hot duck and fled. Gillette chased Yan to Chinatown as the latter juggled the smoking bird from one hand to the other, blowing on it to cool it as he ran. His thick-soled sandals finally caught on a stone and he stumbled. The duck flew through the air several feet before landing. Yan crawled forward on his hands and knees and had just retrieved the duck when the policeman collared him.

Still carrying the fowl, he was given a free ride to jail in the patrol wagon. At the police station, he refused to part with his prize and was finally allowed by the good-natured cops to take it into his cell.

Relatives of the kleptomaniac at once furnished bail for his release but Yan Sing refused freedom until he had polished off the duck to last bone.

Chong Suey, twelve-year-old orphan, whose father had been killed in a tong war, was another headache to the police force. Chong's specialty was the stealing of horses and buggies, horses and wagons—anything pulled by a horse. On one occasion while the skinner of a six-horse ore team was refreshing himself in Gus Fitchen's saloon on Main Street, leaving the horses tied outside, young Chong climbed up on the driver's seat and drove away with the outfit. He had the horses and heavy ore wagon tied up in front of his home on Colorado Street, several blocks away, when caught by the police. Anytime a horse or horses were missing in Butte, the police looked for Chong.

His climaxing theft was the purloining of Barney Shannahan's hack from in front of an undertaking establishment. He drove it, loaded with kids of the neighborhood, to the Nine Mile House, south of the camp. For this offense Chief Jere Murphy was planning to send the juvenile horse thief to the State reform school. Relatives and members of his late father's tong came to Chong's rescue by agreeing to send him to a military school with a cavalry troop, where the lad would be assured of plenty horses to ride.

For most of the first quarter of the new century, Chinatown was peaceful, its population gradually dwindling. The activities of the race had become accepted as a matter of course. They were becoming more and more Americanized and most had cut off their queues and eliminated much of their Oriental costumes. Many had raised large families and were sending their children to public schools. Some had become Christians and now attended the Chinese Baptist Mission in the heart of Chinatown. The bulletins on the scarlet sheets of paper caused but passing interest—merely the notices of tong and lodge meetings. The native

New Year was celebrated, but not with the fanfare and glory of earlier days. Chinatown was lacking the old mystery and glitter.

Then suddenly in 1922 the bulletins gained a new and fearful meaning. The Chinese stopped to read, then scurried to hiding places. A war of national scope between the Bing Kong and the Hip Sing tongs had broken out.

On the evening of February 11, 1922, Hum Mon Sen, an elderly merchant, was sauntering down China Alley puffing his long, Oriental pipe, when from a doorway, a .38 caliber automatic barked five times and Hum Mon Sen was the camp's first tong war victim. Within a few weeks there were four more killings in the same alley, two of them credited to the Hip Sings and two to the Bing Kongs.

The Celestials refused, or dared not talk. The police were powerless. They were certain that the killings were the work of imported gunmen, but because of the reticence of the natives to testify, the murderers went unpunished. The entire colony feared for its life, doors were padlocked and barred with heavy steel. Special white guards, armed to the teeth, accompanied many Chinese about the streets.

A fifth killing was chalked up when Chong Sing, a fifty-three-year-old poultry dealer was shot down on the threshold of his place of business on the edge of Chinatown. Two youthful Chinese, strangers to Butte, were seen to flee the scene. A .38 Colt automatic was found near the body.

After an investigation by Chief Jere Murphy and Undersheriff Jack Duggan, which included a trip with native guides through underground Chinatown—the first ever made by police officers—two suspects, Quang Quak Key and Louie Gar Fook, both eminent tong men, but newcomers, were arrested and charged with the murder. Their trial opened March 22, 1922.

An impressive array of counsel appeared for the two defendants, but the court procedure developed into a travesty because all witnesses either refused to testify or evaded questions. The trial attracted large crowds of both whites and the Chinese, many of whom drove to and from the trial in armored cars surrounded with white bodyguards. Finally after ten days of testimony the case was given to the jury which brought in a verdict of acquittal within an hour. The trial had cost the state several thousand dollars.

The war ended as suddenly as it started. Through the intervention of powerful national and local forces, a truce was arranged between the tongs. The gilt and scarlet posters once more covered the walls of China Alley, but this time they called the residents to feasts celebrating the treaty of peace that was about to be signed.

Then for over a decade, Chinatown lapsed back into a humdrum existence, until in 1936 it once more leaped to page one prominence in the nation's press. This time it was narcotics. A federal narcotic agent, after a two-and-one-half year investigation that puts to shame the most sensational detective fiction, had unearthed an international dope ring, assertedly the most far reaching to be ever brought to trial. Butte's Chinatown was the hub from which the spokes of the dope ring radiated to every part of the United States.

A pioneer merchant, Tom Chinn, was discovered to be a top official in the Hip Sing Tong, one of the two leading tongs of the world, and also the directing genius of the vast dope syndicate.

During the investigation, a Federal officer, posing as the head of a huge narcotic buying ring, had spent several months in Butte, where he was frequently entertained by the camp's Celestials. A short time before, the agent had so wormed his way into their confidence in Chicago, that, at a meeting attended by Chinese from all parts of the nation, he was admitted as a member of the Hip Sing Tong, the first white man ever to be so honored.

At any rate, Tom Chinn was arrested in his store on the corner of China Alley and taken to New York city for trial with scores of other Chinese, from different parts of the country, implicated in the ring. He was convicted and sentenced to a Federal prison.

All is quiet in the copper camp's Chinatown now. The population has dwindled to a handful. Most of these are now withered patriarchs who sit over their long pipes and talk about the good old days.

The red, weirdly charactered posters are still on the walls of China Alley. But ask a resident about them today and he will proudly tell you they are notices from the tongs telling their members to enlist in Uncle Sam's forces and help vanquish the despised Japs from the face of the earth.

Finlandia

THE FINNS, now the camp's fourth largest foreign group, began arriving in large numbers around 1900. Most of them came from the copper mines of Michigan, principally Calumet. Stout, sturdy men, with years of experience in the deep mines of the Great Lakes country, they readily found employment. Excelling in the dangerous shaft timbering and sinking operations, these Finns and their fellow emigrants who followed, can be given a great deal of credit for the present development of the Butte mines.

Clannish, because of their difficulty in speaking English, the Finns early formed their own community—three or four square blocks on East Granite and Broadway Streets, where boarding houses, saloons, stores and, of course, the inevitable bathhouses soon predominated.

By 1917 it is estimated that there were 3,000 Finns in the colony.

Both the baths and boarding houses are important in the Finn's design for living. Every day is a holiday at a Finn boarding house, where the tables are loaded with food and there is no stinting. A mystery among restaurant men is how the boarding-house keepers provide such a quantity of food at such low prices, and still show a profit. The answer apparently lies in the enormous volume of business, for three or four hundred boarders eat at each of the larger boarding houses.

Good eating is a passion with the Finns, and heavy trays of food are carted to the long tables as long as the boarders can consume it.

The boarders are by no means all natives of the land of Sibelius. Long ago miners of all nations learned of the excellent fare, and moved in. In addition to the three regular meals, it has always been a custom of the Finn eating houses to serve a lunch for miners off the night shift. They call it a snack, but the heaped-up table more resembles a small banquet.

Another practice, appreciated by the miners, is the rule that the regular boarder who pays his bill promptly need have no fear of periodical shut-downs in the mines. As long as the Finn landlady has a cracker in the house or a dime in the bank her regular boarders will eat. Countless times the boarding houses have served meals until finally closed by the sheriff.

Their grocery stores have the same rule. Scores of miners can tell of an East Broadway grocer, in his day worth thousands of dollars, who during the depression said that while there was one can of tomatoes on his shelves, his regular customers would be kept on the books and not allowed to go hungry. So well did he keep the promise that by 1933 he was on the verge of bankruptcy. He is still in business, however, and grateful customers are paying up as rapidly as they can.

The Finns have a superstitious fear of death and the unknown. The funeral of a departed friend or relative is never held from the home, but the body is rushed to the funeral parlors with all speed. It is the same down in the mines. A Finn will perform any sacrifice or act of heroism to rescue a disabled comrade, but once dead it is strictly hands off the corpse.

The bathhouse or *sälma* is as much a part of the Finn as his left arm. If he were given a choice between eating, drinking and bathing, it is probable that the bath would be his selection. The ritual of the bath has been instilled into the Finlander for generations. In the old country, no hamlet will be without at least one bath.

The Finnish bath is a model of simplicity. A large room with an open fireplace or pit in which a roaring fire is kept burning around several huge rocks is all that is needed. As the rocks are heated, steam is created by pouring cold water over their surfaces. Here the nude bathers, men and women together, revel in the torrid vapors, while they whip themselves with tied bundles of evergreen or willow branches to increase circulation.

After an hour or so in this humid atmosphere, the bath is completed with a plunge into a tank of icy water. Finns credit the baths for their racial hardiness, and certain it must be for very few are ever seen suffering from a common cold.

In the mines, the Finns usually work in pairs. They are expert miners although inclined to be somewhat careless. They are not an imaginative race, and this perhaps accounts for their willingness to work in the most dangerous places. Most Finns are fatalists. A story is told of two who had been working a mining claim outside of Butte for nearly a year and had saved most of their earnings.

Arriving in the camp with their large stake, each bought a new pair of shoes and then began partaking of East Broadway hospitality. In two days, both were broke and had terrific hangovers.

Sitting on the curbstone in front of a Finn saloon, one of the pair was bemoaning their fate, when his partner encouragingly assured him: "It's tough all right, bardner—but anyvay, vot de hell, ve got new pair shoes."

In the homes of the Finns, the woman of the household is boss, and she rules with an iron hand. No matter how big, or strong, or what the provocation, there are few Finns, foolhardy enough to dispute their helpmate's dictates.

A certain Finlander was discovered spending his mine check in an East Granite Street resort by his spouse. The lady went into action, and after severely pommelling the wayward husband led him home by the lapels. The following day the chastened Finn, who weighed around two hundred pounds, excused his display of meekness:

"Vell, vot could I do? She's better man dan I am, ain't she?"

Crazy over Horses

THAT September day in 1899 when Tom Newton, a local machinist, drove a home-made, snorting, gasoline-propelled contraption up the main street of the camp, there must have been a thousand horses parked along his line of progress. They reared up on quivering legs at sight of the smoking monstrosity, straining to tear themselves from the hitching posts.

Newton's "horseless carriage" was the first "gas wagon" to bounce over the cobblestones of the copper camp. A few months later John Gillie introduced the first factory built car. Up to that time, Butte had been a city of horses and if copper was king, certainly the horses had a large part in making it so.

The first placer miners had arrived by pack trains. In their wake followed more; this time, long strings of freight wagons with jerk-line skinners and six- and eight-horse teams. Then the stage coaches. But always horses and more horses. Livery stables were erected and the great barns of the ore-hauling contractors were built. The first mines were sunk with the aid of the equines.

Horses pulled the cables that wound and unwound the first mine windlass. Horses were sometimes used to pull the mine cars underground. It was the countless strings of six-horse teams with their tobacco-chewing, whiskey-drinking, blasphemous "skinners" that hauled the first copper ore to the smelters on Butte's Flats. More and more this animal became a part of the camp and its progress.

An old-timer remarked when the statue of Marcus Daly was unveiled:

"Arrah, they should have put him astride a big, phite harse. Marcus was always wild about horses!"

And Marcus Daly, like the men and women about him, did love horses—all horses—but his real love was for the fleet thoroughbreds which he brought from the great race tracks for the thirty- to ninety-day meets at the Butte track, southeast of the camp.

It is doubtful if there was a city its size anywhere that could boast of finer racing programs, faster horses, larger or more colorful crowds or greater

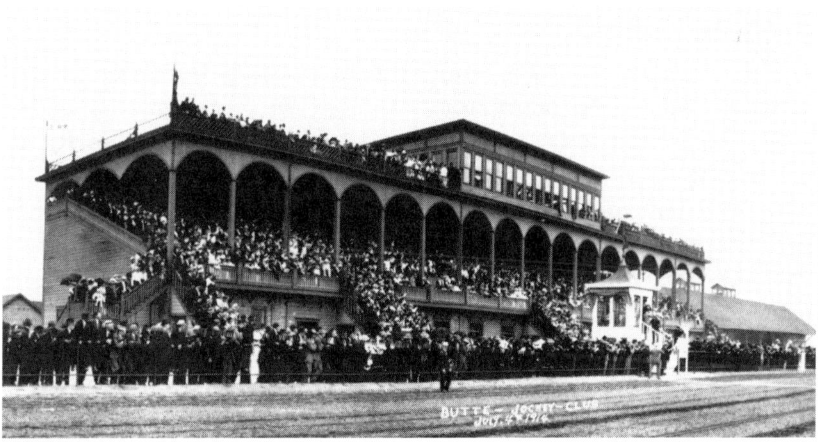

MONTANA HISTORICAL SOCIETY, HELENA

A full crowd at the Butte Jockey Club, July 4, 1914 (detail of panaroma).

amounts of money changing hands in the betting rings, than at the Daly race track at the turn of the century. The cry: "They're off at Butte!" echoed through the poolrooms and sporting halls of the nation. Several times during each race meet it was Marcus Daly's custom to give his miners the shift off—with pay—that they might attend the sport of kings.

Who among the survivors of early Butte can remember without a pang of nostalgia, the endless parade of six- and eight-horse ore teams straining at their harnesses as they pulled the heavily laden ore-wagons? There were few pavements in those days and it was not uncommon to see the giant, five-ton wagons mired hub-deep in the sticky gumbo that filled the streets after the first spring thaw. It was then that ladies, horror-stricken, put their hands over their ears and scurried from within sound of the irate teamsters. The skinner prided himself on a vocabulary that was at once both classical and profane, and the true-to-his-profession ore-hauler remained on his high-seated perch until every expletive and adjective had been thoroughly exhausted. Only then, would he climb down and offer material aid to the pawing and struggling animals.

And who of those old-timers can remember without regret, the cold, dismal whine of those frost-stiffened ore-wagons as the wheels screamed their mournful way up and down the hill in mid-winter with the thermometer registering anywhere from twenty to forty degrees below zero? This dolorous shriek on an early winter morning made one doubly appreciative of a snug, warm bed.

They were hardy citizens, those copper camp ore-team skinners. They braved the cold wrapped in many layers of clothing over which was frequently worn a shaggy, buffalo coat, cinched tight at the middle with an enormous brass-studded leather belt. Buckskin gloves covered horny hands. They wrapped reins around their wrists, continually pounding arms across chests to keep up circulation. As further protection against the cold, nine out of ten skinners kept a quart bottle of bonded whiskey in the wagon box within easy reach. The quart, full at the beginning of the shift, was tossed aside, empty, when the ten-hour day was finished.

Gus Fitchen's saloon, near the business section, was the teamster's hangout, the rendezvous of hundreds of skinners. Here hard-bitten ore-haulers talked horse, drank heartily to the horse, and from all reports certainly must have smelled of the animal. Here, during a convivial evening, more ore was hauled than the yearly output of all the mines of the world. Fitchen's doors never closed. It wasn't unusual for a skinner to leave the saloon in the early dawn staggering to his work, to return again ten hours later and repeat the performance as long as his pay check held out.

There were more than a hundred grocery stores in the camp, and as there was little "cash and carry," each grocery used from one to a score of teams on their delivery wagons. The mining-company-owned department stores also had many teams, as did the hardware stores and the coal and fuel merchants. Add the laundry wagons, surface teams from the mines and smelters, milk wagons and similar conveyances and it can easily be seen that there were close to ten thousand horses about the streets of Butte early in the century. In those days, too, whether it was the heat, the humidity, throbbing heads or hangovers, the copper camp used tremendous quantities of ice. Some three hundred head of draft horses were used to keep the thermometer below the danger level. Another hundred or so horses were used each winter to harvest this ice from ponds that bordered the outskirts of the town.

At that time the business district had every type of paving, cobblestones predominating. Brick, slag, wooden blocks, concrete, asphalt, and even sawdust were experimented with by different graft-seeking city administrations. The result did little to ease the strain on the feet of either man or beast. Four days a week, according to pioneer teamsters, was the length of time the average horse could take it. The remaining three days were spent in the barn for rest and repairs.

There were fifteen livery stables in Butte, each with from twenty to a hundred horses for rent by the hour or day, used largely for funerals. The horses were often rented out for as many as three funerals a day. In addition to the funeral business, the hacks carried passengers to and from the railroad depots and were in demand for christenings, weddings, parties on the Flat and elsewhere.

At one time, the story goes, the Populists of the camp, their numbers depleted by a Democratic landslide, held their convention in Barney Shannahan's hack, nominating an entire county ticket.

Langlois' livery stable rented saddle horses and the young bloods were steady customers, but there was another variety of customer, whose favorite saddle mounts were kept by the liveryman in sleek condition, always ready for call.

"Angels on horseback," the boys on the Hill called the lovely equestriennes from the "line," who liked to while away the long afternoons and perhaps forget for the moment the tawdriness of their nights with a canter on the outskirts of the camp. These painted damosels [sic], clad in up-to-the-minute riding togs might well have stepped from the pages of *Vogue.* After a brisk gallop through the mountain air, they met for a "tea and lemon" at Browne's Cafe on Park Street (wine room for ladies in the rear). The horses were left in the alley and tended by willing newsboys at four bits a head. They were ladies of the night, but somehow or other they were a flash of color on a bleak canvas, and even their horses formed a deep attachment for them.

Long before the advent of the modern rodeo, E. B. Turner, the camp's foremost horse-breaker and trainer, was presenting a thrilling show at his corrals on the Flat. It was all in a day's work for Turner, even though his only audience was a few barefoot kids perched on top of the corral fence, or occasionally a bleary-eyed barfly from a neighboring saloon. When Turner or his assistants broke a horse, it stayed broke. No nag was too tough, and the word "outlaw" was never heard at their stables. "E. B." broke horses for either saddle or harness. Many a bitterly fought battle of man versus mustang was fought in the corral with Turner always the victor. The training stable did a remunerative business in the nineteen hundreds, often breaking and training as many as twenty horses in a week.

The brewery horses were the camp's pride and without them no parade was complete. The flashy teams were of blooded and registered Clydes and Percherons, and the brewery owners combed the horse markets of the country to buy the finest of these animals to draw their monster beer wagons. In gleaming brass-studded harnesses, the four-horse teams of matched coal-black, dapple-gray or snow-white were the pride of the camp.

Then there was the horse-drawn patrol wagon, variously termed the "Black Maria," the "hurry-up wagon" or just the "wagon." The reverberating clang of its bell could be heard as it raced through the streets. One harness bull perched on the driver's seat, another stood on the rear step, his coattails flying to the wind as the galloping horses pulled it to the scene of crime.

It was a motley array that rode in its wire-mesh enclosure. Plain drunks, bediamonded pimps, bleary-eyed vags, fighting and bloodied miners, perfumed, attractive ladies of the parlor houses or their bedraggled sisters from the Cabbage Patch, cringing hopheads, Chinese hatchetmen, murderers, thieves, confidence men, ace-in-the-hole gamblers—all the backwash of the copper camp, and many of the good, at some time experienced the patrol wagon's jolting sway over the rough cobblestones.

The patrol horses were intelligent beasts. They saw and knew the town at its worst. The wagon was rickety and ill-smelling, but many a roughhouse, free-for-all, incipient riot, neighborhood quarrel, or common street-brawl was brought to an end with the approach of its determined clang.

"Pup Milk" Gertney, originally from Tipperary, was a Butte dairyman during the late nineties and the first decade of the new century. Patrick J. Gertney was his voting name, the "Pup Milk" having come about by a queer turn of events. The sign on his nondescript wagon originally read, "Pure Milk Gertney." Perhaps it was the poor quality of paint used, possibly the elements, but most likely it was the work of some prankster. In any case, the final lettering of the word "PURE" was somehow obliterated, leaving the word "PUP."

Gertney never bothered to change it, "Pup Milk" Gertney it remained, and "Pup Milk" Gertney he was thereafter known.

"Pup Milk" had a dairy located about five miles southeast of Butte. Twelve cows graced his stables. Gertney also had several beautiful daughters—"a daughter for every four cows," he liked to boast, "and each and everyone a prize winner." Whether he was referring to the daughters, or the cows, or both, is not known.

It was Gertney's horse, though, that offered the main attraction. At one period in its life, the aging animal had been in a dancing horse act in a circus. The years had not been kind to the beast but a proud memory of a glorious past kept the head erect and the tired body upright between the shafts of Gertney's milk wagon.

Music alone served to revive and bring the old spirit to life. At the first notes of a band or orchestra, once again the old horse was a prancing, dancing steed, pridefully re-enacting the routine of an old circus act.

Forgotten then was Gertney and his milk wagon and his twelve cows and daughters. In their place were the wide canvased-acres of the big top, the applauding thousands, the blare of the circus band, the sawdust and the menagerie, the tights and the tinsel.

Gertney for the instant was metamorphosed from a wizened, plodding old milk wagon driver to a bowing, smiling equestrian director, resplendent in frock coat and high silk hat.

The milk man's horse lived for these moments. During holiday parades and at circus time the animal capered to the music of the band. Everyone stopped to admire and applaud, for "Pup Milk" Gertney's horse had become as well known as the corner policeman.

This was, of course, good advertising for the dairy business. As word of the dancing horse spread, more and more customers were added to the route. His herd increased, and it was not long until he had eight cows for each daughter.

In August, 1912, Ringling Brothers' circus was in town. This was the day of the circus street parade. As usual Gertney and his equippage was bringing up the end of the procession. As it wended its way up Arizona Street the proud steed was once again living in the old circus days. Through dim eyes a glittering past was once again parading. The heart was there but the tired old body was unequal to the task. As the bands blared and the calliope shrieked, the aged horse made a final, pitiful, proud effort—then fell dead between the shafts of Gertney's milk wagon.

"By Gar, she's the best damn horse in City of Butte! Dat horse—she's know more than any damn lawyer in Silvair Bow County!" The remarks, accompanied by a two-handed French Canadian flourish, might have been heard any day on the streets of Butte forty years ago.

It was Joe No-Legs, tin-can rustler, extolling the virtues of an animal as well known on the streets of Butte as the mayor himself. Joe was a French-Canadian, born in Ontario. He came to the camp in the early nineties, together with scores of other "Canuck" woodchoppers, who supplied the smelters and mines with firewood and timber.

Joe's baptismal name was Joseph Baptiste Meloche, but no one ever called him that. To every man, woman and child in Butte he was Joe No-Legs.

Both of Joe's legs had been amputated slightly above the knees. It is not certain just how the appendages were lost for he told many different stories. At times, Joe would state that they were frozen off. At others, his story was that a fast railroad train had severed them. When in an expansive mood he claimed that he wore them off holding back a team of horses that had become unmanageable at the top of a steep hill.

"I stop dem horses," Joe would explain, "but I wear dem damn two leg off using dem for rough-lock!"

Notwithstanding the lack of limbs, Joe was a powerful figure. He allowed his loss in no way to interfere with wood chopping, and up until the time the mines and smelters had no further use for the wood, he did as much, if not more work as he put it "dan any damn Cayuse Frenchman in dam hills."

Joe was a lover of horses. He knew and understood them; and most horses, in turn, knew and understood Joe.

With the cessation of the wood-chopping industry, Joe moved into town. Out of discarded railroad ties, he built himself a comfortable, if not pretentious, house directly southwest of the city, near Clark's Butte Reduction Works. He also built a sturdy stable of old ties.

It was at this time that No-Legs came into possession of his first horse, a fine, big bay, which he hitched to a light wagon as he entered into his new business, the rustling of tin cans. He sold the cans to the copper precipitating plants, which at that time were making their appearance. Joe was doing well for himself. He and his horse were comfortably quartered. Tin cans commanded a high price and the world took on a rosy hue for Joe No-Legs.

The winter of 1905 brought with it a record-breaking spell of forty to fifty degree below zero weather. The camp shivered and froze up. Humans and livestock suffered intensely and No-Legs and his horse were no exception. Although Joe boasted that because of the loss of his legs, "I only get half so damn cold as oder Cayuse Frenchmen," he had plenty of reason to remember the winter of 1905.

Upon going out to the stable to care for the horse one exceptionally cold morning, No-Legs was shocked to find that the animal had frozen to death during the night.

Joe was heartbroken. Making sure the horse was dead, he stepped back and surveyed the frozen carcass mournfully.

"I don't know about dat damn horse," he wept, "she's nevair do dat before. By Gar, I feex 'em. I buy new horse. She's stay in de house with Joe. She's freeze 'em up—Joe's freeze 'em up too!"

He was as good as his word. Shopping about, he purchased a sprightly four-year old mare, which he at once stabled in his bedroom. Moving his own cot to a far corner of the room, the remainder of the space was turned over to the horse. Joe built no stall, used no rope or halter. Straw was scattered about the room, and from then on, the horse had the run of the house.

As might be supposed, the horse, raised under such an environment soon developed unusual intelligence. "She's bettair housekeeper dan me!" Joe said—and judging from the condition of the house, it was no idle boast.

By the simple method of grabbing a mouthful of bedcovers and pulling them off the sleeping Frenchman, the horse would awaken him each dawn. Joe's first duties were the feeding and watering of the animal. These chores completed, the horse was turned out for her morning canter over the hills. In an hour or so after his own breakfast, a mighty "Haloo-o-o" from Joe called the animal in and they were ready for the day's tin-can rustling.

As time passed the bond between man and horse grew closer. The horse developed the ability to spot an empty tin-can much farther than her master. Spying a can, the mare's habit was to stop and allow Joe time to retrieve it and throw it in the wagon. Very few cans were passed up. The animal needed no guiding line and the streets of Butte were an open book to her. Every alley, gulch, and vacant lot were known and explored by the pair.

In the hot summer months, and in the winter too, Joe was often tempted to slack his thirst at many of the taverns that lined their route. Whether from instinct or force of habit, the horse possessed an uncanny knowledge of where the largest five cent scoops in town were located, and would invariably stop the wagon before these establishments.

"By Gar, dat horse, she's smarter every day," Joe would blarney the bartenders. "She's know where the biggest and coldest schoonair of beer in Butte is sold." This flattery usually brought forth a return beer from the complimented barkeep.

During the winter No-Legs wrapped the beloved horse in several layers of blankets. Great wads of burlap sacking were tied around the animal's feet. Sometimes a lady's shawl was tied around its head. The bundled equine caused many smiles as it proceeded on its tin-can rustling way.

Pat Mullins was mayor of Butte and No-Legs was one of his most ardent supporters. Election day came and Mullins' name was the ballot. Joe was registered from a South Butte precinct. Early on election morning, he and the familiar horse and wagon were parked in front of the voting booth. Joe was the first voter to present himself when the booth opened. Great was the election clerk's astonishment when Joe demanded two ballots.

"One for me, Joe No-Legs," he explained, "De odder for dat horse."

The clerk, at first amused and later indignant, attempted to explain that horses, no matter how intelligent, had not as yet been granted the right of franchise, not at least in his precinct. But No-Legs was insistent.

"By Gar, dat horse, she's know more dan any damn votair in Silvair Bow county. She can't vote for Pat Mullins—neider can Joe. You keep dat vote!"

Joe stalked out and Pat Mullins lost a vote.

The years passed, No-Legs became fonder and fonder of the big five-cent "schoonaires" that "dat horse fin' for me." There were times when Joe had one or two "schoonaires" too many. Friends took care of him on these occasions by safely stowing him in the back of the tin-can wagon. That was all that was necessary. The horse took charge from there. A slap on the rump and she would unerringly trot the mile and a half to the shack. The ride home usually revived Joe sufficiently to enable him to unharness the animal at the latter's "all out-end-of-the-line" whinny with which she invariably ended the homeward journey.

It was one of these unguided trips that eventually spelled disaster for both Joe and the horse. The night of January 26, 1928, brought an exceptionally heavy fog to the mining camp. A dense pall enveloped the town. In the middle of this Joe was once more *hors de combat.* All was well until the intersection at Montana Street was reached. Here, a southbound streetcar failed to see the horse and wagon in the gloom. In the crash, the horse was killed instantly. Joe died the same evening at a local hospital.

No-Legs and the horse were given separate funerals, the horse being buried in the rear of the shack that she had so long shared with her master and Joe was laid to rest in Holy Cross Cemetery.

Many people said it would have been nice if the horse had been buried beside him. Joe No-Legs would have liked it that way.

In the '90s one street carnival hit Butte under unfavorable circumstances. There was much competition—horse and dog racing, league baseball, championship prize fights—all in progress along with faro banks, poker games, the pool rooms which listed odds and the results at every track in America, and unlimited saloons and honkytonks.

The "take" was small and the carnival soon went broke. A local Don Juan stole Fatima, the "hoochie koochie" dancer. Other ladies of the troupe proved willing consorts for various miner's parties, leaving the show short of pulchritude, and possibly of talent. The manager of the carnival tried to recoup at the roulette games. The cashier also tried his luck at the race track, but neither of them clicked. Two spielers from the carnival took over the merry-go-round for their back pay. They were joined one evening by a local miner—a good fellow and a good spender. All three spent a convivial evening.

Next, morning the local man, a Jim Conrad, awoke to find the eleven hundred dollar roll he had started with missing from his billfold, and in its place, a crudely drawn bill of sale for "one merry-go-round." Conrad scoured the town for his carnival acquaintances, but they had left camp while the leaving was good.

Conrad had his merry-go-round hauled to an iron works, where he had it overhauled, and then set it up on a vacant lot near the center of town and opened for business.

Scores of women and children, eager for rides, made the opening day a fair success.

The second night coincided with pay day for many of the large mines. A crowd of hilarious miners collected. Some one promoted idea of making every ride a sweepstake—the wooden horse stopping nearest to the engine, winning the pot for its jockey.

The whooping and yelling brought hundreds to the lot to watch the fun and soon there were scores of customers clamoring for a ride. Conrad raised the price to twenty-five cents, but it would have made no difference if he had asked for a dollar. Some of the miners astride the horses with a bottle of beer, sent boys around the corner for another and stayed in the saddle for the next sweepstake.

Not till far past midnight would the crowd permit the merry-go-round to stop. In three nights Conrad cleared more than his eleven hundred dollar "investment," then sold his contraption for some fifteen hundred dollars and retired from the carnival business. Miner's luck they called it.

The Bohunk Scare

IN BUTTE everything seems to occur in cycles. For instance, chronologically there came the placer mining era, the era of silver mining, and later that of copper. In politics there have been periods of success for the Republicans, Democrats, Socialists, and then the Democrats again. Nationalities also arrived in cycles. After the first Yankee settlers, came the "Cousin Jacks" and the Irish. In later years Missourians came from the lead mines of Joplin, followed by silver miners from Lead, South Dakota. World War I brought Mexicans and Filipinos, and the latest invasion has been that of the "Arkies" and "Okies" from the dust bowl.

The year 1910 marked the beginning of what is known as the "Bohunk" era in Butte. Developments of later years proved that the period was more of a scare than anything else. These "Bohunks," as immigrants from the Balkan nations were called, dropped their earlier mode of living. Hundreds of them later married, settled down, built their own homes and raised families, which are today among the most respected citizens of the camp.

There never could have been such a scare in the first place, if it had not been for the avarice of a few foremen on the Hill, who let the fact that they had idle cabins to rent, lead them into a nasty mess.

On July 24, 1910, the Butte *Evening News*, a Heinze-owned newspaper, broke a full, front-page story titled "The Story ofThe Butte Bohunk." To this day, that issue of the *News* holds the record for a single day's sales. Ninety thousand papers were printed and distributed in Butte and other cities of the Northwest.

Splashed with photographs and art work, the story caused more than the usual copper camp sensation. The following paragraphs are taken from the expose:

> "Butte, thrice cursed after its years of pride and prosperity, writhes under a malady which only the white light of publicity will help.
>
> "This condition will not be improved as long as it goes unnoticed. The Butte *Evening News* will tell it all. It has looked a calamitous situation squarely in the face and is going to tell the truth.
>
> "This story tells of the bohunks, three thousand strong, who are driving the white man slowly but surely out of the camp. Many never saw a bohunk; they only know that the bread-winner is out of a job and some mysterious form of foreigner has taken his job. . . .
>
> "The newspaper which by direct or indirect means attempts to defend or justify the condition of affairs which is cursing Butte is criminal in its attempted deception.
>
> "At the word 'bohunk' every other paper in the city but the *News* cries 'hush.' The alarming feature of the bohunk problem is that every other paper seems to be willing to see Butte turned into a cheap foreign settlement even as Dublin Gulch has already become 'bohunk valley.'

"There are 3,000 bohunk miners in Butte today. Of these, 2,175 are working and the balance are being supported by their brothers and are ready to slip into every job where a white man is laid off.

"There are hundreds more en route from Europe ready to come to Butte and live on their friends until they can edge into the mines. . . .

"The bohunk miner is the low grade foreigner who buys his job from the foreman and pays him for keeping it; who lives in a cabin; who never adapts himself to American life any more than does a Chinaman. . . .

"Gambling, white slavery, prizefighting, licensed prostitution, horse racing, and every ill, alleged or otherwise, that one can conjure up palls into insignificance before this black peril which has Butte by the throat and is dragging it down to the level of a grading camp.

"That these black men from across the water are buying their jobs is a secret so open that he who runs may read; yet the operations of this accursed peonage are guarded with all the secrecy of the blackhand and in the end are just as fatal.

"These men buy their jobs for cash; buy their jobs because they board in certain places; because in some instances they buy groceries in certain places; they buy their jobs by renting rooms of people related to the men who employ them; they buy their jobs by paying a rental for cabins far in excess of their worth, content to give up these various tolls to hold their jobs. . . .

"Walk into Dublin Gulch today and you will see what a bohunk is and how he lives. Six of them live in one cabin, not a stone's throw from the Anaconda Mine, and each one of them is paying a rent of $10 a month. One could rent a luxurious mansion for $60.

"Imagine what $60 a month for a one room cabin means to the owner, especially if he has a group of them. He can cut it in two with the foreman and still get rich in a short time.

"Another story is that eight bohunks occupy one cabin, each paying $10 a month. The room was owned by a foreman who drew down $80 for a room that would ordinarily rent for about $10.

"In some places the peonage has been pretty open and above board. Two bohunks were each paying $20 a month for a room in which they were sleeping. This brought $40 for a room worth about one fourth the price. One morning one of the pair notified his landlord that he had secured a cabin in Walkerville for five dollars a month and proposed to live there. When he got over to the mine he was promptly bawled out by the foreman who told him his time was in and go to hell and work in Walkerville.

"The buying of jobs has continued. These foreigners who have walked into the Butte mines and who have taken away jobs from under the very noses of the white men employed in Butte are no part of the community interest in this camp. The foreman who put them to work have no use for them; they cannot carry on a conversation with the other miners of the camp; they do not associate with the other miners; they herd like cattle in the cabins of the gulch and other parts of the town.

"The bohunk colony proper lies in that portion known as 'Corktown' and 'Dublin Gulch.' North Wyoming street, from Copper street north to the B.A.&P. tracks is a regular bohunk hot-bed. Every available house, cabin or shack that can be procured is rented by this element, and between shifts in the mines they are herded like cattle day and night.

"How they sleep is no mystery. The ones on the night shift occupy the same bed that the day shift uses, and the bedding never has a chance to get cold. The other curl themselves up in a dirty blanket on the floor, and feel as refreshed when the alarm goes off as if their cot was of feathers.

"Another shack has eighteen bohunks and for filth it is a marvel. Suspended from the ceiling of the kitchen are several greasy pieces of dried meat. On the claret-soaked table is a dirty deck of cards, while around the table a number of bohunks engaged in some game that is popular in their native land. The walls are smoked and grease-stained and the smell of filth is frightful. The very air reeks with the sickening odors of foreign tobacco and unwashed bodies, and through it all one of their number is kept busy keeping a roaring fire under a coal-oil can with the top cut out and which is used to boil soup in.

"At another house, where over fifteen of them lived, one of their number lay in bed with consumption. Day after day he lingered, with no hopes of rising again, and yet the other bohunks gave little heed to their brother in misfortune, and while each day brought him nearer to the grave, they let him die without the care of a doctor or nurse and even shared the same bed and the same room with the patient.

"Since the bohunk influx to Butte began it has never ceased. Day after day, night after night, as the trains pull into Butte, the bohunks step off at the station. Once landed they are met by one or two old time bohunks who immediately take them on the long hike to 'Cork-town' or the 'Gulch.' Carrying their luggage, blankets and belongings with them, they make a spectacular procession up through Utah Avenue.

"As they step off the train there is no hack driver asking them to have a cab; no baggage man asks for their luggage; and the conductor on the streetcar beats no jangle on the foot bell to give them warning that the car is about to start for town.

"They know it is but a waste of time and words.

"Every train that dumps these foreigners off as it pulls in takes just as many old-timers aboard as it pulls out.

"Up the gulch, 'mother and the kids' watch daily for the postman to see if father has found employment in some place where a white man can live and earn his living. Up the gulch, boys who were born and raised there are kissing their gray-haired mothers good-bye and are leaving for pastures new.

"In an effort to ascertain the effect of the bohunk invasion on the business of Butte a poll was taken of the various business men. The grocer shrugged his shoulders and said, 'We did not get any of his business; there's a bohunk grocery.' The bakers say the bohunks do not eat white bread and have their own bakery; the butchers say the bohunks eat dried sausages and dried meats; the fuel dealers say the bohunk steals coal and rustles railroad ties for his fuel; the clothier says one suit of clothes lasts a lifetime; the bohunks are not fancy dressers.

"There are bohunk saloons and tobacco stores where the invaders buy their drinks and smoking tobacco. Doctors and druggists get little or no patronage from these people. For light in their dingy cabins, candles stolen from the mines are used. These people shave themselves and cut each other's hair. They rarely ride on streetcars; they attend no theatres except perhaps in a wild splurge of extravagance they go to a moving picture show. It will readily be seen that there is not a commercial interest in Butte that profits by this invasion of this class of foreigners."

That, and more, was the story the *Evening News* plastered in scarehead type over the front page on that Sabbath morning in July, 1910. Sensational is a mild word for the effect the story had on the residents. Foremen and shift bosses scurried for cover and made vain attempts to cover up. Surprised foreigners were ousted from their cabins without any explanation, their few belongings tossed into the streets. There was an epidemic of resignations by foremen. "Pink slips" by the hundreds were passed out to the bewildered immigrants.

A few of the guilty foremen attempted to brazen the matter out. Among the latter was a foreman of the High Ore Mine, whose cabin renting proclivities were well known. Monday morning, following the *News'* story found him at the collar of the shaft as usual. Inwardly, he was seething at the turn of events, but outwardly, a malevolent glare told the hundreds of miners gathered around the shaft that for once silence would be golden. At this precise moment Matty Kieley delivered a short oration that was to make him famous, and in later years became a classic of the camp.

On this particular morning, Matty noticed the brooding foreman standing near the shaft. Turning to the assembled miners, with his back to the foreman, Kieley removed his hat, bowed low in mock deference and addressed his remarks to the huge gallows frame which stood over the shaft.

"Good morning, Mr. Gallows Frame," greeted Matty in a voice that could be heard all over the mineyard. "Have you any cabins to rent this morning?"

The High Ore was one mine in the camp in which Matty Kieley never again worked.

The *Evening News* expose had its effect in correcting the situation. Cabins were vacated and fumigated. There was a wholesale exodus of the foreigners from Butte. Stores catering to the "Bohunk trade" silently folded up. Many of the foremen journeyed to California, supposedly for their health. But a minority of the foreigners, as stated before, stayed with their jobs and in time became some of the camp's most respected citizenry. Butte opened its arms to them as soon as fear and its companion, Intolerance, were vanquished.

Kids of Butte

IT MEANS something to have been a kid in Butte. Aside from copper, kids have always been the camp's most bountiful crop. Whether born in the nineties or the forties, Butte kids possess the same reckless, strange characteristics. They are individualists, yet of a pattern too.

From the slopes of Big Butte on the west, to the farthest reaches of the slough ponds of Meaderville on the east, you'll find them jealously proud of their home neighborhoods, but battling valiantly as a unit if the prestige of Copper Camp is in anyway questioned.

In early days a large majority were born in their own homes without benefit of maternity ward. They were brought into the world by such loved and efficient early-day physicians as Drs. Gunn, Whitford, Tremblay and a host of others. In those days, once a kid had survived the first uneventful six years and had started to school, he was on his own. At once he began viewing, through more mature eyes, the first real glimpses of the wide-open camp. There was plenty to see—if the smelter smoke did not blot out the high lights.

The smoke was bad. Many days in the winter it hung over the camp like a yellow, sulphurous pall. The school teachers often found it necessary to light their coal-oil lamps in the middle of the day. Many mothers brought children to and from school for fear they might be lost in the heavy fog. The braver of the youngsters, however, chanced it and rapidly developed sharpened senses for finding their way in the thick smoke.

A mine superintendent who was a school kid during the early days of the camp tells: "The Butte school teachers of that time were a rugged race. Their harshness was born of necessity and self-preservation. They could and would slap a kid down and tan his britches as soon as look at him if the kid but hinted at monkeyshines. Most of the teachers kept a big switch alongside their desks and would wear out three or four of them during a semester. A few of these women are still teaching here, for the misery dealt out by the early-day youngsters must have given them cast-iron constitutions."

The old time schoolrooms of the camp were cold and drafty. A big, pot-bellied wood-burning stove stood in the center of the room. The older boys had the job of keeping it filled with lengths of cordwood. The girls often complained of the cold, so the teacher permitted them to stand close to the stove and thaw out. Most girls wore their hair in pigtail braids, and it seemed that the majority of them were named Mary or Annie. A monitor passed around a tin water bucket and a dipper several times a day.

MONTANA HISTORICAL SOCIETY, HELENA

Fourth grade class in Meaderville School, 1892.

Some of the kids were known to sprinkle pepper on the hot stove while the teacher's back was turned. The smell of the burning pepper, mingled with the odor of the asafetida bags that many pupils wore around their necks as a preventive of disease, plus the scent emanating from some of the "Polack" youth whose mothers sewed them in their underwear for the winter and whose lunchboxes were generously stuffed with garlic, was overpowering. With the windows closed tightly to keep out the sulphurous smelter smoke, the combination stench sometimes left the less-rugged of the girls slightly peaked beneath their pigtails. It never bothered the boys. Like their fathers in the mines and smelters they appeared to thrive on the pungent atmosphere, and grow tougher with each year in school.

It took a school kid about the first four years to really get his bearings. From that time on events began crowding. He concluded that the switch alongside the teacher's desk was "kid stuff," and that the autocratic dictates of the woman in the front of the schoolroom might be open to an occasional argument. He ceased calling the teacher "Miss"; thereafter referring to her as "Old Lady" whatever-her-name-might-be. If she wore glasses, the pedagogue immediately became "Old Lady Four Eyes." As an educator said: "It took fifty years before we succeeded in getting the Butte boys to address their teacher as 'Miss.'"

Once this stage was reached, the next procedure of a Butte kid was to get a nickname and join a gang, of which there were several score in the camp. Then, on the last day of school, he took off his shoes and for the remainder of the summer, with the possible exception of Sundays and holidays, went barefooted. One store, in the summer of 1904, was advertising boys' sturdy shoes at fifty cents a pair—with no takers. The kids wouldn't wear them.

School over, shoes discarded, and with a "livery stable" haircut—the kids were ready for the first of their daily migrations to Bell Creek, the camp's old swimming hole. From the slopes of Walkerville, Chicken Flats, Centerville, Hungry Hill, Corktown, Boulevard, Dublin Gulch, East Side, Parrot Flats, the Hub, South Butte, McQueen Addition, Silver Bow Park and Meaderville, after the last ring of the hated school bell, the gangs began to gather for the year's first foray on the clear and winding waters of the little stream on the Flat.

Barefoot and tattered they moved in from every direction, with South Butte the focusing point. Through the Northern Pacific Railroad yards where red-hot rails blistered grimy feet, still tender from the winter wearing of cramping shoes, they came. Across the copper water ditch from the mines, toes slipped on the insecurity of a rickety single-pole bridge. The last barrier was a muddy swamp, on the other side of which at last was green, rippling, inviting Bell Creek. It was only three miles long and just deep enough for swimming and diving, but what a recreational paradise!

Each gang had a favorite nook, bend or hole on the stream and encroachment by another gang meant warfare. First necessity was a fire. The gang scurried in search of dry and weathered "buffalo chips," with a moment's pause while parched and aching feet were sunk in the moist and soothing depths of any occasional fresh cow chip. This, they believed, was an old Indian remedy for foot ailments. At last the fire burned cheerily, the acrid, blinding smoke providing incense to their nostrils.

Clothing was discarded down to the skin. Clothes were piled in heaps along the bank where alert eyes could guard against any alien tieing of knots. Next came the sacred annointment of urine applied with proper incantations to legs and back as a positive prevention of cramps and sunburn. Finally a lusty challenge: "Last one in is a nigger baby!" A mighty splash, and Bell Creek, Butte's great, outdoor swimming pool of the early days, was open for the season.

There were countless happy hours spent beneath a smiling sun, for Bell Creek to the kids was the last outpost of civilization. North of them was the turmoil and blare of a frenzied mining camp. To the south stretched the vast gray expanses leading to the foothills beyond Timber Butte with its sprawling mills and the stinking Cree Indian encampment. But here, by the mountain-fed stream was freedom from parental dictates—freedom from the hated pedagogy of the classroom. Here was a revel of swan dives, jackknives and belly-floppers—an orgy of front and breast strokes, floaters, mud-baths, dog-strokes and belly-crawls.

But it was poor pleasure without the flavor of combat. It might have been a stone cast in the direction of another gang's hole. Or perhaps, someone crawled up, Indian fashion, swooped down on a garment pile and threw it into the fire or creek. Anything could start the fight which, lightning-like, would spread the length of the creek.

Clothing was thrown on with fireman-like speed. Bottles, stones, bricks, clubs, were hastily gathered in the rush to the firing line. It was everyone for himself, with the honor of the gang at stake. Corktown Irish fought shoulder to shoulder with Anaconda Road Serb. Centerville Cousin Jack battled in hand-to-hand or club-to-club combat with East Granite Street Finn. Silver-Bow-Park Austrians and Poles joined forces with Meaderville Italians. Silver Street Negro and Mercury Street Chinese battled valiantly against the combined odds of Boulevard French and Dogtown Slav.

Skirmishes, attacks, retreats. Broken heads and blackened eyes. As suddenly as it started, it was over. A perfect day concluded, the gangs returned to their respective homes to nurse and gloat over every battle scar.

But the Bell Creek pilgrimages were not always unprofitable or for pleasure alone. There were frogs to be caught in the nearby swamps, their legs to be sold to French restaurants of the "district" at thirty-five to fifty cents a dozen. There were also, for those in on the secret of their location, mushrooms to be gathered and sold for fancy prices to hotels and cafes. And within close distance there was the old slaughterhouse dump with its heaps of stinking refuse, beneath which lay millions of fat, crawling maggots. When cleaned with cornmeal and placed in tobacco tins the squirming grubs sold readily to fishermen at the railroad depot for twenty-five cents a can. Profit could almost always be combined with pleasure by the kids.

At the west end of Bell Creek lay a big dam creating a pond of several acres. This area, which in places was twenty feet deep, was taboo. A half-dozen boys had been drowned there at different times, but in the absence of the caretaker the kids would chance it. Two large rafts had been built from old railroad ties, and no prouder ships ever sailed the seas than these Bell Creek craft.

One memorable naval battle was fought when Lutey Brothers' grocery store dumped unnumbered crates of ancient eggs into its depth. The eggs floated. And so the kids chose sides, climbed on a raft and the battle of Bell Creek was on; odorous to be sure, but the kids didn't mind that.

During the horse and buggy years the camp supported well over a score of livery stables. No effort was spared to keep the animals spick and span—frequent washings with soap and water, constant curry combing and daily brushing being part of a regular routine for the "rent" horses.

Once each year, usually in the early spring, the equines were shorn of the winter's accumulation of heavy hair. Hand-clippers were used for this task, while a huge wheel, about a yard in diameter and attached to the bellows supplied the power. Rapid turning of the wheel forced air into the bellows, which in turn passed it through a long hose and into the mechanism of the large clipper attached to the end.

At horse-clipping time the livery stables were a mecca for the camp's juvenile gangs. As time for the first horse-clipping approached, word traveled along the grape vine, and at once the shearing of the gangs was under way. With visions of the annual livery stable haircut or "baldyshine" as they called it, they gathered at the barns.

Attendants at the various stables encouraged the lads in their quest for tonsorial attention. To them, the visits meant willing hands to turn the large wheel. They knew full well that there would be a surplus of labor. When one youth tired another relieved him.

The last horse, having been shorn, the long-awaited moment arrived. A convenient bale of hay was dragged forth to serve as the barber's chair. A grimy horse blanket answered the purpose of an apron. Each youth in turn perched himself on the improvised seat. The livery stable hostler, clippers in hand, gave the signal and a member of the gang started the huge wheel in motion.

Up one side of the victim's head and down the other—curls or pompadours—blond or brunette—red or sorrel—the wool fell to the stable floor. Another quick zip or two and the job was finished, leaving the youthful cranium with all the aspects of an enlarged, irregular, billiard ball.

Prominent scars and bumps, proud souvenirs of contact with the brickbats and clubs of other gangs, stood forth to be admired.

Often, the large clippers, intended for the coarser hair of horses, would snag when run through the more or less silky locks of youth. An agonizing yell, quick stopping of the machinery, adjustment, and the wholesale shearing proceeded.

The numerous cats who made the livery stables their home gathered around in curiosity. These, the barbers jokingly assured the youngsters, were merely waiting a possible tid-bit in the form of a severed ear or so. With plenty of minor nicks, a slight scratch or abrasion, but thankfully no missing aurical organs, the shearing progressed, until the last lad had parted with his once crowning glory. Ostracism awaited the member of any gang foolhardy enough to refuse the gratis haircut.

The livery stable workers reveled in the sport. It was the year's big entertainment to them—even if later they found themselves facing many an outraged mother.

It was rare, but not unheard of, for a girl to be inveigled occasionally by a persuasive brother or admirer into parting with her curls. Moments like this were indeed tragic for all concerned. Usually, however, the girls would have no part of the orgies—or the livery stable itself, for that matter.

The *en masse* hair cutting was often followed by irate parents' vigorous chastisement applied with a board or razor strap, yet the gang's return for their livery stable shearing the following spring could always be depended upon.

But life was not all a round of pleasure in earlier times. Parental discipline was strict, and there were many duties for a kid to perform at home. Life was hard for a miner, and after ten hours in the hot boxes he had little liking for chores about the house. As soon as a kid was old enough, he gave the old man a lift.

There was for instance, the matter of fuel. A subject for neighborhood gossip was the home which need buy fuel except in the coldest months of the winter. Every kid spent a portion of the spring, summer and fall days rustling wood or coal. Like an African ant hill, the mine dumps teemed with kids, wheelbarrows, and home-made wagons. Discarded mine timbers were snatched, piled on the makeshift vehicles and carted home to dry in piles in the back yard, later to be sawed and chopped into stove-length sections. It was a similar scene in the railroad yards. As fast as the section laborers dragged out an old tie to replace it with a new one, some kid was on the job to seize and carry it home.

Coal was gleaned, ostensibly, from the railroad and mine-yard track where it had fallen from the cars. But harried watchmen were continuously on the prowl, for the conscience of the kids was very flexible. They were not above climbing into the cars and throwing coal off by the ton to pals on the ground. Indeed, in certain localities, it was no novelty for an entire railroad car of coal to disappear overnight. At times as the trains pulled into the East Butte yards, kids and women were seen to fairly swarm over the cars, throwing coal off while the train was still in motion.

The kids of those years were ruthless.

There were other chores. In many of the mines, on the day shift, miners come on surface to eat their lunch. A hot meal was appreciated and it was the kid's job to carry the old man's lunch pail to him. It was the same at the smelters and other outdoor jobs. Kids carried the lunches but they made it pay. There were few lads who did not return from this chore without the lunch bucket filled with three or four pounds of copper ore or other scrap metal purloined from the scrap heaps of the works. Here again, a flexible conscience came in handy. The camp did not look upon this as dishonesty—it merely showed that the kid had potential business talent.

Many early day families possessed a cow. Rumor had it that certain of the dairies were not above adding chalk and water to their product, and, as a matter of self-preservation, the need of home dairies was soon realized. Kids, of course, became custodians of the family cow.

Barns had to be cleaned, manure hauled, the cow milked and the milk kept in a cool and sanitary condition. Any surplus milk would be delivered to neighbors not so fortunate as to own a cow of their own. All this meant added labor for the kid, but he accepted it gracefully. To save on feed bills, many cows were driven out and staked to graze on pastures along the lush creek banks on the Flat. This chore meant a three-mile hike in the morning and the same on returning at night.

Youngsters with an eye to business made dickers with the Indians, obtaining for themselves cheap Indian cayuses with which they herded the cows to and from the creek. Many kids built up considerable herds which they tended at a charge of a dollar a month.

It was common to see these convoyed bovines, their bells ringing, complacently strolling through the business district of the camp, competing with traffic and antagonizing the hard-swearing skinners of a constant stream of ore-wagons.

First, last, and at all times, the kids were breadwinners, but it wasn't always bread. When times were flush, they found cake. A boy, in those days had a thousand angles, everyone of which was remunerative if skillfully handled. The problem of spending-money for the kids was never a worry to the household budget. Mothers or fathers had little occasion to dig down in the family sock to supply Junior with money for the weekly show or a frequent lollypop.

All varieties of bottles could be sold, and bottles were as plentiful in the copper camp as pine needles in the Big Woods to the north. Quart beer bottles were sold at three for a nickel. Whiskey bottles were the same. Gunny sacks, without holes, were two for five cents, and it needn't be known that they came from Mrs. Murphy's back porch where they were placed to wipe the mine mud off her old man's feet.

Mike Gordon's "High Class Junk Shop" was open for business six days a week and you could find him at his home on Sunday if the call was urgent. Mike bought anything that didn't have the stamp of a railroad on it.

On Saturday during the school year, and practically any day during the summer vacation, the gangs went "rustling." Each group claimed undisputed jurisdiction over the alleys in its own particular territory. Encroachments meant war but on rustling days, business came before pleasure. The late Chief of Police Jere Murphy, or any police chief who preceded him, could have written a book on those rustling forays. Some of the names they could mention later found their way into the halls of Congress and the President's Cabinet. It was a poor gang that couldn't split at least a ten-dollar bill at the end of a day of rustling.

The lads conjured a thousand money-making angles. At the railroad depots chewing gum, candy, fruit and magazines could be sold to passengers on the trains. Most anything in the line of food could be peddled at the depots to the passengers on "Jim Hill's Bohunk Special," which were trains of Bulgarian emigrants on their way to work as laborers on the Great Northern Railroad. These strangely garbed foreigners were particularly fond of giant loaves of French bread, bologna, strong cheese, onions and garlic. They purchased in quantity, and many of the kids earned bountiful spending money catering to the Bohunk wants.

In lull moments "hopping hacks" offered a chance dime. Hopping hacks at the depots meant carrying passengers' luggage from the hacks down to the trains. Practically all of the hack drivers tolerated the practice except Fat Jack and Barney Shannahan. Barney thoroughly hated the kids. And frugal Fat Jack figured if there were any stray coins to be picked up, he might as well have them himself.

Ice, salvaged from the refrigerator cars, was easily sold. The price was low, however, and only the younger kids would bother with it.

The copper precipitating tanks, just starting operations with mine water pumped from the Hill, offered a ready market for scrap iron or tin cans. They purchased unlimited quantities and did not draw the line at railroad iron, which precipitated almost pure copper just as well as any other scrap.

Live chickens were salable at the Chinese noodle joints. But only certain gangs living in the vicinity of the Cabbage Patch specialized in these.

The camp's half-a-thousand saloons purchased prodigious amounts of sawdust at twenty-five cents a sack. Carpenter shops in the mineyards gave it away to the kids, the haul to the saloons entailed only labor to convert it into cash. One juvenile corporation, with the aid of an Indian cayuse and a wagon, established a volume business in this commodity.

"Rushing the can" was another sideline that offered many possibilities. Residents of cabins in the eastern and southern sections of the copper camp, male and female, were ever willing to pay an honest, alert youngster from fifteen to twenty-five cents for the safe delivery of a growler of beer. The kids who went in for the can-rushing trade had a set scale of prices, a percentage of the cost of the can. Delivery of hard liquor was charged for at the rate of two-bits a pint.

In those days growler rushing was much practiced especially in summer. After a tough ten-hour shift in the hot boxes every miner felt in need of a cooler and a lifter-upper. Many with homes and families did not wish to stop in at the saloons on their way home from work. The temptations were too great. Growler rushing, therefore, was the answer to the problem. The oldest kid was dispatched to the nearest saloon with the old man's dinner pail and a quarter, for there was no law against selling beer to minors in those days.

Beer was usually consumed with the evening meal. When friends or neighbors dropped in for an evening's visit, it was the custom to offer liquid hospitality. So, once more it was the kid's chore to make the trip around the corner to the Dutchman's. The tricks to can-rushing, such as rubbing lard on the inside of a bucket to prevent accumulation of suds, were common knowledge to most Butte kids.

And so it was a rare occasion when a youngster didn't have a couple of coins to rub together in his much-mended pants pockets. There were jobs for all who wanted them. Six or eight messenger forces in the city alone hired up to a hundred boys. The job paid thirty dollars a month and tips were high. An alert messenger boy could easily make as much as a miner. There were many temptations on the job, but the kids knew their way around and very few succumbed.

Grocery stores hired scores of lads as "swampers" on their delivery wagons. A kid had to be tough to hold down this job, as gangs in certain sections of the city made a practice of raiding the wagons. It was the lad's duty to hold the horses and guard the groceries while the driver made deliveries. The swampers frequently sported black eyes.

The camp's various dry-goods stores hired a number of youths as "cash boys." This was looked upon as a "sissy" job and only accepted in dire emergencies, or when some kids' mother became possessed of the idea that the job might aid in making a gentleman of him.

Theaters hired boys as ushers. This was considered a first class position as it entailed but a few hours work in the evening, and the kids got to see all the shows.

There were paper routes galore, as the camp supported four newspapers. Many of the more ambitious kids carried routes for both morning and evening papers. Carriers who delivered the morning papers had to be on the job at four A.M. Most kids, however, considered this early rising as sport, for there was plenty of riotous activity and much for an inquiring eye to see at that time of the morning.

By far the greater part of the Butte kids of those years were self-supporting. Nearly every small store or butchershop had work for one or more boys, and there were countless other jobs to keep a kid in spending money before the time arrived for him to go down in the mines.

In election years a young fellow had additional opportunities. During the Heinze-Amalgamated campaigns, and earlier, during the Clark-Daly battles, the kids were in clover. Rallies then were held every night in some neighborhood. Kids furnished firewood for the bonfires. It mattered little whose back yard fence went up in smoke when the pay was ten dollars, spot cash, for the evening's supply. Election banners also were carried at so much an hour. A smart lad could carry a banner for both parties on the same evening if he knew the right angles. There were election cards, too, to be passed out. The supply of political jobs around voting time was almost unlimited, depending more on resourcefulness than anything else. Heinze tossed handfuls of silver to the kids. He was a great favorite with them.

Weddings and christenings were petty rackets. It was a poor sport who wouldn't donate heavily on his wedding day. The old time ear-dinning charivari had a distinct nuisance value, and tribute paid by the bridegroom often was occasioned by the realization that discretion is the better part of valor.

The camp's newsboys are a story in themselves. With four news papers—the *Standard* and *Miner* in the morning, and the *Inter Mountain* and *Evening News* in the evening—and with thousands of people on the streets night and day, money-making opportunities for the scores of urchins who cried out headlines were limitless. There was a fair margin of profit to be made on each paper, for the sports about town thought little of tossing out a quarter for a paper. Many miners' sons made more money selling papers than their fathers made in the mines. Stories are numerous of kids who put enough money aside to finance their way through college. Many of today's professional and business men in Butte gained an education through money earned hawking papers.

Butte newsboys of that era had a club which gained national prominence. It was founded by the late J. R. Wharton, a sincere friend of the newsies. The club had its own mayor, chief of police, aldermen and police judge. They patterned the grown-ups in campaigns for the election of officers, and their campaigns were just as bitterly fought.

The newsboys saw plenty on the streets of the camp, as they were barred from no place except the red-light district, and many of them sneaked in there when the police were not watching. Papers sold fast to the habitants of the early-day district and their tips were generous.

A former newsboy tells of an incident that happened on a summer morning in 1907. He and two other kids were on their way uptown to sell the morning editions. They took a short cut through an alley behind a saloon and music hall on the edge of the red-light district.

Suddenly the youths heard a groan coming from the darkness of the alley. They were frightened, but their youthful curiosity got the best of them and they investigated. In the shadows they saw the faint outline of a human form. They lit a match, and there stretched out in the alley was a big rawboned cowboy, boots and all. From his groans they knew he was alive, but they could see that somebody had given him a terrific beating. His face was smashed to a bloody pulp.

The cowboy's trousers had been pulled down over his shoes, and protruding from the lower mid-portion of his anatomy was the handle of one of the biggest guns either of the youngsters had ever seen.

Frightened, the two lads hurried from the alley in search of a policeman. At the first corner they ran into big Jim Larkin, captain of detectives. They told their story and he accompanied them to the scene. After looking things over, the detective hurried to a patrol box and called the police wagon. On its arrival, as he and the driver lifted the cowboy, gun and all, into the wagon, Larkin turned to the driver:

"Well sir," he remarked, "I've often heard of a gun toter being threatened that way, but this is the first time I've ever seen the threat actually carried out."

As mentioned before, there was continual warfare among the different gangs of kids—more for the sheer love of combat than anything else. Ever-belligerent gangs of Corktown and Dublin Gulch Irish would swoop down over the mine dumps on a Finlander gang to the southeast. The hardy Finns would retaliate. Up and down, through the streets of the colony, the battle would rage. Sticks, stones, brickbats and chunks of "first class" from the mine dumps were the usual weapons. Windows were broken and fences demolished. The women and girls, true to the Finn tradition, fought valiantly at the sides of their sons and brothers. Storekeepers closed their doors, bartenders deserted their saloons to witness the fray. The cop on the beat, helpless against the onslaught, phoned frantic calls for reinforcements. The clang of the patrol wagon bearing its load of reserves was the signal for the end of hostilities. The Gulch and Corktown warriors retreated back up the hill, through the mine-yards and across the waste dumps. The battle was over for the time but it might break out again the next day or remain dormant for a month. That was in the laps of gods.

This situation existed among other gangs. The kids of South Butte would attack the Parrot Flat gang at the slightest provocation or the reverse might be true. The juvenile mobs of Centerville and Walkerville were natural enemies. Kids from the tough East Side weren't particular, they would fight any gang, any time or any place. Small wonder that many of the old time residents proudly display such well-scarred noggins, not all accounted for by the fall of loose rock in the mines.

But let outsiders start anything. Local differences ceased immediately and the kids of copper camp presented a united front. As Berton Braley wrote in his autobiography, *Pegasus Pulls a Hack*: "Outsiders were never allowed to get tough in Butte. That was a local privilege. "Many were the circuses and carnivals that learned this to their sorrow. There were few juvenile baseball or football games that did not end in a free-for-all. The old "wood yards" on the site of the large, new high school stadium was the scene of hundreds of hard-fought battles. The "Red Barns" and the "Cinders," two other well-remembered juvenile playgrounds of old Butte, also soaked up a good share of juvenile gore, shed in the perpetual warfare of the time.

For unexplained reasons early-day kids had a violent dislike for the Chinese. The appearance of a laundryman or vegetable peddler was the signal for an onslaught by the gangs whose territory was trespassed upon by the hapless Chinese. In wintertime the violence might take the form of a barrage of frozen snowballs. In summer the terrified Oriental might be greeted with a bombardment of rocks and cobblestones. Many Chinamen finally obtained permission from the authorities to carry guns. Thereafter several Butte kids died from blazing guns in the hands of the infuriated Orientals.

A favorite sport of many of the gangs called for visits to noodle parlors of Chinatown. There, quantities of strange foods would be ordered and hurriedly devoured, the gang making a frantic exit for the street without paying for the meal. It was dangerous, attendant with real risks of bodily harm, as any unfortunate lad who failed to make the door with the rest of the gang could testify.

In later years the Chinese protected themselves against such imposition by attaching patented drop locks on their doors, and demanding pay in advance. A North Wyoming Street gang one evening kidnapped a youthful waiter from the Mai Wah noodle parlor and transported him to a deserted shack in Corktown where he was securely bound with ropes. Miners coming off shift the following morning heard his frantic cries and released him.

Syrian rug vendors and Afghan tamale peddlers were also objects of attack. Some of the Syrians carried small arsenals, while the Mohammedan tamale vendors depended on curses to Allah and a two-foot razor-sharp Afghan cleaver, a sort of glorified bolo knife, for protection.

In dark neighborhoods, thin wires stretched across sidewalks would trip an unsuspecting tamale man as he came down the street crying; "Hot ta-ma-le!" The gangs hidden nearby, swooped down to loot his cans as they fell to the ground.

Looking back, it seems remarkable that half the kids weren't assassinated before they came of age.

Barney Shannahan, a Butte hackman with a violent temper, was made a target of abuse by the gangs. Barney hated the kids, and their cry of "Barney, give us a kiss!" was like a red flag waved in the face of a bull. Why the request should so anger the hackman was never explained, but Barney's reaction to the cry was violent. Up the streets and alleys Barney would drive his hack, lashing his horses and uttering oaths, in pursuit of his tormentors. The unfortunate youngster whom the cabman cornered was out of luck. Barney carried a special whip and he was not backward about laying it across his victims.

Cushman, the iceman, a huge Hollander, was another who developed an intense hatred and suffered considerable plaguing as a result. Cushman carried a heavy leather bullwhacker's whip on his wagon seat and would use it at the slightest provocation. His method was to leave his horses in the middle of the street and, whip in hand, take out after the kids. Being an athlete, he often ended up by catching one of the culprits, and to be caught once by Cushman was a lesson that a kid remembered all his life.

Another victim of the gangs was a gentleman named Powers, who for some reason or other saw red at the cry of "Pretty Powers!" He carried a lather's hatchet in his hip pocket and had a habit of throwing it into the midst of a gang of tormentors. Bylo, the rotund individual who peddled "hokey pokeys," an ice cream confection, came in for his share of attention from the kids.

One person is still living who, perhaps, was better acquainted with the Butte gangs and in return received more respect from them than any other individual. He is Frank O'Brien, railroad detective for the B.A.&P. Railway which operates between Butte and the smelters in Anaconda, twenty-six miles away.

The kids steered clear of O'Brien and his savage, ninety-pound bulldog. Part of O'Brien's bailiwick was the notorious Dublin Gulch, and O'Brien knew by name every juvenile resident of that hard-boiled neighborhood. Keeping the kids off the railroad property which ran through the Gulch was part of O'Brien's job, and he relates that the major portion of the gray hairs decorating his thatch was put there by "those kids."

O'Brien tells of a day when some of the gray hairs first made their appearance. That was the afternoon when over a score of Dublin Gulch kids climbed aboard a flatcar loaded with heavy steel rails and released the brakes.

The car of rails had been left on the main line of the little railroad opposite St. Mary's Parochial School between Corktown and Dublin Gulch, where the "hill hog" was scheduled to pick it up on its next trip into Butte. Long before the arrival of the engine, however, the kids had climbed aboard and turned the car loose. For five miles the track was downgrade, and it was for that distance that the runaway car careened on its mad trip with a load of wildly yelling passengers. Out through the west end district of Butte and around the foot of Big Butte the car tore at a speed estimated at fifty miles an hour. Fortunately the Butte-bound engine had not yet left the yards and the line was clear.

It was fortunate, too, that the runaway car was noticed at the start of the trip, and the dispatchers in the little division town of Rocker notified. Never were such preparations made for the arrival of a train as on that eventful day, O'Brien tells. A switch engine tore madly up and down the yards fighting against time to clear the main line for the arrival of the onrushing car. It was a miracle that car remained on the tracks; it must have been the heavy rails that kept it upright, but somehow it did and it passed the Rocker station doing better than sixty miles an hour, its load of passengers seemingly not in the least terrified but yelling and waving like Comanche Indians.

Down into the Rocker yards the juggernaut rushed and then onto the track cleared for its arrival. For over a mile it bumped and jolted before finally coming to a stop. Kids scattered in all directions, none of them stopping until they were deep in the foothills several miles west of the camp.

A popular rendezvous where the kids were able to combine business with pleasure was the old Marcus Daly race track. They scoffed at the idea of paying admission to the track for there were many convenient holes in the mile-round fence, and where apertures did not exist, it was a simple matter to tear off a loose board. Kids were banned from the betting ring—that is P. J. Gilligan, Butte juvenile officer, was stationed at the track to keep juveniles from making bets —but there were ways of getting around the vigilance of "P. J." The "combination book" accepted fifty-cent bets, and it was at this betting stall that the youngsters did their wagering. Many became fairly expert in picking winners, in the optimism of inexperience often doing better than many of the professional horse pickers. There also was work to be done around the track, stables to be cleaned, and horses to be cooled. Several of the smaller kids became jockeys and made reputations on the nation's larger tracks.

The kids missed very few of the early-day prize fights for which the camp was noted, and, of course, never paid admission fees. The two large arenas on the Flat were patronized by youths who somehow, despite attendants, managed to be perched in the better seats when the bell rang for the main event.

One resident recollects climbing a fifty-foot pole to be among those present at the memorable Battling Nelson-Herrera fight. He tells that it was necessary to make a ten-foot leap from the pole to attain the topmost edge of the arena. The danger of a possible fall merely acted as a preliminary thrill to the excitement of the show. There were a hundred or more kids who saw the fight by making the same climb and jump, he says.

Nearly every kid was the owner of a dog. Breeding mattered little, just so the canine possessed four legs. The animals were as wild and tough as their owners and were ever ready to battle other dogs of the neighborhood. Very few of the kids ever purchased a dog license.

The city employed two colored dog catchers named Sampson and Brown, and it was a harried life the kids dealt out to them. Although both carried arms, it was not unusual for the two to come back to the city corral without wagon, dogs, or guns, and thoroughly beaten up in the bargain.

The colored men were persistent, and reoutfitted, they would soon be back about the streets. One afternoon, being particularly courageous under the inspiration of what allegedly was several "slugs" of square-face gin, the two dog catchers decided to go into Dublin Gulch, where the canine population averaged two dogs to each family.

Sampson's wagon had some twenty dogs imprisoned in its screened enclosure when it drove up Wyoming Street into Dublin Gulch. The men had a wired pole for a snare. Sampson wore a large tin star on his vest and each of the dog catchers carried pistols on their hips.

"Sampson, ah don't feel lucky in this paht of town. These kids up heah are plenty tough," complained Brown to his partner.

"No need to be scairt long as I has this star sayin' I'se an officer of the law—and besides we's both got these big smoke wagons jes' in case of emergency," declared the six-foot Sampson. "At foah bits a dog, we is goin' to make a good afternoon's work up heah."

By this time they were in the heart of the Gulch. Sampson spied a nondescript mongrel dozing at the side of the road and in a moment was down off the wagon and had the dog lassoed. The cur yelped, a ragged urchin shrieked an alarm, and in a twinkling the two colored men were surrounded by a half-hundred kids, a dozen neighboring

WORLD MUSEUM OF MINING, BUTTE

Butte boys try their luck at mining.

women, and several husky miners who came running out of an adjacent saloon.

Although Sampson drew his gun, he was promptly knocked down; his gun, star, the captured dog and half his clothes were taken from him. A kid bounced a rock off his head and the terrified dog catcher went down with half the Dublin Gulch gang on top of him. His partner Brown, at the first onslaught, had promptly climbed aboard the wagon and whipped up the horses, leaving his partner to the mercy of the gang. The dog cage on the rear of the wagon, however, had been yanked off by a dozen hands, and the twenty yelping curs released.

Thoroughly subdued, the huge Sampson escaped and streaked down the road after the wagon, eventually catching up with it some distance down the hill. Between gasps he shouted at the trembling Brown, "You is canned, you is canned—leavin' me up dar to be killed by wild Irishers!"

"Ah ain't canned a-tall," Brown insisted. "Ah done quit dis job when you-all grabbed dat first dog."

The leading theatrical attractions and road shows of the country played at the old Broadway Theater, at that time one of the best equipped in the Northwest. Few kids ever missed a show. The theater had a large skylight directly over the second balcony, or "nigger heaven" as it was known to them. A fire escape on the side of the building in the alley led to the roof of the theater and the skylight. To the second balcony seats it was about a ten-foot drop from the skylight, which could be opened from the outside by prying with a heavy stick. Scores of kids made the perilous drop at every show, little minding the fact that they often landed on the necks of cash customers. In wintertime the fire escape was usually covered with a heavy coating of ice. A slip might mean death in the alley below, yet there is no record of any kid being killed while making the ascent. Copper camp kids were as sure-footed as Walkerville cats.

The gangs were in evidence at all celebrations. The Fourth of July, to them, was a gala day. For weeks before, many made a habit of loafing around the mine-yards awaiting an opportunity to walk away with supplies of dynamite, caps and fuse. The loot was saved for the big day. It was far more exciting and much louder than shooting off mere firecrackers.

Other gangs purchased large quantities of potash and sulphur from the drug stores. The two ingredients when properly mixed and placed a double handful at a time on an iron anvil produced a terrific noise when a heavy iron horse-weight, attached to a long rope and pulley, was dropped upon the mixture. Many a kid journeyed through life minus fingers, hands, arms or eyes as a result of these strenuous Independence Day celebrations.

Torpedoes, "borrowed" from the railroad yards, and placed close together on the streetcar tracks also made excellent celebration material, even if the series of explosions took years from the motorman's life and frightened his passengers half to death.

Summertime picnics offered further opportunities. Here again, kids mixed profit with pleasure. Most of the picnic resorts paid for the retrieving of the thousands of beer bottles that lay scattered over the grounds. At the then-current rate, five or six dollars could be garnered for a few hours' work. And all the picnics featured sporting events—foot races, jumping, and the like. An athletic kid might knock over several of the cash and merchandise prizes offered for the events. From necessity, most of them were good foot-racers.

Thomas Hosty, now nearing seventy, was a Butte kid—one of the first, he says, and as "tough as any then, or those who followed." Hosty was raised in "Chicken Flats." When twelve years old he was making a nuisance of himself around the mine-yards and as a result had gained the enmity of one "Swede" Johnson, head ropeman on the Butte Hill. This day Johnson had boosted Hosty out of the mine-yard, using his broad right toe. Hosty retaliated by coming back in the yard and throwing a double handful of iron nuts through the rope house window, one of them striking the Swede behind the ear. Johnson came out wild and flying and in a few steps caught young Hosty and this time booted him the entire distance to the mine-yard gate.

"Well, I was good and sore," says Hosty, "and swore to get even with that big Swede. Now, in those days they used to use clean cotton instead of toilet paper in the mine-yard toilets. So I waits my chance and gets a big handful of the waste and soaks one end of it good in turpentine. Then I put it back in the toilet. Happily, Johnson was the first one to go in the place, and I hid outside to watch the fun. It was only a short time before that Swede let out one of the loudest yells I ever heard in that part of town. He came out fighting mad and in a state of undress, as you would say. I didn't stick around, but high-tailed it over the hill to Chicken Flats as fast as my legs would carry me.

Hallowe'en presented the greatest opportunity of the kid's busy year. All the hell raising that couldn't be crowded into the other 364 days was saved up for this one dreadful evening. With fear and foreboding civic authorities of the copper camp awaited approach of the night. Special police were added to the regular force. Extra deputies augmented the sheriff's staff. Mounted squads of officers patrolled the streets, but their activity did not in the slightest deter the kids.

Gangs of fifty to a hundred boys pillaged the various neighborhoods. Anything movable was carted away. Whole sections of fences, sheds, outhouses, wagons, buggies and hacks were either toppled over, demolished, or hoisted onto telegraph poles or railroad bridges and street-car viaducts. Often windows were smashed. Cows were sometimes tied to front doors. Horses were lassoed and forced into church and school vestibules. The brakes on ore or coal cars were released and the cars allowed to run away, sometimes being wrecked in the descent.

Streetcar tracks were painted with axle grease, forcing the cars out of control on the steep downgrades. Trolleys were often pulled from the wires; smoking chimneys, plugged with gunny sacks, almost asphyxiated the occupants of many homes.

Many of the more hot-headed residents protected their property with shotguns and more than one Hallowe'en celebrant carried bullet scars through life as a momento of a night of vandalism. Several kids were killed on different occasions. The jails were filled but the kids were usually turned loose the next day. A term at the "hookey school" on the Flat was the worst punishment meted out.

Of the many gangs, the combined forces of the South Montana, South Main and Iron Street gangs had an enviable reputation for originality. The year previous to the Hallowe'en of 1903, they had caused a "Missourian" prospector, living in a small shack on the outskirts of the town, considerable grief and annoyance. He had sworn that on the next Hallowe'en he would "blow to hell" the first kid who came close to his place. The kids had heard of the threat and made preparations accordingly.

Late in the afternoon of Hallowe'en, while the prospector was away from his shack at work, several members of the gang obtained a heavy three-inch rope from a nearby mine. They placed this around the upper part of the shack, in the form of a huge slipknot, with about a hundred feet of rope left over. This long end they laid out and hid in a clump of bushes some fifty feet away.

Dusk came and the prospector returned to his cabin, failing to notice in the darkness the rope that encircled his home. His first act after completing his evening meal was to break out his shotgun and a supply of ammunition. He then sat down to wait.

The kids also waited until about nine-thirty when the electric ore trains running to Clark's Smelter at the foot of the street were due. At that time, the heavy and powerful ore trains ran straight down Montana Street through the center of the town and often carried as many as ten or twelve cars on their evening trip.

At last the ore train came clattering down the street and stopped at the B.A.&P. railway crossing to allow a freight train to go by. As the ore train stopped, several of the gang slipped silently into the bushes and retrieved the end of the long rope which they pulled into the street and attached securely to the last ore car on the string.

The freight train finally cleared the crossing, and the electric ore train slowly started. The rope grew taut, and as the train picked up momentum, a grinding, crashing noise could be heard. Then hell broke loose. Over and over tumbled the flimsy wooden shack with the prospector and his gun still inside. Escape was impossible. For four blocks down Montana Street, the cabin crashed and tumbled, stopping only when the motorman of the ore train heard the terrific din at the end of the drag.

They dug the prospector out from between the chimney and the rafters of his crumpled cabin. Miraculously, he was alive, but considerably bruised. They moved him to a hospital, and the entire sheriff's office, with the police, combed the neighborhood for hours seeking the perpetrators. The kids, however, had transferred their activities to another part of town. Newspapers carried stories and editorials decrying the brazenness and enormity of the affair, and that was about all that was ever done about it. The "Missourian" prospector built himself another cabin, this time out in the foothills, far away from the kids.

The law had been most lenient with the camp's gangs but by 1904, city and county officials decided that something must be done. They erected the Industrial School on the Flat, a two-story structure with a ten-foot fence. It was intended as a correctional institution. Joseph R. Jackson, now a Washington attorney, was placed in charge. The kids dubbed it the "Hookey School."

Ed Colligan and William Bebee were chosen as truant officers and they at once became the nemesis of the gangs. Scores of the more active and prominent members were rounded up and herded before Judge Mike "Long Distance" Donlin. Judge Donlin lived true to his moniker and handed out sentences of from one to three years at the school on the Flat. There was never a dearth of pupils. As a correctional institution the hookey school curbed to a great extent the exuberance of the camp's youngsters. The kids at the institution had their own gardens to tend. There also was livestock, and in the manual training shop many of the boys were taught the rudiments of useful trades.

Many boys developed the wanderlust. Not having the easy access to travel by automobile of modern youth, the question of what lay on the other side of the mountain demanded a satisfactory answer; and to find out, many of the kids, singly and in groups of two or three, climbed aboard the rods or blinds of the transcontinental trains and set out on trips that sometimes ended in cities hundreds and sometimes thousands of miles away. Butte kids, however, had little trouble getting along. They scorned riding on freight trains—it was a fast passenger train or nothing. Most of them came back via the same method when time for return to school rolled around. The strenuous training received in the copper camp enabled a kid to find his way around any place and in any company.

Putting up hay in the Big Hole ranching district was another profitable vacation pastime for many of the boys. Hundreds of them journeyed to there each summer and drove the rakes, mowers and hay boats of the Big Hole cattlemen. The latter had a lasting regard for them, usually hiring Butte boys in preference to older hands.

Many of the early-day kids remained in school and obtained an education. The closing exercises of the various schools at the end of the school year were usually held in the theaters or at the city auditorium. Pupils fortunate enough to obtain diplomas were cheered by pals who attended in force.

One closing exercise of a local parochial school was held in the Butte Civic Auditorium. The opening ensemble arranged by the Sisters of the school was a tableau depicting one of the girls dressed in long, flowing white robes as Miss America, leading in song pupils representing the other nations of the world.

The curtain was down and Miss America, with her back to the audience, was in position to lead the opening chorus at the curtain's rise. At the signal for the start of the show, the curtain began to slowly rise, and with it, the skirt of Miss America. Some one had tied it to the curtain. The astonished audience were treated to a full rear view of a vivid green pair of pantaloons. Amid an uproar the curtain was stopped about half way in its ascent and rung down. Miss America fainted, and it was some time before the show went on.

Despite the numerous other vocations and avocations, the largest number of kids, however, on finishing grammar school or on reaching their sixteenth birthday, made a bee line for the "Hill" to "rustle" a job in the mines. Some, with influence, went to work in the shops on surface as apprentice machinists, blacksmiths, boilermakers and other trades. A few went wiping engines and eventually became hoisting engineers. They were the fortunate minority. The greater part of the kids hired out for underground work as nippers, carmen or shovelers. They were paid a man's wages and at once began living a man's life. Their kid days were over. Those who survived are now Butte's old-time miners.

One Butte kid who didn't intend to go in the holes was "Heinze-Clark."

He was a member of the South Butte gang. His real name was Dennis Donovan, and his old man had the "con." He was a queer kid but tougher than nails.

It was because of the queer things he said and did that the kids gave him the nickname, "Heinze-Clark." His gang was sitting around talking one day about the usual things kids talk of. Some of them were wishing they could hurry up and get old enough to get a job in the mines when this Donovan kid pipes up.

"You fellows can have your mines. Not for me. I've learned a lesson from my old man. Look at him, he's spent the last ten years in the holes, and what has he got? Can't eat anything, coughing his lungs out night and day, always looking like he's half-dead. No mines for me. I'm going to be a big guy like Heinze or Clark and own my own mines, and I'm not going to get them by working in them either."

That sounded pretty funny coming from a kid like Donovan, so right away the kids nicknamed him "Heinze-Clark," and that's the only name any of the kids ever called him after that. His mother didn't like the name, but they called it to him just the same. Heinze-Clark was a long, stringy kid. Maybe he'd grown too fast. There was something wrong with his eyes and he had to wear glasses. He wasn't any sissy though, and he was just as tough or tougher than any kid in the gang. He looked funny when he dressed up on Sundays for church. His long, skinny legs in the short, tight pants the kids wore those days made him appear twice as tall as he really was.

Heinze-Clark was always after his mother to buy him a suit of long pants, but I guess his mother didn't like to see him grow up. A kid had to be old enough to vote in those days before they'd let him wear long pants, anyhow. Heinze-Clark was persistent though, and he was saving every nickel he could earn. He said as soon as he had enough money, he was going to have a talk with his father and see if they couldn't argue his mother into letting him have the long pants suit.

Heinze-Clark was peculiar in a number of ways. He was interested in birds and was always searching for birds' nests. He'd also pick up every sample of ore he could find and had a big box of specimens in his room. "Heinze-Clark" was a very appropriate name for him.

Along about the time he had enough money saved to buy the long pants suit, Heinze-Clark met with a lot of hard luck.

It was in the spring of the year, just a month or so before vacation began. A dreary evening, it had been raining a slight drizzle all day, and the gang was moping around the neighborhood without much of anything to occupy their time because of the rain when Heinze spotted a sparrow's nest up on the cross arm of a high telegraph pole.

Nothing would do but he should climb the pole and see if there were any eggs in the nest. The gang warned him against it because they knew there might be some high-powered wires up there. Heinze-Clark wasn't afraid of anything though, and he insisted that someone give him a boost up the pole so he could reach the first of the iron footholds that led to the top of it. It was no use arguing with him once he got a notion, so they gave him a boost, and up the pole he went.

He made it to the top of the pole all right, but just as he reached the sparrow's nest and leaned over to look in it, his foot slipped, and he reached out his hand to save himself from falling.

There was a big lightning-like flash as his hand touched a wet wire, and poor Heinze-Clark fell from the top of the pole to the ground.

The gang thought he had been killed, but as they rushed over to him they could see that his body was jerking. They were an excited and frightened bunch of kids. A peculiar kind of bluish-gray smoke was coming from his hand that had touched the wire. Someone called his name and tried to get him to talk, but Heinze-Clark was out cold.

Just about that time, a teamster drove up. When he saw what had happened, he was frightened as the kids and told them to help him lay the lad on a blanket in the back of his wagon.

It wasn't far to the hospital. The teamster lashed his horses with a whip and made all possible speed for St. James Hospital. "Copper Ditch" Dugan, a member of the gang, piled in the back of the wagon and sort of held poor Heinze-Clark's head. The injured lad never made a move, and Copper Ditch thought for sure he must be dead.

When they drove up to the hospital, a couple of doctors came rushing out with a stretcher. They wanted to know all the particulars. The boy was carried into a big room and the door shut behind him. His gang waited out in the hall.

Somebody must have told Heinze-Clark's father and mother what happened because in a few minutes they came rushing in. His mother was crying and carrying on, and his father looked pretty sorrowful. A nurse came up behind them and ushered them into his room.

The gang waited out in the hall for near an hour before finally his father came out. He was a big man, his face was pale and drawn, and he had to stop and cough every few words he said. He kept opening and closing his hands as he talked.

"Dennis is in bad shape, fellows," he said. "He's alive, but the doctor is not sure for how long—maybe it would be for the best if he didn't live."

The poor guy sort of gulped at those last words. Big tears came to his eyes and he finished:

"The doctor says, if he should live—he'll never be able to walk again."

Then the father broke into a fit of coughing. It was terrible. The whole gang had big lumps in their throats and anyone of them would have given anything to bust out bawling, but Butte kids didn't cry very often in those days, so they just stood there helpless and looked at Heinze-Clark's old man.

"There's nothing much you can do here, boys," he said. "You might as well go home." He gulped and wiped his eyes. "You might say a little prayer for him—if you know any."

It was a couple of weeks later when they brought Heinze-Clark from the hospital. Copper Ditch Dugan and several others of the gang went over to his house to see him. His mother let them in. She looked sad, but she tried to smile and act happy.

Heinze-Clark was propped up in bed. He looked like a pretty sick boy, but he smiled at his friends kind of sad like. "Hello, fellows," he said, "I guess I didn't find out if there were any eggs in that nest."

His visitors smiled back, but couldn't find anything to say. They just sat there feeling sort of choked up and fooled with their caps and watched their ailing friend. After a while they got up to go. He asked Copper Ditch Dugan to stick around.

As Copper Ditch told it afterwards, after the rest of the gang had gone he turned to him and said: "They can't fool me. There isn't any feeling in my legs, and I know I'm going to be a cripple. I'll never be able to wear that long pants suit. I'm finished up. I'll have to lay in bed all my life or be pushed around in a wheel chair. I'll never be like Heinze or Clark."

Then Copper Ditch said, for the first time in his life he saw Heinze-Clark bust down and bawl like a baby. Copper Ditch tried to change his mind. He told him there were big hospitals in the East where they cured people. He did his best to make him look at things differently, but Heinze-Clark wouldn't listen.

"I don't want to be a cripple," he said. "Of all the gang, you are my best friend and pal. I'm going to give you my box of specimens."

The talking was too much for him, and he fell back on the pillow all tired out. His mother came running in and Copper Ditch left the room.

The gang tried to cheer their pal as best they could. They went out to Bell Creek to pick bunches of johnny-jump-ups, his favorite flowers. Copper Ditch took him over a pot of growing shamrocks his old man had brought from the Old Country. The gang chipped in and brought him plenty of fruit, but Heinze-Clark didn't seem to be getting any better. He just lay in bed and stared at the ceiling all the time.

One evening Copper Ditch and the gang saw Heinze-Clark's father rush out of the house and in a few minutes come back with the priest. Right then they knew things weren't so good. The gang went over in front of the house and stood by the front gate. In a little while they heard Heinze-Clark's mother give a small cry. Then the priest and Heinze-Clark's father came out on the porch. His father was leaning on the priest. His eyes were red, and he was sobbing kind of quiet-like. He saw the boys down by the gate and he walked over slow and said:

"Heinze-Clark has gone forever, boys."

The gang walked away. Nobody said a word, and pretty soon, one by one, they all went home.

There was a wake and his old gang went into the house to have a look at him. There he lay, looking just like he was asleep. He had his glasses on, and they had him dressed up in a long pants suit.

Six of the gang were pallbearers. They looked odd with their skin-tight haircuts and sunburned faces and the shoes hurting their feet because they had been going barefooted all summer.

Heinze-Clark was buried out on the Butte Flat. If you look you can find his grave in the cemetery out there. The headstone says, "Dennis Donovan—Born May 3, 1891—Died July 12, 1905."

But to his gang he's always been "Heinze-Clark," just another Butte kid.

Disasters

AT ITS safest, mining is a dangerous occupation, and the average miner accepts its dangers with a fatalistic attitude. Like most men engaged in dangerous work, he is apt to scoff at it, although the nearness of death is always foreboding.

It is not known what early-day humorist christened loose, hanging slabs of ground with the name of the camp's leading undertaker; but for years, "Bar down the 'Larry Duggan!'" was a common expression for a dangerous slab or rock hanging over a miner's head. Larry Duggan's mortuary on North Main Street was a landmark for years. The old-timer will add that when the safety campaign began to make the mines safer, Larry had himself elected sheriff.

When the cantankerous "Buzzy" air drills first came into operation with their clouds of deadly silicosis-breeding dust the miners promptly labeled them "Widow-makers."

In referring to "missed-holes," or dynamite charges that have failed to explode, it was not uncommon to hear a shift boss tell a miner, "There's a couple of 'requiem high masses' in that stope. Better keep an eye for them." Anything for a laugh.

But joke though he might, the experienced miner early adopted his own safety measures designed to keep accidents at a minimum.

Not counting the unavoidable major disasters the copper camp's average of fatal accidents throughout the years of operation probably created fifty to a hundred widows annually. That's why the cemetery population exceeds the 1940 census. The camp remembers best the big accidents that can't be laughed off.

Butte's first major mining calamity occurred on November 23, 1889. A fire broke out in the shaft of the Anaconda Mine, sending smoke and gas through the workings. Fortunately, the fire occurred between shifts with most of the miners out of the workings. Only six were killed and two badly injured.

It was the custom that when a fire broke out in any mine for every mine on the hill to blow its whistles, setting up a piercing wail that usually scared the town out of its wits, causing understandable fear to those having friends or relatives underground.

"When the mine whistles blew in chorus," says a veteran of the period, "every woman in Butte, whose old man was down in the holes, would throw her shawl over her head, grab a couple of kids, and hit out lickety-split for the mine he was workin' in—dead certain that he was being burned alive."

A fire broke out in the Silver Bow Mine in the spring of 1893, causing the miners to scurry for safety. All but nine escaped. A public funeral was held for the victims with the entire town in mourning, a large sum was collected for the dependents of the victims. Since then Butte has dug deep into its pockets on many similar occasions.

The next big mine fire, while not claiming lives, was the cause of considerable inconvenience. It was in August, 1900 when the hoist and entire surface workings of the Parrot Mine were destroyed by flames. The miners' change dry was among the buildings burned down, and with it, the clothing of the miners. Considerable money and valuables belonging to the miners working in the mine at the time were reduced to ashes.

John Harrington of Centerville, a veteran of that blaze who lost his roll and a "new tailor-made suit" in the conflagration, tells of his experience.

> "I had been workin' day-shift at the Parrot and the night before the fire, I had just paid for a new tailor-made suit, and I put it on and went for a stroll around town. I had a piece of change in me pockets, and it wasn't long before I was sittin' in a faro game.
>
> "Well, sir," continued John, "I never had such luck in me life. I couldn't lose, and long about six o'clock in the mornin', I was winners, a thousand dollars.
>
> "I says to meself, this is one time in your life you won't be a damn fool. You'll save this money and make a trip to the old country. So I has it changed into a thousand-dollar bill and puts it in the inside pocket of me new tailor-made suit.
>
> "It was gettin' late in the mornin' and I didn't have time to change me clothes, so I grabbed me bucket at the boardin' house and hurried up the hill to the Parrot.
>
> "I changed into me diggin' clothes in the dry and left the tailor-made suit and the thousand-dollar bill in the mine-locker, went down into the mine, and put in a tough shift, what with me not havin' a wink of sleep.
>
> "To make a long story short," ended Mr. Harrington, "When I come up out of the mine that evenin', the dry was burned to the ground and with it me thousand dollars and the new tailor-made suit. It was the first and only money I ever saved in Butte," he added sadly, "and I never did get to make the trip to the old country."

Evidently 1911 was a jonah year for mine accidents. On April 24 the engine at the Leonard Mine, while lowering the shift, got out of control. This caused the mine cage with its burden of fourteen men, nine on the upper deck and five on the lower deck, to fall from the surface to the sump, some fifteen hundred feet. The five men on the lower deck were killed outright. The nine on the upper deck were more fortunate, but all received injuries that kept them in the hospital for many months.

Again that year disaster struck the camp. This time at the Black Rock Mine on September 3, and sadly, the victims all were little more than boys.

Before the introduction of child-labor laws, it had been the custom in the Butte mines to hire boys of school age as "nippers" or toolboys. It was their job to go from place to place in the workings of the mines and pick up dull or damaged tools, including drilling steel, and to replace them with tools that had been sharpened and repaired. Each level in the mine had its own nipper.

The nippers carried the damaged tools to the stations on the various levels where they were pulled to the surface, usually about a quarter of an hour before the men were hoisted at the end of the shift. At that time, and before the introduction of "safety-boats" (a container to prevent drills from falling through the grating on the floor of the cage), the collected steel was piled none too carefully on the decks of the mine cages.

Although it was strictly against safety rules, it long had been the custom of the nippers to ride to the surface on the same cage with dull tools and steel, thus gaining a fifteen-minute advantage over the rest of the miners. It was to gain this fifteen minutes that eight Black Rock nippers, not one of whom had reached his twentieth birthday, piled aboard the tool cage on that fatal Sunday morning.

On its trip to the surface, in some unexplained manner, the steel became loosened from the bottom of the cage, and one or more pieces of the heavy, sharp metal forced its way through apertures and protruded into the shaft. The cage rising to the surface at express train speed, became a grinding, tearing juggernaut, pulling the shaft's timbers and wall-plates from their moorings in its wild ascent. The eight nippers were literally ground to pieces. But two were alive when the twisted and battered cage reached the surface. Both were horribly mutilated.

The years 1915–16–17 in turn witnessed the three most devastating disasters in the camp's history, climaxing with the Speculator fire of 1917 that remains to date the most disastrous in the annals of all quartz mining.

On October 19, 1915, sixteen shift bosses and assistant foremen on surface for their lunch hour were grouped around the shaft of the Granite Mountain Mine awaiting the 12:30 whistle to announce the time for lowering the mine cage to take them down below to their work. Beside them on the surface turn-sheets a small hand-truck with twelve cases of forty-per cent dynamite also was waiting to be lowered.

At the first blast of the whistle, from a cause that has never been determined, the twelve boxes of powder exploded with a roar that could be heard for miles. The sixteen men standing around the shaft were blown to atoms. Fingers with rings attached were found a mile from the scene. Undertakers scoured the surrounding hills for days, seeking portions of bodies. What they found was sealed in caskets and a combined public funeral was held.

Shortly after the explosion, several undertakers were engaged in searching for fragments of the victims' bodies. As small parts were found they were placed in one large basket. A well-known character, drawn to the scene with thousands of others, watched with morbid fascination.

"Hm-m-m," he commented to a bystander, "Puttin' 'em all together in one basket—Corkmen, Far-downs, Cousin Jacks, Democrats, Republicans, Masons, and Knights of Columbus. There's goin' to be a helluva mix-up there on Resurrection Day!"

Early the following year fire broke out in the workings of the Pennsylvania Mine. Fortunately, it was undergoing repairs at the time and no great number of men were working. Twenty of the forty or so in the mine at the time fell victims to the deadly gas. Once again Butte mourned and combined funeral services were held with the entire city in attendance.

The United States had been at war over two months on the night of June 8, 1917. War industries were clamoring for copper. Every mine in Butte was working to capacity. Among them was the big Speculator, with close to two thousand miners employed on the two shifts.

Oddly, it was at the Speculator where the "Safety First" campaign had been most stressed. A crew of safety engineers was employed. All modern safety improvements and practices had been installed, and motion pictures showing safety methods were periodically shown to the employees. Attendance was compulsory. The "Company" was desirous of keeping accidents at a minimum and did not tolerate the slightest infraction of safety rules.

But on that June evening, the night shift of some nine hundred men had been lowered and were at work. During the late afternoon and evening, ropemen and shaftmen had been lowering a huge, insulated electric cable to operate the ventilating fans on the lower levels. The heavy cable had somehow become fouled and was hanging suspended in the shaft. For some time the workers had been vainly trying to free it. The assistant foreman on the night shift had descended to aid in the difficulty. The cable was an old one, with the insulation in some places frayed and worn. Sallau, the assistant foreman, his carbide light in hand, was examining it in an endeavor to find some way of breaking the tangle and getting it started down the shaft once more. In some inexplicable manner, his carbide light came in contact with the frayed edge of the insulation.

Like a lighted match dropped in gasoline, the insulation burst into flame. Acting as a chimney, the draft in the up-cast shaft pulled the flames toward the surface, and in an instant the entire length of the cable was ablaze. As the dry shaft timber caught fire, it was but a moment before the entire three thousand feet of shaft had been turned into an inferno.

At the first flash, Sallau and his assistants hurriedly descended out of danger, below the path of the flames. But now the damage was done. Any effort on their part to prevent the spread of the fire was hopeless and would undoubtedly have lead to their cremation. It was but a few moments before the flames were shooting out of the mouth of the shaft on surface, consuming with incalculable speed the timbers, and forcing the deadly smoke and gas onto every level in the mine.

An instant before the cable was ignited the mine cage with two station-tenders aboard had been lowered into the mine. Hardly had it disappeared from surface before flames bellowed forth from the mouth of the shaft. The hapless men had been lowered into a flaming furnace. Too late, the engineer on duty discovered their peril. It was some time later that the white-hot cage was brought back to surface. A few charred bones and metal overall buttons were all that remained on its scorched deck.

Underground, on every level, the scene was the same. Many of the miners, smelling the first whiff of smoke had made a run for it and escaped through the levels of other mines adjoining the Speculator. Fortunately there were connections to neighboring mines on almost every level. These men were quickly hoisted to surface.

On the eighteen-hundred-foot level of the Speculator, two hundred men escaped into the Badger State Mine by battering their way through a fifteen-inch concrete bulkhead with sledge hammers and heavy timbers.

On surface at the mouth of the blazing shaft, any rescue work until the fire had burned itself out, was impossible. Word was sent to all other mines in the camp for rescue crews.

In answer to the call came ambulances, trucks and other vehicles carrying first-aid and fire-fighting equipment. The presence of "dead wagons" and hearses offered a grim foreboding. News had spread rapidly in the city, and thousands came to the mineyards. Scenes were pathetic as those having loved ones below gazed with frantic appeal at the smoking shaft.

Statements gathered from the rescued as they arrived from the other mines were practically all the same. Miners had been compelled to feel their way in the darkness of the drifts and cross-cuts. One of their number who knew the way advanced ahead of the others. Those behind formed a human chain, each holding to the one ahead of him, and staggered blindly through the gases that were becoming stronger minute by minute. The rescued told harrowing tales of hundreds of their fellow-workers lying dead throughout the mine where they had fallen.

Without number were the stories of heroism of the miners. If feats of bravery could have saved the scores of entombed men there would have been but few fatalities, for never were more heroic sacrifices made in any mining catastrophe. Many in the copper camp are alive today because of the deeds of their fellow workers.

Gas from the Speculator had swept into the Diamond Mine almost immediately. Luckily, however, most of the miners employed in this mine had time to reach the safety of the mine cages and were hoisted to the surface. Not all were so fortunate. Con O'Neil, foreman of the mine, and three miners were trapped by the on-rushing gas and died gasping in their tracks.

Hours later, as the fire in the Speculator burned itself out, an attempt was made to enter. Over a dozen volunteers were loaded on the mine cage, among them, the assistant foreman, Sallau, whose carbide light had inadvertently caused the blaze. As the cage reached its destination and the rescuers stepped off, they were met by a blast of the deadly gas and all perished on the turn-sheets of the station. Further attempts at rescue were abandoned until fresh air had been pumped into the mine.

Butte was stunned and shocked. A rapid check of the survivors indicated that over two hundred miners had been trapped below. Barring a miracle, all had perished, for survivors had reported seeing the drifts and stations strewn with dead. Scenes in the mine yard were heartrending. The hospitals were crowded with the injured. Thousands crowded frantically seeking word of some loved one. Regular army soldiers, stationed on guard duty in Butte at the time, were pressed into service and endeavored to keep some semblance of order.

Two days and a night had passed since the first flames had swept up the shaft. Fresh air was being pumped into the mine, and safety engineers decided that at last it was safe for rescue squads to descend to bring up the bodies of the victims. All hope of anyone being alive in the mine had long been abandoned. It was then that a small miracle happened. Sitting in his chair in the engine room, the engineer of the Speculator was astonished to hear a signal flash from the depths where a moment before he had been positive there was no living person.

Somewhere below, someone had escaped the deadly gas.

Again the signal flashed. Startled into instant action, he threw the various levers and throttles. The giant engine hummed, the cable unwound from the whirling drums, and the cage descended to the level the engine-room indicator showed the signal had come from.

A brief pause—and again a signal—this time to hoist.

Up came the cage. Before the astonished eyes of the hundreds who had crowded around the shaft, nine men—blackened—haggard—stepped from the cage, blinking in the sudden sunlight but bringing the joyous news that sixteen more of their fellows were alive below and waiting to be hoisted.

Down the shaft and up again traveled the cage, until in all, twenty-five miners had been brought back from the dead into the sunlight of the mineyard.

It was a startling tale these survivors told—a story of the heroism and sacrifices of one man who died that others might live—the story of Manus Duggan, a common miner; a simple tale of heroism, but twenty-five Butte miners owed their lives to Duggan's act.

Within an hour after the fire started, the twenty-five-year-old miner marshalled a group of twenty-nine men and gathered them together in a cross-cut into which the deadly gas had not yet penetrated. Hastily erecting a makeshift bulkhead of timber, canvas, clothing and dirt, he took charge of the little group of men in the small, cramped cross-cut, keeping up their morale and preventing them from making break for a supposed safety that would certainly have meant their end. As tiny apertures appeared in the bulkhead, Duggan forced them to strip their clothing from their bodies to plug the gaps and keep out the gas.

As the long hours passed, breathing became more and more difficult. When Duggan saw at last that it was only a matter of minutes before they would all succumb, he decided to seek a path of safety for his charges. Taking three of the men, he set out to find a safe path into some other mine, intending, if successful, to come back and guide those left behind. Manus Duggan and his three followers never returned. Days later their blackened bodies were found in a drift where they had fallen.

The remainder of the little band, after waiting a reasonable time for Duggan's return, decided to chance everything in a rush for the station. Any risk was better than slow death in the cross-cut. Desperately they set out in a group. To their joy and surprise on reaching the station they found pure air. The air pumps had done their work well. Frantically, delirious with joy, they gave the station signal and rang for the cage.

Butte received news of their rescue with elation. Houses of sorrow were changed into homes of rejoicing as the rescued men returned. On all sides were words of praise for the hero, Manus Duggan. His wife and three small children were offered the sympathy of the city.

For weeks the copper camp mourned. Both private and public funerals were held. Identification of the one hundred and sixty-three bodies recovered was difficult, and many were never identified. The North Butte Mining Company estimated damage to the mine at a million dollars. Compensation to dependents of the victims totaled $800,000; about $4000 for the life of each miner. To date, it is the camp's greatest disaster. There has not been a major accident since, but the town knocks on wood—the mines are never too safe and anything can happen underground.

The city itself has also had its share of fires, the most disastrous being the million-dollar conflagration of Sunday, September 24, 1905. The fire started in the basement of Symon's large department store. It burned to the ground all of the lower side of the business district of Park Street from Montana Street east for nearly a block. The north side of Park Street extending up to Broadway, another important business street including the Public Library, also was badly damaged. Nine people were injured, but there were no deaths.

John L. Sullivan, famed pugilist, was in the city making a personal appearance at a vaudeville theater. Sullivan accepted the fire as a tribute to his own greatness and later remarked to a San Francisco newswriter: "A hell 'av a fine place—that Butte. They burned down half the town in my honor when I played there last fall!"

Another hot time was the Hale House fire of March, 1898. The Hale House was Butte's largest miners' boarding house, and the fire broke out when most of the miners were asleep in their rooms. In less than five minutes after flames were discovered the entire building was a blazing inferno. Many of the scantily clad miners jumped from the upper stories. A score were killed in the attempt or burned to death, while half a hundred others were injured.

Ten barrels of bonded whiskey were among the many articles destroyed by the blaze. Hearing of this, a grizzled miner bowed his head reverently over the smoking ruins and said: "The ashes of hard-rock miners blessed with hundred-proof whiskey—'tis indeed consecrated ground!"

There are many in the copper camp who compute their length of residence so many years before or after the "Big Explosion." To many a brawny Celt, it succeeded "The Big Wind In Ireland" as an event from which to date all occasions of note.

It came as a terrific shock to the young camp, and it is doubtful if there was a single home in the city that was not in mourning for a relative or friend.

January 15, 1895, marks the date when the entire fire department with the exception of three men and one horse was instantly killed. Scores were blown to atoms and no trace was ever found of them. The property loss reached an estimated $200,000. Practically every window in the city as far north as Walkerville was shattered. In some instances whole families were wiped out. Hundreds were injured by the shrapnel-like rain of steel, timber and hardware that followed the blast. There are several residents of Butte who to this day carry small pieces of nails or steel in their bodies as souvenirs of the occasion.

A local newspaper reported: "Never did a field of battle present a more appalling spectacle at the first light of morn. Butte has more the appearance of a besieged city in the days of war."

The fire started at 10 P.M. in a flour warehouse, a wooden structure, which burned fiercely, casting a great glow in the winter sky and drawing hundreds of people from all parts of the city. The fire department had just arrived and was preparing to attach hose lines when a gust of wind caused the flames to jump from the flour warehouse to the Kenyon, Connell Commercial Company, a wholesale hardware concern next door. Unknown to the crowds that continued to gather, this building stored three hundred and fifty boxes of dynamite.

As the firemen attacked the flames, a small explosion occurred. This acted as a warning and some of the bystanders set up the cry that there was powder in the building. The crowd fell back somewhat, but the warning had come too late. With a mighty reverberation that could be heard for miles, the first big blast killed scores. Bodies were thrown into the air as high as three hundred yards. Mingled with the screams of the dying and wounded could be heard the roar as a rain of steel and timber fell for blocks. A huge railroad-car wheel was blown for eight blocks. Parts of bodies were found a mile away.

The full force of the explosion had hit the members of the fire department. All but three, including the chief, were instantly killed. The fact that their duties called the three of them some distance from blast was all that saved their lives.

On hearing the blast, hundreds of Butte residents rushed to the scene. They at once entered into the work of rescue. Hacks, buggies, and vehicles of all descriptions were being pressed into service to remove the wounded to the hospitals when another mighty explosion took place killing many of the rescuers and pouring steel, timber and debris upon those wounded by the first blast.

Still a third explosion occurred shortly after the second, adding further horror to the holocaust. The street adjoining the place of the explosion was a scene of carnage. Many bodies had been decapitated by the

MONTANA HISTORICAL SOCIETY, HELENA

Busy volunteers in Butte after multiple explosions on January 15, 1895.

flying steel making identification impossible. Great timbers lay across many of the wounded. Now fearing another explosion, rescuers dared not approach close to the flames for more than an hour.

The camp presented a grim scene the following morning. Hundreds filed through improvised morgues seeking loved ones. Mass meetings were held and provisions made for burying the dead and relieving the distressed. Many private homes, hotels and lodging houses were turned into temporary hospitals. Doctors and nurses worked valiantly. Messages of sympathy with many money contributions came from all parts of the country. Private funerals were held for those who could be identified; a combined, public funeral, attended by almost every resident of the city, for the others. A public funeral also was held for the members of the fire department. The business of the saddened city finally resumed its regular trend.

Skibereen's One Mile Limit Ranch: Mountain Oasis

THIS copper camp was anything but a farming community; yet, in the minds of those who were young bloods at the turn of the century, Skibereen's One Mile Limit Ranch directly back of Columbia Gardens, in the rock-faced mountains east of the city, is indelibly recorded.

"Skibereen" Mullins, or "Skib" as he was better known, was a descendant of the ancient Danes who landed on the Emerald Isle. Wild, blue eyes with a glint of the sea, and a mop of wind-blown hair, red with the flash of a summer sunrise proclaimed him of that adventurous race which had settled, survived and multiplied centuries ago on the wild, bleak stretch of Irish coast known as the County of Skibereen.

Men of Skibereen, the famous, battle song of the Irish, bespeaks the caliber of men who called this seacoast home. And Mullins was indeed a "Man of Skibereen. "

Measures of weight were not computed in pounds and ounces in Skibereen. Nothing less than a "stone" counted and a stone was fourteen pounds. Skibereen claimed fourteen stones, Irish weight, and every ounce of it was weather-hardened bone and steel-ringed muscle. A fine figure of a man he was, with a voice on him that could have been heard o'er the roar of the breakers of the windswept shores of his native heath.

Skib was twenty-five when he came to Butte. With hope in his heart and a fight in either fist, he followed the route usually taken by his countrymen. Skibereen to Queenstown; Queenstown to Boston; Boston to Butte; Butte to the Mountain Con Mine, where Jim Brennan was ever willing to give any "lad from home" a job—if he had big shoulders and could push a car of ore up the steep grades of the drifts.

Skib had the big shoulders, he could and did push cars, and his daily tally was satisfactory to Jim Brennan. He did his daily stint in the mine and made it pay, but his heart was not in his work. He who is born of the open spaces, quickly found the stuffy confines of the Mountain Con not to his liking. On off days from the mine, it was Skib's custom to roam the hills around the camp. The mountains and gulches adjoining Columbia Gardens were a particularly favorite haunt of the homesick Irishman.

Columbia Gardens was a popular resort and thousands of residents visited the natural playground each week end. The management, with the approval of the city council, passed a law prohibiting the sale of intoxicating liquors in or within a mile of the park. It was at this time that Skibereen's active brain gave birth to an idea that led to his famous ranch.

Stepping the distance off with great strides, he measured an exact mile from the outer fence of the park. At odd moments, somehow or other, Skib had obtained a smattering of the whys and wherefores of mineral law. He now placed this knowledge to work. At a point an exact mile from the Garden's fence, he posted a mining location notice. This gave him the mineral and surface rights to claim approximately six hundred by fifteen hundred feet. He named the site after himself and his homeland, "The Skibereen." That the mineral contents of his claim were negligible, bothered Skib not a whit. He had other ideas.

With the aid of cronies, giant pine logs were cut and hauled down the mountainside. In a short time, a huge, barn-like building made its appearance on the site. Fences were erected, enclosing the entire property. A tunnel (the "mine" proper) was started into the mountain. A cool, natural spring was sidetracked and the course of its stream changed so that it ran through the tunnel. Skibereen had his own ideas as to the use of the spring, too.

Rustic home-made furniture was installed in the big cabin. A crude bar was carved from rough pine slabs. Butte breweries sent many wagonloads of brew to be stored in the natural refrigerator provided by the tunnel. Many bottles and jugs were also carted to the mountain retreat. Sawdust was sprinkled on the floor in quantities and Skibereen was ready.

MONTANA HISTORICAL SOCIETY, HELENA

Columbia Gardens, ca. 1925.

It had been his intention to name the resort "Skibereen's Mine" but as he reasoned— "They got enough of the mines all week. 'Tis something to take their minds away from thim on Sunday. A ranch or somethin' would be more to their likenin'!" And a ranch it became. A large sign over the gate entrance proclaimed in large green letters that this was "SKIBEREEN'S ONE MILE LIMIT RANCH."

"'Twould be a hell of a rancher who didn't have a big hat," he explained to a customer, so Skib outfitted himself with a large Stetson which became a permanent part of his wardrobe. Hillside historians will tell you that Skibereen at one time had added a pair of spurs to his ranching regalia, but while acting as arbitrator between two of his sportive customers, he had accidentally roweled one of the gentlemen with the sharp points and, deciding they were unsportsmanlike weapons, discarded them.

Livestock on the ranch consisted of a placid Holstein cow. That is, the animal had been gentle when first it came to the ranch, but the extraordinary carrying-ons soon changed her into a surly and suspicious beast.

Skibereen was never a man to make a secret of his ranch. He and the big hat were much in evidence on the streets of Butte. The strapping Irishman would have been picked by the casual stranger as a prosperous cattle baron. He and the hat were always present at the livestock conventions of the State.

The ranch prospered. Miners from the hill and many other thirsty citizens welcomed it as an oasis near the arid Columbia Gardens. The many parties were large and hilarious. The biggest crowds came on Sundays and holidays. But regardless of size, Skibereen ruled his domain with an iron hand. All arguments were held under house rules and fighting in the barroom was forbidden. Those insisting on avenging their honor or having good clean fun via the fisticuff route were directed to the corral. On these occasions, the cow, if present, was turned out and the brawlers had at it in the enclosure. Skib always insisted that combatants part as friends—after the usual formality of "setting them up" for the house. Few permanent feuds ever developed at Skibereen's Ranch.

Skibereen operated the ranch only in the summer. During the winter, taking the cow with him, he moved into Butte and worked in the mines. Because of a generous nature each winter found him broke, and the job in the mines was imperative.

He continued to run the ranch into the years of prohibition but the Volstead Act sounded the death knell for the business. Uncle Sam tolerated no nonsense, as Skibereen soon learned. Besides, the automobile was making the clientele of Columbia Gardens dwindle, as more and people were able to drive out of the camp on holidays. In 1920 Skib dismantled his equipment, tore down the building, filled in the tunnel and returned to the mines.

But Skibereen was a child of the open. Hot boxes and dusty raises played havoc with the giant Irish body. Soon the silicosis cough of "miner's con" indicated failing health. Skibereen died four years later, another addition to the population of the cemetery on the Flat.

Girls of the Line

THE words of a favorite bawdyhouse ballad of early-day Western mining camps went:

> "First came the miners to work in the mine,
> Then came the ladies who lived on the line."

And Butte was little different from the other camps. With the first hundred miners settled and working for their pay checks, mysteriously, out of nowhere appeared the mademoiselles to help spend them. As the population of Butte City grew in bounds, so, also, did the ranks of the "sporting girls."

As a grizzled old veteran of that period told it:

> "They were like bees attracted to the honey. Let a strike be made anywhere, and before sun-up the next day, there would be a dozen or more of them set up and ready for business."

Another old-timer adds this information:

> "They were a necessary evil. They did little harm—and maybe some good. Many's the miner who'd never wash his face or comb his hair, if it wasn't thinkin' of the sportin' girls he might meet in the saloons."

And for the first year or so in the existence of the infant camp, it was in the saloons that the girls circulated and solicited their trade. The Clipper Shades at Wyoming and Park Streets, a combined dance hall and saloon, harbored many of these courtesans.

The Butte *Miner* on January 12, 1899, reported on the death of one of the proprietors:

"Pete Hanson, the 'King of Galena street' is dead. He was a notorious man. Under his management and that of his partner, J. W. Kenny, the Clipper Shades acquired such a reputation that letters dropped in letter boxes throughout the country addressed merely to 'The Clipper Shades'—without mention of city, county or state, arrived at their destination.

"Hanson was reputed to be a 'druggist'—that is, he made a practice of drugging men who came into his saloons with money so that they may be 'rolled' in safety by the horde of pickpockets that clustered about his place of business.

"Pete always denied the drugging. 'When a man is determined to get drunk,' he would say, 'the safe course is to allow him to get drunk. No drugs are needed in such instances.'

"Report has it that when a man with money was found touring the twilight zone, a string or wire was pulled that rang a bell in Hanson's. Apparently each house had its own bell because the ring immediately brought a crook or robber to relieve the visitor of his roll."

By 1884, the first "line" had been established on the south side of East Galena Street between Main and Wyoming Streets, within a hundred yards of the main street of the camp. It consisted of a few hastily constructed shacks and tents. The earlier occupants were largely negresses and mulattoes, with a sprinkling of half-breed Indian squaws and a few Mexican and Spanish.

Of the latter was Carmen, self-claimed as the original pioneer of the industry in Butte. An early-day writer described her as a "full blossomed Spanish rose who would just as soon stick a stiletto into your gizzard as stand at the bar and have a drink with you."

Another pioneer of this period was a dusky-hued charmer known as "Nigger Liz." Both Liz and Carmen were pioneers of the earlier gold camps of Virginia City and Bannack. Both remained at their profession until they were withered, toothless hags. Carmen died in the early nineteen hundreds, while Liz lived to be well past eighty and died in 1917. Commenting on their longevity, a resident remarked: If, as the preachers say, 'the wages of sin are death', those two old girls had a hell of a long wait for payday."

With the opening of more mines and the influx of more and more miners, several influential members of the community, never adverse to turning an honest penny, bought up at ridiculously low prices considerable land on the lower side of Galena Street. In an area only a few blocks from the heart of town they proceeded to erect a long line of one room wooden shacks which were promptly rented to the women at exhorbitant prices. Indeed, it is no secret that more than one Butte fortune was founded on profits from the rental of these hovels.

Still other "speculators" and "investors" turned their idle capital and benevolent attention to the north side of Galena Street, and, in a fortnight or so, myriads of cheaply constructed saloons, music halls and gambling joints made a mushroom appearance. This one street became one of the wildest and most wide-open districts in the United States, ranked by many with the Barbary Coast in San Francisco and Corduroy Road in New Orleans.

Prominent on the street was The Casino, a combination saloon, dance hall, prize fight arena, theater, and brothel. It is estimated that at its peak, more than a hundred girls worked out of this one establishment. Its doors never closed. Gun play was common and many killings were chalked up against the resort. Prize fights were held there each week. Stanley Ketchell, later middleweight champion of the world, at one time worked in the Casino as a bouncer and received much of his earlier ring experience there.

The story is told that Ketchell, while employed at the Casino, became involved with one of the dance hall girls and as a result was arrested and charged with vagrancy. A Butte police judge handed him "a floater," which meant twenty-four hours to leave town. Ketchell shook the copper dust of Butte from his heels, so embittered at the Butte police that he would never return, although he was offered thousands of dollars to do so when he later became champion. Neither, it is said, would he allow the name of Butte to appear in any of the stories of his life.

On the south side of the street close to a hundred girls were crowded into the tiny cell-like compartments or "cribs." All nations and races were represented. On the door of each compartment was emblazoned the name, or "nom de crib" of its occupant. Names such as Blondetta, French Erma, Austrian Annie, Dotty, Jew Jess, Mexican Maria, and scores of others as descriptive and colorful are remembered by those who were Butte's gay young bloods during those years.

A dozen saloons in the district did a thriving business. Every crib had an electric call-box system hooked up with the various saloons. Beer sold in the cribs for a dollar a pint bottle, and nearly a score of messengers or "runners" as they were better known, were kept on the move day and night, answering calls and delivering drinks. It was a bonanza for the girls, many of them earning as much as sixty dollars an evening. A contemporary observer described it:

> "I've often seen it on the old line with the girls late in the evening walking up the street, their stockings so weighted down with silver dollars that it was all they could do to navigate. I've seen them having to use both hands to keep their stockings from falling and let money spill out over the street."

The district was well patrolled by the police, and petty thievery, holdups, fighting, disturbance and rolling of drunks were kept at a minimum. The late Chief of Police Jere Murphy delighted in telling of an occurrence involving a certain police officer patrolling the district when Murphy was a captain.

It seems that the chief at that time had suspected the officer in question of spending entirely too much time hobnobbing with the girls of the district. He sent Murphy down to investigate.

It was a bitterly cold winter evening, and although he searched the street thoroughly he could see neither hide nor hair of the cop who should be patrolling his beat. Inquiries brought forth the information that the missing policeman had been seen entering the crib of a certain blonde.

Murphy soon found the place and pounded upon the door. There was no reply. Murphy pounded again.

"Open it up, or I'll kick it down!" Murphy bellowed.

This brought results, and a disheveled damsel poked her head out the door. Murphy rudely pushed her aside and entered the crib. There was no policeman in sight.

"Where's the flatfoot that should be out on the street poundin' his beat?" Murphy growled.

"No cops in here, Jere. This is a respectable crib—and there's no money in cops—they want everything on the cuff."

"Never mind the funny stuff," Jere countered, and continued his search. No cop—but Jere's keen eyes noticed that peculiarly enough for such a cold night a window into the alley was partly open. Reposing beneath the bed were a pair of number twelve brogans.

"Well," Murphy would laugh when telling it, "the blonde stuck to her story, and I never said a word about the open window or the shoes, but I purposely stood in the open door questioning her for nearly an hour. The two of us were about half froze, but not a sign of me brave bobby.

"To make a long story short," Murphy would continue. "The next morning one of our policemen was down in the hospital with a bad case of pneumonia. He was never suspended. The chief and I figured that his sickness was punishment enough. When he got well, he was transferred to pounding a lonesome beat down in South Butte where the temptations weren't so great."

Another inmate of the district was the notorious Jew Jess, who police claimed was one of the cleverest pickpockets in the Northwest. The girl was personable and smart as a whip. Times without number she had been arrested, but rarely convicted. Jess was a drug addict, and when "junked up," her crafty brain and nimble fingers were capable of anything.

The story is told of Jess being hailed before a police magistrate on the usual charge of petty larceny and vagrancy. The evidence on this occasion was rather vague. The man who accused her of rolling him was not able to prove the charges, and the judge was forced to dismiss her.

Apparently under the influence of a recently administered "shot," Jess, in gratitude, threw her arms around the broad shoulders of the surprised judge.

Embarrassed, his honor finally disengaged her and blushingly endeavored to rearrange his disheveled clothing. A few moments later he discovered that his watch, wallet, tie pin and lodge emblem were missing.

A police officer was sent to rearrest the girl, but not a trace of the missing articles could be found. Indignantly, she asserted her innocence, and without a single shred of evidence to convict her the chagrined judge was forced to release Jew Jess again. About a week later a messenger delivered a package containing the missing articles to the judge's chambers. There was no explanation.

Down on the line, Jess could usually be found sitting in the window of her tiny room knitting or sewing, the picture of domesticity—that is, when she wasn't otherwise occupied.

Another girl of the district was the much publicized Mabel Ford, alleged to be the one-time wife of Bob Ford, who shot Jesse James. She delighted in recounting lurid details of "the shooting," at which she claimed to have been present. Her story was that she deserted Ford because of the cowardly killing.

Wesley Davis, early day Butte journalist and author, describes in his *Sketches of Butte*, a typical Galena Street crib:

> "A bed in one corner, in another a stove, a coal hod and bundle of kindling. A small dresser with a wash basin against the wall.

Permeating everything a mixed odor of disinfectant, hair oil and cheap perfume. On the walls, a few art pictures, oddly enough, usually of some pastoral or equally innocent scene, never a picture of a pornographic nature. A photograph or two, usually of other prostitutes or the favorite pimp of the moment."

In another chapter of his book, Davis describes the street itself:

"It seemed like a street leading into hell. Young men, boys, old men; hundreds of them wandering about. Girls in the doors and windows soliciting in honeyed words. Young girls, some looking as though they should be in school. Beauty, withered hags, Indian squaws, mulattoes, Japanese, Chinese. Every race and color. Here and there a Chinaman with a wash basket. Indians with gay colored blankets. Noise. Ribaldry. The shrill shrieks of a police whistle. The clang of the patrol wagon. Drunken cries. Maudlin tears. Bodies for sale."

A pioneer of the camp enlightens the scene with this description of Galena Street:

"'Tis well indeed I remember the old time Galena Street. It was a tough hole if there ever was one. 'Twas sin and virtue crawling through the stinking street—where Salvation Army girls were passing the tambourine and trying at the same time to convert the painted hussies in the dives. And where sneakin' pickpockets were waitin' in dark corners and doorways to give the drunken miners a knock on the head and take their money.

"There were some sprightly lookin' lasses down there too. A lot of them prettier by far than the theater and society ladies with their pictures in the paper. But there was plenty of tough lookin' blisters too. A man could have got hydrophobia from even lookin' at them. The better lookin' ones—a man could take them up town to a dance and not be a bit ashamed. They knew how to act like ladies when away from the district—and did it too. I seen one of them up and give a poke in the face to a masher on Park Street one afternoon, when he, not knowin' who she was, tried to flirt with her. They might have been bad, but most of them always knew their place.

"And another thing—not that I'm stickin' up for them, for there were some real divils amongst them—but a lot of them wore

> more clothes sittin' in their doorways waitin' for business than some of the women do nowadays on the streets.
>
> "And you'd never see them up against the bars in the saloons up town. Down on Galena Street—maybe—but when they wanted a drink up town they went in the side or alley entrances and drank in the wine rooms out of sight. The one thing that gave a lot of them away was that they were the only women you'd ever see smokin' cigarettes."

This was the copper camp's "line" in the 'nineties.

But already murmurs of reforms were being heard. The blaring street was on the direct path to two churches. On the Sabbath, worshippers from the East Side had to pass directly through the district or else take a roundabout course. These murmurings soon became cries of indignation, and finally in 1903 the City Council ordered that the district be moved from the street into the alleys.

None of the girls was compelled to undergo any great inconvenience. The conversion was simplicity itself. The windows and doors opening on Galena Street were merely boarded over and new doors and windows cut into the rear of the shacks. Sidewalks were laid in the alley and presto, Butte's new line came into being.

The camp was still growing rapidly, and the new line, if not quite as open, became far larger than the old. Hundreds of girls arrived to share in the prosperity. There are records of girls from homes of refinement in other parts of the country, allegedly attracted by tales of easy money. Their intention, the old-timers say, was to remain in the business long enough to accumulate a stake, and then return to their homes without anyone being the wiser. This, some of them succeeded in doing, although the greater part drifted until they became permanently a part of the life.

Several real estate men reaped a harvest from this new district. Substantial buildings were erected to replace the crumbling shacks and to accommodate the influx of the demimondaines, second stories were later added to many of the buildings. Utilizing available space still further, excavations were dug, and what was known as the "subway" appeared. Girls were charged rentals of as high as five dollars a night for the cribs, many of which now had hot and cold running water.

It is conservatively estimated that during the period from 1904 to 1917 there were close to a thousand girls quartered in the district at one time. Some boasted that it was the largest red-light district in the United States after the closing of the Barbary Coast in San Francisco.

On Saturday nights and pay-nights it was not unusual for as many as three or four thousand men to be crowded along the "Board Walk," "Pleasant Alley" or the many "terraces" which made up the enclosure. To be sure, there were many more single men in the camp at that time than there are today. But that the visitors were not all bachelors may be gathered from a remark made by one woman at that time: "If it wern't for the married men, half us girls would starve to death."

Each inmate, for a fee of ten dollars a month, was issued a license by the city. The law regarding the license was strict, and fines and jail sentences were meted out for nonpayment.

Pimps, known to the miners as "P. I.'s," "McGoofers," or "John McGuimps," were not encouraged. The late Jere Murphy as chief of police constantly harried them, and fines and jail sentences trimmed down their earnings and leisure time. It was impossible to keep a line on all, however, and it was no secret that scores of the silk-shined gentry lived about the city and waxed fat on the earnings of their women.

Soon after the opening of the new district, the color line was drawn. All Negroes were forced to move a half-block farther south on an alley. Here, scores of the dusky-hued damsels plied their trade. A scattering of whites, mostly those whose youth and charm had fled, were also located on this street. Aptly, it became known as "Four Bit Alley."

On the north side of Mercury Street, between Main and Wyoming Streets, were the de luxe establishments or "parlor houses." These were not ordinary brothels. It is doubtful if in the city there were any more elaborately furnished residences than the pretentious "parlor" establishments.

The finest of silken draperies and upholstery, art treasures worth a small fortune and ornate furniture went into the furnishing of the superbagnios. Neatly clad colored maids and Chinese servants greeted the guests at the doors. Each house operated by a bediamonded "madame," had a score or more of attractive, well-groomed girls. One of the most pretentious houses, operated by the famous Lou Harpell, openly advertised on theater and race track programs—long before Earl Carroll made the slogan famous—that "the most beautiful girls in the world" were located at her place of business. Old-timers are ready to admit that the statement was pretty close to being the truth.

If the old Galena Street and the new line were the playground of the miners and the common man, the parlor houses were the stamping ground of the millionaire copper kings and their friends. It was nothing out of the ordinary for the rich playboys to spend several thousand dollars in an evening. Champagne was the common beverage, and diamonds, the least of gifts bestowed upon the lovely ladies.

Besides Lou Harpell's place, Belle Rhodes, Mabel Loy and Molly DeMurska had similarly ornate establishments. Each house was known by the name of the madame who operated it. In later years the aforementioned ladies were succeeded by Beryl Hastings, Pansy Brasier, Lucille Howard and Mae Malloy, who christened her place, "The Irish World."

At the corner of Galena and Wyoming Streets stood the Copper King, a three-story structure built in 1892. While never a brothel or parlor house, the hostelry was home for many of the girls who operated in the cribs. It served as headquarters for the locality and practically all the girls received their mail at the place. A large barroom was conducted in connection with the hotel business.

A reform wave hit Butte during the first World War, and without warning the entire district was closed by civic order.

Hundreds of girls were turned out, many of them homeless and penniless. They turned to the hotels and rooming houses. Many openly solicited on the principal streets of the city. This situation continued until the early nineteen-thirties when the old line was reopened. But is now only a shadow of its once-famous self. Seldom now are there a half-hundred girls to be found on the one small thoroughfare which is dubbed "Venus Alley."

The Old Comique

THE copper camp was operating high, wide and handsome in 1893. The lusty camp of a dozen years earlier had discarded its swaddling clothes and won a place among the leading cities of the West. Miners were flocking to the town from every point of the globe. In their wake trailed more and more of the camp followers from the cesspools of the world—gamblers, thugs, confidence men, madames and their gay-lady charges; panderers and procurers, the riffraff of every underworld from Corduroy Road in New Orleans to the Barbary Coast of San Francisco.

As a honey bee to a hive, this flashy element flew to the music halls of the camp.

Earlier there had been the notorious "Clipper Shades," situated at Wyoming and Park Streets and the equally unsavory place which had operated under a dozen names but was most generally known as "The

MONTANA HISTORICAL SOCIETY, HELENA

The Comique Theatre as depicted in the Holiday Miner, *1887.*

Wide World." The latter was located on East Park Street between Main and Wyoming Streets in the heart of the city. Both offered entertainment and feminine companionship of a sort.

As an old-timer of that period aptly put it: "With a few drinks of the arsenic they sold at those places, a squaw, a Mexican, a nigger wench, or a Barbary Coast blonde, all looked alike—and you could spend your money on one as quick as the other."

But now, as the miners flocked in and Butte assumed the characteristics of a city, something more classy was desirable. So it was in the early part of 1893 that the Comique first opened its doors—and for five long years they never closed. Night and day, week in and week out, this palace of joy catered to the varied tastes of the miners. Month after month, into the hands of diamond-bedecked bartenders, flashily dressed gamblers, painted demoiselles and their John McGuimps, in a never-ending stream poured the hard-earned dollars of the miners.

The Comique was located on the first block on South Main Street, on the west side of the street. Its site is now occupied by the stock and bond division of the Metals Bank at the principal corner of town. In fact, the original building was torn down to make room for the bank.

The music hall was housed in a garish, two-story structure with an ornate front, architecturally patterned after the music halls of the East. In mode of operation, according to old-timers, "hell, itself, might have been used as a model."

The Comique had two entrances, the one off Main Street for the common trade and another entrance off the alley for the use of the "respectable" element who wished to see, but not to be seen.

Steps led up from the alley entrance to the "gallery," in reality a circle of stall-like boxes, each box a separate compartment with an iron bolt on the inside of the door. A small slide and a narrow shelf were attached to the door where drinks could be passed in. The front of the boxes looked down upon the stage and floor below. Completely covering the front of the boxes was a fine-mesh wire screen. Scenes were painted on this screen. An ingenious arrangement, for the occupants could see all that was going on, without being seen themselves.

It was in the boxes that the aristocracy of the town disported themselves, and if credence can be given to countless tales told by those who remember, "the white-collared gentry were not far behind the miners on the lower floor, when it came to passing an evening of hell-raising.

"Sawdust, inches deep, was sprinkled on the main floor. Tables for four were scattered here and there about the auditorium. Girls clad in gaudy, abbreviated evening dresses acted as both waitresses and entertainers. At intervals one would mount a table to sing or dance to the accompaniment of a tinny piano. Without fail the reward was a shower of coins.

Girls visited the boxes in the gallery and the tables on the lower floor with every round of drinks. A red ticket was included with each order. The was the girl's commission. Tipping was lavish. Old-timers agree it was nothing out of the ordinary for a popular singing waitress to earn several hundred dollars in a week dependent, of course, on the ingenuity, pulchritude and persuasiveness of the girl. But the greater part of their earnings invariably found its way into the pockets of the John McGuimps, a luxury which even the poorest of the girls must afford.

The panderers, in turn, dropped the money in panguingui, a game which the miners said "was developed to keep the pimps off the streets." It was an endless chain, but one thing was certain—very little of the money ever returned to the miners.

The Comique stage performances were on the order of a combined vaudeville and burlesque show, with occasional added feature attractions. Often the acts were of excellent quality. Such old time music halls were the forerunners of the vaudeville theaters, and it was in such places that many of the later famous vaudeville and stage stars received their start.

The audience was generous with its applause. All acts received ovations. Encores were demanded by boisterous cheering, whooping, and the throwing of money upon the stage. The entertainment changed weekly, with hit acts often held over for several weeks.

The Comique flourished until 1898, when competition of the theaters and honky-tonks of the "district," half a block away, proved too great. Then the famous music hall was turned into a "more refined" type of variety theater. It continued with varying success under a score of managements, and ended up as one of the first motion picture theaters of the city.

As to the girls, the stories are varied. Many of them, it is claimed, drifted onto the "line." Others married patrons of the Comique. Some of them married into wealth, while many contented themselves with the lot of a miner's wife. Most of the marriages turned out happily, the girls becoming respected matrons and leaders in many fields in the life of the community.

Wakes for the Dead

THE old time Butte miner considered it disrespectful to allow the remains of a friend to make the last trip to the cemetery on the "Flat" without at least two evenings laid out in convivial company.

The old-timers and their wives fully realized, too, that a man can do very little "mourning" over a cup of tea. Intoxicating drinks were nearly always provided at the old time wakes. They were doled out in quantities that insured a maximum of conversation, but an amount that might lead to the maudlin or boisterous was frowned upon.

Death and the dead were respected and held in awe in Butte. Words of praise for the good deeds of the departed were saved for the wake nights much as had been the custom in Ireland and Wales for centuries. There was always some good in a man that would bear retelling at his wake, which was usually held in the home of the deceased, or, if he were not a family man, in the home of a relative or friend.

Probably, in no other city in America have people turned out in such numbers to pay respect to the departed than in the copper camp, nor has the custom been handed down so completely from the "old country." In late years the nightlong wake has become almost a memory, yet there is today, at the funeral parlors and at the homes of the departed, a constant stream of mourners through the evening hours and during the day. Butte is as deeply conscious of death as it is of life.

Politicians have long been noted as inveterate wake-attenders. A local wag, once commenting on the latter fact, remarked: "'Tis no wonder considerin' the number of years they've been votin' the names of the dead on Election day."

Early day residents tell of two of the chronic wakegoers in the old days—"Paddy, the Ghoul" and "Mary, the Ghost." Neither was ever known to miss an important wake. That neither usually had even a nodding acquaintance with the deceased during his lifetime made little difference to the pair. "Mary, the Ghost" was most adept in the rendition of the Old Irish wail or "keen," and was ever ready to shed tear after a preliminary glass or so of "poteen."

Oddly enough, "Paddy, the Ghoul" was remembered in the will of a friend whose wake he had faithfully attended. He used the bequest to take a trip back to the old country, where, he remarked, "They know how to hold a good wake."

The sexes never mingled at a wake. Women gathered in one room and talked over the things that women have talked about since time immemorable. The men congregated in the kitchen, and their conversation was generally words of commendation for the deceased, or of politics and mining. Usually the testimony was sincere and heartfelt despite the shortcomings which the deceased may have had.

Humorous happenings at the wakes were not unusual. A pair of friends of a dead man, one named O'Neill and the other, Patrick Foley, were in attendance at the wake.

Sometime previously, O'Neill had purchased a pair of shoes which proved too tight for him. He presented them to his friend Foley, whose feet were not so large. Foley was wearing the shoes at this particular wake.

The two were seated opposite each other in the crowded little kitchen. After an exchange of greetings, and a word or two about the sudden passing of their friend, O'Neill's eyes alighted on the shoes now adorning the feet of Foley.

"How's the shoes wearin', Paddy?" he inquired.

Embarrassed before the crowded room, Foley mumbled some unintelligible reply, and made an attempt to change the subject. O'Neill, however, was not to be denied.

"You know, Paddy," he insisted, "those were one of the finest pairs of shoes I ever had on me feet. I paid six bucks for them. If it wasn't for the damn things pinchin' me corns, I'd have never given them away."

Every eye in the room was on poor Foley. His face reddened, and he reached down, untied and removed the footwear. Arising with the shoes in hand, and with one wrathful movement, he flung the pair of them into O'Neill's face—turned about—and in his stocking feet, angrily stalked from the room.

O'Neill ruefully rubbed his bruised face, retrieved the shoes from the floor, and in an injured tone addressed the assemblage.

"Now, isn't that a hell of a way for a man to treat ye, after ye've given him the shoes off your feet?"

In the early days, the holding of a wake in an undertaking parlor was practically unheard of. An Irish lady of the old school who had attended one of the modern mortuary wakes remarked to her husband upon arriving home:

"I never felt so sorry for anyone in me life," she lamented. "There they were, turnin' out the lights on the poor divil at tin o'clock, and lavin' him alone all night in the dark."

But today wakes are seldom held in the homes. The funeral homes, as they are now called, provide luxurious accommodations where friends of the departed gather. Liquor is taboo at the modern wake and the discussions are flat and perfunctory compared to the earlier days.

Occasionally a mourner of the old type makes his appearance at the modern wake, and sometimes is the cause of much worry and annoyance to the professional attendants. A story is told by a Butte mortuary employe, who through his many years in the business is as well acquainted with the old wakes as he is with the modern ones.

As he tells the story—one of the old-time miners of Butte had died. A brother and sister were the sole survivors and the wake was being conducted at a funeral parlor. The surviving brother was of the old school. He believed that no successful wake could be held without the addition of some liquid cheer.

In fact, he felt that a drop or two on any or all occasions was never amiss, and, upon learning of his brother's death, he had proceeded to drown his sorrow with all possible haste.

His sister, a righteous individual, had been making strenuous efforts to sober him up and have him in a fairly presentable shape for the wake. His alcoholic supply was cut off, and never for a moment did she allow him to get out of her sight. He had strict orders that under no conditions was he to leave the funeral parlor unless accompanied by her.

His sorrow was complete. Lying dead was his only brother, and he himself suffering from the most vicious of hangovers, with a hovering sister always in the offing to keep a watchful eye on his every move. The evening progressed. Mourners were continually arriving at intervals, and after paying respects to the deceased and offering consolations to the brother and sister, making their departure.

As the hours passed, the sister's watchful eye discerned a gradual change coming over her charge. At first, shaky, silent and morose, his spirits could be noticed to be rising until he was becoming almost jovial in his demeanor, and was fast becoming the "life" of the wake. There could be but one answer to this transformation. His sister went looking for the bottle, but to no avail. Denials met her accusations, and a thorough search of his person revealed nothing. She was certain that he had not been outside of the establishment. There was no place in the parlor where a bottle could be hidden without her knowledge.

She thought it over, and at last a light began to dawn. The brother had been making regular and frequent trips to the men's rest room, purportedly to smoke a cigarette.

She sought out the attendant who made a thorough search of the men's room without finding any trace of the bottle. Not satisfied, she searched the room herself, not missing a corner or cranny, but still no sign of any liquor.

The evening dragged on, and there was now no longer any doubt in her mind. The brother had passed the jovial state, and was fast approaching a stage that bordered on intoxication. Yet the mysterious source of his supply had not been discovered. The very next time he weaved his way unsteadily towards the men's room, the sister followed him.

Down the long, narrow hall leading to the lavatory, she tip-toed on this trail. At the end of the hall, and directly across from the rest room was a door slightly open. Watching in the shadows, she saw the thirsty brother slip through this entrance. Silently, she followed, and as she glanced into the room a terrified scream came from her frightened lips.

In the little room, laid out on a slab was the sheet-covered corpse of an elderly person, and bending over it, and in the act of raising the body from its resting place was the erring brother. Beneath the upraised body, her terrified eyes beheld a quart bottle of whiskey with four-fifths of its contents gone. Here, at last, was his hiding place.

The brother confessed. A sympathetic friend, calling to pay his respects to their dead brother, had smuggled the bottle into the funeral parlors. The safe, if unique, hiding place had been his own idea.

The Callaghans

The Priest and the Bum

THERE were two Callaghans in the camp at the turn of the century. Although they spelled their names differently, they were both men of note in a city of notables. The Reverend Father J. J. Callaghan was a kindly Catholic priest who won the hearts of high and low in the town by his charitable acts and his observance of the Golden Rule. The other was an irresponsible, but nevertheless lovable character who brought many a smile to the old town. He was never known by any name but "Callahan the Bum."

Father J. J. Callaghan was a true man of God. He lived with and for the poorer people of the mining city and erected his Sacred Heart church among the hovels and shabby dwellings of the East Side. He knew practically every boy and girl in Butte by their first and last names. He was a friend of the homeless, the sinner, the drifter and derelict and although an advocate of total abstinence from liquor, he was never known to turn down a shaky alcoholic for the price of an eye-opener. If he did not have the money himself, he often took the mendicant into a nearby saloon and ordered the bartender to fix him up and charge the cost of the liquor to him.

The mining city loved the frail, pale-faced priest. Rich and poor of all creeds doffed their hats in his presence. He organized one of the first parochial schools in the city, and gave up his living room, dining room, and bedroom for class rooms. Through his influence he found hundreds of jobs for the unemployed during "shut down" times. Truckloads of groceries and fuel were delivered to impoverished families through his efforts. To the copper camp, Father Callaghan was no less then a saint.

Never a rugged man, his overworked, frail physique could not stand under the strain and he died at thirty-eight. The entire town went into mourning. Every available hack and buggy in Butte, Anaconda, and Helena was pressed into service to follow his body to the grave. Five thousand people on foot walked in the procession to the cemetery, while eighteen special street cars, each carrying sixty people, slowly brought up the end of the long procession down Montana Street. Thousands of every creed and color stood bareheaded on the streets, as the funeral passed by, many of them from Butte's underworld, with tears streaming unashamed down their faces. White-surpliced altar boys numbering one hundred, and the entire police force headed the procession. Eight thousand people stood outside the cemetery gates while three thousand gathered around the grave. It was Butte's homage to a man beloved by his fellow men.

Callahan the Bum was in his prime in the late nineties and the early years of the present century When not in one of the two jails, his booming voice could be heard in one or another of the cheaper saloons which dotted the business district. No ordinary bum was Callahan. He had an education, and a good one. He could quote Shakespeare or go through portions of the ritual of the Catholic mass with equal ease. Rumor had it that he had once studied to be a priest. But as some said, "the curse of the hard liquor" was on him. He drifted, daily, from saloon to saloon begging for drinks and chanting his eternal psalms until he accumulated a load too great for even Callahan to carry. It was usually then that some flinty-hearted bartender would call up the wagon, and Callahan would be again carted off to the jail "under the [City Hall] clock."

Possessed of a rare wit, Callahan made colorful copy for the newswriters covering the city hall beat. The news files show that there was rarely a week when the name of Callahan the bum wasn't to be found on the pages of the daily press.

It was the summer of 1901. The weather was extremely warm, and unaccountably Callahan had a five dollar note and was "buying for the house" at Jerry Mullin's place on North Main Street. Callahan, when in the money, was generous, and at the moment was acting the perfect host and instructing Jerry to fill them up again, "and see what the boys in the card room will have."

At this instant a salesman came through the swinging doors that served as an entrance to the resort. Callahan, as befitted the host, stood at the front end of the bar, and received the full impact of one of the doors.

The stranger apologized, "I beg your pardon, sir," he pleaded, "I was in a rush and didn't see you standing in front of the door."

Callahan, however, wasn't to be so easily appeased. Swinging from the vicinity of the floor, he hit the salesman full on the button, knocking him to the sawdust. A frantic bartender called the police and Callahan was once more looking out of the hurry-up wagon on his way to the City Hall.

The next morning Police Judge Boyle summed up the charges.

"There was no excuse for your hitting the man," said the judge.

"You admit yourself, he begged your pardon after he accidentally hit you with the door."

Callahan drew himself up and in dramatic tones answered: "Yes Your Honor, admittedly, but that's one time *the pardon came too late!*"

So amused was judge Boyle that he dismissed Callahan with a warning.

While never denying being a bum, Callahan had a heart as big as a watermelon. "The shirt off me back to a friend, if I had a shirt!" is the way Callahan put it. "If I am a better bum than the average, sure it's a God-given talent, and why shouldn't I share up with those who haven't the knack of bumin' at all?"

The following story about Callahan has often been told. There are good church-going people who will deny it, while others affirm it.

They were erecting the new Sacred Heart Church, and the pastor in charge, Father Callaghan, was having trouble making ends meet. The church was nearly completed and there was as yet no bell nor funds to buy one. The kindly priest had instituted a city-wide campaign for money. Times were tough and the amount needed fell short by nearly two hundred dollars.

Father Callaghan had often befriended Callahan the Bum. Indeed the Bum had at times boasted relationship to the good father, although their names were not spelled alike. Walking through the business district one day the priest ran into Callahan. At once, as was his practice, the latter put the touch on the priest.

"Only a 'bit,' father," he pleaded, "till I get me mornin's mornin'. I'm as weak as a cat." Callahan was always honest in his begging, and never said he wanted a bed or a meal when it was whiskey he craved.

Father Callaghan dug into his meager funds and came forth with a dime and a nickel.

"Thank you a thousand times, Father," said Callahan. "This will fix me up and I'll quit the drinkin' and get a job in the Anaconda first thing tomorrow morning. But what is it that makes ye look so mournful?" he added—"sure your face is as long as that of an old country leprechaun."

More to make conversation than anything else, Father Callaghan told Callahan the Bum of his predicament and the hard time he was having to raise the money for the bell.

"Is that all that's botherin' ye?" sympathized Callahan. "A mere two hundred dollars is it? Think no further of it, Father, I'll go out this afternoon and I'll bum that much for ye, and I'll have the money for ye tonight."

Father Callaghan smiled sadly and went on his way. In an hour he had forgotten all about the conversation.

But Callahan the Bum didn't forget. He purchased his "mornin's mornin' " and set to work. Into every saloon in the business district he traveled. Recruiting every bum and derelict he chanced upon, he explained to each Father Callaghan's plight. By noon he had nearly a hundred underworld characters lined up whom he then turned loose with instructions to collect in the highways and byways of the camp, and "make damn sure you account for every penny collected."

Never anywhere had been seen such a motley crew bent on a mission of charity. Hopheads, shaky alcoholics, bindle stiffs, the backwash of the camp—into every saloon, rooming house, gambling joint, shack and hovel, they traveled and the money began rolling in. Callahan, himself went to the restricted district. Not a prostitute was overlooked and all contributed their mite. By eleven o'clock that evening the drive had gone over the top and considerably over the required two hundred dollars had been collected.

All money was turned over to Callahan the Bum, and at near midnight he aroused the priest from his bed and turned over the sackful of bills and coins.

"Here's your bell, Father," he told the astonished priest. "Don't let anyone ever tell ye that Callahan the Bum forgets a friend. Say a few prayers for me and the rest of the lads when ye ring the bell on Sunday mornin's—the Lord knows a prayer or two wouldn't hurt any of us a bit."

The melancholy Indian summer days of the fall of 1904 had arrived in Butte. They affected Callahan the Bum strangely. So strangely in fact that he attempted the famous suicide, mentioned in an earlier chapter.

The business district, in front of a Syrian rug store, was the site chosen by Callahan to call it quits with the world. An awning rope dangling on the street from the store front was the implement chosen for his self-destruction.

Callahan had become well saturated before attempting the journey into the unknown. He tied the end of the awning rope securely around his neck and fell part way to the sidewalk as far as the rope would allow. He succeeded only in choking himself and in his inebriated condition was unable to regain his feet.

The odd part of the performance as reported in the following day's newspapers, was that scores of passers-by saw the hanging Callahan and paid not the slightest heed. His face was turning black, his tongue was protruding and the despondent man was well on the way of succeeding in his venture when the Syrian shop keeper, after the better part of an hour, came out onto the sidewalk and cut the gasping Callahan down. He also called the police and the Bum was once more "under the clock." He later explained, "Hanging ain't such a bad death, if the damn rope didn't half choke a man to death before he passed out."

Little is known of the end of Callahan the Bum. He disappeared from his regular haunts sometime in 1910. There is no record of his death in the City health files. There were reports that relatives had taken him to the East to try and straighten him up. But the name of Callahan the Bum is well remembered in the copper camp.

Naming the Mines

IN THE early days of the camp two partners working a claim, about half way up what is now Anaconda Road on the west slopes of the "richest hill," had decided not to name the prospect hole until they struck paying ore. On this day one of the partners slept peacefully in their small, shabby cabin nearby, while the other puttered around at the bottom of the shaft. It was early morning.

Suddenly the miner at the bottom of the shaft ceased his idle scratching and began to dig feverishly. A glistening ledge of high-grade ore uncovered before him. Hurriedly scrambling up the shaft, he rushed into the cabin and shook his sleeping partner.

"Wake up, Jim, we've struck it!" he shouted vigorously and excitedly.

So "Wake Up Jim" was the name they gave this mine which proved a rich producer.

Names come easy in the copper camp. A city with nearly a third of its population answering to some sort of nickname had little difficulty in finding appropriate names for its mines.

The first successful quartz and silver mine, the Travonia, was originally named for a star. William L. Farlin, its discoverer, had called it the Asteroid, a star-like body. Farlin, when naming it, perhaps believed that this claim stood out like a star among his many other properties. His assumption later proved correct when the mine produced some hundreds of thousands of dollars in high-grade silver ore before it was worked out. To avoid confusion with the Star West, another mine in the vicinity, he later changed it to its present name, Travonia, after a province in the Balkans.

The great Anaconda Mine was named for a reptile as explained previously.

Hickey, the discoverer, with the collaboration of his brother, Ed, named another of his mines the St. Lawrence, after the Saint whose intercession their old mother in Ireland had asked in guarding over her boys in the New World. The benign Saint undoubtedly answered her pleas as the Butte mines made them both independently wealthy.

The miners themselves named the "Neversweat." In the early days ventilation in the mines was not all that it should be. As the shafts deepened, the heat increased. Because of some freak currents of air, this mine escaped the heat, and as a result was called by the miners the Neversweat. In later years as the depth of the mine increased, so did the heat. The name was then shortened to the "Sweat." It is by this nickname that it is known today.

The various Parrot mines were not named after the talkative bird as many suppose. The Parrot lode, and the mines located on it, five in all, were named for the Honorable R. R. Parrott, a one-time prominent attorney who had aided many of the original locators with financial and legal advice.

The Original Mine was named after the first original quartz lode to be discovered in the district. The Stewart and Gagnon both were named after their discoverers.

Romance had a hand in prompting the names of several of the mines of which two or three were fabulously rich. The Emma, Nettie, Cora, Alice, Minnie Jane, Minnie Healy and Little Minah mines were all inspired by the names of either wives or sweethearts of the locators.

The Bell Mine at one time was called the Belle, for a certain belle of Centerville. Some of the early Irish miners of the camp insisted on confusing the pronunciation with that of a portion of the human anatomy. It was then, in charity to the Centerville Miss, that the superfluous *e* was dropped and it became plain "Bell."

The Mountain Con was originally the Mountain Consolidated which proved too much of a tongue twister for many of the early miners who promptly shortened it to "Mountain Con" or "Con," as it is usually called today.

The Moonlight was discovered on the evening of a brilliant full moon. The Balaklava was named after the famous battle where the Light Brigade so valiantly charged. The Speculator was so named by the Largey family for the reason that their investment in the mine was a mere gamble.

N.A. FORSYTH, PHOTOGRAPHER; MONTANA HISTORICAL SOCIETY, HELENA

Miners station at 1600 level, Original Mine.

N.A. FORSYTH, PHOTOGRAPHER; MONTANA HISTORICAL SOCIETY, HELENA

Miners at the Mountain Con.

The Badger, Moose and Buffalo all gained their names from animals common to the West. The Ophir Mine's name was taken from the Bible. The Diamond's from the shape of its location stakes, not from the precious stone. The Pennsylvania and Colorado Mines were titled after the home states of their finders. The Colusa, Berkley, Moulton and Belmont were named after leading residents of the camp, many of whom had invested capital in the enterprises.

Early in 1900 a prospector decided to quit the game. The greater part of his life had been spent tramping the hills in search of riches. He had made one or two small stakes and had accumulated a few thousand dollars and a small holding of real estate in the business district, which he had picked up at a bargain price.

It was to this real estate that he now turned. The mining field was overcrowded, he reasoned. Any money to be made in the growing camp, would come from investments other than that of mining. A small hotel, he thought, would provide a steady income, and he drew plans for a modest two-story building on his property.

For years, a small wooden shack housing a tiny cigar store called the "Smoke House" had occupied the site. This now was torn down, and the excavating for the foundation of the hotel began. Not over ten feet of earth had been removed before they ran into a ledge of solid rock which necessitated blasting operations. The owner grumbled at the added expense, and ordered the contractors to start drilling.

As the powder smoke of the first blast cleared away, the workers rubbed their eyes in amazement. Instead of solid granite, dully shining before their gaze was a twenty-five foot ledge of peacock copper ore.

Gone were all thoughts of the hotel. Here, within a few feet of the surface, and in territory considered worthless as to mineral value, was the richest vein yet uncovered in the Butte district. A shaft was sunk at once, and never a pound of waste was encountered. As miners say, "She was ore to the grass roots."

The mine was named the Smokehouse after the little cigar store that had so long stood on the site of the hidden vein. The shaft was down but a hundred feet when one of the larger mining corporations bought the mine for a million dollars.

The Smokehouse Mine, in the heart of the business district, was a landmark for many years. Several million dollars were taken from it before the shaft was finally "bulkheaded" over, and worked through other shafts of the company. Years later a hotel was really erected on site. Named the Acoma, it stands on the lower side of East Broadway.

A more colorful, if less authentic, version of the discovery of the Smokehouse is that a certain butcher who occupied a small butcher shop on the property, decided to excavate in his back yard for a small "smokehouse" of the variety made famous by the late Chic Sale. Digging a few feet, he is said to have uncovered the rich vein of peacock copper.

The story continues with the recounting of how, in celebrating his discovery, he became uproariously drunk, and, in need of funds to continue the celebration, sold his secret for a few hundred dollars to the man who later filed on the claim. The canny purchaser, the story goes, then claimed the accidental discovery of the mine.

Arguments are still held as to which story is correct. Some authorities say that both are right.

The Green Mountain and the Grey Rock were named for their waste dumps, one a hill of green low grade ore and the other an expanse of grey talc. The High Ore gained its appellation from the excellent quality of its main lead. The Mountain View, because it stood on the top of the hill. The Irish locators of the Parnell, Hibernian, Robert Emmett and Michael Davitt Mines gave them names reflecting their Celtic patriotism.

A prospector on the west end of the camp became a bit sentimental over the remoteness of his claim and called it the Orphan Girl. Later another prospector located a claim within a few hundred yards of the Orphan Girl and promptly named his find the Orphan Boy.

The Nipper was named by a Cornishman for a neighborhood small boy, or "nipper" in Cornish slang, who spent the greater part of his time around the workings.

Despite the colorful selection, seldom was any great thought given to the naming of the mines. To the early locators, it wasn't the name that made the mine. The kind of ore to be found at the bottom of the shaft was what really counted.

Mules in the Mines

"My sweetheart's a mule in the mine.
I drive her with only one line.
On the dashboard I sit
And tobacco I spit,
All over my sweetheart's behind."
—*Old Miners' Ballad.*

TRUER words were never written than the title line of this well-known early-day mining ballad, for the mule and his cousin, the horse, were indeed sweethearts to the mining industry in the late nineties and the first score of years in the present century.

It is certain that the great ore tonnages of those years could not have been extracted from the depths of Butte hill without the aid of these animals. They were as much a part of the mines and mining as were the Irish and Cousin Jack, dynamite and the buzzy.

Around 1910 it is conservatively estimated that in sixty or more operating mines there were at least one thousand mules or horses working underground. Their average work life was five years. Thus over a period of thirty years, close to ten thousand of these animals labored in the mines, each mine using from ten to fifty, with two to eight assigned to each level. They worked in shifts, some for eight hours on day duty, others taking their eight-hour turns on the night shift.

Only the best stock was used for mine work, for scrub animals could never survive the hard labor and intense heat they were subjected to. Like the miners themselves, the mules had what it takes—plenty of strength, stamina, and guts. Big, large-boned, huge-chested, pick of the equine work stock, they were treated with the best of care. Every mine had its own veterinarian and horseshoer. Stables were kept scrupulously clean, with the finest fodder and clean straw bedding provided for them. To slake their thirst, fresh, sweet water was lowered from surface twice daily.

Although the mules lived in perpetual darkness underground, they did not seem to mind. It is doubtful that if given their choice they would trade places with the mules and horses above ground.

Lowering of the animals into the depths was a delicate operation conducted by experienced ropemen. First, the mules were roped in the mine corrals on surface, thrown, and securely tied. Next they were encased in a special rope-harness, resembling a large strait jacket which did not allow the slightest movement. Bound thus, the animals were moved on timber trucks to the collar or entrance to the shaft where they were deftly swung under the mine cage and made secure. Suspended and dangling from the cage in the shaft, they were lowered to their destination from one to three thousand feet underground.

Another method, rarely used, was to place them, strait jacket and all, bodily on the cage. Haunches and tails on the bottom, heads up, the cage door was closed and securely fastened, and the animals quickly lowered down the shaft.

Once underground procedure was simple, the mules being swung out from under the cage and onto the station. The rope strait jacket was removed and the animals turned loose. After a few moments of frightened

N.A. FORSYTH, PHOTOGRAPHER; MONTANA HISTORICAL SOCIETY, HELENA

Mule train working on 1100 level, Rarus Mine.

N.A. FORSYTH, PHOTOGRAPHER; MONTANA HISTORICAL SOCIETY, HELENA

Swamper loading ore car from chute.

scampering, the bewildered beasts were led to the barn, a rock-enclosed aperture in an unused drift, generally some distance from the shaft. A large pole gate kept the animals confined. After a day or two of leisure to accustom them to their new surroundings, the mules were ready for their underground labors. They caught on quickly.

Once they had descended the shaft, the mine was their permanent home. Serious illness, old age, or the suspension of mining operations were the only reasons for a mule's return to the sunlight. Indeed the old-time miner could, with fair accuracy, gauge the duration of shut-downs by whether or not animals were taken to the surface. When the mules and horses came up out of the mine it was a safe bet that the miners would be in for a long period of idleness.

Below ground, the animals were used to transport the ore from the drifts, stopes, and raises to the station where it was "caged" and taken to the surface. Six cars to a train was the ordinary load for the animals, each car containing approximately a ton of ore. The husky animals handled the six-ton trains with ease.

Each mule train was in charge of a "skinner" or driver, and a "swamper" or assistant. The skinner handled the mule; the swamper loaded the cars from the chutes, threw the switches and made himself generally useful.

After a short period underground the animals developed an uncanny intelligence. Old-time miners will swear on oath that the mules could count. At any rate, it is a well-known fact that very few of the animals could be persuaded to pull more than six cars to a train. As each car was loaded, the mules would move up the track the exact distance of one car-length, at the same time taking up the slack of the chain couplings between the cars. This procedure was repeated until the entire train was loaded. The moment the sixth car was full the mule without any urging from the driver was on his way to the station. Let the skinner attach an extra car to the train and the mule would stand stock still in his tracks, not budging an inch until the surplus car was removed. No cajolery, cussing, or beating could change the stubborn beast's mind. It was six cars or none.

The animals became familiar with the different tracks on the level, and in a short time could tell all the low or tight places in the drifts and stoop down or slide over these places as the occasion demanded, as wisely as the miners themselves.

Union-minded, the mules knew to the minute when an eight-hour shift was in. It was an utter impossibility to work them a moment past the allotted time. Another sense told them of the approach of the dinner hour. Although the mining companies allowed a half-hour for dinner, it had long been the custom of the miners to extend this to a full hour. The mules seemed acquainted with this fact and no amount of urging or pleading could get them away from the barn and their oats until every one of the sixty minutes had passed.

On upgrades, where it was too steep to pull the cars, it was customary for the mules to about-face and "breast" or push each car over the grade with their chests, then return to the head of the train, and resume their proper position when the grade was passed.

In most instances a deep affection existed between the skinners and mules. Woe betide the misguided miner, no matter what the provocation, who would dare abuse a mule or horse. Some bitter feuds developed for this very reason.

There were instances where a mule would work for only one certain skinner. Old-timers tell of a white mule, Nellie, at the Mountain Con

Mine, who became deeply attached to her skinner, a young Irishman named Denny. Nellie would absolutely refuse to budge from her barn for anyone else.

Her master liked to celebrate a bit on pay day, and occasionally could not make the grade the following morn. On these days Nellie remained idle. No amount of persuasion from a strange skinner could move her. No Denny, no work. The cars of rock had to be pushed out to the station by manpower. The occurrence was repeated at more frequent intervals, once the wily Denny discovered that the level could not operate efficiently without him.

The gruff foreman, Jim Brennan, finally grew tired of this display of temperament on the part of Nellie and the skinner and presented Denny with a pink slip. Nellie became disconsolate. No human could grieve more than she did over the absence of her adored one. First kindness was tried, and later force. Neither was of any avail. As a last resource, Brennan had to locate Denny and rehire him. The meeting of mule and skinner was most touching. Nellie immediately went back to work and continued to pull the trains under Denny's guidance until he gave up mining. Nellie was then brought to the surface and retired to greener pastures.

Many of the underground mules adopted some of the miners' more pernicious habits. "Peerless," a shredded brand of chewing tobacco, and a great favorite among the underground workers, is noted for its durability and strength. Many miners cultivated the custom of giving the mules a good-sized chew of the weed. The animals formed a liking for the nicotine and would go to any extreme to obtain the biting leaf. An unerring sense of smell would direct them to any miner who had Peerless in his possession. And it was not unusual to see the tobacco-seeking mule nuzzling the miner's clothes with his nose, giving him a thorough frisking. Workers' coats or jumpers left hanging in the drifts or stations were continually being rifled by the tobacco-loving animals. Mules were known to have refused to work unless given their daily ration of chewing tobacco.

Another mulish habit was a craving for pie—any flavor, but apple preferred. All lunch buckets had to be concealed and kept well beyond reach of the animals, for, if left in the drifts or other accessible places, the mules would soon pull them down, kick them over, and scatter the contents to get at the dessert.

A well-worn joke stated the mules could smell-out the buckets put up at a certain large boarding house whose pies and general cooking were of a questionable quality. The point was that the mules would have no part of the buckets from this hostelry and left them unmolested.

Although cruelty to the mules was taboo and practically unheard of, an occasional case of a skinner beating one would crop up. An instance is related by a miner well known as a practical joker.

He was doing some repair work in a darkened manway entrance on the level of a mine when a young Celtic skinner with his mule and a string of empty cars pulled up to a nearby chute for a load of ore. The miner in the dark manway could see the skinner and the mule, but they could not see him. Perhaps the skinner had had a tough night. At any rate, he was in a surly mood and when the mule accidentally backed the train too far from the chute mouth, the skinner picked up a handy pick handle and beat the animal. The frightened mule threw back his ears and bared his lip over his gleaming teeth. The miner hiding in the manway watched the entire performance.

Lowering his voice and in the most guttural and sepulchral of tones, he said:

"You damn Harp son-of-a-bitch, if you hit me once more, I'll kick your brains all over the mine!"

To the startled skinner it seemed that the voice was coming from the mule. Dropping the pick handle, he turned and raced down the drift exclaiming as he ran:

"Japers! He's human!"

The day of the mules in the mines is gone forever. Modern motors and machinery have supplanted the faithful animals, and today in the entire Butte mining district there are only two or three mules to be found. Although still a frequently heard ballad, *My Sweetheart's A Mule In The Mine* pertains only to fond memories of the past.

Men of the Mines

MATTY KIELY: He Dug The Mines.

"B-r-r-r-r-r-r-r-r-r-r-r-r-r-r-r-r-r-r-r-r-r-r-r-r
I rustled at the Diamond—I rustled at the Bell;
I rustled all summer—and I rustled like hell.
B-r-r-r-r-r-r-r-r-r-r-r-r-r-r-r-r-r-r-r-r-r-r-r-rl"

It was Matty Kiely, wit, all-around miner, minstrel, Paul Bunyan of the camp and perpetual headache to the bosses on the Hill, performing for a crowd of miners and muckers at the Moonlight Saloon on East Broadway.

The "B-r-r-r-r-r-r-r-r" was Matty's imitation of a buzzy air drill, better known to the miners as a "widow maker." The imitation was an accompaniment to the song he improvised as he went along.

"B-r-r-r-r-r-r-r-r-r-r-r-r-r-r-r-r-r-r-r-r-r-r-r-r-r
I rustled at the Gagnon and I rustled at the 'Sweat'
The Stewart and the Greyrock—and I'm rustlin' yet.
B-r-r-r-r-r-r-r-r—Fill 'em up bartender—this buzzy
can't run without plenty of ile—B-r-r-r-r-r-rl

"I'm a buzzy miner—indeed I am
Old Jim Brennan just gave me the can."

Matty Kiely is in his grave, but of all the big names—Heinze, Clark and Daly included—none was more famous around the town than that of irrepressible, red-faced Matty with his homely Irish grin and his ready wit.

If Matty had lived one more month, he would have spent fifty years in Butte. He was born in Waterford, Ireland, and he hit the town when it was a bleak, but wide-open, hell-roaring camp, and Matty was but a broth of a greenhorn straight off the boat. Marcus Daly, himself, gave Matty his first job, shoveling copper ore on the four-hundred-foot level in his big Anaconda Mine. And this, Matty never forgot. To him, Marcus Daly was both a saint and a guardian angel.

Long after Daly had died and they had placed a statue of him on Main Street, Matty never passed the bronze memorial without reverently removing his hat and breathing a short prayer. In the later years when the camp was undergoing great changes, political, social and otherwise, Matty made semi-weekly visits to the statue and kept Marcus acquainted with every event. One of his worries was, that when erecting the statue, they placed it in such a position that Daly was facing the town with his back to the hill.

"'Tis no luck will ever come of it," complained Matty. "In life Marcus Daly never turned his arse on the mines of Butte or the miners who dug them."

Matty Kiely had worked in every mine, large or small, on the hill, but he never tarried long at any one mine. His irrepressible spirits and too glib tongue took care of that. As he sang himself in rhyme:

"I've been hired and fired tin thousand times,
Tis Matty Kiely who dug their mines!"

Being fired never bothered him greatly. The next shift would find him at another mine, and in the early days, Matty rarely went through the formality of rustling a job as the other miners had to do. He merely picked himself out a mine, and the next morning would find him, lunch bucket in hand, presenting himself to the foreman ready for work. Matty had such a persuasive personality that he usually got away with it and he had another job until he was once more fired or ready to quit.

It was very little work that Matty did while below ground. He was a past master at finding ways and means of avoiding any exertion This would not have been so bad from the bosses' point of view, but while Matty was on a mine level he kept everyone else from work while he sat around telling tall stories of his exploits.

There must be a thousand stories of his doings. Wherever Butte miners sit to "take five," another new Matty Kiely story bobs up. At one time the San Francisco *Leader* ran a lengthy article written by a Butte resident chronicling many of Kiely's exploits, jokes and witticisms.

Matty pulled one of his best-known pranks while working for Jim Brennan, the colorful foreman of the Mountain Con. It was at a time when Brennan had just made one of his periodical cleanups and had "canned" most of his crew, hiring in their stead a green gang of miners recently arrived from the mines of Joplin, Missouri. None of newcomers knew Matty Kiely. The fact that they had replaced many of his old buddies at the mine rankled him.

At that time the ordinary miners used candles for illumination while working underground. The only one privileged to carry carbide lamps or "blue lights" as the miners called them, were the shift bosses and foreman. In some way Matty Kiely obtained a carbide lamp and smuggled it down into the mine.

He waited until the shift boss of the level had made his rounds in the early part of the shift and then he started out on his rounds. The first place he visited was a stope where two six-foot Missourians were busy behind an Ingersoll drill boring into the body of ore. Matty flashed his bright light on them.

"Who told you to drill there?" he demanded.

"Why, our boss did," explained one of the miners, "he told us to put in a round of holes here and to blast them when we go off shift."

"Of all the blankey blank fools!" returned Matty. "He won't be your boss any longer, I'm foreman of this mine, if you don't know it, and I'll fire him to hell out of here as soon as I see him. Tear down that machine, and set up and drill over here," he continued as he indicated a place on

N.A. FORSYTH, PHOTOGRAPHER; MONTANA HISTORICAL SOCIETY, HELENA

Ready to blast at 1900 level.

the hanging wall of the stope which was valueless waste. "We need waste to fill the gob—and see that you get it done and blast at quittin' time or up goes the two of your tails!"

From stope to stope and from drift to drift on the level, Matty made his way repeating the performance wherever he encountered any of the Joplin miners. On the sills, he varied his orders. Here he set the Missourian mule skinners who had been hauling waste to hauling ore instead, and instructed them to dump it in the waste chutes. Those who were pulling ore were instructed to change to waste and to dump in into the ore chutes. The orders might have sounded screwy to some of the Missourians, but they all obeyed orders. After Matty had reversed the working procedure of the entire level, he sneaked back to his own working place and hid the carbide light under a pile of waste rock.

That afternoon as the shift boss in company with the real foreman made his next round, the level was in bedlam. Neither of the bosses would believe the Missourian's fantastic tale of a mysterious boss and they fired the newcomers right and left. On all the levels, Matty Kiely was the only one who had obeyed the boss' instructions. They asked him if he had seen the pseudo-foreman.

"You two are the only ones I've seen," said Matty. "You can't pay any attention to them danged Missourians—they're always seen' things. It's the hunger they brought with them from Joplin that makes them have visions!"

A few shifts later, it was discovered that Matty had been the perpetrator of the hoax, and he was promptly fired, but what was another pink slip in the life of Matty Kiely?

Another time Matty was shoveling up in a stope of the Anaconda mine. As fast as he shoveled a car of ore into the chute, the loader down below was pulling it out. Matty couldn't make any headway, so he rolled over an enormous mine timber and pushed it down into the chute, completely blocking it. Then he sat himself down on the muck pile for a rest and a smoke. The sweating, cursing loader vainly attempted to remove the heavy timber from the mouth of the chute below.

It was not long before the shift boss, making his rounds, came upon the loader who told him of the difficulty. The shift boss had had all his teeth pulled out a day or so previously, and was in none too happy a frame of mind.

He climbed part way up the manway and yelled at Matty, "What the hell is the idea of throwing this timber down the chute, and how in the hell do you think we're going to get it out?"

Matty, by this time, had finished his pipe, and aware of the boss's dental troubles, complacently strolled over to the chute, and using his hands as a megaphone, bellowed down at him:

"How in hell should I know—pull it out with your teeth!" Once more Matty Kiely was looking for a job.

Another time a foreman asked Matty for the measurements of a piece of timber the latter had ordered for a certain cross-cut.

"It's the breadth of me two hands plus the width of two wedges plus the length of half a tamping stick," Matty blandly informed him.

As an old crony of Matty's, when told of the latter's passing said, "So poor Matty Kiely's gone—God rest his soul. Many's the laugh he gave the old town—and many's the ton of first class ore he broke for the company in the saloons of Butte."

An eastern magazine writer wrote in an article: "In the lusty gang of thick-thewed giants one met in Butte, the ordinary sized man was considered a runt. Height and bulk and 'he-ness' ruled in office, shop and trade."

There were many strong men in the camp. Most notable was the trio known to every miner who carried a lunch pail up the hill in the early days, namely, "Con the Horse," "Mike the Mule," and "Steamshovel Steve."

"Con the Horse" was a mule skinner in one of the mines when he received his sobriquet. Of prodigious size, and with shoulders twice the breadth of the ordinary skinner, he closely resembled a cartoonist's impression of Neolithic man. Con's duties at the mine consisted of guiding a huge white horse that pulled a train of six ore cars from a chute on an inside drift out to the station, a distance of nearly a mile. Each car contained a ton of first-class copper ore.

One night, coming on shift, Con noticed that his horse was suffering from the colic. Instead of reporting the horse's condition to the boss, as other skinners would have done, Con decided to leave the horse in the barn and take the ailing animal's place himself. This he did, pushing two of the loaded ore cars at a time out to the station. From that night on he was a marked man and carried the name, "Con the Horse," to his grave.

"Mike the Mule" was a mine station tender. Part of his duties were to load heavy timbers onto the mine cages. In stature and general appearance, Mike resembled "Con the Horse" and he scorned the help of any working partner in juggling the enormous timbers. The miners claimed that he was equal in strength to "Con, the Horse," but possessed a better appetite. Mike carried two lunch pails to work, both filled to the covers with an assortment of nourishment which he consumed in an eight-hour shift. Mike ate from his lunch buckets in the manner described by the miners as the "cave-in system"—from the top town. For instance, if pie was on top of Mike's bucket, pie was what he ate first and then worked his way to the bottom.

One day Mike the Mule attempted to lift the end of a heavy, five-ton mine motor, and knocked something awry in his great body. Hundreds of miners followed him to his grave.

"Steamshovel Steve" was a giant Serbian with handlebar mustaches. He was listed on the mine payroll as "Steve Murphy" because the timekeeper couldn't spell his right name. Steve's entire vocabulary of English was four words, "Yes," "No," "Payday" and "Anaconda Mine," but what the herculean Steve lacked in loquaciousness, he more than made up by his dexterity with a "muck stick," the miner's term for a shovel.

Steve worked in the toughest, gassiest drifts on the Butte hill as a contract shoveler, long before the present contract system became general in the district. Shoveling "rough-bottom" or from the top of a muck pile, the six-foot Serb was equally at home. Sixty or seventy mine cars, each car containing a ton of the heavy copper ore, was an ordinary shift for him.

Steve worked steadily for over five years, and saved his money intending to take a trip to the old country. When he had accumulated a stake of some five thousand dollars, the Serb went on a gigantic bender from which he never recovered. Booze did what the muckstick failed to do—it put Steve under six feet of good earth "out on the flat" where Butte's departed miners rest.

Another "good little man" of the old days was Tommy Coughlin, usually called "The Man Eater." Standing slightly over five feet, and never weighing over 140 pounds, the Man Eater possessed all the characteristics commonly attributed to the wild cat. As his friends put it: "There never was born a man, be he miner, shift boss or policeman who could make the Man Eater take a back step." His name graces many pages of police court news in the yellowing newspaper files. The charges are invariably the same—fighting and disturbance with an occasional mayhem charge thrown in for variation.

Coughlin was the owner of a number of mining claims in the Highlands, south of the camp. It was his custom to work the claims during the summer, returning to Butte to work in the mines in the winter. At one time an Idaho sodbuster moved in on the "north forty" adjoining Coughlin's claim. Annoyed, the Man Eater staked mining location notices about the farmer's property.

This angered the man from Idaho, and he appeared with a sawed-off shotgun, poked the weapon in the vicinity of the prospector's intestines, and ordered him to take the notices to hell off his property or else.

Not daunted, the scrappy Man Eater attempted to push the gun aside saying: "I never saw a blankety blank Idaho sleeve-gilder who had the guts to pull a trigger on a gun. Put it away or I'll grab you by the tonsils and turn you inside out!"

The man from the Gem state pulled both triggers and the contents of two barrels hit the miner in the stomach. They took the farmer to jail and the Man Eater to the hospital where the doctors took one look and shook their heads.

But they did not reckon with the recuperative powers of the Man Eater. In a month, he was out of the hospital. He refused to appear in court against his assailant who was turned free. Coughlin's first act on reaching his mining claims was to beat within an inch of his life the six-foot Idahoan.

The Man Eater received his greatest recognition several years later when annoyed by a large pack rat that was prowling around his cabin, he fired a shotgun at the rodent and hit instead a case of dynamite that was stored in the corner of the place. The explosion could be heard in Butte, twenty-six miles away, but once again the Man Eater's life was saved. The cabin was blown to smithereens, but the durable Coughlin received not a scratch. By some freak or other, the force of the explosion escaped him and he was found by a neighbor several moments later badly stunned, still sitting in his chair amidst the debris of the cabin with the shotgun lying in the wreckage beside him.

When death came to the Man Eater, it was from natural causes.

Early Butte boasted of some of the most colorful shift bosses and foreman to be found in the mining world. Among them was Mickey Carrol, Marcus Daly's superintendent at the Anaconda, St. Lawrence, and Neversweat Mines. When Carrol fired a miner, he often did so with the admonition, "—and don't let me catch ye on *my* side of the hill again!" Joe Laird, foreman of the Green Mountain, and Jim Brennan, of the Mountain Con, were two tough, gruff individuals who would fire or fight a miner on the slightest provocation. "Savages" was the term applied to them by the miners—when well out of hearing distance. Brennan's great passion was the saving of nails and spikes, and it was the pink slip for the miner whom he might catch wasting a sixty or eighty penny spike by using it to hang up his lunch bucket or jumper.

"The "Rimmer" O'Neill who worked himself up from tool boy to superintendent was a colorful and also a respected boss. The term "savage" was never applied to the Rimmer. He numbered his friends in the camp by the thousands.

A favorite story of the Rimmer has to do with the recurrence in Butte of the name "Sullivan" which leads any other name in the directory or phone book.

The Rimmer was making a tour of inspection of the St. Lawrence Mine. Half way through his rounds he chanced into a slope on the ten-hundred-foot level where he was confronted by a frightened miner who was in the act of quitting the slope and had his lunch bucket under his arm.

The Rimmer asked the lad why he was quitting.

"Japers! Mr. O'Neill," he pleaded. "That place ain't fit for a human to work in. The place is full of loose slabs and boulders, anywan av thim which might come down and crush a man in a minute."

The Rimmer surveyed the slope and attempted to assure the man.

"I wouldn't worry, if I was you. If one of them slabs has your name on it you'll get it. Otherwise, you're as safe as if you were home in your bed."

"I know that well," complained the miner, "and that's what worries me most. With a name as common as mine, I'm a cinch to get it. You see, me name happens to be Sullivan."

Another shift boss was "Rags" Daly, whom the miners accused of getting his working clothes from the "poor box," a receptacle in front of the "drys" (change houses) for discarded clothing. Daly is the boss who is reported to have one time fired a balky mule. Daly, the story goes, wrote out a pink slip for the stubborn animal, attached it to his harness and ordered the mine ropemen to hoist the mule to surface, and then ordered two greenhorn Serbian car trammers to take the animal's place.

"Tango" Cullhane was a shift boss and foreman, who had the unpleasant habit of blowing out his carbide lamp and sneaking up the manways into the scopes in the hopes of catching the miners and muckers "taking five." A greenhorn shoveler put an abrupt end to this practice when he dumped a wheelbarrow filled with "first class" down the manway and put Tango in the hospital for several weeks.

There was a Cornish foreman at the Mountain View or "Saffron Bun," who would hire none but Cousin Jack miners and always told the Irish rustlers, "Thee are in the wrong line, my boy!"

The "Big Bull" and the "Little Bull"—foreman and assistant foreman of the Grayrock Mine were particularly pugnacious. Their favorite admonition to the miners and shovelers, "Pin back your ears!" is well remembered by the old timers.

"Savages," or whatever the miners preferred to call them, there is no getting away from the fact that the old breed of bosses knew their business. They were miners and producers and, in spite of all, had respect of their men. Theirs was a great contribution to the building of the camp.

In few places was there more color, humor and sometimes pathos than in the miners' wards of the two Butte hospitals. Mining being the precarious occupation that it is, the wards were usually filled with miners suffering or convalescing from accidents.

One old timer put it: "It was often a better performance than any of the vaudeville shows put on by Uncle Dick Sutton." It was a trial to the nurses but they accepted the rough horseplay and humor of the miners in their stride and gave back as good as they received.

One memorable night in a St. James Hospital miners' ward is recounted by a Butte miner, Pete McNulty, who at the time was recovering from a leg broken by a fall of ground in the Diamond Mine.

The ward was crowded, every bed occupied, but some of the convalescents were able to hobble about on crutches.

A friend of one of the patients had that afternoon brought down several quarts of Three Star Hennessy brandy which he had won on an election bet. The liquor had been cached under a mattress. That evening word came that the Sister Superior had been taken down with a cold, and the boys prepared to make merry. Some one placed a heavy chair against the door, to keep out inquisitive nurses, and the bottles were passed from bed to bed.

Tony Pasquale, a diminutive Italian from Meaderville, who had stepped into a chute at the Leonard mine, had an accordion under his bed. After a third helping of the Three Star, Tony brought out the instrument from its wrappings and soon the strains of *O Sole Mio* were ringing through the ward, a dozen voices joining in on the chorus. Nurses came on the run, but the chair-barred door prevented their entrance.

Soon Tony's music box changed to a lilting Italian tarantella and several of the crippled miners, aided by their crutches, grasped each other as partners and began dancing around the room. Some of those unable to get out of bed, joined their voices in raucous chorus, while others pounded on bedpans and water pitchers, cheered the dancers along. The ward was a bedlam. The nurses banged frantically on the barred doors. Doctors hurried to the scene, and in the ward the Three Star kept making the rounds until the last drop was drained. It was over an hour before the nurses with the aid of the hospital janitor succeeded in opening the door. By that time things had quieted down and the miners were back in their beds, most of them dead to the world in a three-star stupor.

Melting Potpourri

WITH some half-hundred nationalities working, playing and drinking together it was only natural that there should be many odd individuals in the copper camp.

Characters such as Jimmy July, Whistling Sammy, Butt Block and Whiskey, Mohammed Murphy, Johnny the Swede, Dago Jim, Telephone Tschaikowsky, O. B. Anderson, Nick Portulis, Hughie Evans, Dutch Nick and hosts of others, representing a myriad of nations, added much to the color of the camp once the immigrants of Europe and Asia began arriving in the Rocky Mountain region.

To bring a smile of reminiscence to the faces of old-time miners one need but mention the names of "Butt Block" and "Whiskey," an inseparable, indestructible pair of Finn miners who for years worked as partners, in nearly every mine on the hill. Both were diminutive, nearly as broad as they were long, and one was seldom seen without the other. The two worked, played, drank and even loved together, it being claimed that at one time both were smitten with the same girl, a buxom Finnish hasher at one of the Finn boarding houses on East Granite Street. Neither would accept a job in the mines unless the other was hired as partner—a Damon and Pythias combination if there ever was one.

Although the pair were top-flight drinking men, they never drank together, but alternated, Whiskey getting drunk one night and Butt Block the next. In this way a shift was seldom missed. If one suffered hangover pangs, his partner was able to carry on—an ideal arrangement for them.

Butt Block and Whiskey were excellent miners, absolutely fearless. There was no place underground too dangerous for the pair. The dangerous occupations of catching up caves and blasting "hung-up" chutes were their special forte. One time the two were working on the eighteen-hundred level of the old Black Rock Mine, under Joe Foley shift boss. In some manner a two-hundred foot transfer chute used in moving first-class ore from one level to the other, became blocked about fifty feet above the level. There were nearly a hundred tons of ore in the chute, so Foley sent for Butt Block and Whiskey.

Such chutes usually have a manway running parallel alongside them, and the usual procedure in freeing them is to bore a hole through the manway into the chute, then to pole with a long steal bar until the rock is free. Failing in this, dynamite is forced through the hole into the mass of rock and the obstructed area blasted.

But such methods were too slow for the chunky Finns. Butt Block climbed up and looked into the yawning mouth of the chute. Far above him he saw the huge boulders holding back the tons of ore. The slightest touch might start it rolling, but it was too far up to reach with a bar.

"Veesky," Butt Block called to his partner, "go to bowder house and get me all the bowder vot you can. Bring fuse and caps too!"

Whiskey was on his way, and in a few moments returned with a powder sack filled to the brim with forty per cent Hercules dynamite, nearly twenty-five sticks in all. Butt Block took the sack of powder, fuse and caps and throwing the lot over his shoulder crawled up into the mouth of the chute. One misstep might have brought an avalanche of ore down upon him, but he crawled on upward unmindfully, while his partner, Whiskey, disdainfully gazed up into the chute, holding his miner's lamp so its rays fell on his partner as he worked far above. Soon there was a smell of burning fuse, and in a moment, down out of the chute scampered Butt Block. He and his partner were barely in the clear when the mine level shook with a terrific reverberation.

After the smoke had cleared away, the two returned to the chute. Tons of ore lay scattered about the track below. Butt Block had done his work well, not only had he freed the ore, but the vast amount of powder had blown out the mouth of the chute along with its doors. A portion of one side of the chute and manway was also carried away. There would be shoveling for many days before the mess could be cleared.

Butt Block gazed pridefully at his partner, smiled and then with brawny fists pounded, Tarzan-like, upon his hairy chest.

"Now, Who's the Who?" he boastfully asked of Whiskey.

Another inseparable foreign pair was "Johnny the Swede" and his pal, "Dago Jim." Neither were miners. A wizened runt of merely five feet, the Swede was a woodcutter who sawed fuel for the miners at so much per cord. Dago Jim, a slight, moustachioed Italian of particularly villainous appearance—he had but one eye—was of the "idle rich." He disdained work of any kind, living off the rent of three makeshift cabins which, with Johnny the Swede's help, he had built of plaster and discarded railroad ties.

Dago Jim was an ardent Socialist. He could usually be found perched on some miner's woodpile, expounding his Marxian theories to his Swede friend, while the latter sawed wood and marveled over the Italian's vast store of knowledge. A woodcutting job completed, it was the habit of the two cronies to celebrate with the proceeds of the job. Dago Jim on these occasions, usually drank himself stupid. But the Swede, having greater physical resistance, never left Jim to the mercy of heartless saloonkeepers. He simply loaded his comatose partner into a rickety, old iron wheel barrow, and weaving unsteadily through the streets, hauled the latter to his cabin. As this homeward journey usually took place in the morning hours, and as the noisy wheelbarrow was in need of axle grease, the resulting din, more than once caused the pair to be cursed by neighbors whose sleep had been disturbed.

Jimmy July, an aged, withered and toothless Chinaman, cut quite a figure in the early days of Butte as a vegetable peddler and sawyer. His bid for fame came from the fact that he was the only naturalized Chinaman in the camp, having taken out citizenship prior to the enactment of the law that forbade Chinese to become citizens.

Because Jimmy July was proud of his citizenship he invariably wore an American flag in his lapel. He was in turn respected by the white men, suffering none of the abuse so frequently piled in those days on the heads of his countrymen. Jimmy was also quite a Lothario, newspapers frequently mentioning his affairs of the heart. He had been a successful placer miner in the early days and was reported have accumulated a considerable stake. Many of the ladies knew this.

It was for the 1896 Fourth of July celebration, that Jimmy was chosen principal speaker of the day; in his broken English he recited the Declaration of Independence from start to finish.

Before his death Jimmy July became a Christian. He is buried in the Catholic cemetery.

Another notable who trod Butte streets for over sixty years was Sammy Alexander, known to thousands of residents as "Whistling Sammy." Sammy was a Polish Jew who came to the camp in 1875, ran the first restaurant and at his death was the town's best posted historian. Short of stature, not weighing more than a hundred pounds, Semitic nose, and inevitable derby hat, Sammy was a living likeness of the popular vaudeville version of a Yiddish money lender. This in fact was Sammy's principal occupation, although he dabbled in stocks and mining as a sideline.

Sammy was a lovable eccentric who possessed the fighting spirit of a bantam rooster. It was this latter propensity which often led him to grief in his contacts with much larger men.

No end of wonder to the kids of the town was the huge chain of gold pieces which Sammy sported across his waistcoat. The coins graduated from the smaller two and a half dollar gold pieces up through fives and tens to several glittering twenties in the center of chain. The little money lender was never without the glistening array, and it was considered remarkable that he wasn't ever hit over the head and robbed, because his business dealings took him to every corner of the camp.

At one time Sammy proudly displayed a four-carat pin in his tie. At the old race track, one afternoon, directly in front of the grandstand, Sammy was seen to be in trouble. Emitting feeble bleats he was observed to clutch the neckband of his silk shirt with one hand, meanwhile violently waving signals of distress with the other. Finally a track detective noticed his plight and walked over to learn the cause. Sammy pointed to where once had been a flowing cravat and a four-carat diamond. The tie had been cleanly cut off at the knot as if by a razor. Sammy insisted that the officer search every person at the track. All he got was sympathy and a story in that evening's papers. He never again saw the diamond.

On another occasion a husky Irish stockbroker who had some difficulty with obstreperous Sammy in his offices in a local business block, picked him up, kicking, squealing and fighting and threw him down the elevator shaft, a drop of three floors. The stockbroker went to jail and Sammy to the hospital.

The whistle which gave Sammy his name, was continuous and entirely without tune. From the manner in which he contorted his facial muscles it must have cost him considerable physical effort. An apocryphal story is that Sammy offered twenty-five dollars to anyone who could name the tune he whistled. As stated, Whistling Sammy was considered an authority on the early-day history of Butte. He often boasted of his prowess as an Indian fighter, too, having joined the troop organized by W. A. Clark when the Nez Perce trouble broke out in 1877. Although he is reported to have seen no action, Sammy claimed to have several arrow wounds from that conflict. The town sincerely mourned his passing in the early thirties and hundreds followed the eccentric little money lender to his grave.

Telephone "Tschaikowsky" wasn't his right name—Matt Konarsky was the way it was listed on the mine pay roll. The fame of his big, innocent, good-natured Pole who could shovel as much ore as any other two men on the eighteen-hundred level of the Diamond Mine came from the odd manner in which he received his monicker.

When off shift, Matt entertained himself by picking out with one finger Polish melodies on the untuned, tinny-sounding boarding house piano. Some wag at the eating place at once christened him "Tschaikowsky," by which name he was known around the mines thereafter.

Tschaikowsky had become ruptured while trying to lift a loaded mine car on the track and the doctors had fitted him with a truss. Shortly after he started wearing the truss, made with a black metal part somewhat resembling a telephone transmitter, he was taking a shower in the mine change room. A big Hibernian spotted the Pole's accessory and remarked so everyone in the change room could hear

"Lord, God, will ye have a look at the tiliphones on old Tschaikowsky!"

From that day on it was "Telephone Tschaikowsky," an appellation of which the good-natured Pole seemed proud, for he readily answered to it on all occasions.

"Big Jerry," a graduate miner with degrees from half the mines in the camp, was proprietor of the famous Eagle saloon on the road to Centerville.

Six foot-two, red of face and black bristled, Big Jerry was a tough, two-fisted, black Irish "divil" who ran his popular establishment on the same plan. Jerry was honest though rough and crude and unfortunately most of his most classic comments are unprintable.

On one occasion, after the front window of his place was kicked out by a couple of celebrators, Big Jerry printed a card-board sign and put it up alongside the window: "DON'T LEAN ON THE GLASS—THERE AIN'T ANY."

On another occasion a young matron campaigning for her husband's election to congress, stopped into his saloon and asked politely if she might place one of her husband's election cards in the saloon window. Jerry was in a particularly vicious mood that morning. He looked approvingly over the shapely young woman and answered in his gruffest manner.

"You can—and you can put your pretty little arse in there if you have a mind to!"

"Stuttering Alex" was a Nova Scotian or "fisheater" as they were termed in the camp. In a town of tough men Alex was conceded all honors in rough and tumble encounters.

When sober there wasn't a more peaceful man in the camp, but with a few drinks aboard, Alex was a one-man blitzkrieg, having once killed another miner in a saloon brawl with a single punch. Alex' specialty was fighting three or four men at one time, policemen preferred. It was a bullet from a gun held by one of the latter that laid Alex low in a Chinatown noodle parlor after he had literally taken the place apart.

Fernando Mendez was a Mexican tailor. On the shelves of his little shop was always an assortment of bottles of bay rum, hair tonic, rubbing alcohol, lemon extract, liniment and a half dozen varieties of patent medicines of alcoholic content. But one day it developed that Fernando was not in the drug, grocer or barber supply business. As a side line he was selling his assorted nostrums to Indians from the camp out on the Flat and a thriving business it was—until Fernando inadvertantly sold a tribesman a bottle of wood alcohol which subsequently blinded a portion of the Indian camp.

O. B. Anderson, a giant red-faced, tobacco-chewing, profanity using Norwegian was an early-day railway car inspector on the N. P. railway. As far as is known, "O. B." was the only Norwegian in the camp who talked with an Irish brogue, a phenomenon he explained by saying he had come over from the old-country in the steerage of a ship occupied exclusively by Irishmen. "When I hit New York," explained the Norwegian, "I was talkin' exactly like them Harps, and sure I've been doin' it ivir since."

Nick Portulis, a Greek carman at the High Ore Mine, had a heart as big as the Hill, and he invariably kept a fully paid meal ticket at an East Park Street Greek restaurant for the exclusive use of several orphan newsboys. Nick's knowledge was a little vague as to the exact meaning of the word "orphan." He explained the sad plight of the youngsters this way:

"No fodder—no mudder—poor little bastards!"

Another miner known as "Dutch Nick" was a surface man at Jim Brennan's Mountain Con Mine. A short, fat German of the comic-strip type, he dearly loved his schnapps and often sneaked out of the mine yard over to a Main Street saloon for a few quick ones. This particular time, Nick had obtained a pint bottle and when noontime came, Jim Brennan, the foreman, found him laid out in back of a pile of timber.

Brennan kicked the prostrate German's foot, "What's wrong with ye lad, why ain't ye workin'?"

Nick was equal to the occasion. Opening one eye, he groaned as if in pain, "I tink I gott sthruck mit der sun, yet."

Brennan was sympathetic. Reaching into his pocket he took out a silver dollar and passed it to a worker standing by.

"Rush over to Main Street and get a pint of the best whisky ye can buy. It's the only cure for sunstroke."

The worker was back in a very few moments and Brennan pried open the German's jaws and poured over half of the pint down his throat. This finished the job. Dutch Nick was out cold and the mine ambulance had to take him to the hospital where he spent the better part of the week sobering up from sunstroke.

Napoleon Bertrand was a French-Canuck whose job was cleaning and taking care of the "toilet cars" at the Original Mine when they were brought to surface. Because of the odium connected with his occupation, he was the brunt of many jokes and had been christened "Jump In The Pond."

When excited or angered, Napoleon, whose English was never any too good, became helpless and was almost unintelligible.

The Frenchman was boarding at a French-Canadian boarding house out on the Boulevard. The landlady kept a cow, a flock of chickens and several turkeys, including a huge gobbler which had taken a violent dislike to Napoleon, and attempted to attack him whenever the Frenchman came close to it. Tiring of the turkey's antagonism toward him he decided to teach the gobbler a lesson. At the first sign of offensive tactics on the turkey's part, Napoleon rushed in, grasped the gobbling bird, and shoved its head deep down into a pile of cow dung alongside the barn.

After the startled turkey had extricated its head, the Frenchman strutted over and pointing his finger at it admonished:

"Ha, ha, Mistaire turkey gobelet! Where you been from—ain't it?"

Others among the countless foreign-born characters who have contributed so much color to the camp was Mohammed Murphy, an Afghan rug peddler, who had the court change his name to its present form "for business reasons."

Still another "Spuds," a Chinese waiter at a noodle parlor, who for six months went on a straight diet of potatoes, nearly killing himself while so doing—all because a big Irish patron of the noodle parlor had told him that was the way to become big and strong.

Then there was "Hughie" Evans, the Welsh butcher, who left his shop untended while taking on a few at a nearby saloon. Upon being cautioned by the proprietor of the shop, the next time Hughie felt a thirst coming on, he locked all meat save the hamburger in the icebox. Then he scrawled and placed a sign on the display case: "Hamburger Is All We Have Today. Help Yourself—Will Be Back Later."

Sports in the Early Days

WHEN there's rock in the box and the lads who put it there are off shift, that's the time when the camp's sporting blood shows itself. Sport in Butte never saw the day when it meant sitting around sipping tea and indulging in a quiet game of parcheesi. The lads from the mines required lusty diversions.

Bull and Bear Fight

The following event which took place On July 4, 1895, at Columbia Gardens illustrates this. Though it happened less than fifty years ago, yet it could have taken place in the medieval bear pits of London in 1595 before much the same type of crowd.

Nearly six hundred spectators assembled at the Gardens that day to see a huge black bull turned loose to face a shaggy bear. The bear retreated before the thundering charge of the bull and before it could be driven back into the pit Sheriff Sam Reynolds stopped the fight. Spectators threatened a riot unless their three dollar admission fee was returned. They were quieted when the word was quickly and cautiously passed among them: "Tomorrow."

The next day the same crowd gathered again. This time the bear did not retreat. Instead, its giant paw slashed out and ripped a great chunk from the bull's shoulder. Then it grasped the bull in a deadly hug, at the same time gouging dripping red flesh from the bull's flanks and rumps.

When the bull broke loose it was gory with blood, but it charged the bear repeatedly. At last the bear slipped in a pool of blood. Like a great juggernaut the maddened bull hooked, gored and stamped the bear into a pile of lacerated flesh and broken bones. When the bear's last feeble clawing ended, the bull stood watching its dead adversary with glazing eyes. Sheriff Reynolds arrived—too late. As he entered the arena with his deputies, the huge bull wobbled, dropped to its knees and rolled over-dead, but, nevertheless, the victor. The crowd, sickened by the brutal and gory sight, silently filed out to buoy up their spirits at the nearest saloon.

That was Butte.

Drilling Contests

". . . there were giants in those days."

There were indeed giants down in the mines where men did their daily stint with single jack, double jack and steel to bore the holes for the charges of powder that blasted out Butte's wealth in high-grade ore. These giants stood out and it is only natural that tales come down of their prowess in putting rock in the box. It was only natural, too, that arguments developed between men of different mines—arguments that had to be settled through contest backed by cash as hard as the rock they worked in.

Today, mechanical drilling machines, known as buzzies and Leyners, have replaced the old-time hand driller and have rung down the curtain on this more dramatic side of the mining game. But even some of these mechanical wonders are incapable of duplicating the drilling achievements of the men who hammered the steel home by muscle, speed and precision.

Walter Bradshaw, an old-time Butte double-jack man and co-winner of the drilling championship of the world, has often told that the easiest drilling contest he engaged in was against one of the mechanical drilling machines.

Bradshaw's eyes twinkle as he relates, "It was in Spokane, the day Joe Freethy and I won the world championship by drilling fifty-five inches in fifteen minutes. A salesman bet that his drilling machine could outdrill us for fifteen minutes. We took the bet and then took a look at the machine. The salesman, in turn, took a look at the hard piece of granite and paid off. His was a coal drilling machine." Bradshaw believes that had the salesman's drill been of the hard-rock type, he and his partner could have outdrilled it for the short period of fifteen minutes.

"That's where the machine is better than the man," said Bradshaw. "It can drill twenty-four hours a day, seven days a week, if necessary, without tiring."

Before mechanical rock drills were adopted, most blasting holes in mines were drilled by hand. The practice gained in swinging a hammer day after day, developed many expert drillers. A majority of the best drillers either made Butte their home or contested in the Mining City. Drilling contests were held regularly in Butte in the early 1900s. Mining companies donated prizes, the drillers made large-sized bets, and they were backed by their followers with money in important amounts.

When a drilling contest was held, everybody came to Butte. Saloons did a thriving business and, after a bit of communing with John Barleycorn, the miners would argue loud and long on the merits of the various drillers. By the time the contestants appeared "on the rock," nearly all the spectators had something at stake on the result. The larger the mining camp, the greater were the prizes; and Butte was the greatest of them all.

There are two principal types of drilling contests, double hand and single hand. A double-hand hammer, or double jack as it is generally called by miners, is gripped and swung with two hands. This kind of drilling calls for two men, one to strike the drill steel and the other to hold it in the hole and turn it after each blow. In single-hand drilling one man both strikes and turns the drill steel. Double-hand drilling is the more spectacular of the two and more exciting to watch. The two members of the team alternate at striking and holding for a period of fifteen minutes, making the change every minute or less.

The change calls for a high degree of cooperation. The top-notchers of the old days could execute this difficult maneuver so expertly that their actions had to be seen to be believed. There are fifteen pieces of steel in a set for a fifteen-minute contest. Double-hand drillers allow three inches difference in length for succeeding steels. This means that if each piece of steel is driven three inches in one minute, a hole forty-five inches deep would be the result at the end of a fifteen-minute period.

A small stream of water was directed into the hole by a helper to make the steel easier to turn and clean out the cuttings. A team of Butte drillers, Page and Reagan, first introduced what is known as the splash method of cleaning the hole. The records disclose that they were also the first to change steel without missing a blow and that they originated the maneuver known as "fostering." This is the striking of two blows by each man as they change. Each has a hammer in his hand and both strike two blows while shifting.

Changing steel at minute intervals is a man's job. To throw a long piece of steel from the hole and replace it with a still longer one while the striker is raising his hammer, requires strength, skill, coolness and extremely fast action, especially when the striker is swinging at the rate of as many as eighty-five to ninety blows per minute. This is where the rhythm comes in. The used steel flashes into the air and the replacer is smacked to the bottom of the hole a split second before the hammer descends on it.

Mike McNichols and Walter Bradshaw were considered by many as the best drillers in the business. Both won the majority of contests they entered and amassed small fortunes in prize money and wagers won. Bradshaw won over $13,000 in prizes alone in drilling contests held at Butte, Missoula, Mullan, Goldfield, Bisbee, El Paso and Tonopah.

It was in Spokane on October 25, 1901, that Bradshaw and Joe Freethy, another Butte driller, drove fifty-five inches into hard rock in fifteen minutes, a world record that has never been surpassed. Some old-timers refuse to accept this achievement as a world record, claiming that Gunnison granite was not used. This type of rock, quarried at Gunnison, Colorado, is known as the hardest of granites. Old-timers contend that no marks were considered as official unless Gunnison granite was used. Ed Chamberlain, Cripple Creek, and Carl Maka, Leadville, drilled what is said to be the deepest hole ever put down in Gunnison granite by two men. Their record is 46 5/8 inches, made at Bisbee, Arizona, in 1903.

Drilling contests were not confined to the professionals. Many impromptu matches were held, usually to settle arguments between miners. One of these, which caused a small flurry of excitement in Butte in 1888, was a match between Henry Page, brother of the professional driller, William Page, and Pat Kelly. The match was for $250 and was held back of the Parrot Mine before a crowd of some five hundred miners. The Anaconda Mine workers offered odds of five to three on Page with few takers. Page weighed 156 pounds and Kelly 160. Kelly drilled 14 ° inches in granite in ten minutes. Page then followed and won the match by drilling an 18-inch hole.

No story of rock drilling in Butte would be complete without reference to Harry Rodda and Mike Davey, two blind men, former Butte miners who lost their sight as a result of an explosion in the mines. To see them drill was an unusual experience. Their timing was perfect and their stroking a work of art. They engaged in many contests and finally turned their talents to exhibition drilling in all parts the country, including an appearance in Madison Square Garden, New York.

Drilling contests are now a memory of yesterday. The single and double jackers, with few exceptions, have passed away. A perfect tribute to their prowess stands in Mount Moriah cemetery in Butte. The monument to the drillers who have passed on is the historic stone on which many single and double jackers won and lost their laurels at Columbia Gardens.

Coursing

While rock drilling contests came directly from the mines, many of Butte's sports had an indirect connection in that they were brought from the homelands of those who came to work in the mines of the camp. Such were the sports of the Cousin Jacks who came from the mines of Cornwall in the "Old Country."

Times were hard in Cornwall and, as conditions became more acute, the sons of Cornwall betook themselves to the United States where "a mon could get 'imself a meal and 'is dog a bloomin' bone." They carried with them fond memories of coursing and in a short while, when enough money was accumulated, the Cornishman would send 'ome for 'is cousin 'Airy and tell 'im, "Be sure to bring along the racin' dog."

So many Cornishmen were named Jack, and so many sent passage money to their cousins of the same name, that it wasn't long until Cornishmen, no matter what their given names, were called Cousin Jacks. Thousands of them settled in Butte, where their mining talents were in demand.

It was but natural that the favorite sport of their days in Cornwall be revived. In 1898, the first coursing track was built in Butte. Named the West Side Coursing Track, although it was located in the south-eastern part of the city, it was to see twenty years of prosperity. During its heyday the track drew from five to six thousand persons on Sunday afternoons.

Two dogs were usually matched in a race, although at times three were allowed to compete. The speed of the dog, while important, was not always the most important quality. A dog's ability to turn the rabbit, or keep it away from the holes in the hedged side of the track and on a straight course counted for more in the judge's opinion than any other feature. Of course the dog fast enough to catch the rabbit before it was turned was usually considered the winner. A judge on horseback followed the dogs around the course and checked points on turning, catching, and general behavior. Some dogs were so well trained that they would hurdle the competing dog's body to get the rabbit.

In 1902 the sport reached the peak of popularity in the camp. That year disagreements among dog owners and the track officials were many, but, contrary to the usual rule, such arguments only added to the publicity and the coursing fans increased in numbers. The Silver Bow Coursing club was organized that year, composed mostly of owners. This group forced the resignation of Judge Carter as the recognized official at the track. Other officials were appointed in his place, but all proved incompetent, and the following season Carter was again astride the horses, checking the greyhounds for points.

The coursing track was closed temporarily in 1905 when the competition of horse racing with free admission drew many supporters of greyhound tracing away. From 1906 to 1917 there was a revival of the sport and the betting booths at the coursing track were crowded on Sunday afternoons.

Two booths were provided for bettors, one booth for each dog. Many bets were also accepted on the rabbit, but very few were paid as the majority of the dogs made a kill. There were times when the last of the match races on a card would have to be called off because of lack of rabbits.

When Owen P. Smith, a former coursing man, invented the electric rabbit in 1918, the sport deteriorated in the minds of most Jacks. There were some, however, who entered their dogs in the new sport but most insisted that the old way was the best. As one old time Cousin Jack puts it, "You give the 'are 'is 'ole and you give thee 'ound hay treat 'ee hunerstands. Both the blighters get a chance, my son, in coursin.'"

Cornish-style Wrestling

Cornish wrestling was another popular sport introduced to Butte by the Cousin Jacks. Any native of Cornwall, transplanted to the hills of Butte, the mountains of Michigan or the South American steppes, will tell in unforgettable language how "the bloody ways of the fahncy blokes cahnt compare to the 'eel and helbow gents indulgin' in a bout of Cornish-style man throwin'!" And many who aren't Cornish will agree.

Strangler Lewis, Farmer Burns, Joe Stecher, Man Mountain Dean, and even Butte's old favorite, Pat Connolly, are relegated to the wrestler's limbo when Cornishmen recall the early-day champs of the Butte camp. Nick Crewell, Tony Harris, Tim Harrington, the Chapman trio, Charley Vellenweth, Bill Andrews and many others, all had backers among the clans, and bravely went out to toss or die, lest their friends lose the homestead on the match.

A thousand dollar side bet was a common wager of the Cornish wrestlers and many more thousands would change hands among their followers, a considerable sum when it is recalled that an audience of three hundred was a large crowd. The scene of most of the matches in Butte was the Arena, on Talbot Avenue in the rear of Union Hall, a swing-door emporium that vied with the Michigan House in pleasing the thirsty fans.

In 1900, Tony Harris was the popular champion of the Butte camp acclaimed by every Cornishman on "the Hill" as "the best man to ever wear a jacket." So confident of the prowess of Harris were the Cousin Jacks of Butte that plans were made to bring the English champion, Pierce, to the mining camp and wrest away his hard-won laurels. The Englishman, however, was not to be tempted and refused all offers to show his ability in Butte.

Gaelic Football

The Irish, like the Cornish, had their favorite sport—ancient as the Emerald Isle itself, and just as fascinating. Even the bards recorded it in their songs:

> "Ye champions of fair Lusk and ye of Swords,
> View well this ball, the present of your lords,
> To outward view, three folds of bullock's hide,
> With leather thongs bound fast on every side,
> A mass of finest hay concealed from sight.
> Conspire at once and make it firm and light."

This poem was chanted by a master of ceremonies in 1721 as an introduction to a game of the famed Irish sport between the villages of Lusk and Swords. Gaelic football was then no infant sport, as it had been played in Dublin as far back as 1521.

It has been a long time since the beginning of the sport, but the rules of the game and the spirit of competition remain much the same. However, there have been a few changes. Today, there are fifteen men to a side, whereas, up to 1884, the entire male population of a village engaged in a contest. In 1884, the men of Tipperary met those of a Waterford, 34 to a side, near Carrick on the Suir. The fierce game ended in a scoreless tie when one of the players kicked the ball, or the *lithroid coise,* as it was then known, out of the neighborhood.

As played in the copper camp, there have been occasions when exceptions were taken to the rules, one of the most notable being a disregard for many of the finer points of the game and the vulnerability of the players' bodies in a match between the Wolftones of Butte and the Emeralds of Anaconda in 1911. Such present-day notables, at that time hard-rock miners, as Judge Jeremiah Lynch, John "Sherrig" Sullivan, alderman and tavern owner; "Firebug" Murphy, mine shiftboss; "Pidgeon" Shea, United States Forest Service worker and captain of the team, and John Sheehan, present-day saloon keeper, were members of the Wolftones and played with the same tenacity of spirit as shown by that Irish patriot, Wolf Tone, for whom they were named.

The game was played in Anaconda before several thousand spectators, who received much more amusement than they were entitled to at fifty cents per head admission. Fortunately, no fatalities were recorded, but the fierceness of the contest was something to behold. The aggressiveness of the players spread to the stands and "a fine old Irish time was had by all." The Wolftones were victorious by the score of 4 to 3, and were heralded as the Gaelic football champions of the Northwest and the winners of the Gaelic league's gold medal. The Emeralds took consolation in the majority of victories achieved by their backers in the fist fights that took place among the spectators.

The game retained its popularity in Montana until the year 1926. After a strenuous tussle won by the Wolftones from the Emeralds at the close of the 1926 season, the teams disbanded. Except for occasional games in more recent years, little attention has been given the sport and the old Gaelic war cry, "Schlam bath to boo tay" (pass or push the ball), is no longer heard. The younger Irish-Americans, whom the natives of the "Old Sod" sometimes refer to as "narrowbacks," together with a liberal sprinkling of Croatian, Italian, English, Scottish, and Lithuanian offspring, have taken the zest out of the game for the old country Irishman, who refuses to waste his time watching such "sissy goin' ons."

Boxing

Boxing was as big a favorite in Butte's early days as football. All the town did homage to a fighter, if he was a good one; and all were ready to shell out their money to watch their favorites in the ring. Such an outlay of ready money attracted the world's best over a period of two decades. Champions, near champions and aspiring champions were eager to show their wares in Butte where they were assured of a square deal and a purse large enough to insure them of something more than a few square meals.

And so they came—all the great ones from John L. Sullivan to Jack Dempsey; the champions in exhibition bouts and the future champions and near-greats in many grueling encounters that either took them up or set them back a rung on the ladder of fistic fame. Local boys served as trial horses—Mose and Sil LaFontise; Mike, Dan, Montana Jack and Twin Sullivan; Eddie and Willie McGoorty, Jack Munroe, Maurice Thompson, "Boy" Robinson, Jack O'Keefe, Buddy King, Stanley

Ketchell, Battling Nelson, Leo Flynn, Spider Kelly, Jerry McCarthy, Ike Hayes, Joe Simonich, Dixie LaHood, Thor Olsen and a hundred others whose names are lost to oblivion. Some were born in Butte, others were attracted, called it home, and were recognized as Butte boys.

In 1894, the Boston strong boy, John L. Sullivan, came to Butte and found a bit of tough opposition in an aspiring youngster dubbed "Boy" Robinson. Robinson, weighing but 155 pounds, was to receive one thousand dollars if he stayed four rounds with the mighty 225-pound Sullivan. "Boy" was knocked down all of fifteen times before he went down for keeps in the last twenty seconds of the fourth round. But Sullivan knew he had been in a fight, bruises on his body showing the telling effects of the skinny "Boy's" hitting power. Robinson and his many followers contended that he had received a "short count" and could have stayed the entire distance. All Sullivan had to say was a terse, "Mebbe so."

On the same card, Kid McCoy, the reigning middleweight champ, met Dave Cusick, another Butte lad. Cusick carried away the honors in the first round and had McCoy on the floor for a short count. The second round was judged even up to the last seconds, when McCoy got Cusick in a corner and knocked him against a second's chair which had been prematurely placed in the ring. The Butte man stumbled and went to his knees. As he was rising, McCoy let go with a sizzling right to Cusick's jaw. Cusick claimed a foul and thought the referee had agreed with him. He went to his corner and had removed his gloves by the time the bell sounded for the third round. Not prepared to continue the fight, Cusick was disqualified and McCoy declared the winner. The majority of those who saw the affair called it skullduggery. The men never met again.

It was in December, 1902, that Jack Munroe, the fighting Butte miner, gave James J. Jeffries, the undisputed heavyweight champion of the world, a Christmas present in the form of a four-round bout that earned the Butte man the right to meet Jeffries the next year in a championship fight.

With the camp at its zenith of feverish activity and with gold and silver pieces bulging the miners' jeans, the year 1903 was a big one for the fight game in Butte. Two fight cards a day were offered in more than one instance to the sport loving public. On June 13, Jimmy Britt, the California lightweight sensation, fought a twenty-round draw with Jack O'Keefe, a Butte regular, before six thousand howling fans. That same evening, Aurelia Herrera, the Mexican lightweight flash and a Butte favorite every time he showed, scored a fourth round knockout on Kid Broad at a local theater. All four contestants were of championship caliber and thus able to satisfy the hunger of the fans.

Consecutive fight cards seemed to meet with approval and July, 1903, saw Butte as the scene of two world championship fights. Joe Wolcott, the great welterweight champ, put his crown at stake for Mose LaFontise, a Butte product, to shoot at. The fight was scheduled for twenty rounds the night of July 3 at a Butte theater. Joe Gans, the lightweight champ, was to meet Buddy King, another local boy on the afternoon of the Fourth. Both fights drew maximum crowds, with the SRO sign in evidence. Butte, the sporting town, was fight mad.

As an aftermath to this Fourth of July celebration, Joe Wolcott and his second, Jack Johnson, who was later to carve himself a niche in the fighting hall of fame, found themselves locked up in the Butte bastile. They were charged with malicious mischief.

The colored gentlemen, admitting a professed love for chicken, stated that their dogs, given to them by Butte admirers, preferred the delicacy of rabbit. Unselfishly, they had given their dogs free access to a pen of the choicest Belgian hares at the Butte coursing track where the rodents were confined as future lures for racing dogs. Upon payment of a hundred dollar fine each, the two pugilists were released.

It was during this same period that a future middleweight champion of the world came to Butte and started his sensational fighting career by taking on the job as bouncer at the Copper King saloon. His name was Stanley Ketchell and he provided the fans of Butte and other sport centers with a thrill every time he donned the padded mitts. Another promising middleweight, Maurice Thompson, had gained a certain amount of fame and made Butte his headquarters. Thompson met Ketchell three times in Butte rings and beat him each time. Thompson was the only man to beat the great Stanley in a second meeting. At that time Thompson was an experienced boxer while Ketchell was green.

Between 1903 and 1905, Ketchell showed repeatedly in Butte with varied success. Most of his fights took place in the old Casino theater where he defeated such able ringsters as Kid Tracey, Jimmy Quinn, Harry Maguire, Joe Mudro and Jack Grimes. Montana Jack Sullivan, Butte electrician, fought Ketchell twenty rounds to a draw at this time. From Butte, Ketchell's fistic endeavors took him to Goldfield, Nevada, and then on to California and the world's championship. Ketchell never returned to Butte as a champion but corresponded frequently with his many Butte friends.

Stanley Ketchell met an untimely end early in the fall of 1910 when he was murdered while visiting at the ranch of his manager, Wilson Mizner, in the Ozark mountains of Missouri.

Battling Nelson, the durable Dane, who was later the world's lightweight champion, met up with Herrera, the Mexican flash, in a twenty-round Labor Day bout on September 5, 1903. Both men were crowd pleasers and the battle was a slashing, punishing affair. One round might be a clever exhibition of the finer points of the game and in the next science would be forgotten and the men would trade blow for blow. That's the way it went, round after round. The crowd became hysterical. Bets on the outcome were made right up to the last round. Nelson was declared the winner. There was some dissatisfaction with the decision, but all agreed it was a fight to be remembered.

Nelson returned to the Mining City in 1907 and appeared in an exhibition four-round affair which has been described as desultory. The bout was arranged after the arrival of Nelson, the purpose of his visit being to find a crooked gambler who had fleeced him out of a considerable sum of money.

Horse Racing

Sunken in the untended outer stretches of a little Catholic cemetery in Butte, crazily askew and rapidly crumbling from the deteriorating effects of years of rain, snow, wind, and sunshine, a granite marker struggles to maintain a slight bit of recognition. It is a memorial to Sam Lucas, horse trainer, horse lover, and Kentucky gentleman.

Inlaid in the floor of the buffet of the Montana Hotel in Anaconda is the replica of a horse's head. It is done in colored hard woods, a thing of rare beauty. It is a reproduction of the head of Tammany, a thoroughbred racehorse, owned by Marcus Daly, the copper king in the 1890's—a memorial to one of the greatest of the performers on the turf. Tammany was Marcus Daly's pride and joy. Sam Lucas was Tammany's trainer.

A streamlined speedster, Tammany was treated with all the respect shown to royalty. Tammany was housed in quarters that would have satisfied an Indian potentate, and he shared his quarters with Lucas. Carpeted floors, shining brass rails, modern plumbing—nothing was lacking to make Tammany's home stable at Hamilton the grandest in the world. Tammany accepted the setting as a natural heritage. Lucas was unawed by the palatial splendor and tolerated it only because it provided a fitting background for his one great love, Tammany.

When Marcus Daly brought from the East a highly recommended horse trainer and placed him in charge of the Daly stock farm, Lucas rebelled; not openly, but like a hurt child. He took the orders of the new boss and lackadaisically performed his duties. He nursed his injured feelings and sought solace in the company of the great Tammary as he exercised the racing beauty on the private oval track. This track was five-eighths of a mile and had a base of eight inches of solid loam, cushioned with tan bark and a surface of sod. The track was entirely roofed over and the temperature was kept constant.

When Cosgrove, the new trainer, selected Inverness to be the Daly entry in the Ashley Plate race at Newmarket and relegated the great Tammany to the starting post in an unimportant race, Lucas fumed and stormed, but Cosgrove had his way. Inverness ran third in the Ashley Plate and Lucas was vindicated. He was also successful in keeping Tammany from contending with the selling platers.

Sam's great love for Tammany was shared by Marcus Daly. Poor judgment on the part of Cosgrove brought down on him the wrath of the mining magnate. Daly summoned Cosgrove to his office, counted out twenty thousand dollars in bills of the one-thousand dollar denomination, and brought back Cosgrove's two-year contract. Sam Lucas was called in and told by Daly to take charge of the stables. He was given complete authority. He was to nominate all horses from Daly stables for all races and supervise their training. Daly asked but one thing in return—winners. No contract was made as these men were content with each other's word. The salary was ten thousand a year, plus all expenses and a percentage of the stakes won by Daly's horses.

It was then that Lucas came into his own. He haunted the leading race tracks of the country, flashily dressed in the top styles of the gay nineties. He was the emperor of a domain of from 90 to 120 horses. Lucas mingled with millionaires, professional men, gamblers and hangers-on of the turf. He would never give a capitalist nor a stable boy a tip on a race, but he was an easy touch for anything from a five-spot to a thousand-dollar bill.

Lucas' sudden affluence, though it changed his mode of living, did not alter his success as a trainer. In a few days less than four months, Tammany was winner in four out of five starts on New York, Coney Island, Brooklyn and Kentucky tracks. The Withers, Lawrence Realization, Lorillard and Jerome stakes were won by the long loping strides of Tammany. Charade beat him the fifth time out in the Tidal stakes at Coney Island.

Lucas took the defeat by Charade as a personal rebuke. Firm in his belief that Tammany was unbeatable, he set about correcting the one error. He watched over Tammany like a mother. He wouldn't allow a groom or swipe near Tammany and personally attended the animal. For three weeks Sam was missing from the tracks as he cared for every whim of the great horse. Four weeks from the day that Charade had beaten Tammany, Lucas saw Tammany give the same Charade seven pounds in weight and come thundering down the stretch, a winner by three lengths.

All of Lucas' attention was not given to Tammany. From the Marcus Daly stables the same season Montana led the four-year-olds in twelve starts, with four winners and six thirds. Montana was the horse that came from behind in the 1892 Suburban Handicap with Snapper Garrison up, to pass a top-notch field in a driving finish. The Daly horse trailed the field until the great Snapper started booting him home in the run down the stretch. Since that race, in any line of sport when a competitor comes from behind to win, it is known by the tag line—a Garrison finish.

There were other Daly horses; some that were great. Among them were Scottish Chieftain and Bathhampton. But there was only the one Tammany. He was the horse for whom the whole town of Anaconda celebrated with a big party when he defeated Larne Lighter in a match race. He was the horse the old-timers of Butte and Anaconda still tell tales about as if he had been a temperamental human artist who had reached legendary peaks.

With the season over, Sam Lucas took a much needed vacation. He had his pockets lined with money and headed for Butte to have a bit of fun.

His popularity with the sporting gents of that day proved his undoing. Many a toast was drunk to Tammany, to Daly, to Lucas, to life, to anything and everything. For three days the party continued and increased in tempo. At the height of the gaiety Lucas received a telegram from the Hamilton stables. So that his fun would not be interrupted, Lucas declared, "I won't open it. A man deserves a vacation and a vacation should not be disturbed by business."

The next morning Sam ordered the bellhop to bring him a morning eye-opener. Ever meticulous about his appearance, he ordered the bellboy to take his suit out to the tailor shop to be pressed. As he emptied out the pockets, he came upon the unopened telegram. He opened it and read, "Tammany sick. Return immediately."

The eye-opener remained untouched. Lucas hurried to Missoula and from there to the Daly stables at Hamilton—but too late. Tammany had been dead three hours when he arrived.

After that Sam was never the same. He had truly loved Tammany and had cherished hopes of making him the greatest winner of all time. He blamed his own negligence as the cause of the horse's death. But for his sincere loyalty to Marcus Daly he would have tendered his resignation. Daly, too, lost a great deal of his interest in horse racing with the death of

Tammany. Notwithstanding, Daly horses continued to win with astounding regularity on tracks in all parts of the country.

Lucas' sorrow was somewhat assuaged when Daly took him to Anaconda and showed him the artistic reproduction of the noble racer's head which he had caused to be carved and imbedded in the floor of the state's leading hostelry at a cost of thousands of dollars. Both men, the millionaire mining magnate and the former stable boy, stood with heads uncovered in silent meditation as they paid tribute to their friend, the animal they believed to be the super-horse of all time. In later years, neither Daly nor Lucas would visit the hotel without pausing in reverence at the replica of Tammany.

In 1900 with the death of Marcus Daly, a pall fell over the famous stock farm. Without Daly's guiding genius and enthusiasm, activities lessened. Settlement of the Daly estate caused the sale of the thoroughbreds and the complete wrecking of Sam Lucas' fond hopes for a champion.

Sam drifted over the country, following horses and racing meets. He made occasional bets and sustained himself comfortably, but not in the fashion of his heyday. With the passing years, his small fortune faded and he returned to Butte in 1918, a broken, disconsolate hanger-on at pool and bar rooms.

In January of 1929, Sam became ill. Without funds, he was removed to the county hospital where he passed away, March 29, 1929.

Sam Lucas and Marcus Daly were high lights of an era. There were other race track celebrities in a smaller way, of course. They too, did their part in the heyday of racing in Montana and some wrote track history.

There was the great sprint horse, Bob Wade, who, in 1890, carrying 122 pounds, ran two furlongs in 21˘ seconds, still a world's record. And sixteen years later there was Atoka, another sprinter, who, carrying 105 pounds, ran three furlongs in 33° seconds, another world's record. These records, both made on the Butte track, stand unbroken to this day.

Jockeys, too, came from Butte, and some acquired great fame. The greatest of them all was Red Pollard, who was usually up on the immortal Sea Biscuit and was much sought after by the turf kings of the present day.

Cock Fights

"Hens are made for the kettle and cocks are made to fight."

This terse statement expressed the attitude of the men, and the women, too, who followed the cockfight circuits and gambled their money on the prowess of their favorite birds in the pits. It may have been the sight of fresh blood, the element of chance or the belief of all cockfighting addicts that their birds are potential champions that caused the cock owners to lead a gypsy life and travel hundreds of miles to pit their birds against reputable opponents. Whatever the reason, a cockfighting enthusiast will argue that the game gets in the blood and becomes a vital part of one's existence.

Thirty years ago, a recognized center of the game was the booming, sport-loving mining camp of Butte. Austere bankers, mining magnates and sedate professional men matched their favorites against cocks owned by brothel keepers, panderers and tin-horn gamblers. Hundreds of dollars would exchange hands on a single match. Many a cockfight was decided not by the birds, but by the owners and backers who fought tooth and nail to prove that a recently killed bird was the victim of a foul.

Such personal encounters added zest to the sport and increased the interest of the followers. As enthusiasm mounted, attendance at the matches, frowned on by law, increased. In the early 1900's cockfights were held in several widely separated spots. The Chicken Flats of Walkerville, the Boulevard district, Meaderville and west of the city from Crystal Springs to Gregson Springs were favorite gathering places of the followers of the sport. Illegal, the pits for fighting were enclosed in some obscure hideaway. A few scattered raids were made by law officials at the behest of disgruntled neighbors, who believed the sport to be brutal. There is no record of convictions, however.

Cockfight fans contend that the sport is not brutal and is quite as humane as chopping off a chicken's head to make it ready for the pot. When a bird is badly injured and suffering pain it is speedily decapitated and put out of its misery. Old-timers in the game tell with relish of a certain prominent Butte businessman, who scorned to use a knife or his hands on a badly disabled cock's neck. He made certain of the cock's entry into a warrior's heaven by placing the head of the bird in his mouth and severing it from the body by a quick crunching of his jaws. Any blood or feathers were washed away by a copious gargle of whisky.

The bravery of the cocks in the pits is something to behold. One law of the sport appears to be an unbreakable one—the law of courage. It spurs the cocks on to fight, even when badly gashed and the life blood is streaming from their veins. A game cock never knows when he is beaten and thousands of the birds literally commit suicide in their attempts to rise and have one last slash at their opponents. It is indomitable courage of the birds that attracts followers to the sport and causes them to back their favorites to the limit in the battle pits.

Wysteria, a Rhode Island Red, smaller than most fighting cocks and winner of thirty consecutive fights in the Butte and Anaconda rings, is credited with passing to the great beyond in a suicidal manner. This demon of the pits was the property of a businessman of Butte. The little bird is said to have won more than eight thousand dollars for his owner. His success in the pit was attributed not so much to his stamina as to his lightning-like speed when released by his handler. Like a bolt of feathered lightning, Wysteria would flash across the ring to meet his opponent. The zenith of his rush invariably took place just as he reached the breastbone of his opponent, and the very speed and fury of his rush would drive the other back, off balance. A flash of steel and Wysteria's spur would strike home in a vital region, usually the foreneck of the luckless opponent. It is claimed that Wysteria never varied the location of the fatal blow by more than an eighth of an inch.

His last and fatal fight was lost by this gallant cock, not through incompetence but rather through over-eagerness to complete the coup. He rushed his opponent, Crocus, a much larger bird of unremembered breed, in the usual manner and with almost the usual result, but his timing was off and the spur, instead of reaching the foreneck of Crocus, became lodged in the breastbone. Ever the fighter, Wysteria attempted to use his other spur and in doing so went to the gravel. Attempting to rise, his own spur, somehow, became engaged in his own neck. His owner and many of his backers insisted that Wysteria, incensed at his slight error in timing, considered himself disgraced and committed hara-kiri.

Other cocks were as prominent and successful as Wysteria, but none was respected as much as this bantam of the pits, according to old-timers.

Two or three hundred men and a light sprinkling of women comprised the average crowd at the early-day Butte fights. As many as thirty matches were fought on one card, but the average card consisted of ten fights. Cock owners were not confined to Butte alone, but came from Anaconda, Missoula and Helena to fight their birds. The better type of fighting cock was valued often as high as $500. Many of the cocks fighting in the Butte area were imported from Ireland and Scotland, but the majority were from the Carolinas and Tennessee. Wagers on the outcome were made at the pits between individuals, although in later years a few bookmakers took up the sport and conducted a profitable business in the manner of horse racing bookmakers.

Cocks are trained and cared for with the same diligence afforded a first-class fighter. While training, the birds are not spurred for fear they might inflict injury on each other. Certain diets are prescribed and very little water is allowed a high-class fighting cock. Many owners give their birds liberal doses of whisky. Whisky, too, is often used as a stimulant to revive a battered bird so that he may live to fight another day. In the early days of the sport, hypodermic injections were used for the same purpose but are now banned as unsportsmanlike.

The spurs used are of fine lightweight steel and are kept honed to a razor-like sharpness. These spurs are curved like talons and are made to fit over the cock's natural spurs. The birds are handled in the pits by individual handlers, usually the owners. When the word is given to go, the handler releases his tight grip on the cock's sides and the bird wings his way to the center of the ring. A judge decides the winner and disqualifies a bird he considers too weak to continue. On many occasions the decisions of the judges are disputed, but to no avail as the judges are as dictatorial as the umpires in major league baseball.

In many instances the death of one of the contestants decides the battle without a dispute. Considering the ferociousness of the fights and the vulnerability of flesh to cold steel, it is surprising the number of birds that come out of the pits alive.

The tension of the crowd can be sensed and is a part of the proceedings. In but few cases are there any shouts of encouragement to the birds. Cockfight fans contend that such solemnity is a tribute to the courage of the birds. Neither is there heard any sound from the cocks as they go about their deadly business. Immediately following a match, however, the victor invariably gives forth a lusty crow.

Cockfights are still an attraction in some parts of Butte and also in surrounding towns, but the popularity of the game has dwindled considerably.

Dog Fights

Dog fighters, or the men who own the animals and bet their money on their fighting ability, will tell you the dog fights because it is his nature. "A bulldog of this breed enjoys the thrill of battle," they insist, "and if retired from the pits, will gradually lose interest in life and waste away." Others who have observed dog fights are of the opinion that the dogs fight, even to the very death, just to please their masters. Certain it is, that a dog, if a winner, will look to his master for praise, and if a loser, will crawl to his corner in a cringing manner, willing to receive his master's condemnation.

The owners of the dogs held their respective fighters on short leather straps or leashes and with the word "go," they hastily unloosened the spring latch and the fight was on. Low, ominous growls heralded the opening lunge as they parried for position like well-trained boxers. During the actual fighting the dogs remained quiet. Occasionally, a dog would squeal or give a low growl, but such occasions were few. The throat was the main objective of the fighters, but the dogs had their peculiarities and many of them preferred to cripple an opponent by crunching the bones of the leg. With an opponent crippled, it was only a matter of time until he was virtually helpless and the stage was set for the kill. The average dog fight lasted about ten minutes, but dog men tell of fights that have lasted for an hour and a half.

One particular fight the old pitmen like to talk about was a battle that raged for an hour and five minutes and resulted in the death of both contestants. Blubber, an imported English bulldog, and Mighty Thor, a nondescript dog, partly English bull and mostly common cur, were the participants. The fight took place at the old Hog Ranch, a notorious rendezvous of the period for gamblers, tired businessmen, playboys, harlots, and other seekers of amusement.

It was a summer evening in the year, 1909. The roadhouse was jammed with customers. Only a select few, however, were aware of the main attraction and were permitted to attend the fight which took place in a small building adjoining the main structure.

In the early part of the evening, with liquor flowing freely and the owners of the dogs boasting of the abilities of their fighters, enthusiasm waxed hot and it was "put up or shut up." Continued argument boosted the wagers until each owner had planked down $550 on the outcome. This was only a small part of the money wagered. Patrons of the establishment chose their favorites and backed them with cash to the amount of over five thousand dollars, according to one spectator. A few women gained admission to the fight arena and are said to have greatly enjoyed the brutal proceedings.

With the dogs in their corners and the fight about to begin, it was necessary to postpone the start. Mighty Thor became violently sick and regurgitated the contents of his stomach. It was rumored the dog had been fed raw hamburger and stale beer. Accusations were made and hastily denied. As a fighting dog receives no food for three hours before a fight and is given only a scant amount of nourishment for two days preceding an encounter, it was believed that the match would have to be postponed. However, Mighty Thor's owner, an early-day Butte saloon keeper, asked for only an hour's delay in which to get his dog back in shape.

Perhaps it was this sickness that caused the defeat of Thor, as was claimed by many who had bets up on him. His owner, however, admitted that the dog put up the stoutest battle of his career and lost the fight by only a few seconds time.

Mighty Thor was the aggressor throughout most of the battle and repeatedly sank his fangs into the English bull's throat, only to be shaken off and forced to withdraw to save his legs from punishment. At the end of an hour both Thor and Blubber were in bad shape. Thor was limping and had lost the use of his right forefoot. His beautiful brown coat of hair was dyed a sickening bloody hue, and one ear was all but completely chewed away and hung limply. Blubber was in very much similar shape, bleeding profusely from the hindquarters and with stomach and throat shredded to bloody ribbons. It was apparent that the fight was all but over and stamina alone was to decide the winner.

Still with courage that had no par, both dogs continued to tear away at each other for another five minutes. At this juncture, Blubber caught Thor by the throat and sank his teeth home in a death grip. The Mighty Thor sank to the floor slowly and breathed his last.

It took all of three minutes to release the English bull's hold. The victor was Blubber. He was carried by his master to the corner where hot, raw whisky was forced down his throat. His wounds were bathed and dressed, but to no avail. He went out of this world to an accompaniment of shouts and cheers for Blubber, the champion, as his backers returned to the barroom to spend their winnings—winnings gained at the cost of a brave dog's life.

Interest in fights between animals took an unusual turn in the fall of 1891. Followers of dog fighting engaged in an argument as to the relative speed and fighting qualities of dogs and wolves. To decide the matter, a wolf was captured and the fight was held at the race track on November 8, 1891.

A cage containing the wolf was brought to the center of the paddock and the door of the cage was opened. The wild animal leaped out and started to run. When he had a start of about two hundred yards, two greyhounds and a bulldog were unleashed.

The wolf ran around the enclosure several times, looking for some place of escape. The fleet hounds, clearing several yards at a bound, were soon at the heels of the wolf. Finally they overhauled the frightened animal and dogs and wolf rolled over in a tangle, snapping and snarling at each other.

Soon the wolf was up and off again, pursued closely by the dogs. Again he was overtaken and another scrap resulted. This performance of alternately fighting and then chasing the wolf went on for nearly an hour. At last the wolf eluded the dogs and disappeared among some buildings on the grounds. He was found later in a badly chewed condition and was shot. The dogs came out of the series of battles showing no evidence of bites or scratches.

Italian Boccie

National pastimes peculiar to the natives of European countries found their way to the new world and many have become associated with the American way of life. One of the more popular sports with the Italian immigrants is boccie, a variation of the old English game of bowls and having many of the aspects of the American school-boy's game of "folly-taw."

Meaderville, the Italian colony of Butte, is a favored locale for the boccie addicts. Today, only the old-timers indulge in the sport, but in previous years hundreds waited their turns on the alleys. In former days interest in the sport was amplified by the high wagers made. Today, a glass of beer or a shot of *grappa* is all that hinges on the outcome. Yet, the vociferousness of the players and spectators would lead one to believe that an event of national importance was in progress.

Boccie is played on a hard earthen floor, six feet wide and ninety feet long. As many as eight contestants usually take part in the game, sometimes individually, and at other times in partnerships of two or four. Wooden or light steel balls, known as the boccies, are used and each player is allowed the use of two balls. Another ball, the jack, is rolled down the alley by either the lead-off man or a spectator and is the target at which the contestants shoot. Players maneuver to jockey the opponent's ball out of position and away from the jack, or to blockade the next player's ball from the area of the jack. The winner is the player whose ball is closest to the jack at the conclusion of the game.

Players become adept at curving the ball and much skill is shown by the expert boccie tossers in making the ball do their bidding. English similar to that used in the control of a bowling ball, as well as "return" balls and "jump" balls are a few of the deliveries executed in edging up to the target ball.

Forty-three boccie alleys dotted the vacant lots in Meaderville and the Austrian- and Slav-inhabited McQueen addition in the 1920s. Many Austrians also took part in the sport and played in match games with the Italian colonists. Today, three alleys are used occasionally. However, the followers of the sport are adept at makeshifts. At picnics of the Cristoforo Colombo and other Italian societies, the click of the boccies and the sounds of "viva," "bravo" and an occasional Bronx cheer are to be heard as the game is played on a greensward, hastily staked out by a few, not-to-be-denied, boccie addicts.

Curling

The ancient ice sport of curling has had its followers in Butte, chiefly among those of Scottish nationality. The game originated in Scotland centuries ago.

The game is played on a strip of ice one hundred and thirty-eight feet in length and ten feet in width. At each end is a circle, ten feet in diameter, with a twelve-inch circular spot in the center. Before a match starts the ice is prepared by being scraped twice and sprinkled with warm water through a perforated nozzle. This produces a pebbled face. The equipment for the game consists of stones of polished granite not to exceed thirty-six inches in circumference, four and one-half inches in height and forty-four pounds in weight; also a number of ordinary household brooms. The stones have curved handles.

A match is played with four players on a side. Each player casts two stones from a backline toward the ten-foot circle at the far end of the lane. The players propel the stone forward by a sliding push, while teammates hasten the progress of the stone toward the circle by energetically sweeping the ice before it with their brooms. After the stone has entered the circle, opposing players try to cause it to pass beyond the circle by sweeping before it. By twisting the handle in one direction or the other when casting the stone, it can be made to curve "in" or "out."

The object of the game is to place as many stones as possible closer to the inner circular spot than those of the opponents. A point is scored for each stone not cancelled by an opponent's stone with a better location. At the completion of the round the direction is reversed. Fourteen rounds are played and then the total score is taken. In reality, curling is lawn bowling on ice.

Considerable practice is necessary to acquire the right speed with which to cast the stone. If thrown with the speed the average bowler uses in delivering a ball at ten pins, the stone will pass through the circle and out of the playing lane.

The game has been played nearly every winter in Butte since the early 1890s. The principal opponents of the Butte curlers have been from Anaconda, where the sport also has had enthusiastic participants. Tournaments in curling are known as "bonspiels" and there were many in the years back between curlers of the two cities.

In 1911, the Butte curlers became so enthusiastic that they entered a team in the annual bonspiel at Winnipeg, which is to curlers what the annual American Bowling Congress is to ten-pin bowlers.

Among those who were prominent in the bonspiels between Butte and Anaconda were: Martin Martin, E. P. Mathewson, Pat Allen, N. B. Braley, T. H. Wilson, D. W. McGregor, N. A. McMillan, Dr. McGregor, Gene Moulthorpe, Malcolm Gillis, E. J. Barker and D. McMillan.

A few other pastimes of the miners were sometimes splashed with drops of red blood.

One such contest indulged in by the miners around holiday time, were the turkey shoots. Live turkeys were used as targets in these shooting matches. The bird was put in a box, its head sticking through a hole in the top, and the marksman who snipped off the head, won the turkey. Often the unlucky gobbler lost his beak inch by inch before losing his life. But no one heard of the miners registering any complaints about the cruelty involved. Sport was sport and let the feathers fly where they may. A turkey was a turkey, and didn't he have to bleed thoroughly before he was fit to eat?

Another Saturday afternoon pastime indulged in by the miners who were lovers of horse flesh, providing the livery stables would rent their horses for such a purpose, was called "Pogrom in a Hencoop." Along a street live chickens were buried, except for their heads, and the horsemen galloped by endeavoring to wring the fowl's neck without toppling from the saddle or pulling the entire chicken from the ground. This sport, the miners had borrowed or inherited from the plainsmen, and it called for great dexterity and a certain amount of expert horsemanship. But with a few generous snorts of whiskey aboard, many of the miners would have a try at the sport. The fact that they did not know one side of a horse from another did not deter then. Broken bones and even broken necks often resulted from the strenuous competition, not to mention the wear and tear on the chickens.

A sport requiring less skill and often indulged in by the early-day sports in East Side resorts was "Rat Baiting," brought to Butte, no doubt, from some of the waterfront dives of the East and West coasts. Enthusiasts of this pastime locked a hungry terrier or thoroughly starved and fighting-mad tomcat in a pen with a dozen or so large and famished rats and wagered on how long it would take the dog or the tomcat to polish off the rodents. Thanks to some of the more humane citizens of the camp, a line was drawn on this sadistic sport, and it was prohibited, with drastic penalties inflicted on any caught participating.

The old time devotees of sports in which the animal gets it in the neck or other vulnerable parts of its anatomy, were wont to excuse their interest in the sport by maintaining that the excitement of the chase or fights blinded the victims to pain and fright. Objectors to cruelty in sport stated that the soul-tearing sounds made by a tortured, dying animal have never made such an argument convincing.

Another sport in which the miners played little part, but from which the big-wigs of the community obtained many a thrill, was trap shooting with the shooters blasting away at live pigeons. This was considered the ultimate in a refined, Sunday afternoon pastime.

These were a few of the sports of Butte in the early days. For variance, there were always the Sunday afternoon grudge fights, fought with bare knuckles in some vacant lot or alley. Peculiarly, the law did not object to brutal exhibitions when the participants belonged to genus *homo.*

Copper Camp Cuisine

WITH Butte's polyglot population originating in practically every country of the globe, it was a certainty that many strange dishes would be found on the local menus. Each nationality brought its favorite dish from the old country and through fraternization between nationalities, many of them were soon adopted by the entire community.

The best example is that epicurian masterpiece of pie crust, beef and vegetables which Butte, with pardonable pride, claims as its very own—the Cousin Jack pasty.

The pasty, as prepared here, is beyond description in mere words. An Oscar of the Waldorf or a Rector could not begin to do it a full measure of culinary justice. Made strictly according to Cornish ritual, it is both a thing of beauty and nourishment to body and soul. No earthly mortal could delineate for a moment on its delights without waxing eloquent.

It is not exactly certain when the first pasty came into being. Mayhap it was the gods on Olympus, who in a palate-jaded moment, first concocted the delicious morsel. History is silent on the subject. The only thing that is at all certain is that it was to be found as the *piece de resistance* on Butte tables as far back as the oldest inhabitant cares to remember.

The old-timer, when in a retrospective mood, will tell you that the first pasty made its appearance in the camp simultaneously with the arrival of the first Cornish housewife who followed her husband to the mining city direct from her hearth in Cornwall. And that is many score years ago.

Be that as it may. The camp at once adopted the pasty as its own. Today it is as much a part of Butte as the ore dumps. There are few other cities where it may be found. Possibly among the copper mines of Michigan or the Coeur d'Alenes. Elsewhere it is alien. Restaurant keepers and waitresses look bewildered when a native of Butte asks for it. They have never heard of it.

Neither the making of a pasty nor its ingredients are complicated. Your true pasty maker will insist, "It is not so much what you put into them as how you put it in."

It would be the height of presumption, and an encroachment into the fields of art to attempt to give the various details as followed by a true pasty baker who has the "gift." The following directions, furnished by a Cornish woman, are intended as a guide to the novice, in hope that a hidden talent might be uncovered—that after diligent practice, another pasty maker might be given to the world.

The meat in a pasty is of vast importance. It must be beef of an excellent grade, Montana preferred. The finest cuts, tenderloin or sirloin are insisted upon. The meat should be diced to approximately the size of the third joint of a Cornish woman's little finger. It should weigh about three or four pounds. You do not make pasties in infinitesimal quantities.

Enough for the meat. Next, eight or ten fair sized Irish potatoes, peeled and diced—never sliced—into cubes of a size similar to the meat. The same procedure for whole, firm onions, in about half the quantity of the potatoes ... these are the ingredients.

And now the crust. The usual pie crust made with the addition of a breathed prayer or two will suffice. Keep praying. Mix thoroughly the meat and vegetables. Now, take generous heaps of the latter and wrap with dough that has been cut in the shape of a semi-circle about four inches in radius. Crimp edges and place in hot oven, not forgetting an added sprinkling of more prayers.

That is all there is to it. Sounds simple—but in the hands of the inept—or if sufficient prayers are forgotten—the result might turn out to be but a soggy mess. Expertly handled, however, the finished product is something to cause the true gourmet to contemplate on thoughts, ethereal and unworldly. A real pasty does those things to a human.

Serve it piping hot, with lashings of brown gravy, and it would indeed be an incurable dyspeptic who could not consume three or four at a single sitting. Served cold as a midnight snack, or at luncheon, a pasty always speaks for itself.

Fortunate indeed, is the miner so steeped in connubial bliss as to possess a better half, who in her loving care, as a token of her affection, places a pasty or two in the lunch box of her miner spouse. "A letter from home" is what the miners term such a setup.

A noted breakfast dish introduced in the late nineties was referred to as "stirabout," simply old-fashioned oatmeal mush, thinned with milk to the consistency of a medium-heavy gruel. It was, no doubt, the thousands of Irish miners who followed Marcus Daly to the town, who first introduced this acclaimed cereal.

In the early days, the single men of the camp far outnumbered the married, and it was for the unmarried that the many large miners' boarding houses sprang up. Famous among them was the Florence Hotel, known to the miners as the "Big Ship," the Clarence, dubbed the "Mad House," and the Mullin House in Centerville. Each of these hostelries fed several hundred miners daily, and prominent in the kitchen of each was the huge "stirabout" pot from which countless bowls of the gruel were ladled out each morning. At the Big Ship, an ingenious cook contrived a sort of chute arrangement on the copper "stirabout" pot from which the breakfast bowls were filled by simply pulling a lever. A one-time manager of the Big Ship tells that in the early days of the hotel, the daily consumption of "stirabout" was never computed in pounds but in tons. Nearly every boarder, he says, consumed at least two or three bowls of the succulent gruel at a sitting. Naturally, this custom added to the profits of the dining room, as the average miner who paid his board by the week, when fortified by several bowls of the filling cereal, had little appetite for the hot cakes or ham and eggs. At the Big Ship, this former manager claims, the time and services of a special cook were needed for the preparation and serving of the oatmeal. The miners were very particular, and were not above registering loud complaints if the "stirabout" was burned or not properly prepared.

So popular was the food that many of the miners insisted on having a bowl of the mush included in their dinner bucket for consumption down in the mine. The custom was to add the "stirabout" to their tea and drinking water, the miners believing that the mixture would act as a deterrent to weakness or heat cramps that often attack a miner underground. A pinch or two of salt was often added. That there was a certain amount of preventive value in the salt at least, has been later proven by scientists who have discovered that the cramps are caused by a loss of salt from the system due to the excessive perspiration. Butte miners who worked in the 100-degree "hot boxes"' also had the custom of salting their beer long before science learned the sound reason for the practice.

A story is told of one of the early-day miners, who upon taking his lady friend to one of the higher-class cafes for an after theater bite, became indignant and departed from the place in a huff because he could not find his beloved stirabout listed on the bill of fare.

Another food peculiar to the early-day Cornish, Welsh and Irish and to which a certain amount of superstition was attached was "boxty." As it is told, boxty was made from the first milk taken from a cow immediately after calving. This milk, a thick, clabber-like substance was strained thoroughly and then mixed with eggs and cornstarch or flour and steamed into a kind of pudding. At that period many families owned their own cow, and boxty was an annual treat. The eating of the pudding was supposed to bring luck to the eater, strength and virility to the males, and a degree of fecundity to the female members of the family. It was another Copper Camp food that had its origin in the old country.

Another dish that decorated the tables of many families was the Christmas Eve potato cake. Not to be confused with the potato pancakes of other communities, which were made by adding mashed potatoes to pancake batter, the Butte potato cake was a substantial affair a half-inch thick and baked in an oven.

The afternoon of Christmas Eve would find hundreds of Butte housewives preparing the potato cakes. A steaming vessel of golden, mashed and buttered potatoes was made ready and then flour kneaded in until a heavy, unleavened dough resulted. Carroway seeds were added to the mixture which was rolled out with a rolling pin until a great slab a half-inch thick lay before the housewife. The cakes were then cut out from this slab into triangular shape about four inches across the base. They were then placed in a large baking pan, popped into a hot oven and let bake until a golden brown.

For serving, the cakes were brought to the table steaming hot, where each diner cut them in half, lengthwise through the center, and added plenty of butter. The cakes served as the principal part of the meal and if any were left over they were saved until after Christmas when they were cut in half and reheated in a frying pan on the top of the stove. It was rarely that the potato cakes were served at other than Christmas time.

A favorite in Butte with the Scotch, Nova Scotians and many of the Irish miners was the oaten cake—a mixture of oatmeal, milk and water, pressed into a cake and baked to an iron hardness over an open fire. The oaten cake was claimed to give one great staying qualities and is said too often to have proved a staunch stand-by during periods of shutdown or depression.

Peculiar to the Serbian miners of the camp, but joined in by their friends and neighbors of other countries, was *povitica*, a sweetened, unleavened cake, blessed by the Orthodox priest. It was, and still is for that matter, the principal dish at the Serbian Christmas and Easter celebrations, set by the Julian calendar, which are observed some days later than the Christmas and Easter observed by other churches.

As is the custom on Serbian holidays, the womenfolk remain at home to prepare the feast, while the male members of the family visit in the homes of Serbian friends. A long table, covered with straw, symbolic of the manger, is set in the dining room of the Serb home. The povitica is set on a large platter at the head of the table. Baked hams, roast pork, beef, mutton, chickens, turkeys, geese and ducks are spread out on heavy chinaware surrounded by cakes and spiced sweets with decanters of wine, whisky and native plum brandy called *slivovitz.* A single large candle burns on the center of the table as a symbol of the star of Bethlehem.

The custom is for the male visitors to start with the *povitica* at the head of the table and then to sample a little of every variety of food displayed, ending up with a small glass of either whisky, wine or native *slivovitz.* It is the custom for all the neighbors and friends of a Serbian family to join them in the celebration of the holiday. It is accepted as a mark of esteem and friendship that the neighbors drop in some time during the day to wish them the season's greeting and partake of the feast. All through the day the visitors come and go, the women remaining standing while guests are present. Not until late in the evening when the last visitor has departed do the ladies of the household finally sit down for their share of the repast.

Unique also were the miners' lunch periods as enjoyed hundreds feet underground. While allowed but a half hour for lunch, it was the usual custom in the old days to take a full hour and sometimes longer. The lunch hour on both the night and day shifts began the instant the shift boss and foreman took the cage for the surface and ended when they were again lowered into the mine.

The miners congregated in groups for the meal hour, and usually found a cool, dry place in the fresher air on the sills of the level, away from the dust and gases of the stopes and raises where they worked during the shift. Each miner procured a clean, dry "laggin," the latter a three-inch plank about six feet long and sixteen inches wide. This was propped up and made into a comfortable seat, which at the conclusion of the lunch was usually turned into a bed.

Illumination for the feast was furnished in those days by the miners' candles stuck into the surrounding timbers by a sharp-pointed steel candle stick. The lunch hour was always a period of conviviality and story telling. Many of the tall tales attributed to the miners had their inspiration at these lunch-hour gatherings.

Mixed among the groups of underground diners might be native Americans from all points of the country, with Finns, Irish, Serbs, Cornish, Swedes, Norwegians, Welsh, Canadian, Scotch, Manxmen, Cleetermores, Italians, Poles, Austrians, and perhaps an old Mexican or Chilean miner. And as variegated as the nationalities were the different foods laid out in front of the diner.

Ham sandwiches, cake, fruit and apple pie might comprise the contents of the American's buckets, while his Irish workmate might face practically the same array with one exception. The son of Erin would be washing his food down, not with coffee, but with strong, black tea sometimes fortified by the addition of the aforementioned stirabout.

Holding prominent place in the Cornish miner's lunch bucket would be the well-browned, generous-proportioned pasty or "letter from 'ome." Next in prominence might be three or four slices of yellow, Cornish saffron bread—or might be saffron buns. Either one or the other, liberally dotted with currants or raisins, were almost certain to be included in the Cornishman's mid-shift repast. Black, English tea with cream and sugar washed down the meal.

The buckets coming from Italian or Austrian homes were sure to be filled with a generous supply of home-made salami sandwiches, a button or two of garlic and perhaps a whole Bermuda onion. Instead of tea or coffee, the Italian buckets were invariably filled with Italian claret or "dago red." That is, if a miner of some other nationality had not found his way to the wine before the dinner hour. Hunting for buckets containing "dago red" was a popular underground sport.

The repast set before the Finns might contain strips of dried fish or pieces of "jerky" (home-cured beef or venison). A delicacy highly prized by the Finns of those days was a sausage prepared by the Finlander housewives by pounding the marrow from venison bones which were then ground up with jerked meat, and all stuffed into casings made from the entrails of deer or elk. This was a holiday food for the Finns and was often passed around to the other miners at Christmas time.

The Scotch, Welsh and Canadian miners often munched on their oaten cakes, and at Christmas time shared slices of their beloved "haggis," a heavy, steamed meat pudding, cooked in the stomach of a sheep.

The Mexican and Chilean buckets were almost certain to contain liberal portions of frijoles and tortillas. The Serbs dined on a menu entirely of their own conceiving—thick, greasy chunks of home-boiled brisket of beef of a cheaper quality, enormous half loaves of outdoor-oven baked bread, and garlic and onions in quantity.

It was undoubtedly through these underground lunch hours and the interchange of food that has made Butte one of the nation's most cosmopolitan cities in its dining tastes. The average Butte housewife's weekly menu might include any of a dozen foreign dishes.

Unusual is an inadequate word as used in describing the free lunch as served by the town's thousand or so saloons in the pre-prohibition days. For quantity and variety, it is doubtful if these gratuitous repasts could be equaled in any city of the country with the possible exception of New York's Bowery. There never was any shortage of saloons in Butte and they vied with each other in obtaining the patronage of the thirsty miners. The enormous scoops of five-cent beer together with platter upon platter of every variety of luncheon delicacy imaginable was the answer. The larger the scoop, and the bigger the lunch, the greater the ring-up on the cash registers. The saloon men extended themselves in providing every viand the market afforded.

The Council Bar, an enormous, barn-sized saloon over whose bar some thousands of schooners of beer daily found their way to the thirsty throats of nearly as many miners, may be used as an example.

At one end of its half-block long bar, behind which six or seven bartenders toiled, was a section partitioned off. For twenty feet beyond, was an array of food that might tempt any gourmet. To a hungry miner or ill-nourished transient, it was manna in the desert.

Great platters of bologna, liverwurst, anchovies, summer sausages, pickled tripe, pig's snout, sliced corn beef, frankfurters and a half dozen other varieties of cold cuts gleamed up beside plates and platters of a dozen kinds of smoked, pickled and kippered fish. Domestic and imported cheeses of every variety cut into appetizing cubes and slices. Five varieties of bread were stacked on large trays, rye, white, wholewheat, graham and pumpernickel with added plates of salted and plain crackers.

Pickles were grouped with whole and sliced beets, radishes, tiny green onions and also the sliced Bermuda variety. Over this array of food, a white-coated attendant kept the plates filled and saw that all who desired had their fill. It was a help-yourself arrangement and everything was free. The only requisite was that the diner have purchased a glass of beer.

The Council was but one saloon purveying the free grub. Hundreds of others offered as large a variety. Several featured a so-called merchant's lunch during the noon hour, offering a fair sized meal of stew, baked beans, or roast beef, gravy and mashed potatoes for ten cents including the usual scoop.

Still other saloons specialized in free barbecued beef, pork, and mutton on Saturday nights, the meat sliced off steaming hot by an attendant. Buffalo and bear meat were often served in season and the food was advertised by hanging the fresh hide of the animal in front of the establishment. On Christmas and Thanksgiving Day nearly every saloon offered free roast turkey with the beers. Other saloons served chili con carne or steamed frankfurters the year round. There was little occasion for a miner to go hungry if he could provide the five cents necessary for the accompanying glass of beer.

No treatise on copper camp cuisine would be complete without mention of that potent drink as old as the city itself, called by the miners for some obscure reason, a "Shawn O'Farrell," or to use the Gaelic spelling, a Sean O'Farrell.

A sacred tradition in a town of traditions, the Shawn O'Farrell cannot properly be termed a single drink. It is two drinks for the price of one, a full ounce glass of whisky followed by a pint-sized scoop of beer. Both are served in the saloons that cater to the miners' trade for a thin dime.

Shawn O'Farrells are not served at any hour of day or night, but are reserved for the hours when the miners are coming off shift, and to be eligible to purchase one the buyer must have a lunch bucket on his arm to prove that he has spent the day working in the mines.

The "Shawn O'" as it is often abbreviated, is the miners' cure-all for the fatigue of the working day. As they explain it, the whisky is to cut the copper dust from their lungs, and the cooling beer is to slack the thirst accumulated during eight hours spent in the "hot-boxes."

One Shawn O' is refreshing tonic. Two makes a new man of the miner and calls for a third for the new man. Imitations of the Shawn O' have bobbed up in other industrial centers where they are sometimes referred to as "boilermakers."

During the years of prohibition the countless speakeasies continued to serve the old stand-by, the difference then being that the price was upped to a quarter, and moonshine and home brew were offered instead of legal liquor. With the coming of repeal, many Butte saloons revived the practice. In the recent issue of the Miners' Union newspaper, the *Miners' Voice*, considerable space was given to a "blacklist" containing the names of certain Butte bars which had abandoned the practice.

Tom Howie and Billy McCarthy for a quarter of a century operated what was known as "the smallest restaurant in the world," the Success Cafe on East Broadway. When crowded to the doors, it held four customers squeezed in on either side of its one small table. The Success was three feet wide and thirteen feet long, half of the length being taken up by the kitchen. And most of the kitchen was taken up by either of the proprietors who were also the chefs and waiters. The place was never empty and to the camp's newspapermen, nightlooming hack drivers, gamblers, and men-about-town who patronized the cafe, it was known as "Little Waldorf Astoria."

Another famous eating place was "Leu's," the Chinese noodle parlor in China Alley, patronized by half the town. The place was greasy, ill-kept, and reeked of Chinese incense. But Leu served the finest noodles, chop suey, and chow mein in the camp and the young blades for many years flocked to his place after shows and dances. As the unofficial mayor of Chinatown, Leu was as well known as the mayor of the city proper. Three times a year without fail, he got thoroughly drunk—Fourth of July, St. Patrick's Day and Chinese New Year's. On these occasions he was host to hundreds of friends, his Chinese rice wine flowing like water. Leu was a banker, of sorts. He was never deaf to a plea for a loan, if the borrower was likely to meet his obligations. A good judge of human character, he often loaned thousands of dollars to his white friends. He charged no interest, and boasted that he never lost a penny. The restaurant man, mayor, and banker remained in Butte until overtaken by old age; then he journeyed back to China, that his bones might rest with those of his honorable forefathers.

There were many other notable eating places in the old camp, the greater portion of them operating twenty-four hours a day, just as they now do.

McCabe and McLelland were proprietors of the Creamery Cafe. In early days it was located in a basement on Main Street and known to the miners as "The Dump"; for no better reason than many a man's nickname, as it was one of the cleanest cafes in the camp.

Kenoffel's Spokane Cafe is known to every miner who ever worked on the Hill. Sam's bid for popularity with the miners came from his ruling that during strikes, the cafe would refuse to prepare a lunch bucket for any strikebreaker.

The old Iona Cafe on East Park Street had an odd approach. "Get the money, Mollie!" was the cry of the waiters upon the seating of any down-at-the-heels customer or newsboy. "Mollie" was a huge German woman who acted as cashier. The cry was her order to receive payment in advance of the serving of the meal and Mollie never failed.

The Chequamegon is another noted cafe which has been in operation for more than fifty years. The name, derived from an Indian word, was a tongue twister for the early day miners, many of whom called it the "Chew Quick and Be Gone Again" and let it go at that. It was the lunching place of many of the Copper Kings.

The Mudros, Joe and Charlie, Austrian emigrants, were other well-known restaurant operators. The boys worked up successively from miners, dishwashers, cooks and waiters to the ownership of two of the leading cafes in the camp.

Fabulous Females

HUNDREDS of the camp's old-time residents can remember their parents frightening them as youngsters with the warning that they would be turned over to "Crazy Mary" if they did not behave. Crazy Mary was a demented Syrian girl who roamed one end of Butte to the other in the early days. She lived in the Syrian colony near Ohio Street, and the poor creature was perfectly harmless, but she did present a terrifying aspect to the children. Mary had skin the color of old saddle leather, a set of gleaming white teeth and only one eye, and a glaring, open socket where the other eye had once been. Stories were circulated that when an infant, her father obsessed with the belief that she had been born with an evil eye, had taken a red hot poker and burned the eye from her head.

Crazy Mary had a disconcerting habit of walking unannounced into people's houses seating herself in their living room, and refusing to budge until served with refreshments. Her plea, "Mary like some tea and cake," seldom went unanswered.

Oddly enough, though the Butte kids of that period bore tough reputations, it can be said that, except for one rapist (and he was an adult from out of town) they never molested the afflicted girl. She lived to middle age in the mining camp.

Where the tobacco smoke was thick and the red of bourbon and the amber of beer stood out above the mahogany, where oaths were heard and racy stories told and loud guffaws of vulgar laughter reverberated, came Captain Tillie Noble of the Salvation Army with her tambourine.

When Tillie entered a Butte resort the voices at once died down, and those who did not greet the Salvation Army lass with a cheery, Hello Tillie," or, "How's she going, Tillie?" accorded her a silent respect.

Half intoxicated men ceased in the midst of ribaldry, profanity was stilled, and saloon loungers were careful of the way they blew the smoke from their ill-smelling pipes.

Yet there was no glint of gilded uniform about Captain Tillie Noble—no imperious mien, no harsh, unfriendly word, no remonstrance, no complaint.

For Captain Tillie Noble was a lady in a poke bonnet, the costume of the Salvation Army women. Soft voiced and of rare judgment, she had learned to read the hearts of rough and drunken men with an understanding few could ever know.

Tambourine in hand, Tillie collected money for the Salvation Army. Saloons, cigar stores, brothels and at the cribs in the twilight zone, everywhere that men congregated, Tillie Noble pursued her way in the afternoon and evening.

In later years Tillie claimed to have collected an average of fifty dollars a week and contrary to the supposition of many she did not work on a percentage. She was paid a wage of one dollar a day.

If she averaged fifty dollars in her twenty-five years enlistment, Tillie's tambourine must have collected close to seventy-five thousand dollars in the saloons and dives of Butte. This money was all spent in the city and devoted exclusively to the Army's charitable purposes.

Time was in the early days of Butte when Tillie took in more money than in later years, and the receipts for the week often touched the three century mark. Those were the days when there were more single men and less mouths to feed. Gambling was wide open and in poker or faro game, checks would frequently be dropped into her tambourine and Tillie would cash them at the gambling house "bank."

Tillie was of simple taste, of modest ambitions and great loyalty to the Army but she was never theatrical, and was no fanatic. She has been dead these many years but the camp was better for her presence.

Hundreds now living in Butte remember the town's two Annies, "Shoestring Annie" and "Nickel Annie"—and the peculiar fact disclosed at their deaths—neither's right name was "Annie." "Shoestring Annie" was Mrs. Rose Herron and "Nickel Annie" was Margaret English.

Shoestring Annie was a big, strapping woman weighing well over two hundred pounds. Proportioned like a steam shovel, she also possessed a pair of blacksmith's arms, either which packed the kick of an army mule, as any unfortunate male who received their force could testify. A jutting, iron-clad jaw, a pair of eyes that could flash fire or lightning, and a tongue which for vituperation, had no equal on the waterfronts of Liverpool—or any other waterfront for that matter—completed her makeup, that is with the addition of the crutch which she always carried. Some folks were uncharitable enough to claim she carried it for defensive or offensive purposes only. Annie never wore stockings and usually had her feet encased in an oversized pair of men's shoes. She usually wore a house dress or "mother hubbard." In cold weather a man's heavy bathrobe was added. An out-moded, shapeless felt hat, without ornament, was her usual headgear. A small cigar-box filled with shoe laces displayed her wares.

WORLD MUSEUM OF MINING, BUTTE

Shoestring Annie peddling her wares.

Shoestring Annie came to Butte from Colorado around 1910. She brought her husband, a blind broom vendor, whom she called "My John" and whom she guided about the city with his load of brooms for many years. Her husband was a quiet inoffensive man who bore the brunt of many of her tongue lashings. He ended up in the State Hospital for the insane at Warm Springs, finding it no doubt, a peaceful haven of refuge as compared to the life lived with Annie.

On his death, Annie went into the shoestring business, if business it might be called, because Annie put up a terrific argument if any donor to her cause had the temerity to demand a pair of shoestrings in return for his contribution.

It was at the pay office where the miners received their weekly pay envelopes that Annie became best known. Week after week, rain or shine, she could be seen perched on a canvas stool at its entrance, her box of shoestrings on her lap, offering her indignant plea, "Buy a pair of shoe laces, you God damned cheap skate!"

And if any miner took offense, Annie had her decks cleared in a second. The crutch would at once go into action, raining blows on the helpless individual. The crowd of miners usually cheered her on until the victim retreated beyond range of the wrath of the harridan.

Policemen and detectives were especial victims of her temper. The average Butte cop would walk two blocks out of his way to avoid passing Shoestring Annie and the embarrassing dressing-down he was certain to receive.

One spring day during prohibition Annie was standing in front of a Main Street speakeasy, when the Chief of Police and a Federal prohibition Agent walked past. Preoccupied, they paid no heed to Annie as they passed by.

Turning to the crowd and within hearing of the two officers, Annie opened up her floodgates.

"Look at those two dirty, hightoned sons of bitches!" she shrieked. "I'm not good enough for them to talk to when they meet me on the street. When they had me over to the city jail last week the two of them begged for to sleep with me all night!"

The crowd roared. The police official's face turned red, and he started for Shoestring Annie. The prohibition agent, the calmer of the two, grasped the irate officer by the arm and persuaded him to keep going.

Annie's preposterous statement did her little good. The police official gave orders for his men to pick her up on the slightest provocation and Annie spent many nights in the city clink that she could otherwise have avoided if she had kept her mouth closed.

That the Chief was not of the vindictive sort is shown by his kind treatment of Shoestring Annie in her last days. Hearing that she was seriously ill in her cabin on the fringes of the Cabbage Patch, he had the police car pick her up and remove her to the hospital. The Chief paid all her expenses at the institution out of his own pocket. Shoestring Annie died there about two weeks later.

"Five cents please!"

Spoken in a plaintive voice by a forlorn elderly lady clad in a sun-faded black dress, many a resident of old Butte remembers:

"Five cents please!"

She never asked for more.

Yes, the copper camp remembers Nickel Annie. For many of her eighty years she shuffled along the streets, haunted church doors, always muttering, "Five cents please."

Unobtrusive, never in trouble, the little old lady remained a mystery to the town. Many rumors circulated. Some said that she had been deserted by a wealthy husband. Others claimed that somewhere she had a fortune in nickels and dimes hidden away.

The truth came out at her death after forty-five years of begging. She had been well educated and was of a prominent St. Louis family. When she first came to Butte she had been employed as a housekeeper for the late Senator W. A. Clark. Then she had other jobs.

Her employers had thought well of her, praised her cooking and her passion for neatness.

For years she had lived with a Mrs. C. H. Bucher in South Butte and helped with the housework, but had gradually drifted away from the Bucher home. She left early in the morning and returned late at night. Always, rain or shine, she carried a frazzled old umbrella.

She never married, nor had she ever accumulated any great fortune. When the authorities removed her to the county home, some three years before her death, she turned over to them her every cent, some three hundred dollars, to help pay for her keep.

While at the county home, the nurses were kind to the tiny old lady. One day she disappeared from the hospital ward and was not seen for several days when she returned with a man's handkerchief filled with nickels, dimes and quarters. This she presented to the nurses in gratitude. During the time she had been away she had gone from house to house in Butte with the old familiar plea, "Five cents please."

Shortly afterwards Nickel Annie died at the home.

WORLD MUSEUM OF MINING, BUTTE

Nickel Annie.

Myra Quarles was a colored woman who ran a small ranch out behind Big Butte, northwest of the city, and who for years drove a milch cow harnessed to an old-fashioned barouche through the streets of Butte.

Strange to say, little attention was ever paid by the residents to the queer turnout as it passed through the business district or remained tied to some hitching post while Myra did her shopping.

Myra herself, was almost as strange a figure as the equipage she drove. Always dressed in the habiliments of a by-gone century, she might have come out of the pages of an eighteenth-century novel.

She claimed to have been born a slave. As to why she used a cow as a beast of burden, or how she trained it to pull her coach, she never offered an explanation. Pictures of her, the cow and barouche are to be found in the files of old-time newspapers.

Another woman who achieved prominence during the stormy days of mining litigation was Mrs. Charles Gyman who operated her husband's mine while he was in jail. As far as can be learned she was the camp's first and only female miner.

Her husband, Charles Gyman, operated the Yankee Boy Mine on the Hill. He had become mixed up in the turbulent litigation of the moment and had violated a court injunction. The court had sentenced him to thirty days in jail for contempt.

Mrs. Gyman was left alone with the Yankee Boy on her hands. Instead of shutting down or hiring someone to manage things, she decided to run the mine herself, and accordingly dressed in miners' clothes, took charge and handled the property successfully until her husband's release.

With a miner's old slouch hat, covered with copper-water stains and candle grease, a miner's jumper and candle stick, she made regular trips through the mine, climbing ladders into the stopes and raises, inspected workings, directed production and development, ordered supplies, estimated timber, superintended the operation of the Yankee Boy concentrator and looked after the disposition of the output of mine and mill. During this time she also looked after her home and continued to be a very womanly woman, despite her employment.

When Gyman was released from jail he found the mine and mill in as good condition as when he left, and the output of ore was actually greater than the month previous.

The year was 1905 at the old Butte High School. The second year English class was in session. It was near the end of the school year and the pupils, with visions of vacation just ahead, were in hilarious mood. Their teacher made little attempt to curb their boisterous spirits. She, herself, was thinking and planning for the happy months ahead. But there was one pupil who did not join in the merrymaking. A frail, flower-like wisp of a girl who scarcely looked her seventeen years. As her pencil flew over the manuscript before her, a strange look came over the child's odd, sea-green eyes. The girl was Mary MacLane, and the manuscript over which she worked was *The Life Of Mary MacLane*, which in two years was to make the pale, fragile student famous the world over.

This, her first story, written at odd moments in the classroom and during long evenings at her home on West Broadway in Butte took the nation by storm. In reality, it was nothing but thinly veiled sexuality handled in a precocious manner, but superbly written. It was essentially the same, if not as crude, as the confession stories which became popular a generation later.

The critics were divided, but the book was condemned by church and school. It sold by the thousands and edition after edition was printed. Mary MacLane became overnight a world figure, and was lionized throughout art and literary centers. She moved East and remained there where she wrote several other novels which had a slight success on the reputation of her initial effort. And then, years later, disillusioned, she came back to Butte, a world-wise woman of thirty-five, attempting to recapture the spark that was present when she was eighteen. It was then that Mary MacLane showed that she was a showman of ability. She saw to it that her every move was news. She lived alone. She took long walks out on the Flat in the middle of the night. She spent many nights in the Butte cemeteries "communing with her spirit" as she told reporters.

The book, *I, Mary MacLane*, was finally finished. Advance ballyhoo made it another sensation. A motion picture was made of the story and Mary acted the title role herself. The picture had only slight success—and Mary MacLane never again wrote a line that caused more than passing interest.

Play Boys

THERE have been countless playboys—miners and millionaires—in the copper camp.

The old time miners put it this way: "Sure, what is money for but to spend? Isn't that why we went down in the hot boxes to dig out their ore—to get the money to spend on a good time? And when it's gone, won't we go back down again and work like hell to get some more to spend? Easy come, easy go, I says, and you can't take it with you."

Best known among the prodigious spenders of the old days, of course, were the sons of the Copper Kings. Their fathers had obtained it the hard way; there was plenty of it, and the young gentlemen, never having known a want in their lives, cut a real swath through the pater's millions.

Senator W. A. Clark's sons, "Willie" and "Charlie," as they were known to the camp, were artists in the circulation of money. "Drinks for the house" was the rule whenever they entered a saloon or sporting house. An old time friend of the family once remarked: "I've seen Willie and Charlie with their arms lame from the elbow down, from signin' checks on the old man's banks to pay up for a shindig they threw the night before."

The story is told of a hack driver who had driven their father, the Senator, up from the depot. At the hotel, he handed the cab driver a dime tip.

Disappointedly the cabby turned to the Senator and complained, "Why your sons always tip me a dollar."

"Yes, I know," answered the Senator, "Willie and Charlie have a rich father—I haven't."

The Largey boys, Creighton and Sellars, heirs to the millions of their Copper King father, Pat Largey, are remembered pleasantly among old-timers as spenders and good fellows without a par in a town noted for its spending. They still recount the party staged by Sellars to celebrate his twenty-first birthday, rumored to have cost in the neighborhood of fifty thousand dollars.

The boys went broke after spending more than five million dollars at a rate of almost a million dollars a year. They never whimpered. Creighton got a job driving a truck and made good at it. Sellars went to work for a California manufacturing concern and worked his way up to a foremanship. They typify well the spirit of the camp: "Spend it when you've got it, and don't cry when it's gone."

Early-day spending wasn't confined to the wealthy. There are numerous tales of the high, wide, and handsome spending engaged in by miners who unexpectedly came into the money, or who spent a month's pay in a few hours.

Larry Mullins, for example, was a shoveler in the Bell Mine. An uncle in the East died and left him $3,500. Larry's first act was to obtain a suite of rooms at a hotel that catered to the sporting element. This he stocked with the finest of liquors. Next, he visited a leading parlor house and contracted for the services of five of the house's most beautiful girls. "Mix 'em up," ordered Larry, "and see that there are two blondes, a brunette, a red head, and one Jap or Chink."

His order filled, the young heir then installed the harem in his suite of rooms, playing public host until his legacy ran out, three short days later.

"Benzie" was a nipper at the Anaconda Mine during prohibition. He unexpectedly fell into a fortune of some four thousand dollars. Benzie quit the job, purchased a second-hand car, picked out three friends from the mine, and, along with two barflies from a speakeasy and several gallons of bootleg whiskey, set out to tour the United States. After riotous celebration along the way, they eventually arrived in Los Angeles where Benzie's money ran out. The entire party came back by freight.

There were many, many others, but the stories generally ran the same. The atmosphere of two extremes—easy money, or money earned the hard way in the sweat boxes underground—was conducive to free spending. In the one case, the wealth stored by nature for millions of years, when reaped, flowed so fabulously as to fever the most thrifty. In the other extreme, hard work begat hard play. "What the hell, we're here today and gone tomorrow," reasoned the miner, who remembered a fall of rock the previous shift which had narrowly missed his skull. The next one might connect.

Limbs of the Law

HIZONNER, the Mayor, Pat Mullins was as popular a subject for the early-day cartoonists as was Fat Jack, the hackman. Built like a roly-poly top, Mullin's legs graduated from small, neatly shod feet into a immense belly which tapered off again to a smallish head surmounted by an iron grey moustache and goatee. Mullins was always warm, and even on the coldest day could be seen energetically mopping his brow with a large handkerchief. He was a "Heinzeman," but eleven of his aldermen were of different political faith. Known as the "solid eleven" they voted against his every suggestion. The malcontents led the mayor a harassed existence and it was few smiles that Pat Mullins found in the city hall until the eleven were finally defeated by an entire council of Heinze-blessed candidates.

It was on the last day of the tenure of office for the defeated aldermen that Pat Mullins took his revenge. He was host at a banquet held in the council chambers of the city hall, given by him personally for the eleven men who had fought him so bitterly.

A sumptuous repast was prepared. Mullins had the town's leading caterers provide every delicacy. Rare wines and liquors were provided in quantities. As the aldermen were seated around the groaning banquet table, the mayor arose, mopped his brow and pointed to the assortment of foods: "Eat, drink and be merry, gentlemen," he said. "For by God this afternoon you're dead ducks—and it's Pat Mullins who' be havin' the last laugh at your wakes." He then ordered a photographer to take a picture of the assemblage.

MONTANA HISTORICAL SOCIETY, HELENA

W.A. Clark and Mayor Mullins (front right), Fat Jack atop his carriage in crowd.

Judge O'Mara, police judge in 1878 and Alex McGowan, Charlie Boyle and General Charles S. Warren, who later presided over the Butte police court made copy for the newswriters in those colorful days. They all with the exception of O'Mara were tough on the pimps of the redlight. (O'Mara sympathized with them and called them sportin' gintlemin.") Ninety days was the usual sentence doled out to this gentry when found guilty, and six month sentences were not unheard of.

To the miner who might celebrate a bit too much, they tempered justice with mercy. Judge Warren who was Butte's first police judge 1880, and 26 years later was again elected to the office, often made the assertion that a hard-working miner was entitled to one rip-roarin drunk a month. Few underground workers were ever fined in his court, unless it was for disturbance or some more serious offense. But the judges without exception were poison to wife beaters. Boyle once walked down off the bench and invited a big husky charged with beating his wife to take off his coat. The man's wife, a little woman not weighing over a hundred pounds, turned to Boyle vehemently, "Just lay one hand on my husband, you big brute, and I'll beat your brains out with this umbrella!"

From that time on Boyle was not as severe on wife beaters, claiming there were often extenuating circumstances.

Judge Warren always looked at a prisoner's hands. If he had, as Warren called them, "piano player's hands," he gave him the book, while a calloused, work-grimed paw might win an acquittal or a suspended sentence.

O'Mara, one of the few early day judges of which there is any record, made colorful copy. As already stated he was in complete accord with the P.I.'s or "sportin' min" and had a soft spot in his heart for their women, but he did not believe that the girls should be beaten and would dole out severe sentences to any pimp found guilty of the offense. As he told one culprit who attempted an explanation, "Cut it short, bye, cut it short. Ye're guilty as domnation. The limit of me jurisdiction is a fine of $100 or thirty days in the jail. I give ye that. But be the sacred toe-nails of Moses, if ye weren't a sportin' gint, I'd give ye five times me jurisdiction!"

So sympathetic with the sportin' life was O'Mara, that he made a girl of the half-world, one "Lilly the Lush," his bride at a public ceremony in the courtroom. After the ceremony he turned to the audience and proudly remarked. "Remember boys, the gur-rl is Lilly the Lush no longer. She is Mrs. Judge O'Mara from this minute on and I'll thank ye to treat her according to her high and exalted social position."

Of the famous that trod Butte's streets in that bygone past, few were better known and respected than the big, gruff Chief of Police, Jere Murphy, known to the underworld and police from Maine to the Mexican border as "Jerry the Wise." Chief Murphy stood well over six feet and weighed around two hundred pounds. His hair was coal black. He had brown, piercing eyes, prominent features and a powerful body. His stride was manly, head held high above a robust chest and his striking appearance set him apart in any company. His greetings were cordial and generally accompanied by a bit of wit. He was always what is known as a "snappy" dresser. Never gaudy, but exceptionally well groomed.

He came from Kilkenny, Ireland, and joined the Butte police force in 1893, appointed by Mayor E. O. Duggan. Old-timers recall the dapper policeman who stood at the corner of Park and Main Streets. The gimlet eye was in evidence from the start, they say. His exploits as a police officer were many and colorful, and many of them gained him national recognition.

Chief Murphy had an uncanny ability to get information on crooks, big timers, small timers and all. As a friend of his said some years before his death: "Murphy doesn't wait for something to happen. The minute Jere learns of the presence in Butte of a tough gang, he immediately carries the law to them. They never even get started on their jobs."

A typical instance was when he knew some gangsters were stopping at a Butte hotel. He went to the room door, knocked, and when the door opened said: "My name's Murphy. There's a train leaving here at 3 o'clock. See that you're on it." It was not necessary for Jere to explain that he was chief of police. All the mugs in the country knew him by name and reputation. For this reason the camp was usually left off their schedule.

The chief was not only poison to big-shot gangsters, murderers and their kind, he despised the petty crook, chiseler, phony and pimp and made life unbearable for them. This natural abhorrence of "slickers" first came to notice in the early nineties when Jere was employed by Marcus Daly at the latter's famous race track south of Butte. Daly learned that his track was infested with touts who were trying to "fix" races. He hired Murphy to clean them out.

Spotting the gentleman with a checkered suit and polished finger nails, with possibly a "caddy" hat tipped sidewise on his head, Murphy was apt to saunter up to him. "Who are you, where did you come from?" was almost certain to be his greeting. Usually the conversation didn't last long. The tout knew it was time to leave.

Murphy's memory for faces was outstanding. Always a great hand for prowling the city, he often spotted men—and women too—that he knew he didn't want in "Our Village," as he called Butte. Ordering his driver (Murphy never drove a car himself) to pull into the curb, he would call his man to the side of the walk and give him his orders, usually "get going!" But not always. Frequently he would take his man for a ride to headquarters. In such cases the chief probably had an idea that his quarry was up to something. His questioning of such individuals led in more than one instance to the uncovering of some major crime.

Murphy not only never forgot the face of a criminal but he had the same memory of those who had proved "on the up and up." He loved children, although he was not ostentatious in that regard. A man of sympathetic nature, Jere Murphy at most times presented a gruff exterior. Criminals quaked when he interrogated them in his blunt and caustic manner. Those who knew him realized it was no bluff. Behind his command was the highest type of physical courage.

He rarely pulled his gun. He not only had a horror of shooting anyone, he relied more on quick action with his fists in a dangerous situation. He demonstrated this latter trait many times. One time was when an Indian attacked him with a foot-and-a-half butcher knife. Instead of reaching for his gun, Chief Murphy dropped the Indian with a solid right to the jaw.

WORLD MUSEUM OF MINING, BUTTE

Jere "the Wise" Murphy (center) with two Butte law officers.

Like many another man who became a leader in Butte, Murphy shoveled his share of rock in the mines on the hill. He worked in the Anaconda Mine for a time after coming to Butte, and later operated a lease. He had always the deepest understanding of the troubles of the miner.

"Shooting people is bad business," Murphy used to tell his friends. "It doesn't matter how it is done there's always retribution. There is a commandment that reads: 'Thou shalt not kill.' There is a passage in the bible that says: 'He who lives by the sword shall perish by the sword.' I don't remember that any exemption is made for peace officers. Of course it is sometimes a case of kill or be killed. That's something different. But just to shoot people because you have a gun in your hand and can get away with it before the courts is rotten. And the man who does a thing like that will pay for it."

One of Murphy's noted exploits was the capture of a Butte man who made a fly-by-night attempt to defraud a friend. This man had seized a large sum of money which should have been used to pay his obligations and fled to Canada. Murphy was engaged to run him down. He did it so effectively that he not only located his man but learned how he carried his plunder. The man was arrested by the Canadian police and released when they found no money on his person.

"Search his shirt," Murphy wired them. "It has a double back. The money is carefully spread between the two thicknesses of cloth." The fugitive was re-arrested and Murphy's information was found to be correct. The chief would never divulge how he obtained his dope.

No Butte resident will ever forget Chief Murphy in a car, particularly if it happened to be the "Black Maria." It was that right foot of his. Invariably it was out on the fender, much as if he was holding himself in readiness for a quick jump for the street—in which there was much truth.

Murphy did a great deal of prowling, and his driver had no easy time of it. The chief, who invariably kept up a running conversation, was apt to order the car stopped at any moment, or possibly to speed up, but more often to "Swing in there and see who that bird is." His eye was ever roving. He missed nothing. No man or woman passed up or down the street that he did not see. The name "Jerry, the Wise" fitted the chief like a glove. Always he was watching for enemies of "his village."

Often he was called on to settle a dispute over accounts, particularly amounts due as wages. While his office was not a collection agency, the chief liked to lend a hand to the working man without entailing him with expensive court costs.

It was during the prohibition era that a man of foreign extraction came to Chief Murphy's office at the police station and asked for a hearing.

"Come in, son," the chief greeted the man. "What seems to be the trouble?"

"Well, Mister Murphy," the man replied in broken English, "I worked for a man down the street and now he won't pay me."

"Now isn't that too bad; we'll have a look into this. What kind of work did you do for him?"

"Well," replied the petitioner, "I built a cabinet for him," and he gave the address of the place.

Now the premises named had been suspected of housing a blind pig and Chief Murphy's interest in the place increased. Taking a scratch pad, Chief Murphy drew a square and asked where the cabinet was located.

The man indicated on the diagram the location of the cupboard and further explained that it was opened by an electric switch located in the far corner of the room.

Folding the diagram and placing it in his pocket Chief Murphy said: "Now, young fellow, we'll see that you get your money. Go with this officer," the chief instructed as he indicated a policeman, "and show him the man who won't pay you." To the officer he directed, "Get that money or bring the man in."

Some weeks later Chief Murphy was visiting with a federal prohibition agent. He had occasion to seek a paper in his pocket and in the search came upon the diagram, almost forgotten since he had received it.

Changing the subject, Chief Murphy asked the federal agent to accompany him. "I think I have got something that will interest you," he said as the two left the station. In less than an hour the two officers returned. They had in custody a man and a large quantity of contraband liquor.

On entering the place where the wage dispute occurred, Chief Murphy stepped into a corner and reached for a button. Across the room a secret panel flew open, almost striking the agent.

Inside the cabinet was the liquor that officers had tried time and time to locate on previous raids.

Flabbergasted, the federal agent asked the chief, "How did you know where to look for that stuff?"

"Foresight, my boy, foresight," was the chief's reply.

It was Murphy's reluctance in pulling a gun that brought an end to his career. Called to the offices of the Montana Power Company to quell a crazed foreigner who was terrorizing the offices with a loaded gun,

Murphy attempted to wrest the weapon from the man's hand and in the scuffle fell to the tiled flooring, fracturing his skull. He lingered for weeks, but finally succumbed on September 19, 1935. Butte had lost one of its most colorful residents.

For downright color Butte's procession of county sheriffs has been something to comment upon. The sheriff's office is considered the best political plum in the mining camp and election to the office is eagerly sought.

Rough, red-faced John Quinn served as sheriff during some of the hectic days of the copper kings. Quinn was an inveterate tobacco chewer and it is reported that at one time he masticated on an average of a pound of the weed each day. It was commonplace for Quinn to interrupt proceedings involving millions in Judge Clancy's court while he borrowed a chew from the bewhiskered judge. The sheriff was particularly fond of the long-twist brand which the magistrate imported from Missouri.

Another picturesque sheriff was the suave, debonair John K. O'Rourke, known to the camp as "Jawn K." A handsome, distinguished man, the picture of sartorial perfection, he might easily be mistaken for a middle aged movie star. His gorgeous cravats were reported to have been imported and to have set him back five dollars a copy.

Through his loyalty to the underground worker, O'Rourke became a successful politician. He later took over the management of the Florence Hotel, or the "Big Ship." It was O'Rourke who is said to have given it the nickname when he proclaimed that there was enough liquor drunk there on weekends to float a ship—and "a big ship, too," he added.

When the First World War was over and the Butte boys came back from France, the sheriff acted as host at a party in the city auditorium that will go down as one of the most hilarious ever held in the town. The boys attended in uniform and O'Rourke turned over to the servicemen the entire supply of liquor confiscated under the new dry law, later estimated at some hundred or so gallons of beer, bourbon and "dago red." There were also great quantities of victuals supplied at the sheriff's expense. The party lasted for three days and three nights, and the doors of the auditorium were barred to prevent anyone's departure. Veterans of the Argonne will tell you they took more punishment during the extended party than on any battlefield in France. The sheriff, himself, remained during the whole festivity.

Another Butte sheriff was Tim Driscoll, a kindly, honest miner, elected to the office in 1913. Driscoll's only "error" was that he refused to give his deputies orders to fire on rioting miners on the night in 1914 when the Miners' Union mob dynamited the Miners' Union Hall. Driscoll was impeached along with the Mayor, Lewis J. Duncan.

Larry Duggan, the town undertaker, was elected to the office in 1917. Larry's had been a colorful career since the early days. He came up the hard way and had been a mucker, miner, mortician and sheriff in turn. His first act was to order the shooting on sight of any who dared don the Ku Klux Klan robes and pillow slips, or who attempted to burn any fiery crosses within the county. There were several notable executions of criminals during his three terms of office. As some of the miners remarked: "As undertaker and sheriff, Larry gets them comin' and goin'!"

Sheriff Angus McLeod was a Nova Scotian who became a hard-rock mine foreman. He prided himself in being one foreman for whom every miner on the hill had a good word. McLeod was noted for his lenient treatment of prisoners convicted of liquor law violations. While he was sheriff, the various Butte bootleggers, distillers and peddlers led a de luxe life in the county jail.

They were quartered in a private part of the jail building and had their own chef, commissary and waiters. Fine foods were provided, and there was no dearth of liquid cheer. At times paid entertainers were brought to the jail to provide amusement for the prisoners and one time a wedding was held, an imprisoned bootlegger and a Butte girl being joined in marriage. Invitations were sent to many prominent Butte people, and a banquet was served while an orchestra furnished music for dancing. McLeod had little regard for the Volstead act, and could not regard its violators as ordinary criminals.

In Centerville was the town marshal, one Tim O'Neill, who proclaimed that he was "The Limb of the Law" and was thus known to all. One night in front of Hibernia Hall in Centerville he was endeavoring to persuade a lady who had been imbibing too freely to go home and get off the streets. To the amusement of the throng gathered in front of the hall, Marshal O'Neill got his tongue twisted and pleaded with the woman as follows: "Come on home and go to bed with me now like a good woman!"

Cabbage Patch Corsage

COVERING an area of six square blocks on the east side of town at the foot of the Colorado Mine dump, and bordered by lesser waste-ore heaps, cheap saloons and shabby flophouses, the Cabbage Patch was for a score of years the commanding eyesore of the copper camp.

The Patch was originally settled in the early eighties by squatters who erected makeshift homes, cabins and lean-tos, and then dared the mine owners to evict them. The principal street in the settlement was named Mahoney Alley. At that time the district was known as the Hesperus Lode, and the mines in its vicinity numbered some of the richer of the camp. Although there was a decent element residing in the Cabbage Patch, consisting largely of miners who erected comfortable homes there for their families, they were far in the minority. Most of its residents were the backwash of the camp, hopheads, dipsomaniacs, worn-out prostitutes, paregoric addicts and a dozen other varieties of derelict humans.

There were two distinct eras in the ten-acre hell's kitchen—before prohibition and during prohibition. Before the Volstead Law, the more noted of its inhabitants were such untouchables as Nigger Riley, George Breen, the king of the Patch; Little Annie Rooney, Mary Koski, Liz the Lady, Pat Friel, Red Foley, Chicken Lee, Happy Henry, Fighting Steve, Blasphemous Brown, and a host of lesser lights who continually found their way into the police courts through an assortment of weird and willful predicaments.

"*You Made Me What I Am Today, I Hope You're S-A-T-I-S-F-I-I-I-E-D!*" South Main Street, three o'clock in the morning, the year 1910, "Nigger Riley," copper camp's premier hophead baritone and elocutionist, under the impetus of a shot of "happy dust," is making the welkin ring.

The voice, if not tuneful, carries ample power.

A slamming open of windows of rooming houses on each side of the street. Touseled heads, sleep-glazed eyes, raucous voices, male and female, call down curses and imprecations on the stovepipe-hatted, coal black singer.

"That Goddamn Nigger Riley is all snowed up again!" "Hand me my pants and the shotgun!"

"Pipe down or I'll blow your damn black head off!"

"Call the bulls!"

The singing continues: *"You dragged and dragged me down until the s-o-oul within me died!"*

A barrage from both sides—lumps of coal, chairs, water pitchers, chamber pots, books, and kitchenware.

A direct hit from a chunk of Rock Springs, and the high hat rolls in the gutter. A well-aimed pitch of a rolling pin from the hand of a southpaw blonde, and a bump the size of a goose egg appears on the kinky wool-covered pate of the singer.

Clang-Clang-Clang! The patrol wagon arrives. Nigger Riley, his art once more unrecognized, is hauled away to sleep off his "goofer" jag in the Hotel de Clink. Windows on either side of the street slam shut again. The night is once more silent. It will be thirty days when he faces Hizzoner, Judge McGowan, in the morning.

"Nigger" Riley was at one time a resident of the deepest Cabbage Patch, but in an affluent moment he moved to the outskirts of the settlement, and from then on looked askance at the hopheads who shacked up on Mahoney Alley in the Patch proper.

Hats were Riley's sartorial speciality. He possessed three, a high "stovepipe," and two straw sailors, one without a brim, the other with a brim, but no top. He wore the stovepipe in the summer and the straw hats in winter. When the weather was exceptionally cold, he wore the one with the brim. "It kept out the wind," he explained.

Riley possessed a remarkable vocabulary and was an orator of some ability. When "snowed up," the dusky gentleman was ever ready to orate his way into any argument, discussion, or public address. Riley was an imposing figure, as black as the eight ball, usually arrayed in a long frock coat, once black, but turned green with age. At times he affected horn-rimmed spectacles and might easily have passed as a colored revivalist.

Considerable of his time was spent in the "clink" in allotments of thirty, sixty and ninety days. Riley had a way with him, however, and often talked "My friend, Jeremiah, the Wise, Murphy" into reducing his sentence if he washed all the windows in the City Hall. Riley was industrious and often did odd jobs for many of the prominent residents of the town.

Riley had a pal, another gentleman of color, prominently known about the mining city as merely "Liz the Lady." Liz's only claim to fame was that he was an hermaphrodite. Liz had a woman's voice and walked like a woman. Otherwise he or she wore male attire and conducted itself as one of the masculine sex.

There were many other notables among the hophead colony. In those days "happy dust" could be purchased at most any drug store or in the dens of Chinatown. A silver dollar would buy enough "dream powder" to furnish an evening of high jinks for the entire clan. To obtain funds, the addicts combed alleys, garbage cans and back yards in search of anything that was saleable, Brooms, mops, shovels, or any tools were never safe in back yard or woodshed when the hopheads were on a foraging expedition.

Pat Friel, one of their number, gained nationwide notoriety when he moved off with a red-hot, smoking stove from another hophead's cabin. The police apprehended Pat with the still-smoking stove as he was on his way to an Arizona Street second-hand store. The newspapers played up the caper on their front pages and the Associated Press picked up the story and placed it on their wire. Friel woke up in the city jail the following morning to find himself famous.

Another of the colony who made his headquarters on Mahoney Alley in the Cabbage Patch, and as constantly in the police court news of the city was Chicken Lee, a six-foot colored gent, whose specialty was the raiding of hen coops and who, when with an overload of narcotics aboard, terrorized the colored colony with a cutlery display of a half-dozen razors always kept in condition for "social purposes" as he put it.

Then there was "Happy," a gruff, seedy individual who never was seen to smile; "Fighting Steve," who weighed ninety pounds with his shoes on, and who made up what he lacked in weight in gall and pugnaciousness; "Blasphemous" Brown, who, in a town of hard-swearing, rough-talking men, was conceded all honors. There were a dozen or so others, and why they came to Butte or why they remained is a mystery. They spent the greater part of their time in jail.

Around 1904 Police Judge Alex McGowan had the idea that all the hopheads might be cured of the drug habit and ordered the police to arrest them. He had them placed in the basement of the old county jail with orders to leave them there, deprived of their dope until cured. The plan didn't work. The hopheads made the days and nights in the vicinity of the courthouse hideous with their maniacal screams. Finally, the country commissioners could stand it no longer; so they ordered the basement unlocked, and for weeks the hopheads roamed the streets begging and stealing for their supply of dope in the daytime, returning to the jail for their meals and sleeping quarters at night. For weeks, the unfortunates led the life of Riley. There were women among them. Oddly, the majority of the hopheads lived to reach their seventies and eighties, which was more than could be said of those camp characters whose affliction was the continual tipping of the bottle.

Prohibition brought a new era to the sordid locality. Most of the old characters had died off and a new cast came into being. Mexicans and

Filipinos moved in, and with them came the new self-appointed Mayor, one McNamara, a hard-hitting Irishman who ruled the district with an iron hand, incidentally controlling the bootlegging privileges of the six-square-block area. McNamara was law, and the law forces gave him free reign in policing the district. Under his administration blossomed forth such benign public characters as "Mexicali Rose," a half-Indian and half-Mexican beauty, who was mixed up one way or another in five murder cases, but never convicted; Fay, the lady barber, a tall, dark, sloe-eyed charmer who when not busy at shaving was strongly suspected by some of doing away with three or four of her suitors. Fay, with a cargo of McNamara's liquor aboard, journeyed out to Columbia Gardens one Sunday evening and shot up the dance hall. A large crowd was present at the time, but fortunately Fay's aim was good and out of five shots, she succeeded in bringing down the man she was after, her paramour of the moment. No one else was injured. Her lover survived his wounds, and Fay was turned loose with a reprimand when the victim refused to appear against her.

During this era of the Patch there was one Goldie Davis, a coal-black vixen who was most proficient with a razor. Goldie, at various times, slashed a half-dozen of McNamara's subjects. One evening, her ire aroused, Goldie went forth with her razor, bent on doing a little "cutting up." A certain white friend of hers had done her wrong, and she entered a South Arizona Street resort, Dinty Moore's, in search of him. Seeing a sleeping drunk at one of the tables, Goldie rushed over and drew his head back and neatly cut his throat from ear to ear. Goldie erred, because her victim was not her erstwhile boy friend, but a total stranger. Nonplussed at the mistake, Goldie apologized to the bleeding man and explained her error. The victim was sewed up and Goldie did a trifle of six months for her social blunder.

McNamara's reign in the Patch came to an end when a still he was working on blew up, killing him instantly.

And there was George Breen, an earlier majordomo of the Cabbage Patch, who stole dogs—any and all dogs he could lay his hand on—not for any monetary value they might possess, but because he loved dogs. His cabin in the Patch usually harbored a dozen canines of assorted breeds. Jere Murphy, the chief of police, accused Breen of taking the dogs to bed with him in the winter-time, which may or may not have been true. Breen one time astonished East Park Street by upbraiding a Greek whom he caught mistreating a dog.

"If you want to kick a dog, kick me!" he said angrily as he rescued the little animal and escorted it to his cabin in the Patch.

The Hopheads' Ball

The Butte *Miner*, July 12, 1898, carried a story telling of a ball held at one of the roadhouses on the Flat and attended by Butte's underworld. The article states: "Gathering from the character of those arrested, it could have been termed 'a hophead's ball.'" At the festivities one "Nick the Greek" had been shot by a character named "Smokey." The two had quarreled over a blonde.

It must have been a grand occasion
That night in ninety-eight,
For the papers of the township
Next morning did relate,
How on the Flat, far from the city
In a certain roadhouse hall,

All the hopheads of the district
Gathered for their yearly ball.
All the junkies were invited,
Yes, every gink and muff.
Not a single one was slighted
If they were on the stuff.
Invitations were presented
To every hustler and her man.
They even sent up invites
To the hopheads in the can.

The hall was decorated;
The committee had done well.
'Twas fantastic and artistic,
Most like a scene from hell.
Paper streamers and festoons
Fell in fifty-seven tints.
Chinese lamps gleamed from the ceiling;
O'er it all, blew Chink incense.

At eight, they began arriving
On wheel or rig or hack.
Some came in liv'ried splendor,
While others rode horseback.
There were bicycles and tricycles,
And mules that wouldn't balk.
Eight or ten rode in one wagon,
And there were some who had to walk.

At last, they were assembled;
'Twas indeed a motley crew.
There were some fifty couples,
We'll but try to name a few.
Callahan the Bum was present
In a long-tailed coat and vest.
Jew Jess from Pleasant Alley
Was dolled up in her best.

Frisco Kate was there with Baker,
He, of the diamond tooth;
Coal black Liz and "her" boy friend,
And a dame called Laudanum Ruth;
Junkie Joe from near the woodyards
Brought along his crutch and cane.
Seattle Sal from that town's skidrow
Came all the way by train.

Some were clad in silken raiment,
More, in tattered shoe and sock;
A few wore full-dress garments
They'd just redeemed from hock.
In rags and tags and ruffles,
There ne'er was such a sight
As presented by those junkies
Out on the Flat that night.

Three fiddlers from the red-light
And some junkie with a flute
Were hired to play such music
Like ne'er before was played in Butte.
They'd appointed a committee;
It's chairman took the stand:
"Gents and ladies choose your partners,
Then take your partner's hand!

"But, before they play the grand march
Let each dancer have a shot;
It will act as stimulation,
And should make the dancin' hot."
So from scores of hiding places
Guests brought forth their hypo gats;
From sleeves, brassieres and bustles,
Some even hid them in their rats.

Not all the cokies used the needle,
Some from their opium pipes did whiff;
Others drained their paregoric,
A few of "happy dust" did sniff.
Opium pills or hasheesh
Came forth from many a sock,
And some twist from China Alley
Brought out her old yen hok.

You may live to be a hundred,
But you'll never see again
Such a spectacle presented
As when the dancing did begin.
The fiddles wailed forth wildly
As the hopheads got in swing;
Gavottes, quadrilles, and polkas,
They even tried the Highland fling.

Waltzes, mazurkas, two-steps,
They never passed one by;
There ne'er was dance invented
That the hopheads didn't try.
The fiddlers kept on fiddling
Like they didn't give a dang;
When one of them was tiring,
He just took another "bang."

A cokey from the Clipper
With the rhythm of a fish
Steered a henna'd damsel
Through a gay schottische;
While a gal called "Round The World"
Showed a dame, the guys called "Mooch,"
The forty-seven movements
Of the dance known as the kootch.

And there would have been no trouble,
For all were satisfied,
If Nick the Greek, a snifter,
Kept his hands off Smokey's bride.
Now, this Smokey was a killer
With two notches on his gun,
And, when hopped up like a million,
Would shoot just for the fun.

So when he saw his peroxide darling
In the arms of the Greek,
Out came his old persuader,
And Smokey made it speak.
Rat-tat-tat in quick succession;
Three shots, and then no more;
But when the smoke cleared from the ballroom
Nick the Greek lay on the floor.

At once, the hopheads set to screeching;
You could hear them up the Hill
Yelping, yowling like Inferno;
Their cries were weird and shrill.
There ne'er was such commotion
As heard there in the hall,
And it brought a sudden ending
To the hopheads' annual ball.

For news got to the sheriff
To get there without fail,
So he came with three big wagons
To cart them off to jail.
In the dungeon, dank and dismal,
The revelers sat to think
How their simple, social gathering
Had ended in the clink.

Frontier Belascos

BUTTE has always been a great show town. For the richness of its theatrical past, it owes a debt of gratitude to a strolling Irish minstrel who followed closely behind the gold-seekers of the sixties. John Maguire gave the camp its first recorded theatrical performance in 1875, coming to Montana from County Cork by way of Australia, San Francisco and Salt Lake City.

While in the latter city Maguire managed the famous old Salt Lake Theater, built by Brigham Young.

The building in which he first appeared in Butte was a rough one-story false-fronted structure on the principal corner of what is the present business district, then occupied by the King and Lowry gambling hall.

No orchestra or music was deemed necessary, Maguire being a whole show in himself. His act consisted of a series of monologues and recitations. Favorites of the camp were his recitations of *Over the Hill To the Poorhouse* and *Shamus O'Brien.*

In appearance John Maguire was a typical showman of the school, slight of stature, bespectacled, always clad in the latest New York fashion, high starched collar with ascot tie and black pearl pin, a form-fitting broadcloth coat of vivid purple surmounted a pair of fawn-colored trousers and patent leather shoes.

On a second visit to Butte a year later, Maguire appeared in a frame Main Street building, on ground later occupied by the Brophy Grocery Company. This time he had an orchestra—a volunteer trio composed of Hank Young, violinist; Simon Hauswirth, cornetist; and a trombone player whose name is forgotten.

Planks resting upon empty nail kegs served as seats, and candles secured by nails driven in a scantling furnished the light. Maguire later appeared in a frame building on the present site of the Hirbour Building. In 1880 Owsley's Hall was opened by Maguire as a regular theater. Among the attractions he presented there was *Camille, A Case For Divorce, Uncle Tom's Cabin* and *The Banker's Daughter.* The performance of the last play was postponed from September 21 to the following evening because of the death of President Garfield.

During the winter of 1881-1882 the impresario booked entertainments for Renshaw Hall, then operated by John A. Gordon. He also presented entertainments at Speck's Hall in the Caplice Building, which later became Sutton's Union Family Theater.

Appearing about this time, though not at Maguire's theater were Eddie Foy and James Thompson in *Scenes On The Mississippi*, at Gordon's old Comique theater on East Park Street. Foy, later known to a nation of playgoers as a prince of comics, remained in the camp for many weeks at that time. He had come from Tombstone where he played in the famous Bird Cage Varieties. Foy tells of his Butte experiences in his autobiography, *Clowning Through Life.*

William A. Brady appeared about the same time in *The Count of Monte Cristo.* Mr. Brady tells of this period of his career in his autobiography, *Showman* which ran serially in a weekly magazine in 1936.

While one section of the polyglot population found release from workaday cares in the saloons and variety halls, another was grateful for John Maguire's entertainment of a different type, represented from 1880 to 1884 by most of the leading touring attractions at Renshaw Hall.

By 1885 the Irishman had his own theater on West Broadway, where the Leggat Hotel now stands. It was here, at Maguire's Grand Opera House, that the former strolling minstrel made frontier history.

Of that period, the *West Shore*, a monthly published at Portland and Tacoma, said in its issue for August, 1885:

"The Grand Opera House at Butte is the finest opera house on the Pacific Coast outside of San Francisco." It must have been good, for the Coast magazine to place Butte, seven hundred miles inland, on the Pacific Coast.

The very finest shows *en tour* played at the opera house and all the great productions took to the road in those days. To enumerate them, would take a volume in itself. It is enough to say that through Maguire's efforts the miner's and their families were never allowed to become entertainment hungry.

The name of the rococo "Grand Opera House" was not merely a pretentious gesture. It was indeed a home, or at least a transient shelter, for the best the nation had to offer in grand opera. For fifteen years through Maguire's untiring efforts, Butte was never without its annual season of grand and light opera. And there were no empty seats. At many times the entire house had been subscribed long before the opening date. The Grand Opera House burned in 1888 but was soon rebuilt. The new house, with a seating capacity of one thousand, was opened February 28, 1889, with Rose Osborne playing in *A Celebrated Case.*

During the time the "Grand" was being rebuilt, Maguire had opened a short-lived playhouse at Granite and Alaska Streets near the present site of the Silver Bow County courthouse. It was known as the Lyceum.

For a time in 1896 and 1897, Maguire's was known on the billboards, its programs, and the sign over the marquee as the "Murray Opera House." This was in gratitude for financial backing given by Banker James A. Murray. But to Butte's playgoing public it was never anything but Maguire's and in 1898 the old name was restored to the programs. Two later famous actresses, Blanche Bates and Maude Adams received their early training at the hands of John Maguire.

On May 9, 1902, Maguire transferred the lease of his famous opera house to J. P. Howe of Seattle and quietly retired from the town he had helped build.

He went to Salt Lake City, where for a time he was a member of the editorial staff of the Salt Lake *Tribune*, later moving to Monterey, California. He died at San Francisco, March 23, 1907, and was buried at Monterey. Over his grave is a monument, erected by his banker friend,

James Murray. Hewn from a great block of granite, it represents the proscenium arch of Maguire's Grand Opera House. The curtains are parted. Above the arch these words:

"*Ring down the drop—Life's fitful play is o'er.*"

A bust of John Maguire is in the Montana Historical Library at Helena.

Another figure was then entering Butte's theatrical scene. He was Richard Perry Sutton, native of Lexington, Kentucky. There are few residents of a later generation who do not remember the familiar figure of "Uncle Dick" Sutton, as he was affectionately known in the late nineties and the early nineteen hundreds.

If John Maguire was the sartorially perfect beau brummel, Uncle Dick Sutton was his antithesis. Henry Jonas, local tailor, used to say, "There isn't a more untidy man in the Northwest than Dick Sutton. I've often offered to make him a respectable looking suit free of charge, if he would wear it, but he prefers to go about the city in an outfit that a stumble-bum would be ashamed to wear."

Jonas did not exaggerate. Uncle Dick was never seen wearing a tie. A white, starched stand-up collar, usually in need of laundering and a white "dickey" or false shirt front, partly hidden by a nondescript vest on which could be seen the remnants of the showman's last meal, and an ancient coat covered the upper part of his body. A pair of baggy trousers surmounted a pair of Congress gaiters, usually with holes cut in them to relieve pressure on corns and bunions, covered rotund stomach and a pair of flat feet respectively. He was invariably in need of a shave, and a straggly tobacco-stained mustache never knew benefit of scissors or clipper.

Uncle Dick was never without a cigar but no one ever saw the cigar lit. He chewed the cigars and his dickey was usually bespattered with tobacco stains which dribbled down his gray, straggly mustache.

Sutton's only ornament was a diamond stud, half the size of a walnut, which he wore in the false-front dickey. A bowler hat, covered his head.

Uncle Dick first arrived in the camp with an Uncle Tom's Cabin troupe in 1892. He remained to build four theaters and become the owner of the Grand Opera House in Great Falls. In addition he organized the Northwest Theatrical Association, which booked New York stage successes to the Northwest.

Broke when he arrived in Butte, his sole assets were a troupe of hungry mastiffs which posed as bloodhounds in his "Tom" show. Within a remarkably short time, Uncle Dick had obtained a lease on Maguire's

MONTANA HISTORICAL SOCIETY, HELENA

Uncle Dick Sutton.

Grand Opera House, and had also converted what had been formerly known as Speck's in Caplice Hall into the theater known as the Union Family which later was known as "The Family." His new theater, Sutton's Broadway, was opened on September 29, 1901, with *The Belle of New York* playing. The name of the house was changed to the Broadway in 1902. It is now the Montana.

After Maguire, Uncle Dick was the dominant figure in the local theatrical field. He introduced popular-priced stock company performances, and an appreciative public kept his theaters always crowded. At the Grand, one of his companies, in which his daughter Lulu, was ingenue, played one hundred straight weeks—a new play each week. The house later became the home of Orpheum vaudeville, and later still, of the Sullivan and Considine circuit. Road shows played at his newer Broadway. He later erected another theater, The Lulu, across the street from the Grand which he named in honor of his daughter. Here he continued to offer "stock" and later Pantages vaudeville.

In addition to his theaters, Sutton always had one or two companies on the road playing *Uncle Tom's Cabin*, *Jesse James* and other melodramas of the period. He had a private pullman car in which his performers traveled.

Beloved by the theatrical fraternity, Uncle Dick's purse strings were never closed to a hard luck story. It is said that he handed out to indigent actors and actresses well over a hundred thousand dollars during his stay in Butte. He was a sucker for every variety of panhandler and he usually carried a small canvas sack of silver from which he distributed with a lavish hand. The cashier of the old Bartlett's Cafe, a rendezvous for local show people, once stated that there was seldom a time when there weren't at least a dozen meal tickets it the cafe's rack all purchased for someone down on his luck by the generous showman.

So well known was his trait that a story was told in every box office in the Northwest of how one man, a general agent of Kirk LaShelle, a popular actor of the day, reached Butte one morning and in answer to Sutton's cheery salutation of, "Well, son, how much money do you want?" declared he had plenty to carry him through.

Uncle Dick took offense at the answer and was inclined to consider the LaShelle manager in the light of an interloper and a green hand in show business. That opinion was maintained until the same man struck town the next season and having heard the story of how he had fallen from the Sutton grace, "touched" the veteran showman for four hundred dollars which restored him in good opinion of Sutton as a man who had learned many things necessary to the business.

Many a manager of an unlucky venture or "turkey" and many a stranded actor could tell how he reached Butte and got out of the hole through Uncle Dick's devotion to the "perfesh."

As Al Jolson once wrote to Uncle Dick:

> "From the Atlantic to the Pacific, and from Manitoba to Mexico, you are known and loved by the profession as 'Uncle Dick.' And take it from me on this Christmas Day, you are an 'Uncle' in more senses than one. May God bless you and yours Uncle Dick."

Sutton had a trunkful of similar sentiments from the great and humble of the theatrical world.

While noted for philanthropy to members of the profession in distress, Sutton had a particular aversion to the distribution of free passes to his theaters. While a down-and-outer or underprivileged child was always welcome to enter any of his attractions without cost, he hated to be imposed upon by chiselers. Framed in a prominent place in all offices were the following Biblical quotations:

"This generation shall not pass" .... Mark xiii, 30.
"Suffer not a man to pass" .... Judges iii, 28.
"None shall pass through .... Isaiah xxiv, 10.
"The wicked shall no more pass" .... Nahum i, 15.
"Thou shalt not pass by me" .... Numbers xx, 18.
"Though they roar yet can they not pass" ...... Jeremiah v, 22.
"So he paid the fare thereof and went" .... Jonah i, 3.

Uncle Dick was a strong believer in promoting opportunities for local talent. Over a score of local youngsters were at different times featured in his many shows. Old timers of Butte will remember Kitty Brady, "Little Joe" Mulcahey, Cora Morris, Olga Steck and Audrey Phelan (Little Audrey) to name a few. Prominent in his stock companies were such artists as Irene Lorton, Fannie Keeler, Fred Hagen, Lulu Sutton, Charlie Malloy and a host of others.

One of Uncle Dick's proteges, Kitty Brady, who still makes Butte her home, tells of the time that the great John L. Sullivan picked up the major part of his road show from talent supplied by Sutton's Grand, Family and Empire theaters.

On leaving the town, the troupe had been presented with a huge basket of fruit among which some practical joker had placed a small, hard, green citron.

Shortly after the train had got under way, Jim McCormick, billed on the show as "the strongest man in the world," spied the citron, thinking it a small watermelon. Grasping it between his mighty paws, he gave the fruit a terrific squeeze, but failed to dent it. Handing the citron to the famous John L, he suggested the heavyweight champion try his hand at it. Sullivan raised the brawny right fist that had shook fear into the pugilists of three continents, hit the fruit a resounding wallop, and had no better success than the strong man.

Disgustedly, John L. raised the window of the coach and threw the citron out on the prairie, remarking to the troupe:

"Now, who in hell would give a man a green watermelon that wasn't ripe. It's someone who's tryin' to pizen the lot av us."

No one in Butte knew Uncle Dick Sutton's correct age. If one asked when he first entered show business, he would screw up one of his little eyes, bite off a chunk from the end of his "Matinee Special" and answer:

"'Twas before you were born, son."

There was no early-play show business of any description in which he hadn't at one time had a hand. From one-ring wagon circuses to medicine and dime museum shows, the rotund little showman had given them all a whirl. One of the attractions he boasted of taking over the country was an educated sacred "Hindustan bull from down in Indiana." He did his own "orating" for the attraction and as a side line presented a "jigging and dancing act" with himself as principal performer.

Sutton often told of his first circus brought to Butte during the panic of 1893—this was before he had decided to make Butte his permanent home. It was billed as "Richard's Three Big Shows," and as he stated, "that visit was made a memorable one to all connected with the show."

Prior to the date set for the Sutton show, there had been a balloon race advertised at Columbia Gardens which didn't come off. Sutton's circus also advertised balloon ascension, and the citizens decided there would be no more disappointments. There were several hundred tough miners armed with clubs and bottles, around the circus on the opening day. They also had knives to cut the canvas into strips if the ascension was not made. The demonstration frightened the aeronaut, who jumped the show next day and made a dash for Chicago where, as he put it, "he could get satisfactory police protection."

Sutton's decision to make Butte his permanent residence has—like almost every move of his life—a good story attached to it. At the time he had two shows on the road, *The Cradle of the Confederacy* which he played only in the South, and *Uncle Tom's Cabin* which he played exclusively north of the Mason-Dixon Line. It was the latter which he brought as the opening attraction at, as he had been advised, a "new" theater, the Columbia at the corner of Montana and Mercury Streets. The show arrived in time, but when Sutton hunted up the theater he found Barney Quinn's livery stable on the site. He finally located the two would-be promoters who had brought him to town and found their sole property was an immense dog.

The trip had been long and costly, but the failure of the local men to provide a house didn't faze the veteran showman who offered to take the dog and call the deal square as he could use the animal in the "Tom" show. The owner refused, however, and the show was left here with no dates.

The play was finally put on at the old Casino Theater for a three-week engagement. Three days after the close of that run, Sutton leased the rooms in the Caplice Building at Park and Montana Streets and converted it into the Union Family Theater which was the nucleus of his string of theaters.

Uncle Dick retired when motion pictures became popular. Although he had the inside track in the new field, and had shown the first motion pictures in Butte at his Broadway Theater, he regarded them as a "crackpot experiment and fad" and would have nothing to do with them.

He died October 2, 1924, at Ocean Park, California, but his body was returned for burial in the local Mountain View Cemetery.

There were many more of these mining camp Belascos, most of them known from one end of the country to the other or wherever theatrical people gathered.

If any national or internationally famed theatrical star dropped dead between 1900 and 1910, and a photograph was needed by the newspapers, there was one place in the United States where they could be assured of obtaining it—from Mack and Carey's Orpheum Bar in Butte.

The famous barroom on West Broadway, where one of the principal hotels now stands, had on its wall what was authoritively called "the most notable collection of photographs and autographs of stage and vaudeville celebrities in the nation." The result of years of collecting by the proprietors, Danny Mack and Jimmy Carey, the photographs were not picked up at random. Every picture was personally autographed by the giver and was presented to the two partners by actors who had played in Butte. J. Francis Carey, one of the proprietors of the place was a former vaudeville actor and numbered his friends in the profession by the hundreds.

Among the celebrities who occupied a prominent place on the walls of the Orpheum was Charlie Chaplin, who had played in the camp several times on the old Sullivan-Considine circuit in an act entitled *A Night in an English Music Hall.* This was many years before Chaplin achieved fame in the cinema. Chaplin made the bar his headquarters during his stay in Butte and his pictures were autographed with humorous messages to the proprietors.

Charlie Murray, old-time film comedian, then a member of the vaudeville team of Murray and Mack, had his picture in a glass frame. Eddie Cantor, Walter Winchell, George Jessell and Lila Lee were pictured in knickerbockers and rompers as juvenile members of Gus Edward's famous *School Days.*

Another celebrity, and one of the highest priced men in vaudeville, James Morton, had several of his photographs in the collection. Also represented were Frank Fogarty, the "peerless Irish humorist and monologist"; and Bert Leslie, "the king of slang," whose depiction of *Hogan the Painter* and similar roles were one of the biggest successes of vaudeville. McMahon of McMahon and Chappel, another comedian, had his likeness and autograph between that of Julian Eltinge and Harry Lauder. Eltinge was born in Butte and attended school here.

Harry Lauder spent many hours in the Orpheum Bar scanning the gallery of notables when his company played in Butte. Reports of the Scot's penuriousness were not verified by Lauder's actions. Mack and Carey reported that he liked his drink and was considered a good spender.

Willie and Eugene Howard, musical comedy stars donated several photographs to the collection. Albini, famous magician, stood in a three foot frame. Houdini, Anna Eva Faye and Alexander the Great were other magicians and mystics represented.

Patsy Doyle, a former Butte miner who had won renown on the concert stage, had his photograph alongside those of Mat O'Keefe, the famous yodeler, and Manuel Romaine, violin virtuoso. John McCormack and Enrico Caruso were among the concert singers represented.

There were photographs of the Russell Brothers, who stampeded the American stage with *Our Hired Girl.* Pat Riley, pioneer vaudevillian, who headed the first show ever to play in Butte, *The Days of '61,* had his photograph hanging from the back bar mirror close to that of Buffalo Bill Cody, Calamity Jane and Pawnee Bill.

Many of the stars of the old time beer halls and hurdygurdies were also included in the collection hanging on the back bar. John Maguire and "Uncle Dick" Sutton, pioneer showmen of Butte and Sutton's daughter Lulu, were also represented.

More famous stars of that period whose photos were to be found included Chauncey Olcott, famed Irish Tenor, "Noodles" Fagan, King of the Newsboys, V. R. Seaton, famous Indian actor, Tom Mahoney, the comedian; Joe Whitehead and Joe Jackson, tramp cyclists; Ned "Cork" Norton of "B-U-L-I-E-V-E Me" fame. Al Jolson, McIntyre and Heath, George Primrose, and Richard and Pringle, all minstrel men, had autographed their likenesses.

Celebrities from the circus world were James H. Rutherford, clown director for Barnum and Bailey; a group photo of all the Ringling Brothers, autographed; Poodles Hanneford, famous clown; and a large autographed photo of Phineas T. Barnum. Photos of Tom Thumb and several other midgets and freaks were also a part of the collection.

Reece Prosses and Will Oakland, first vocalists to make phonograph records, and Nat Ellis, of, the Burlesque circus, looked down from a side wall,

Other celebrities of the day, Mike Donlan, the baseball star, and his wife, Mabel Hite; "Happy" Jack Gardiner, and N. Manwaring, who brought *Seven Little Girls and the Teddy Bear* through the West were represented in the Orpheum's collection as were Fanny Brice, Trixie Friganza, Lillian Russell, Sophie Tucker, Nora Bayes, Anna Held, Dorothy Morosco, The Four Cohan's, which included George M. Cohan, his father, mother and sister, Eddie Foy and similar old time favorites.

It would be impossible to name all in this collection of more than a thousand autographed photographs personally presented to Mack and Carey over a period of many years.

People from all over the world visited the Orpheum to see the famous gallery, for every photograph had some remark or quip written on it. In addition, Carey, who was something of a raconteur himself, entertained his customers and friends with reminiscences of the stars who made his place their headquarters while in Butte.

With erection of the Leggat Hotel, the Orpheum was dismantled and in 1920 the two partners shipped the entire collection to the Lamb's Club in New York City, where the pictures now hang.

Chronology of Events in Butte, Montana

1856 Caleb E. Irvine, coming through the district in the spring, noted that an attempt at sinking a shaft had been made by some unknown prospector who had used elk horns for gads.

1864 A commission, of which Granville Stuart was a member, was authorized to lay out the town of Silver Bow, seven miles from present-day Butte. Early it the year the first temporary settlers arrived and made camp. The party consisted of Charles Murphy, a man named May, William Graham and Frank Madison. After locating the Black Chief mine they moved on. In May the first permanent residents, G. O. Humphreys and William Allison, arrived to live in Baboon Gulch. On June 12, the first quartz location, the Missoula Mining company, was made by a number of prospectors, including Humphreys and Allison. On August 18, Humphreys and Allison located the Buffalo pacer, in which they were joined by twenty-four others, including Dennis Leary and Henry Porter. The two latter are credited with giving the name "Butte" to the camp by some historians. At this date the population of the place was fifty. This was the beginning of the gold era in Butte. Credit for diggin the first placer ditch is given to J. Garlens, Chastine Humphreys and L. A. Bernard.

1866 The first smelter was built by Joseph Ramsdell, T. C. Porter and William Parks in the north central part of the camp. It was not a success. This same year forty men and five women, engaged in placer mining, erected the only houses in the camp in Buffalo Gulch, northeast of the present city. William Vernon ran the first pony express from Butte to Virginia City. Twenty-five cents was charged for each letter. Christmas Day, this year, the first dance was held in the cabin of Dr. Olman. Fifty men, women and children attended and two fiddlers furnished the music.

1867 Butte City townsite was laid out, and the population reached five hundred. All residents were engaged in placer mining. The first post office was opened in Dublin Gulch, with Dr. Anson Ford as postmaster. The first school, a private institution, was known as Colonel Wood's school, with T. C. Porter as the first teacher. Porter is credited by some with giving the camp its name.

1868 The first mill, the Hendrie, which later became known as the Lexington mill, was erected by A. J. Davis. He purchased the Lexington mine from General Charles S. Warren for twenty dollars and a white horse. The mill was not a success as there was too much silver in the placer dust, whereas the placer miners were interested only in gold. Butte gold was worth six dollars less per ounce than the unusually pure gold of Highland City. The first copper lead was discovered by William Parks in his one-man mine, the Parrot Number 2, north of the camp and near what is now Anaconda Road.

1869 to 1874 Butte was fast becoming a ghost town as a great many of the placer claims were becoming worked out. Many of the houses and buildings had been moved to Silver Bow. Only a handful of placer miners remained—fifty in all. There were no stores and those remaining in the camp had to travel out to the Highland settlement for supplies, a distance of twenty-six miles. Two saloons, however, were still running.

1872 *W. A. Clark arrived.* He at once became interested in the copper deposits and in 1873 and 1874 started work on the Original, Colusa, Mountain Chief and Gambetta claims. He was the first to ship copper in commercial quantities from the camp. The ore had to be hauled four hundred miles by wagon train to Corinne, Utah, the nearest railway point. The first hostelry, the Hotel de Mineral, was opened by Simon Hauswirth.

1874 At midnight on the last day of the year, W. L. Farlin, taking advantage of the new Federal quartz mining laws, "jumpd" the Travonia claim, which he had formerly owned under the name of "The Asteroid," and from which he had taken samples which assayed high in silver. This marked the start of Butte's silver era. News of Farlin's action spread rapidly. The La Plata, Burlington, Lake, Acquisition, Great Republic and a score of other silver prospects were quickly relocated. Farlin soon started the construction of a ten-stamp roasting mill, known as the Dexter, the first to successfully treat silver ore locally.

1875 W. A. Clark completed and successfully operated the Dexter mill, which proved to be the nucleus of his future millions made in mining.

1876 Two Utah freighters traded a team of horses for a Butte mine with ore on the dump. They shipped a sack of ore to Walker Brothers in Salt Lake City for testing. It proved rich in silver. The Walkers decided to investigate and sent Marcus Daly, their mine foreman at Ophir, to look at the property. Marcus Daly arrived and purchased the Lexington and Alice mines in Walkerville, the town being named for the Walkers. Mills were erected on the properties and the ores formerly shipped to Germany, Wales and Baltimore were treated locally. The city of Butte was patented this year. The first Catholic church, St. Patrick's, a small frame structure, was built by Father De Ryckere. The famous Smokehouse lode was discovered by accident. The first Protestant church, the Mountain View Methodist, was started by the Reverend W. C. Shippens. The first community celebration found the entire population, one thousand, gathered at Loeber's hall, where a huge Christmas tree, obtained in Dublin Gulch, had been erected. Butte's first newspaper, the Daily *Miner*, was established in July.

1877 Volunteers left Butte to aid General Gibbon against Chief Joseph at the Battle of the Big Hole. The battle was over before the Butte volunteers arrived.

1878 Butte was incorporated as a city. On June 13 a miners' union was organized under the name of the Butte Workingmen's Union in Loeber's hall. There were 261 charter members. This marked the *beginning of local unionism in Butte.* T. C. Thornton delivered an address at the first public Independence Day celebration.

1879 The first mayor, Henry Jacobs, a Democrat, was elected.

1880 *Marcus Daly bought the Anaconda mine from Hickey Brothers for thirty thousand dollars and sold his stock in the Alice mine back to Walker Brothers.* The first successful smelter, the Colorado, began operations southwest of the camp on the banks of Silver Bow creek. The Bell, Montana and Parrot smelters followed in short order. Marcus Daly sold three-fourths of his share in the Anaconda mine for $30,000 to Haggin and Tevis, San Francisco attorneys representing George Hearst, father of William Randolph Hearst. Daly was appointed manager of the newly formed Anaconda Silver Mining company. Daly leased the Dexter mill from W. A. Clark and treated some eight thousand tons of oxidized silver ore which ran about thirty ounces to the ton. The venture was not a success and the mine was shut down for a time.

1881 February 16: Silver Bow County was created by the legislature out of Deer Lodge County. "Fat Jack" Jones, who became nationally known as a cab driver, operated the first hack in Butte.

December 21: The Utah Northern Railway, first railroad to run directly into Butte, was completed.

1882 The census showed a population of four thousand. The Silver Bow Club, an organization of millionaires, mining magnates and merchant princes, was formed.

1883 July 4: Arrival of the Northern Pacific Railroad in Butte. At a depth of three hundred feet, the first copper in quantity was encountered in the Anaconda mine in a five-foot vein of copper glance. *This was the beginning of the copper era.* Marcus Daly purchased a site near the banks of Warm Springs Creek for the smelter in what is now Anaconda. The site was selected because of the scarcity of water in Butte. Maneuvering for the possession of this water site contributed to the feud which later flamed between W. A. Clark and Marcus Daly, known as the war of the copper kings.

1884 Daly's smelter at Anaconda, capable of handling five hundred tons of ore per day, was completed. The first high school was opened with eleven pupils under A. C. Newell, principal. The first graduating class of six members held exercises in the Miners' Union hall.

1885 Butte boomed. Hundreds of miners of every nationality rushed in from the mines of Michigan, Nevada, and California. Droves of Irish and Cornish emigrants found their way to the camp. Wages were high, and money and pleasure plentiful. The growing population approached twenty-two thousand. In addition to the mines, hundreds were employed in the smelters, or driving the eight and ten-horse ore teams used in hauling the ore from the mines to the smelters.

1886 The capacity of the Anaconda smelter was doubled. Scores of French-Canadian wood cutters were working in the adjacent hills supplying the smelters with fuel and the mines with timber.

1887 Butte had surpassed the Lake Superior copper region in Michigan as a producer of the red metal.

December 22: The Butte Mines band was founded by Sam Treloar. The first library was founded by the Women's Christian Temperance Union.

1888 The Miners' Union became known as the Butte Miners' Union.

1889 *F. Augustus Heinze arrived.* The young mining engineer, recently graduated from the School of Mines of Columbia University, found employment with the Boston and Montana Consolidated Copper and Silver Mining company which owned extensive local holdings. He soon acquired the knowledge of the copper deposits which later enabled him to victoriously battle his erstwhile employer and its allied companies. W. A. Clark and brother purchased the Butte Reduction Works on Silver Bow Creek, south of the city, which refined and smelted the ore from the many Clark mines until 1906, when it was destroyed by fire. The Anaconda smelter burned to the ground on May 4. A new smelter was erected on the site and was operating September 4. In the first public execution, August 23, Henry Roberts was hanged for the murder of Crawford, a teamster. Montana was admitted to statehood, November 8. The Anaconda *Standard* was started by Marcus Daly in Anaconda. The Montana Central Railroad reached Butte this year.

1890 The mines this year produced 25,705 ounces of gold, 7,500,000 ounces of silver and 112,063,320 pounds of copper.

1891 Mines and smelters of the Anaconda Company were shut down due to a dispute with the Montana Union Railway over freight rates from

Butte to Anaconda. About fifteen hundred miners were affected. The shutdown led to the building of the B. A. & P. Railway whose right-of-way Marcus Daly had surveyed. *The Denver Sun*, in a page one article, proclaimed Butte the liveliest town in the United States. The Butte *Miner* stated that the camp had produced three hundred million dollars in mineral wealth since 1864.

1892 The Joshers' club, a famed charitable organization, was founded on Christmas Eve by a group of good fellows celebrating at the bar of Al Green's buffet. For more than a quarter of a century this organization, under the lead of a race horse man, Billy Gemmel, supplied the poor with Christmas baskets and clothing.

1893 The war between W. A. Clark and Marcus Daly began in January. Daly successfully blocked Clark's election to the U. S. Senate by the third Montana Legislative Assembly. Congress repealed the silver purchasing clause of the Sherman Act of 1890. Every silver mine and mill in the camp was closed down. Panic struck the city along with the rest of the nation. The Butte, Anaconda and Pacific Railroad was completed.

1894 Butte entered into the fight for the selection of a state capital, backing Marcus Daly's choice of Anaconda against W. A. Clark's sponsorship of Helena. Helena won. The vote was: Helena, 27,028; Anaconda, 25,118. The first motion pictures were shown on April 14 at the Broadway Theater. The panic was severely felt with only about one-fourth of the mines working.

July 4: A. P. A. riots on West Broadway resulted in deaths, scores injured and several places of business demolished.

1895 The "Big Explosion" killed and injured scores when warehouses on East Platinum Street, containing large stores of dynamite, took fire and exploded on January 15. The entire fire department, with the exception of three men and one horse, was wiped out by the blasts. The Butte Trades and Labor Council was formed.

1896 Butte solidly backed William Jennings Bryan, Democrat and free-silver candidate, for President against William McKinley, gold standard bearer. Because Bryan's platform of coinage of silver at a ratio of sixteen to one meant unlimited prosperity for the silver mines, McKinley's election was a deep disappointment to the camp. F. Augustus Heinze succeeded in having William Clancy elected as a district judge of Silver Bow County. On December 12, the corner stone of a new high school was laid, and seventeen days later the corner stone of the building for the State School of Mines was placed in position. Construction began on Maguire's New Grand Opera House. The Western Federation of Miners affiliated with the American Federation of Labor. The Women's Club of Butte was organized with more than a score of charter members.

1897 An anti-gambling bill passed the legislature and the games in Butte were closed. The population was unofficially claimed to be more than thirty thousand and the camp supported twelve churches, eight schools, a high school, seven theaters and more than two hundred and fifty saloons. William Jennings Bryan, in a colorful reception on August 12, was given the greatest welcome ever accorded a visitor. Albert, king of the Belgians, was given a trip down the mines.

1898 In a raid on a voting precinct in Dublin Gulch, John J. Daly, an election judge, was killed while protecting the precinct ballot box. Patriotically responding to a call for volunteers for the Spanish-American War, several hundred residents departed in thirty-five railway cars for the Presidio in San Francisco. The Hale House, noted miners' hostelry, burned to the ground, cremating several miners. Patrick Largey, banker and associate of Clark and Daly, was shot and killed at his desk by Thomas Riley who had lost a leg in the big explosion of 1895. Largey was one of the owners of a warehouse where some of the powder had been stored.

1899 In February, W. A. Clark was elected to the United States Senate by the Sixth Legislative Assembly after one of the most bitter battles ever fought in a legislative hall. Marcus Daly bitterly opposed the election and thousands of dollars were said to be spent in alleged bribery and vote buying by both parties. Clark's election was contested in Washington. When the Senate threatened an investigation, Clark resigned. The gigantic Amalgamated Copper company, consisting of the Anaconda Copper Mining company, the Boston and Montana Consolidated Copper and Silver Mining company, the Parrot company, the Trenton Mining and Development company, the Butte and Boston Consolidated Mining company, the Washoe Copper company and the Colorado Mining and Smelting company, representing a capitalization of $1,555,000,000 was formed. *Heinze became a full-fledged protagonist in the war of the copper kings*, signaling the opening of the largest scale mining litigation the country had ever seen. In the guise of a friend of labor Heinze began his battle with the Amalgamated. His effective slogan, "Down with Kerosene," referring to the Amalgamated's affiliation with Standard Oil, was the battle cry that resounded through the city, state and the courts for a hectic decade. Butte became one of the most publicized cities in the nation. Columbia Gardens opened in July as a family resort under the management of the Butte Street Railway company. In October, returning Spanish-American War veterans were feted with a mammoth celebration. On the eve of the November election, F. Augustus Heinze and W. A. Clark, riding together in "Fat Jack's" hack, headed a monster street parade. This year, for the first time, Butte was lighted with power brought from the Big Hole River plant near Divide. This last year of the nineteenth century was acclaimed the most prosperous and exciting in the history of the camp.

1900 The State School of Mines was formally opened. The official census gave the population, including the suburbs of Walkerville, Centerville and Meaderville, as 47,635. W. A. Clark, with the support of a Heinze-controlled legislative assembly, obtained his long-fought-for election to the United States Senate. Through a deal with Miles Finlen, Heinze secured the famed Minnie Healy mine, almost immediately striking an immensely rich ore deposit. Finlen brought suit, demanding the return of the mine. John Gillie became the owner of the first factory-made automobile, a "Mobile Steamer." *Marcus Daly died in New York City on November 12.*

1901 In February, the Montana Legislative Assembly passed the Eight-Hour Day bill, which became effective on May 1.

1902 The average daily output of the mines this year was 12,755 tons of ore.

1903 The restricted district was moved from Galena Street to the alley in the rear by order of the city council on January 2. Sutton's Grand Opera House opened October 1. The Minnie Healy case went to Judge Clancy's court and in October he handed down his decision, again finding in favor of Heinze. At the same time in another case, Clancy decided that the Amalgamated Copper company was operating in violation of the laws of Montana prohibiting trusts from carrying on business in the state. F. A. Heinze made his famous speech from the courthouse steps before thousands of irate miners, many of them reported to be carrying guns. Under the spell of Heinze's oratory and personality, they came away cheering for him and were once more his loyal supporters. *May 27*: President Theodore Roosevelt visited Butte.

1904 At the election this year Heinze failed in his efforts to re-elect his hand-picked judges, Clancy and Harney, and as a result his power began to wane. Butte reached a peak in building this year, the building boom having extended from 1895.

1905 The camp's suburban expansion began and hundreds of residences were erected on the flat south of the city. The restricted district in its new location, the alleys in the rear of Mercury, Galena and lower Main Streets, was reported to be second in size only to the notorious

Corduroy Road in New Orleans. It was estimated that nearly a thousand women were quartered in the district. In proportion to population, Butte claimed the largest payroll in the world—twelve thousand men in the mines and mills with a total payroll of $1,500,000 a month. There were now forty-two churches, twenty-five public schools and seven parochial schools. Bank deposits exceeded fifteen million dollars. On September 23, three business blocks, including Symon's department store and the Butte Public library were damaged by a "million-dollar fire."

1906 F. Augustus Heinze, on February 13, sold all Butte copper properties controlled by him to the Amalgamated Copper company for $10,500,000 and left Butte with a fortune estimated at $50,000,000.

1907 D. J. Hennessy, pioneer merchant prince, died January 27. Jimmy July, 82, a naturalized Chinaman and familiar character of Butte, died. William Jennings Bryan again visited Butte during train changes. A lone reporter from the Butte *Evening News* was at the depot to greet him. On Labor Day, a bronze statue of Marcus Daly was unveiled in front of the post office on North Main Street. The statue was erected through popular subscription, the miners and school children contributing more than $5,000.

1908 The long shutdown of the mines ended March 3. Catholic Central High School opened in September. Construction of the new courthouse was started. The Chicago, Milwaukee and St. Paul Railroad was completed into Butte.

1909 April 26: Judge Hunt rendered his decision in favor of the Anaconda company in the famous smoke case brought by Deer Lodge County farmers who claimed the smoke from the Anaconda smelter was ruining their stock and crops.

November 1: Henry Albertson, pioneer gambling house owner, died in Seattle. His body was shipped to Butte and he was given one of the largest funerals ever held in the city. Every hack and buggy in the city was pressed into service.

January 28: Mike Hickey, one of the original locators of the Anaconda mine, died. September 27: President William Howard Taft visited Butte and was given a typical mining camp reception.

F. Augustus Heinze returned to Butte and was welcomed at the depot by twenty thousand cheering residents.

1910 In the spring, Lewis J. Duncan, Unitarian minister, resigned from his church to become secretary of the Socialist party in Butte and editor of the semi-monthly, four-page newspaper, the Butte *Socialist.* The Socialist party in Butte had seventy-five members.

May 14: W. A. Clark sold his principal holdings in Butte, the Stewart and Original mines, to the Amalgamated Copper company for a reported price of one million dollars. A month later he sold his Butte Reduction Works to the same company, retaining only the Elm Orlu mine and his business, banking, lumber and street railway interests. The Amalgamated Copper company was absorbed by the Anaconda Copper company and from that time on was known by the new name. The population of the city and surrounding suburbs this year was 58,818. Carrie Nation, the temperance crusader, visited Butte and was ejected from a Galena Street bagnio by an irate madame.

1911 Lewis J. Duncan was elected mayor on the Socialist ticket. October 11: The camp had the worst snowstorm in its history, twenty-four inches of snow falling in twenty-hour hours. Telephone, power, light and telegraph lines were broken by the heavy, wet snow and for nearly a week the city was isolated from the rest of the world.

1912 The Great Northern Railway built a new passenger depot. The Butte, Anaconda and Pacific Railway was electrified.

March 11: The Butte Chamber of Commerce was organized.

April 10: A half-million dollar fire leveled three blocks of residences and warehouses in South Butte.

July 2: The camp saw its first airplane, piloted by a barnstorming aviator who was killed a few days later while giving an exhibition in Spokane.

August 20: A riot took place at a miners' picnic at Gregson Springs as a result of a disagreement between Butte miners and Anaconda smeltermen over a tug-of-war match. Hundreds were injured by flying beer bottles and one man was killed by a stray bullet.

1913 The area of the city proper was increased to 3000 square acres. September 30: The first electric train was operated over the Butte, Anaconda and Pacific railroad.

1914 June (first week): Trouble brewed in the Miners' Union over heavy assessments made on members for benefits to striking miners in Michigan. Many miners, refusing to pay the assessments and repudiating the conservative leadership of the American Federation of Labor, withdrew from the Butte Miners' Union and organized an Independent Mine Workers' Union, 4,000 strong.

June 12: More than a thousand miners attacked six Miners' Union representatives at the gate of the Speculator mine.

June 13: A Miners' Union Day parade was attacked and broken up by a mob of disgruntled miners. Later the same day, thousands of embittered miners attacked the Union Hall on North Main street and tore out furnishings and fixtures. Later that evening a heavy safe containing Miners' Union funds and records was loaded on a moving van and taken south of the city where it was dynamited.

June 20: Charles Moyer, president of the Western Federation of Miners, arrived in Butte.

June 23: Moyer's men, about one hundred in number, fired with rifles from Union hall upon a mob of thousands of miners gathered in front of the building. The mob fired back. Moyer and his men escaped, but the miners obtained cases of dynamite from the mines and blew up the hall.

July 3: Mayor Lewis J. Duncan shot and killed Erick Lantilla, a Finnish miner, through the abdomen, after first being attacked and wounded by a knife carried by Lantilla.

August 10: Muckey McDonald was elected president of the Butte Mine Workers' Union.

August 20: The rustling card office of the Anaconda Copper Mining Company at the Parrot mine was blown up.

September 1: Martial law was declared in Butte by Governor Sam V. Stewart. Frank Conley of Deer Lodge was appointed provost marshal for Butte. Muckey McDonald fled Butte on arrival of the National Guard. Muckey McDonald and several of his followers were arrested.

September 9: The open shop was declared in all Butte mines.

October 6: Mayor Duncan and Sheriff Timothy Driscoll were deposed from office by Judge Roy Ayers.

November 5: Martial law ended in Butte by order of Governor Stewart.

November 21: Muckey McDonald and Joe Bradley were found guilty by a Jefferson County jury.

November 4: F. Augustus Heinze died suddenly at Saratoga, N. Y., at the age of 45. His estate, consisting of insurance policies, amounted to $1,500,000 and was left to his son, F. Augustus Heinze, Jr.

1915 The winter was the mildest in history, the thermometer never reaching zero. The High Ore shaft was at the 3,400-foot level, the deepest in the district.

January: An explosion of a truckload of dynamite at the collar of the Granite Mountain mine's shaft caused the death of sixteen men waiting to go on shift.

April: Women voted at the municipal election for the first time. The Workman's Compensation Act, passed by the legislature in January, was in effect.

1916 January 11: The temperature had remained below zero for 32 days.

February 14: Fire broke out on the 1,200-foot level of the Pennsylvania mine, asphyxiating twenty-one miners and ten horses on that level.

April 28: Copper reached a new high level of 28 cents per pound and miners' pay was increased to $4.50 a shift.

December 1: Wages were advanced to $4.75 per day by all the Butte mining companies.

1917 April 6: The United States was officially at war with Germany. The news caused very little excitement in Butte.

June 6: A total of 11,603 persons were registered for the Selective Service Act in the city and county. The occasion was a holiday, all stores and saloons being closed.

June 8: At 11:45 P.M., fire broke out in the shaft of the Speculator and in the Granite Mountain mines. In a few minutes the entire shaft was aflame, forcing gas and smoke back into the workings where 415 men were on night shift.

June 9: After 24 hours, mine officials stated that they were forced to believe that nearly 200 miners had perished.

June 10: Twenty-five men in the Speculator mine, given up for dead, were found to be alive. They owed their lives to Manus Duggan, who had marshalled the men into a crosscut and erected a bulkhead to keep out the deadly fumes. Duggan, himself, going in search of a safe exit, was trapped in the gas and died.

June 10: One hundred and twenty-three men of B company, Montana National Guard, arrived to remain for an indefinite period. Their arrival brought the number of troops in Butte to more than 200.

June 15: The funeral of Manus Duggan was held, with thousands of residents paying respects.

The Metal Mine Workers called a strike, demanding wages of $6 per day, irrespective of the price of copper. Martial law was again invoked.

August 1: Frank Little, a member of the executive board of the I. W. W., was lynched about three o'clock in the morning by being hanged from a railroad trestle by six or seven armed masked men who styled themselves "vigilantes." Rewards were offered, but his murderers were never apprehended.

September 8: Forty men, comprising Butte's first draft contingent, left for Camp Lewis to undergo training. One of the greatest demonstrations in the history of the camp was accorded the departing men.

1918 January 14: The first triple hanging took place in the yard of the courthouse. John O'Neil, Frank Fisher and Sherman Powell, the latter a Negro, were executed.

February 1: The camp was observing meatless and potatoless days and was leading the nation in per capita purchase of thrift stamps and Liberty Bonds.

October 2: Granville Stuart, a noted pioneer, died.

November 11: The Armistice was signed, and Butte put on one of the greatest impromptu celebrations in its history, whooping it up for three straight days and nights.

November 20: Martial law ended its sixteen-month reign.

December: Draft boards and army, navy and marine recruiting stations estimated that six thousand Butte men had joined the colors. The influenza epidemic hit the camp with full force. It was estimated that 300 residents succumbed.

December 19: It was estimated that 264 Butte men had been disabled while fighting in the World War and approximately 114 had been either killed in action or had died in camps.

1919 January 1 : Montana's prohibition law went into effect at midnight, December 31. The law was only a few hours old when a pioneer liquor dealer was arrested for its violation.

February 8: A strike was called by mine workers.

February 12: The Silver Bow Trades and Labor Council endorsed the miners' strike. Armed soldiers from Camp Lewis arrived.

February 14: Major General Morrison announced that martial law was not necessary and would not be declared unless conditions became more serious.

February 17: The strike ended when it was officially declared off by the Metal Mine Workers' Union.

February 22: Most of the soldiers stationed in Butte left for their various posts, a platoon from one company remaining.

April 28: Thirty-five thousand people crowded Marr Field to witness the exhibition flights of the Army "Flying Circus." The planes were American, French and German ships that had seen service in the late war.

1920 April 22: A platoon of armed gunmen opened fire with machine guns on pickets assembled on Anaconda Road, killing two miners. Sixteen others were severely injured.

April 23: A company of regular United States Army troops arrived in the city.

April 27: Work in the mines was resumed with military patrols on all roads.

May 12: Mining companies decided to cast out all I. W. W. members from among their employees by recalling rustling cards from members of that organization.

August 18: Franklin D. Roosevelt, Democratic candidate for Vice President, addressed a small audience from the steps of the courthouse.

November 28: Generalissimo Foch of the allied armies spoke in French from the balcony of the old Finlen hotel.

December 16: "Fat Jack" Jones died in California at the estate of W. A. Clark, Jr. Jones was a pioneer cab driver of Butte.

December 30: The camp reached its peak in population. Census figures showed a city population of 41,611 and a county population of 65,000. The count was made in 1920 after the war boom had dwindled. Many authorities claimed the county population was close to 100,000 early in 1918.

January 30: Practically every copper mine in the camp was idle.

1921 March 27: Short dresses and bobbed hair for women made their appearance in the Easter parade for the first time.

April 13: Charles S. Warren, G. A. R. veteran and pioneer resident of the city, died.

April 19: Hunger and starvation was rampant because of the shutdown. The Butte Elks Lodge and the Silver Bow Trades and Labor Assembly worked together in an effort to formulate some plans to aid the needy.

April 25: Ed. Hickey, banker and one of the discoverers of the Anaconda mine, died.

June 3: Federal authorities intimated that Butte led the nation in per capita consumption of illicit liquor.

December 25: The Butte Joshers' club delivered four thousand baskets, a record, to poor families on Christmas Day.

December 29: The Anaconda Copper Mining company and other mining companies made the announcement that all the mines and smelters in the camp would reopen on January 16, with a cut in wages of fifty cents a day, making the wage for miners $4.25.

December 30: Mayor Cocking published a proclamation offering thanks giving for the end of the longest period of industrial inactivity in the history of the camp.

1922 January 16: A majority of the mines resumed operations after a long shutdown. A tong war broke out in Chinatown and the Chinese residents went about armed and many of them were accompanied by white bodyguards. Three Chinese had been killed by tong hatchmen.

April 17: The Chinese tong war broke out again and a Chinaman known as Old Charlie was shot down by Chinese gunmen.

June 20: Thousands of baseball fans mourned because the lid had been clamped down on the daily twenty-five cent baseball pools which had been accumulating posts of $5,000 daily. The pools were again resumed within a few days.

December 31: This marked the end of the first year in a decade that a strike had not been called in some Butte industry.

1923 March 6: Miners were granted another raise of fifty cents in pay, the second within six months.

June 7: One thousand complaints in liquor law violation cases in the city had been filed in the three years of prohibition.

June 29: President Warren G. Harding and party visited Butte for three hours and were given a tremendous ovation.

August 10: All activities ceased for five minutes in Butte while the body of President Harding was laid to rest.

September 3: The first Labor Day parade in nine years was held.

December 22: A naked Indian was caught taking a public bath in the copper precipitating tanks on the East Side.

1924 June 1: "Rimmer" Jack O'Neil, colorful assistant superintendent of mines on the hill for 44 years, was killed by diving into an empty swimming pool at Boulder Hot Springs.

July 22: Several inches of snow fell.

October 1: "Uncle Dick" Sutton, pioneer theatrical man died at Ocean Park, California.

1925 March 2: Former Senator W. A. Clark died at his home in New York at the age of 86. His will was probated, and many Butte friends were given legacies and the Paul Clark Home for children received an endowment of $350,000.

July 10: Slight earthquake shocks were felt.

September 3: Vice President Dawes paid a brief visit.

October 8: Butte's population was given as 42,867 by the census bureau.

1926 Anaconda Copper Mining company, announced that three large hoists would be installed at the company's mining properties which would permit of mining to a depth of 5,000 feet.

July 1-5: Butte swarmed with visitors for the five-day Independence Day celebration.

November 22: The Chicago, Milwaukee and St. Paul railway was sold at public auction to Robert T. Swain and Donald C. Swatland of New York for $140,000,000. There were no other bidders and one of the greatest receivership sales in history took place at the entrance of the Butte Milwaukee depot and was completed in thirty minutes.

1927 February 14: William Gemmell, county commissioner and one of the founders and leaders of the Butte Joshers' club, was instantly killed when he jumped from a window in the Silver Bow block where he was trapped by fire.

May 29: The heaviest snowstorm in twenty-eight years hit Butte. Due to the storm, the Memorial Day services had to be postponed for a week.

September 5: Colonel Charles A. Lindbergh flew to Butte from Boise. Close to 100,000 people saw the flyer while he was in the city.

1928 August 1: The first air mail arrived from Salt Lake.

August 22: The Anaconda Copper Mining company acquired all the holdings of the late Senator Clark in Montana. Included in the sale was the newspaper, the Butte *Miner,* the Montana Hardware company, Columbia Gardens, the Butte Street Railway company, the Elm Orlu mine, the Timber Butte mill and several lesser properties.

September 12: The Butte *Miner,* Butte's oldest newspaper, passed from the field and the Montana *Standard,* combining the features of the Anaconda *Standard* and the *Miner,* made its appearance, narrowing Butte's newspaper field to the Butte *Daily Post* and the Montana *Standard.*

September 17: W. A. Clark, Jr., began publication of the Montana *Free Press,* one of a chain of three Montana papers to take the place of the defunct Butte *Miner.*

September 25: Butte roared its joy at seeing Al Smith, Democratic candidate for President. Thousands swarmed the streets to get a view of the "Happy Warrior."

December 25: The Joshers' Club distributed but 658 Christmas baskets in the now prosperous camp, a new low for that organization.

1929 January 22: The lid was clamped on all gambling.

February 4: The Anaconda Copper Mining company announced wage increase of twenty-five cents per day, bringing the wage of the miners up to $6.00, the highest in the history of the camp.

March 11: Joseph K. Toole, Montana's first governor, died.

May 19: All of W. A. Clark, Jr.'s Montana Free Press newspapers suspended publication.

November 1: Butte keenly felt the stock market crash. Butte's first radio station, KGIR, went on the air for regular daily broadcasts.

1930 January 17: With the temperature down to 47 degrees below zero, Butte was the coldest spot in the United States and Canada.

October 1: Ike Hayes, 67, pioneer colored pugilist who had fought with Peter Maher, died in Butte.

October 15: Winter arrived early, the thermometer falling overnight to 19 degrees below zero.

1931 March 3: With the temperature at 80 degrees above a new winter record for warm weather was established.

March 5: A wild Rocky Mountain blizzard roared in, paralyzing traffic and delaying railroad trains.

October 7: The depression hit Butte. A drive was on for an emergency relief fund.

1932 July 4: Six Butte youths were killed by the premature explosion of a number of sticks of dynamite at the Meaderville baseball park, where they were celebrating Independence Day.

July 19: Thousands of windows in homes and office buildings were smashed by giant hail stones during a violent thunderstorm.

September 19: Franklin D. Roosevelt, at that time governor of New York state and Democratic candidate for Vice President, spoke to a crowd of three thousand people from the courthouse steps.

October 2: Norman Thomas, Socialist candidate for President, addressed a crowd of about 2,500 people.

November 11: In Silver Bow County voters swarmed to the polls and cast one of the heaviest votes in history. Roosevelt and the Democratic ticket carried the city and county by an overwhelming majority.

1933 February 9: The mercury dropped to an all-time low, the official record being 52 degrees below zero. Trask, about ten miles from Butte, recorded a new unofficial low mark for the nation, 60 degrees below zero.

February 10: It was "Springtime in the Rockies" with the thermometer a mere 10 degrees below.

March 15: Butte banks reopened after the bank holiday declared by President Roosevelt, and received heavy deposits. Local breweries began preparations to brew legal beer.

April 5: "Pussyfoot" Johnson, noted dry leader, spoke in Butte and predicted that the beer spree would kill the plan to repeal prohibition.

April 7: Legal beer flowed in Butte for the first time in thirteen years.

April 30: "Colonel" Buckets (James Rutledge), a colorful character of Butte's racetrack life, died of pneumonia.

September 13: W. W. McDowell of Butte was appointed U. S. minister to the Irish Free State.

December 5: The official end of prohibition was received enthusiastically in Butte.

December 20: Butte's state liquor store made its first sale.

December 30: Frank C. Walker was the guest of honor at a banquet at the Finlen hotel as the camp prepared to celebrate its first New Year's Eve since the repeal of the prohibition laws.

1934 January 1: Butte woke with its first post-repeal New Year's headache.

February 6: All pending Federal prohibition charges against local residents, thirty-three in all, were ordered wiped off the docket by the United States Supreme Court.

March 30: All business was suspended for three hours in observance of Good Friday.

April 9: W. W. McDowell, U. S. minister to the Irish Free State and a Butte resident, dropped dead in Dublin, Ireland.

September 19: An agreement between Butte Miner's Union, No. 1 and the Anaconda Copper Mining company was reached and a strike which had lasted six weeks was ended.

October 22: "Shoestring Annie," old-time character, died at the county hospital.

October 29: An inventory filed in the Silver Bow County district court valued the estate of the late William A. Clark, Jr., at $4,982,727.22.

December 25: With the miners' strike settled and sufficient relief being disbursed by federal, state and county governments, the newspapers reported that the camp had celebrated the happiest Christmas since the stock market crash.

1935 January 3: Simon Hauswirth, 90-year-old Civil War veteran, one of the first residents and owner of the first hostelry, the Hotel De Mineral, died.

April 1: Charles A. Hauswirth, Republican, was elected mayor.

April 29: At midnight, wide-open gambling was brought to a sudden shutdown. No reasons were given.

May 13: Gambling in Butte staged a comeback.

June 9: William Mahan, ex-convict, wanted for the kidnapping of George Weyerhauser of Tacoma, Washington, was seen in Butte and chased by Officer James Mooney. He escaped, leaving a car containing $15,155 of the ransom money.

June 13: The first Miners' Union Day parade since 1914 was held with thousands of miners in the line of march.

September 20: Jere Murphy, noted chief of police, died from injuries received while scuffling with a crazed gun wielder in the offices of the Montana Power Company. A working contract with the Anaconda Copper Mining company was accepted by Butte Miners' Union, No. 1.

October 12: Earthquake shocks were felt in Butte and Helena, particularly in the latter city there they lasted for more than a month, intermittently, and caused damage estimated at $3,000,000 and the loss of six lives.

October 25: The W. P. A. program was instituted.

December 25: William Knight, ex-convict, ran amuck at a South Main street rooming house, killing Police Officer Tom O'Neill and Francis Walsh, a store clerk, and seriously wounding Police Officer James Mooney. A day later Knight shot and killed Floyd Wood, a Madison County farmer. Returning to Butte, Knight was cornered at a friend's home on South Oklahoma street, where he had held a woman and several children prisoners for twelve hours. He was shot and killed by Assistant Chief of Police Jack Duggan.

1936 Lewis J. Duncan, Socialist mayor from 1911 to 1914, died at the age of 79.

January 26: Soldiers' bonus blanks were received in Butte.

February 8: The thermometer at the airport reached a new low of 61 degrees below zero.

March 26: William Zaschke, 75, a miner, was tendered a banquet by the Anaconda Mining company on the eve of his retirement after 45 years of service.

July 3: With plenty of bonus money in circulation, the two-day Fourth of July celebration began with a parade.

July 6: The Anaconda Copper Mining Company announced a new group insurance plan for its employees.

September 13: The new Marcus Daly racetrack on the Flat was destroyed by fire.

November 4: Returns from the general election showed that Roosevelt had carried the city and county with one of the largest votes ever cast.

1937 January 15: Butte was "hot" with the thermometer registering 40 degrees above zero.

January 19: Butte was "cold," the thermometer falling to 40 degrees below zero.

February 22: The annual Brotherhood banquet for members of the Protestant, Jewish and Catholic faiths was held at the Finlen Hotel.

1938 April 6: The sale of hard liquor by the drink in bars became legal.

May 18: A freak three-day, spring snowstorm paralyzed all traffic. Snow fell for eighty hours, covering the town with more than two feet of heavy slush. Fifteen hundred W. P. A. workers were mobilized to clear the streets.

June: W. P. A. officials stated that $35,000,000 had been spent by W. P: A. in the Butte zone.

September and October: Five leading mines, the Belmont, Stewart, Mountain Con, St. Lawrence and Leonard, resumed operations after a shutdown of many months.

May: The Anaconda Copper Mining company made a gift of Clark Park, a recreational playground and baseball field, to the city.

1939 July 3, 4, 5 and 6: Butte celebrated the anniversary of Montana's fiftieth year of statehood. It was estimated that 50,000 persons were attracted to the city by the celebration.

November: Copper advanced to 12 ° cents a pound. A majority of the mines were reopened. The Anaconda Copper Mining company raised miners' wages to $5.75.

1940 The Census Bureau gave the population of Butte and suburbs as 53,450.

October: Wendell Willkie, Republican candidate for President, visited Butte and was given a rousing reception.

October 6: Wages in the mines were advanced 25 cents a day. Basic pay was $6.00 per day.

October 29: Youths numbering 7,365 registered for the first peacetime draft.

November: Roosevelt was re-elected and carried Butte and Silver Bow County by a vast majority.

November 18: The first contingent of draftees left the city for various army camps.

1941 January 6: Sam C. Ford became Montana's eleventh governor. One of Ford's first acts was to instruct Attorney-General Bonner to rigidly enforce the gambling laws of the state. Gambling was closed in Butte.

April 7: The city election was held, with Mayor Charles A. Hauswirth, Republican, elected to serve his fourth consecutive term.

April 11: Mayor Hauswirth, 58, died at his home after suffering a heart attack.

May 5: After a stormy session, the city council named Barry O'Leary as mayor.

May 14: A permit was granted to move the statue of Marcus Daly from Main street to the campus of the Montana School of Mines. July 14: Death came to Mrs. Marcus Daly, widow of the late copper magnate, at the Daly estate near Hamilton, Montana. Her estate was appraised at $14,322,891, the Montana holdings being valued at only $163,244.

August 15: Offices for Civilian Defense registration were opened at the courthouse.

August 27: Hundreds of residents went to Stevensville to observe the Catholic centenary in Montana.

December 7: The camp was stunned by the news of the Japanese attack on Pearl Harbor. Many local men were serving with the armed forces in the Pacific.

December 8: Young men crowded the local recruiting offices as the United States declared war on Japan.

December 12: Word was received that LeRoy R. Carpenter of Butte was killed in action in the Philippines. He was the first Butte casualty.

December 17: Plans were made to hold a practice blackout.

Index

Acoma Hotel 206
Adams, Maude 287
Aetna Bank 46
Akara, Mohammed 11
Al Green's saloon 89, 300
Albert, king of the Belgians 301
Albertson, Henry 303
Alder Gulch 14, 70
Alexander the Great 294
Alexander, Whistling Sammy 222, 225–226
Alice Mine 16, 17, 31-33, 297, 298
Allen, Pat 250
Allison, William 14, 22, 30–31, 296
Amalgamated Mining Corporation 38–46, 55, 301–304
American Federation of Labor 301, 304
American Protective Association (A.P.A.)
  elections of 1895 and 1897 48
  riot of 1894 57–60, 300
Anaconda Copper Mining Company 6, 17, 47, 55–56, 299, 301, 303, 304, 305, 308, 310–314
Anaconda Mine 17–18, 28, 33–34, 42, 96, 170, 209, 218, 236, 268, 274, 298, 308
Anaconda Mining company 313
Anaconda Railway 300, 304
Anaconda Smelter 299, 303
Anaconda Standard 35, 39, 44, 49, 50, 107, 114, 154, 299, 310
Anderson, O. B. 222, 227
Andrews, Bill 234
Arena 235
Art Center 11
Atherton, Gertrude 11
Atlantic Bar 9
Auditorium 63, 165
Ayers, Judge Roy 305

B.A.& P. Railway 61, 74, 158, 164, 300
Baboon Gulch 30, 296
Badger Mine 174, 206
Baker, Diamond Tooth 87, 283
Balaklava Mine 204
Bannack 14, 184
Barker, E. J. 250
Barney's roadhouse 90
Barry, "Sheep's Head" 79–80
Bartlett's Cafe 290
Bates, Blanche 287
Battle of the Big Hole 298
Battling Nelson 159, 237
Bayes, Nora 295
Bebee, William 164
Bell Creek 147, 147–148, 149, 169, 298
Bell Mine 204, 268
Belmont Mine 79, 206, 314
Benzie 268–269
Berkley Mine 206
Bernard, L.A. 296
Bernhardt, Sarah 4, 83
Bertrand, Napoleon 228
"Big Jerry" 226–227
Big Explosion 177, 300
Bing Kong tong 126–127
Black Chief mine 296
Black Rock Mine 6, 62–63, 66, 172, 223
"Blasphemous" Brown 278, 280
Blubber (bulldog) 246–247
Bonner, Attorney General 315
Boston and Montana Company 42
Boston and Montana Consolidated Copper and Silver 40, 299, 301
Boulevard 147–148, 228, 243
boxty 254
Boyle, Charlie 87, 200, 270
Bradley, Joe 305
Bradshaw, Walter 230–231, 232
Brady, Kitty 291
Brady, William A. 286
Braley, Berton 3, 76, 100–102, 156
Braley, N. B. 250

Brasier, Pansy 191
Breen, George 278, 281
Brennan, Jim 8, 180, 212, 214, 215, 220, 228
Brice, Fanny 295
Britt, Jimmy 237
Broadwater, Colonel Charles A. 34
Broadway Theater 89, 161, 293, 300
Brophy Grocery Company 286
Brotherhood banquet 314
Browne's Cafe 133
Bryan, William Jennings 5, 83, 300–301, 303
Bucher, C.H. 264
Buckets, "Colonel" 3, 77, 90–93, 312
Buckley, Jerry 7
Buffalo Bill Cody 294
Buffalo Gulch 296
Buffalo Mine 206
Bulgin, Reverend 7, 88
Burlington Mine 16, 82, 297
Burns, Watermelon 3
Butchertown 1
Butt Block 222–224
Butte and Boston Consolidated Mining company 301
Butte Brewery 30
Butte City 14, 15, 183, 296
Butte Civic Auditorium 165
Butte Daily Bulletin 71
Butte Daily Post 310
Butte Elks Lodge 308
Butte High School 266
Butte Hotel 52, 84, 91
Butte Jockey Club *131*
Butte Mine Workers' Union 305
Butte Miner 35, 44, 49, 61, 70, 71, 75, 86, 108, 183, 282, 300, 310
Butte Miners' Union, No. 1 313
Butte Mines band 299
Butte Newsboys Club 102
Butte Railway 300, 304
Butte Reduction Works 65, 136, 299, 304
Butte Socialist 303
Butte Street Railway Company 310
Butte Trades and Labor Council 300
Butte Workingmen's Union 298
Bylo 12, 158

Cabbage Patch 3, 6, 121, 134, 153, 264, 278–281
Calamity Jane 294
Callaghan, Father J. J. 2, 198–199, 200–202
Callahan the Bum 1, 76, 198–202, 283
Cantor, Eddie 294
Caplice Building 286, 290, 293
Carey, J. Francis 293–295
Carl Maka 232
Carmen 166
Carney 85–87
Carrol, Mickey 3, 220
Carroll, Earl 4, 190
Carter, Judge 122, 234
Carter, Thomas H. 34
Caruso, Enrico 294
Casino 185, 238, 293
Catholic Central High School 303
Centennial brewery 65
Centennial Plant 16
Centerville 1, 10, 58, 73–75, 147, 156, 204, 226, 253, 277, 302
ghost 72–76
"Centerville Bull" 95
Chamberlain, Ed 232
Chaplin, Charlie 294
Chequamegon 260
Chicago Railroad 303, 310
Chicken Flats 1, 147, 162, 243
Chicken Lee 278, 280
Chicken Liz 6
Chin Kin Bow 123–124
China Alley 117, 119, 126–127, 259, 284
Chinaman, John 122
Chinatown 114–127
Chinn, Tom 127

Chippewa Indians 105, 108, 110–113
Chong Suey 125
Chope, Tom 91–92
City council 71, 180, 302, 315
City Hall 4, 65, 110–111, 199, 279
Clancy, Judge 3, 42–43, 45, 276, 300, 302
Clarence Hotel 253
Clark, Charlie 37, 267–268
Clark, J. Ross 34
Clark, W. A. 3, 6, 8, 17, 31–47, *35*, 49, 50, 55, 76, 92, 136, 154, 163, 166, 214, 226, 264, 267, *270*, 297, 298, 299, 300–304, 308, 310, 312, 314
  Clark-Daly fight 31–37, 40
Clark, W. A., Jr. 85, 267–268
Clark's Smelter 163
Clifford, Harry 4
Clipper Shades 4, 183–184, 191
Cocking, Mayor 308
Cohan, George M. 295
Cohen, A. B. 30
Coliseum dance hall 4
Collane, Mike 74
Colligan, Ed 164
Colonel Wood's school 296
Colorado Mine 206, 232, 278
Colorado Mining and Smelting company 301
Columbia Gardens 8, 21, 68, 83, 96, 180, *181*, 182, 229, 233, 287, 297, 306, 310, 315
Colusa Mine 17, 33, 206, 297
Comique 191–194
Comstock lode 17, 33
"Con the Horse" 218
Confederate Gulch 14
Conley, Frank 305
Conrad, Jim 139
Cooks and Waiters Union 7
Cooney, Byron E. 98
Copper, discovery of 16–18
Copper Ditch Dugan 168–169
Copper King Hotel and Saloon 191, 238
Copper Kings 31, 37, 260, 268, 298, 301
  sons 267
Cora Mine 291
Corbett, James 83, 94
Corktown 155, 157, 158
Cornwall 233, 251
Cosgrove 240
Coughlin, Tommy 219
Council Bar 257–258
Cousin Jacks 6, 50, 139, 208, 233–234, 235, 251
Cowan 82
Coyle, Mary 86
Crazy Mary 6, 76, 260
Creamery Cafe 259
Cree Indians 103, 105, 108–113, 148
Crewel, Nick 234
Cripple Creek 232
Crystal Springs 243
Cullhane, "Tango" 221
Cumbro, Jerry 82
Curran, Frank 65
Curtis, John 82
Cushman 157
Cusick, Dave 237

Dago Jim 222, 224–225
Daily Bulletin 56
Daily Miner 116–119, 122, 154, 298
Daley, Tabey 50
Daly, John J. 37, 301
Daly, Marcus 6, 7, 9, 13, 17, 20, 28, 31–33, 36–40, 42, 46–48, 50, 55, 76, 84, 92, 106, 130–131, 214, 239, 241–242, 272, 297–298, 299, 300–303, 314–315
Daly, "Rags" 221
Davenport, Homer 80
Davey, Mike 232
Davey, W. H. 11
Davis, A. J. 296

Davis, Goldie 3, 281
Davis mill 16
Davis, Wesley 187
Davitt, Michael 45
De Murska, Mollie 4
De Ryckere, Father 297
Deer Lodge 33, 80, 303
Deer Lodge lode 15
Dempsey, Jack 236
Denny 212
Dexter mill 297, 298
Dexter Plant 16
Diamond Mine 175, 213, 222, 226
Dinty Moore's 281
Discount, Alex 102
Divel, Fred 45
Dixon, Joseph 91
Dixon, Judge 80
Dogtown 1
Donlan, Mike 295
Donlin, Michael 3, 164
Donnelly, Tommy 86
Donovan, Dennis 166–169
Doyle, Patsy 294
Driscole, Julia 86
Driscoll, Tim 63, 70, 276, 305
Dublin Dan 87, 88
Dublin Gulch 37, 53, 120, 140–141, 147, 155, 158, 160, 296, 298, 301
Duffy, Joe 75–76, 85, 87
Dugan, "Copper Ditch" 167
Duggan, E. O. 47–48, 58, 59, 271
Duggan, Jack 126, 313
Duggan, Larry 57, 67, 169, 277
Duggan, Manus 176, 306
Duncan, Rev. Lewis J. 55, 65, 70, 277, 303–305, 313
Durston, Dr. John H. 35
"Dutch Nick" 222, 228
Dynamite (dog) 96–97

East Side 147
Edward, Gus 294
Ehrlich, Jacob 88
Eight-Hour Day bill 302
Ellis, Nat 295
Elm Orlu Mine 304, 310
Eltinge, Julian 294
Emeralds team 235–236
Emma Mine 203
Empire 291
Evans, "Hughie" 222, 229
Evening News 3, 44, 98, 100, 121, 140, 144, 154, 303

Farlin, William L. 15, 203, 297
Fay (lady barber) 281
Faye, Anna Eva 294
"Fighting Steve" 278, 280
Filthy McNabb 6
Finlen Hotel 78, 89, 90, 302, 308, 312, 314
Finlen, Miles 302
"Firebug" Murphy 236
Fisher, Frank 307
Fitzpatrick, Mrs. 3
Fitzsimmons, Bob 83
Flats of Walkerville 243
Florence Hotel "Big Ship" 253, 276
Flynn, Leo 237
Fogarty, Frank 294
Foley, Joseph 223
Foley, Patrick 196
Ford, Bob 187
Ford, Dr. Anson 296
Ford, Mabel 187
Ford, Sam C. 315
Foresco, Dominic 4
Four Bit Alley 190
Foy, Eddie 286, 295
Freeman, Harry C. 15, 16
Freethy, Joe 230
Friel, Pat 278, 280
Friganza, Trixie 295
Frisco Kate 283
Fun Gee 120
Furey, Tom 86

Gaffney, Pig Nose 3
Gagnon Mine 203, 214
Galena Street 184, 187–188, 190, 302, 304
Gambetta Mine 34, 297
Gans, Joe 238
Garlens, J. 296
Gemmel, Billy 88–89, 300
Gemmell, William 310
Gertney, "Pup Milk" 4, 134, 135
Gibbon, General 298
Gillie, John 302
Gilligan, Mrs. 49
Gilligan, P. J. 159
Gillis, Malcolm 250
Glengarry Mine 42
Gold, dicovery of 14
Goldman, J. 124
Gordon, John A. 286
Gordon, Sam 2
Gould, George 46
Graham, William 296
Grand Opera House 287, 290–291, 302
Grand Opera House in Great Falls 288
Granite Mountain Mine 172, 305–306
Grayrock Mine 221
Great Northern Railway 304
Great Republic Mine 16, 297
Greeley, Horace 17
Green Mountain Mine 207, 220
Gregson Springs 10, 60–61, 243, 304
Grimes, Jack 238
Gunn, Dr. 145
Gus Fitchen's saloon 125, 132
Gyman, Charles 266
Gyman, Mrs. Charles 266

Hagen, Fred 4, 291
Haggin and Tevis 298
Haggin, James B. 33
Hale House 177, 301
Hanson, Pete 184
Happy Henry 278
"Happy" Jack Gardiner 295
Harding, President 309
Harney, Judge 302
Harpell, Lou 190
Harrington, "Deaf Dan" 52
Harrington, John 171
Harrington, P. S. 48–49
Harrington, Tim 234
Harris, Tony 234–235
Hastings, Beryl 191
Hauser, Samuel T. 34
Hauswirth, Charles A. 313, 315
Hauswirth, Simon 286, 297, 313
Hayes, Ike 3, 5, 237, 311
Haywood, W. D. 70
Hearst, George 33, 298
Hearst, William Randolph 33, 298
Heinze-Amalgamated struggle 31
Heinze, F. Augustus 31, 38–43, 46, 55, 76, 84, 100, 214, 299, 300–303, 305
Heinze-Clark 166–169
Held, Anna 295
Hempstead, Judge 82
Hendrie Mill 296
Hennessy, D. J. 303
Herrera, Aurelia 237, 239
Herron, Rose 261
Hesperus Lode 278
Hibernian Hall 75, 277
Hibernian Mine 207
Hickey Brothers 298
Hickey, Edward 203, 308
Hickey, Michael 17, 33, 303
Hickman, F. M. 84
High Ore Mine 92–93, 144, 207, 228, 305
Highland City 297
Hip Sing tong 126–127
Hirbour Building 286
Hite, Mabel 295
"Hog Ranch" 3
Hole-in-Blanket 105, 107, 108, 110–113

Holland skating rink 66
Holy Cross Cemetery 138
Hong Huie Laundry 121
Hosty, Thomas 162
Houdini 294
Howard, Eugene 294
Howard, Lucille 191
Howard, Willie 294
Howe, J. P. 287
Howie, Tom 259
Hum Mon Sen 126
Humphrey, Chastine 22, 296
Humphrey, G. O. 14, 30–31, 296
Hungry Hill 1, 147
Hunt, Judge 303

I, Mary MacLane 267
Independent Mine Workers' Union 304
Industrial School 164
Intermountain 44, 97, 100, 154
Iona Cafe 259
Irish Gentlemen 6
Irvine, Caleb E. 14, 296

Jackson, Joseph R. 164, 295
Jacobs, Henry 298
James, Jesse 187
Jeffries, Jim 83, 237
Jessell, George 294
Jew Jess 185, 187, 283
Jimmy July 3, 5, 124, 222, 224, 303
Jimmy Quinn 238
Jimmy the dog 96
Joe Mudro 238
Joe No-Legs 135–136
Johnny the Swede 222, 224–225
Johnson, Elmer. *See* "Lemons."
Johnson, Jack 238
Johnson, "Swede" 162
Jolly, Jack 4
Jolson, Al 291, 295
Jonas, Henry 288
Jones, "Fat Jack" 3–8, 80–85, 152, 269, *270*, 298, 308
Jones, John Codman 80
Joshers Club 10, 88–90, 300, 308, 310
Junkie Joe 283

Kahn, Shad 99
Kane, Stephen 99
Keeler, Fannie 291
Kelly, Con 6
Kelly, Pat 232
Kelly the cat 95
Kennofal, Barney 102
Kenny, J.W. 184
Kenoffel's Spokane Cafe 259
Kenyon, Connell Commercial Company 178
Ketchell, Stanley 185, 238
Kid McCoy 237
Kid Tracey 238
Kiely, Matty 7, 24–25, 56, 144, 213–217
Kilroy, Dick 100
King and Lowry's 91, 285
King, Buddy 238
Klaffke, Joe 48
Knight, William 313

La Plata 297
Labor Day 29, 309
Laird, Joe 220
Larabie, Charles X. 33
Largey, Creigton 268
Largey, Patrick 268, 301
Largey, Sellars 268
Larkin, Jim 155
LaShelle, Kirk 290
Last Chance Gulch 14
Late Acquisition Mine 16
Lauder, Harry 294
Leary, Dennis 16, 26, 296
Lee, Lila 294

Lee, Tom 122
Leggat Hotel 295
Lemons 78
Leonard Mine 17, 171, 222, 314
Leslie, Bert 294
Levy, Sol 94, 96
Lexington Mill 75, 296
Lexington Mine 17, 297
Lilly the Lush 271
Lindsay, John 43
Little Annie Rooney 278
Little, Frank 306
  funeral of 2
  hanging of 71
"Little Joe" Mulcahey 291
Little Stevie 102
Liz the Lady 6, 278–279
Lorton, Irene 4, 291
Lousy Pete 6
"Lovers' Roost" 12
Lucas, Sam 239–242
Lutey Brothers' 149
Lutey the Box Thief 6
Lynch, Judge Jeremiah 235

Mack and Carey 294–295
Mack, Danny 293
MacLane, Mary 1, 266–267
Madison, Frank 296
Maguire 285
Maguire, Harry 238
Maguire, John 286–287, 294
Maguire's New Grand Opera House 301
Mahan, William 313
Maher, Peter 311
Mahoney Alley 278–280
Mahoney, Mike 121
Mahoney, Tom 295
Malloy, Charlie 4, 291
Malloy, Mae 191
Maloney, Mary 6
Manwaring, N. 295
Marr Field 307
Mary MacLane 267
Mary, the Ghost 195
McCarthy, Billy 259
McCormack, John 294
McCormick, Ed 86
McCormick, Jim 292
McCormick, Miss 86
McDonald, Muckey 63, 66, 70, 305
McDowell, W. W. 6, 312
McGowan, Alex 99, 121, 270, 279, 280
McHatton, Judge 59
McNamara 6, 281
McNichols, Mike 232
McNulty, Pete 222
McQueen Addition 147
Meaderville 4, 12, 44, 145, 147, 148, 222, 243, 248–249, 302, 311
Meaderville School *147*
Mendez, Fernando 227
Mercantile National Bank 46
Mesopust 29
Metal Mine Workers Union 71, 306
Metal Mine Workers' Union 307
Metals Bank 193
Mexicali Rose 281
Michael Davitt Mine 207
"Mike the Mule" 218
Mill and Smeltermens Union of Anaconda 60
Milwaukee Railway 303, 310
Miners Union Day 6, 10, 29, 39, 48, 60–61, 63, 304, 313
Miners Union Hall 2, 55, 62, 64, *68*, 235, 258, 277, 304
Minnie Healy case 302
Minnie Healy Mine 45, 302
Missoula Mining company 296
Mitchell, Eddie 78–79
Mobile Steamer 302
Montana Central Railroad 299
Montana Free Press 310–311
Montana Hardware company 310
Montana Historical Library 288
Montana Hotel 239

Montana Legislative Assembly 302
Montana Ore Purchasing Company 42
Montana Power Company 275, 313
Montana School of Mines 315
Montana Standard 56, 310
Montana State School of Mines 20
Montana Union Railway 299
Mooney, James 313
Moonlight Mine 9, 204
Moose Mine 206
Morosco, Dorothy 295
Morrison, Major General 307
Morse, Charles W. 46
Morton, James 294
Moulton Mine 206
Mount Moriah Cemetery 233
Mountain Chief mine 33
Mountain Consolidated Mine 8, 17, 73, 180, 204, *205*, 211, 215, 220, 228, 314
Mountain View Methodist 297
Mountain View mine 207
Moyer, Charles 66–67, 305
Mudro, Joe 260
Mullin House 253
Mullins, Jerry 3, 200
Mullins, Larry 268
Mullins, Pat 7, 137–138, 269–270, *270*
Munford, Frank 59
Munroe, Jack 5, 236–237
Murphy, Charles 296
Murphy, Charley 15
Murphy, Jack 74
Murphy, "Jere the Wise" 6, 64–66, 100, 125, 126, 152, 186–187, 190, 271–276, 279, 281, 313
Murphy, Mohammed 11, 222, 229
Murray, Charlie 294
Murray, James A. 42, 82, 83, 84, 122, 287

N. P. Railway 227
Nanny Goat Hill 1
Nation, Carrie 304
Neversweat Mine 96, 203, 220
Neversweat Mineyard 71
New York Tribune 17
Newell, A. C. 299
Newton, Tom 130
Newton's "horseless carriage" 130
Nick Portulis 222, 228
Nick the Greek 282, 284
"Nickel Annie" 10, 261, 264, *265*
"Nigger Liz" 11, 184, 283
Nigger Riley 6, 278 279
Nine Mile House 125
Noble, Tillie 261
"Noodles" Fagan 295
Norris and Rowe circus 61
North Butte Mining Company 177
Northern Pacific Railroad 147, 298
Northwest Theatrical Association 288

O'Brien, Frank 158
O'Keefe, Jack 237
O'Keefe, Mat 294
Olcott, Chauncey 11, 295
O'Leary, Barry 315
O'Leary, Dennis 37
Oleson, Sam 45
Olman, Dr. 296
O'Mara, Judge 270, 271
O'Neil, Con 175
O'Neill, Rimmer 3, 220
O'Neill, Tim 277
Original Mine 17, 33, 203, *204*, 304
O'Rourke, John K. 86, 276
Orphan Girl Mine 207
Orpheum Bar 294, 295
Owsley, William C. 48, 82, 115
Owsley's Hall 286

Pacific Railway 300, 304
Paddy, the Ghoul 195
Paddy the Pig 3
Page, Henry 232

Parks, William J. 16, 26–29, 296, 297
Parlor houses 190
Parnell Mine 207
Parrot Company 301
Parrot Flats 147, 156
Parrot lode 26, 203
Parrot Mine 17, 28, 170, 203, 297
Pasquale, Joe 24
Pasquale, Tony 222
Pasty 11, 251
Pawnee Bill 294
Pegasus Pulls a Hack 100, 156
Pennsylvania Mine 45, 95, 206, 306
Phelan, Audrey 291
"Pidgeon" Shea 236
Pierce, Howard 85
Pock, Dr. Huie 122
Poodles Hanneford 295
Porter, Henry 296
Porter, T. C. 16, 26, 296
Post 56
Powell, Sherman 307
Powers 158
Primrose, George 295
Prohibition 9, 182, 280, 307, 312

Quarles, Myra 4, 265
Quinn, John 276

Ramsdell, Joe 15, 26, 296
Rarus Mine 42, 45, *208*
Red Foley 278
Renean, George 86
Renshaw Hall 4, 51, 85, 286
Reveille 39, 44
Reynolds, Sam 58, 229
Rialto Theater 93
Robert Emmett Mine 207
Robinson, Boy 237
Rocker Camp 14, 15, 114, 158
Rocker Mine 82
Rodda, Mike 232
Rogers, H. H. 46
Romaine, Manuel 294
Rooney, Crying George 6, 77
Roosevelt, Franklin D. 308, 311
Roosevelt, President Theodore 7, 46, 83, 302, 312
Russell Brothers 294
Russell, Lillian 295
Rutherford, James H. 295
Rutledge, James 92

Sacred Heart Church 200
Sallau 175
Salt Lake Tribune 287
Salvation Army 10, 188, 260, 261
Sampson and Brown 159, 161
Seattle Sal 283
Seldom Seen 1
Shamrock 6
Shanghai Cafe 122
Shannahan, Barney 125, 152, 157
Sharkey the cat 95
Sherman Act of 1890 300
Shippens, Reverend W. C. 297
Shoestring Annie 6, 7, 261–264, 312
Silver Bow 14, 15, 37, 82, 296, 297
Silver Bow Club 2, 298
Silver Bow County 49, 77, 298, 300, 311, 312, 315
Silver Bow Coursing Club 234
Silver Bow Creek 14, 113, 114, 298, 299
Silver Bow Mine 170
Silver Bow Park 147
Silver Bow Trades and Labor Assembly 308
Silver Bow Trades and Labor Council 307
Sketches of Butte 187
Skibereen 180–182
Smith, Al 310
Smith, Owen P. 234
Smoke House 206
Smoke House Mine 206
Smokey 282, 284

Speck's Hall 286
Speculator Mine 62, 172–175, 204, 306
St. George's Day 6, 29, 48
St. James Hospital 167, 222
St. Lawrence Mine 95, 203, 220, 314
St. Mary's Parochial School 158
St. Patrick's Church 297
St. Patrick's Day 6, 29, 48, 102, 121, 259
St. Paul Railroad 303, 310
Standard Oil Company 38, 301
State School of Mines 300, 302
"Steamshovel Steve" 218
Steck, Olga 291
Stevensville 315
Stewart, Governor Sam V. 305
Stewart Mine 203, 304
Stirabout 253
Story of Mary Mac 1
Stuart, Granville 296, 307
"Stuttering Alex" 3, 227
"Success" Cafe 9, 259
Sullivan, Billy 93
Sullivan, John 62
Sullivan, John L. 83, 177, 236–237, 291–292
Sullivan, Mike, Dan, Montana Jack and Twin 238
Sullivan, Sean-Soul 3
Sullivan-Considine circuit 294
Sunday, Billy 2
Sutton, Lulu 4, 290, 291, 294
Sutton, Richard P. 3, 288, 293, 294
Sutton's Old Broadway 61
Swansea, Wales 26
Swiss Home 5
Symon's Store 303
Syracuse Standard 35

Ta-Noose 107–108
Taft, William Howard 83, 303
Tammany, the race horse 239–240
Telephone "Tschaikowsky" 222, 226
Tevis, Lloyd 33
The Four Cohan's 295
The Irish World 191
Thomas, Norman 311
Thompson, James 286
Thompson, Maurice 238
Thompson, William 48
Thornton Hotel 7, 84
Timber Butte 310
Timber Butte Saloon 8
Tolerance Day 2
Tong war 126
Toole, Joseph K. 311
Town Gulch 14
Trades and Labor Council 122
Travonia district 17
Travonia Mine 16, 203, 297
Treloar, Sam 299
Tremblay, Dr. 145
Trenton Mining and Development company 301
Tucker, Sophie 295
Turner, E.B. 133
Twin Bridges 29

Union Family Theater 290
Union Hall 70, 305
United Copper Company 46
Utah and Northern Railroad 16, 82
Utah Northern Railway 298

Vellenweth, Charley 234
"Venus Alley" 191
Vernon, William 296
Virginia City 14, 184, 296
Volstead act 277, 278

"Wake up Jim" 203
Walker Brothers 31, 33, 297–298
Walker, Frank 6, 102, 312
Walker, Tom 102
Walkerville 17, 18, 58, 75, 117, 147, 156, 178, 297, 302

Wall Street Journal 46
Warren, Charles S. 26, 28, 270–271, 296, 308
Washoe Copper company 301
West Grayrock Mine 72
West Shore 287
West Side Coursing Track 233
West Stewart Mine 68
Western Federation 70
Western Federation of Miners 66, 301, 305
Wharton, J. R. 155
Whiskey 223
White, Sam 123
Whitehead, Joe 295
Whitford, Dr. 145
Wilson, T. H. 250
Wolcott, Joe 5, 238
Wolftones 235
Women's Christian Temperance Union 299
Women's Club 301
Wood, Floyd 313
Workman's Compensation Act 305
WPA 11
Wysteria, the fighting cock 243

Yankee Boy Mine 266
Young, Brigham 285
Young, Hank 286